Professional Chef

Level 3 Diploma

Also available in this series:

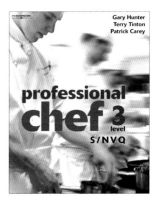

Title: **Professional Chef Level 1 Diploma**	**Professional Chef Level 2 S/NVQ**	**Professional Chef Level 2 Diploma**	**Professional Chef Level 3 S/NVQ**
ISBN: 9781844805303	9781844805051	9781844807062	9781844805310

Virtual Kitchen www.virtualkitchen.co.uk

Winner of the PACE Innovative Learning Materials Award 2008
Finalist for the PACE Innovative Partnership for Education Award 2009

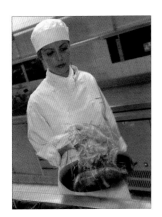

Dedicated online resource for students and lecturers of food preparation and cookery at levels 1–3 including:

- 400 video demonstrations
- theory content
- assessment questions
- image bank

Title: **Virtual Kitchen Level 1**	Virtual Kitchen Level 2	Virtual Kitchen Level 3
ISBN: **9781844807383**	9781844807390	9781844807406

Out now:

Title: Food & Beverage Service Levels 1&2	Hospitality Supervision Level 3
ISBN: 9781408007426	9781408009253

Contact your Cengage Learning Representative for bespoke pricing options

To place your order or for more information, please contact our
College Sales Executive at +44 (0) 1264 342768 or emea.fesales@cengage.com or mail to:
College Sales Executive
Cengage Learning, Cheriton House, North Way
Andover SP10 5BE, United Kingdom

GARY HUNTER and TERRY TINTON

Professional Chef

Level 3 Diploma

DELMAR
CENGAGE Learning

Australia • Brazil • Japan • Korea • Mexico • Singapore • Spain • United Kingdom • United States

DELMAR
CENGAGE Learning·

Professional Chef: Level 3 Diploma
Gary Hunter and Terry Tinton

Publishing Director: Linden Harris

Publisher: Melody Dawes

Development Editor: Lucy Mills

Content Project Editor: Alison Cooke

Production Controller: Eyvett Davis

Marketing Executive: Lauren Redwood

Typesetter: Book Now Ltd, London, UK

Cover design: HCT Creative

Text design: Design Deluxe Ltd, Bath, UK

For product information and technology assistance,
contact **emea.info@cengage.com**.

For permission to use material from this text or product,
and for permission queries, email **clsuk.permissions@cengage.com**

The author has asserted the right under the Copyright, Designs and Patents Act 1988 to be identified as Author of this book.

British Library Cataloguing-in-Publication Data
A catalogue record for this book is available from the British Library.

ISBN: 978-1-4080-3084-4

Cengage Learning EMEA
Cheriton House, North Way, Andover,
Hampshire SP10 5BE, United Kingdom

Cengage Learning products are represented in Canada by Nelson Education Ltd.

For your lifelong learning solutions, visit
www.cengage.co.uk

Purchase your next print book, e-book or e-chapter at
www.CengageBrain.co.uk

Printed by RR Donnelley, China
1 2 3 4 5 6 7 8 9 10 – 13 12 11

Brief contents

CONTENTS

About the authors

GARY HUNTER

Head of Culinary Arts at Westminster Kingsway College, Gary has 14 years' experience of teaching within further, higher and vocational education. Gary has been awarded the City & Guilds Medal for Excellence in recognition of his exceptional work and personal dedication to delivering a continuing high standard of education and training to students and trainees for the catering industry. He recently won the Innovative Teaching and Learning Good Practice Award at the 2009 PACE conference, and has travelled the world as a consultant for Barry Callebaut giving seminars on chocolate and cuisine. Gary is also an experienced international culinary competition judge. As a leading Chef Patissier in the UK, he has won numerous awards and competition medals and has worked with and trained many of today's successful chefs. Gary has recently helped to write the diploma in professional cookery qualification at levels 1, 2 and 3.

TERRY TINTON

A Chef Lecturer and Professional Chef Diploma Course Coordinator in Culinary Arts at Westminster Kingsway College, Terry is a strong and confident chef with many awards spanning a hugely successful career. He has held a senior chef position at the House of Commons and worked extensively across Switzerland and Germany. He holds the Advanced Hygiene Award and is the driving force for developing first-year students at the college.

Acknowledgements

Personal Acknowledgements

Sarah-Jane Hunter   Charlotte Hunter   Estelle Hunter   Hilary Hunter
Phillip Hunter   Paul Hunter   Patricia Long   John Long

Margaret Tinton   Lewis Tinton   Kate Tinton   Paul Lane
Yvonne Hall   Terence Tinton   Ava-Grace Tinton   Liam Lane
Rosaleen Lane   Andy Tinton   George Tinton

College Acknowledgements

Andy Wilson   Geoff Booth   Ian Wild   Allan Drummond
Jose Souto   Simon Stocker   Jonathan Warner   Javier Mercado
Chris Loder   Barry Jones   Alexandra Roberts   Vince Cottam
Paul Jervis   Clare Mannall

Students

Kyle Mcgrady   Tony Hayes   Heather Gil-Abillera   Samantha Doorgachurn
Luke Fouracre   Maxium Shearer   Lucien Bintcliffe   Andrew Giles
Robert Hall   Robert Boer   Luca Boccia   Luke Monaghan
Kirstie McIntyre   Leon Coultress   Selin Kiazin   Ben Arnold

Sponsors

Russums Catering Suppliers   Furi Knives
Steelite Catering Crockery   Barry Callebaut Chocolate   Nigel Fredericks quality meat, poultry and game www.nigelfredericks.co.uk

Chef Contributors

Nick Patterson   Shane Osborn   Martyn Nail   Paul Rankin
Angela Hartnett   David Cavalier   Mark Askew   Andre Garrett
Paul Gayler   Thierry Dumouchel   William Curley   Tony Hoyle
Beverley Dunkley   Javier Mercado

Photography and Resources

William 'Bill' Hull, Professional Photography

Billingsgate Fish Market   Smithfield's Meat Market   New Covent Garden   Compass UK
Westminster Kingsway College   Barchester Healthcare   Russums   Electrolux
Think Vegetables   Eureka   The Ritz Hotel
Susie Mitchell, photographer   Seafish, the Sea Fish Industry Authority

Quality Meat Scotland (QMS) represents the Scottish red meat industry and promotes Scotch Beef, Scotch Lamb and Specially Selected Pork to a national and international audience. Our activities range from helping the industry improve their methods of production and quality of products to increasing customer awareness and preference for Scotch product. QMS also helps in the development of new markets in the UK and around the world. For additional information: www.qmsscotland.co.uk and www.chefsguidetoscotchbeef.org.

Foreword

To achieve success in the competitive world of the modern kitchen environment, it is becoming more and more important to develop a broad range of advanced culinary skills and knowledge. It is vital to have the technical ability to apply these skills consistently to meet the demands of the workplace.

Those making the choice to develop a career in the culinary profession, soon understand that we are fortunate to be part of an industry which offers a fascinating range of opportunities. There can surely be no better environment in which to develop a creative career. It is a profession which enables the resourceful chef to build a reputation through the demonstration of well developed craft skills and techniques and an appreciation of the ingredients and commodities available today.

And this is the profession where reputation is key, where the successful chef is able to blend individuality, flair and technical ability with teamwork, consistency and an appreciation of food trends as well as meeting the complex needs of the customer. These are the key elements that will set the great chef apart from the competent chef.

For those of you setting out on a gastronomic journey into a career in the kitchen, this book will help shape your thoughts and enable you to build a repertoire of complex dishes. It will inspire you to develop advanced culinary skills, exploring new techniques and processes and understanding the characteristics of a broad range of food commodities. For those building on existing skills, it will encourage you to take time to consider further advanced craft techniques and apply the knowledge and understanding you may already have to a wider series culinary challenges.

There are many instructional cookery books available in today's market, all of which outline the skills and knowledge needed to cook competently. What the authors of this book have set out to achieve is to provide a guide to stretch and challenge trainee chefs on the accepted norms of culinary proficiency and techniques. They have set out to define and support the development of skills needed to meet the expectations of the contemporary restaurant environments in today's exceptional hospitality industry. I think they have achieved an excellent outcome.

Enjoy working with the content and the guidance given, this is also the only text of its kind designed to support you in the achievement of the Professional Cookery Diploma at advanced level. Read it, digest it and apply its content in a practical sense and it will enable you to develop the competitive edge so vital to the 21st century workplace.

The great chefs have always set out to go beyond the norm, exploring new concepts and ideas, testing themselves at the frontiers of current practices and challenging existing benchmarks to ensure they achieved success at the highest possible levels.

Take inspiration from their commitment as there is surely no other profession which recognises and rewards true talent like hospitality.

Enjoy every minute!

Geoff Booth, Head of School of Hospitality, Westminster Kingsway College

A quick reference guide to the qualification

The philosophy behind the diploma is the principle that a chef needs to have a sound foundation of high quality skills and to be able to apply these skills across a range of techniques and using a broad variety of commodities.

The qualification has been designed for delivery in a College environment or similar learning resource. It does not replace the NVQ/SVQ but intends to provide learners with a breadth of skills and knowledge and to make them better prepared to meet the modern needs of industry. There is also more emphasis on teaching and learning in comparison to the assessment model presented by the NVQ.

All candidates enrolled on a Diploma in Professional Cookery will follow a specific learning programme, completing a range of theoretical and practical tasks and activities.

Individuals will also receive a final grade for each unit to highlight areas of high achievement.

A quick reference guide to the qualification

The Level 3 Diploma units

The units are structured in a standard format and comprise of the following:

Unit reference number and title – e.g. Unit 308 Advanced skills and techniques in producing pâtisserie and fermented products

Rationale – explaining the aims and purpose of the unit

Connections with other qualifications – e.g. NVQs and Functional Skills

Assessment details – detailing the requirements for the assessment of practical skills and underpinning knowledge

Learning outcomes – specifying the practical skills and/or the underpinning knowledge to be covered

Range – providing detail as to the content of each learning outcome

Guidance – for delivery and best practice

Introduction

The intention of this book is to guide you to the advanced skills and techniques and present the important knowledge required to become a chef in the hospitality and catering industry.

Cooking, serving and eating food has become a major communication practice across the world. Food is prepared as a gift, as a medicine, to create friendship, to nourish, to celebrate, to generate business and to stimulate happiness.

The chef now has the capacity to communicate through their food, initiate fulfilment and joy and conceive relationships. The basic principles of being a worthy professional chef are to combine good ingredients with sound techniques, skills and basic knowledge of culinary science with attention to detail. Only then will you have the basis to show your culinary artistry and creative talents.

This book will also illustrate some of the top chefs in this country whose talent, dedication and energy have helped them achieve a high standard of excellence in the catering industry today. They share their thoughts, recipes and experience with you for you to learn from. It will also provide you with an important reference point to attain the professional skills and knowledge for today's classically based modern cuisine.

Enjoy learning and enjoy cooking!

Gary Hunter

About the book

Mapped to the qualification
Each chapter addresses a specific unit of the Level 3 Diploma in Advanced Professional Cookery qualification.

6
Advanced skills and techniques in producing vegetable and vegetarian dishes (Unit 304)

LEARNING OUTCOMES
The aim of this chapter is to enable the candidate to develop the necessary advanced skills knowledge and understanding of the principles in preparing and cooking vegetables to dish specifications. The emphasis in this chapter is on developing precision, speed and control in existing skills and perfecting more refined and advanced techniques.

INTRODUCTION
The large number of different types and varieties of vegetables enables the chef to give great depth and variety to their menu and to the diet of the customer.

A thorough understanding of the various qualities of each group of vegetables and the characteristics of each type within those groups enables the professional chef to create vegetable dishes that exploit those qualities to their own advantage. This understanding gives the diner a true gastronomic journey through a menu.

VIDEO CLIP
Covent Garden vegetable market

BRASSICAS (BRASSICAEA)
Brassicas, also known as flower heads, are part of the mustard and cabbage family. The main edible parts of these plants develop above the ground. Some varieties are grown for their roots (swede, turnip; see root vegetables).

Learning outcomes at the start of each chapter explain the skills and knowledge you need to be proficient in and understand by the end of the chapter.

Preparation of a parfait

Sautéing onions and herbs

Combining minced meat with onions and beating together

Adding eggs and cream to the base mixture

Blending in a food processor to a course mixture

Seasoning the pâté mixture

Covering the mixture with streaky bacon and plastic film

Step-by-step sequences
illustrate each process and provide an easy-to-follow guide.

Assessment of knowledge and understanding

You have now learned about the health and safety responsibilities for everyone in the workplace. This will enable you to ensure your own actions reduce risks to health and safety.

To test your level of knowledge and understanding, answer the following short questions. These will help to prepare you for your summative (final) assessment.

Health and safety law

1 Discuss the various reasons why health and safety laws exist and the benefits that enforcing these provide.

2 Give three examples of implications of not conforming to health and safety laws.
i) _____ ii) _____
iii) _____

3 State who the Health and Safety at Work Act 1974 covers and why is it in place.

4 Explain why it is important to keep yourself up to date with current health and safety legislation.

Assessment of knowledge and understanding
at the end of each chapter contains questions, so you can test your learning.

PURCHASING SPECIFICATION
- Cauliflowers should have tight and firm flower heads that are white in colour.
- Other brassicas should also have tight heads and bright colouring.
- They should not feel limp and the stems should be strong.

Purchasing Specifications
provide helpful advice for buying commodities.

Recipes Modern and traditional recipes for each commodity.

Ricotta and wild sorrel tortellini with a pistachio pesto and garlic foam

INGREDIENTS	10 PORTIONS	4 PORTIONS
Plain pasta dough	1kg	400g
Ricotta cheese	500g	200g
Pistachio nuts	125g	50g
Parmesan cheese	125g	50g
Olive oil	175ml	70ml
Basil leaves	½ bunch	¼ bunch
Wild sorrel	175g	70g
Garlic	10 cloves	4 cloves
Fresh full fat milk	125ml	50ml
Good-quality salt and white pepper	To taste	To taste

Method of work

CHEF'S TIP

When rolling and storing pasta, use semolina and not flour to prevent it sticking together; this will ensure the strands or sheets are separate and prevent the cooking liquid becoming cloudy and thick with gluten.

1. Mix the ricotta with the chopped blanched sorrel leaves, season well.
2. Roll out the pasta into thin sheets and cut out into circles approximately 5cm in diameter.
3. Brush the pasta circles with water and spoon the ricotta into the middle.
4. Fold the pasta over and pinch the points together (see making tortellini, page 170).
5. Make the pesto using half the oil, lightly toasted pistachios, basil and Parmesan by placing all the ingredients in a liquidiser and pulsing until almost smooth (the consistency should be slightly thicker than a sauce).
6. Blanch the garlic in boiling water for 2 minutes, place the garlic into the milk and bring to the boil; remove the pan from the heat and liquidise.
7. Blanch the pasta in boiling salted water, drain and mix in a bowl with the pesto.
8. Pulse the garlic mixture until a foam appears, spoon over the tortellini and serve.

CHEF'S PROFILE

Name: **ANGELA HARTNETT**

Position: Chef Patron at Angela Hartnett at the Connaught

Establishment: The Connaught Hotel

Current job role and main responsibilities: I oversee all the food and beverage operations at the hotel:
- breakfast
- afternoon tea
- room service
- restaurant (one Michelin star).
Currently employ 110 staff.

When did you realise that you wanted to pursue a career in the catering and hospitality industry?
I always wanted to run my own restaurant from an early age. My grandparents owed a fish and chip shop.

Experience:
1. Midsummer House, Cambridge
2. Gordon Ramsay, Aubergine
3. Marcus Wareing, Petrus
4. Gordon Ramsay Holdings

What do you find rewarding about your job?
I love teaching young cooks and get pleasure from seeing the customers when they have enjoyed dining with us.

What do you find the most challenging about the job?
Finding good staff and retaining them.

What advice would you give to students just beginning their career?
Choose a path you enjoy and are passionate about.

Who is your mentor or main inspiration?
My family and their love of food. Also Gordon Ramsay and Nadia Santini.

What traits do you consider essential for anyone entering a career as a chef?
- Understanding the source of your produce
- People management skills
- Common sense
- Organisation

A brief personal profile:
- Chef de Partie, Aubergine
- Sous Chef, Petrus Restaurant
- Executive Chef, Hilton Creek Dubai
- Chef Patron, Connaught Hotel
- Won Hotel Restaurant of the Year
- Won BMW Newcomer of the Year

Can you give one essential kitchen tip or technique that you use as a chef?
Taste everything.

Chef's Profiles
provide advice from leading industry figures and an insight into what motivated them during their training.

Health and safety boxes draw your attention to important health and safety information.

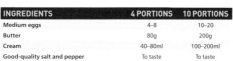

HEALTH & SAFETY

Fire exit doors must be clearly marked, remain unlocked during working hours and be free from obstruction. Fire extinguishers should be available and ready for use in every kitchen.

Video Clip
If your college adopts the virtual kitchen at this level (www.virtualkitchen/level3.co.uk) you will be able to view a video demonstration online.

Scrambled eggs

INGREDIENTS	4 PORTIONS	10 PORTIONS
Medium eggs	4–8	10–20
Butter	80g	200g
Cream	40–80ml	100–200ml
Good-quality salt and pepper	To taste	To taste

HEALTH & SAFETY

Use unsalted butter and low sodium salt.

Method of work

1. Melt the butter in a thick-bottomed sauté pan.
2. Beat the eggs in a basin and season.
3. Add to the pan and cook very gently.
4. When they begin to set, add the cream, remove from the heat and continue to stir until lightly set (baveuse).
5. Serve immediately.

VIDEO CLIP
Scrambling eggs

CHEF'S TIP

Experiment using other marinades, such as tikka or garlic and chilli. Pigeon is a strongly flavoured bird and this will come through even when other strong flavours are used.

Chef's tip boxes
share the authors' experiences of the catering industry, with helpful suggestions for how you can improve your skills.

QUALITY POINTS

- Cock birds have a tendency to be drier and tougher than hens
- Bronze birds can have residual dark feather stubs; these can be removed with duck tweezers
- The flesh should be dry to the touch and without excess blemishes
- If the windpipe is still intact, it should be pliable and not rigid
- The breast should be plump in intensively reared birds and slightly leaner in the rarer organic varieties

Quality Points
provide information to help you assess the freshness of products.

1

Supervisory skills in the hospitality industry (Unit 301)

LEARNING OUTCOMES

The aim of this chapter is to facilitate the candidate in developing the necessary knowledge and appreciation of how to supervise, lead and train teams and individuals in order to develop sound teamwork in a professional kitchen. We will discuss development and understanding of the range of responsibilities required in a supervisory role, including the functions of supervision and the characteristics of leadership.

There is **one** principal outcome to this chapter. At the end of this chapter the candidate will be able to:

▓ Explain how to apply staff supervisory skills within a small team

The definition of supervision is:

1 **Oversee activity**: to watch over an activity or task being carried out by somebody and ensure that it is performed correctly.

2 **Oversee people**: to be in charge of a group of people engaged in an activity or task and keep order or ensure that they perform it correctly.

It is the responsibility of supervisors to directly influence progress and productivity within an organisation. Supervision often includes conducting basic management skills (decision making, problem solving, planning, delegation and meeting management), organising teams, noticing the need for and designing new job roles in the group, training new employees, managing employee performance (including setting goals, observing and giving feedback, addressing performance issues and employee development) and ensuring conformance to personnel policies and other internal regulations.

The scope of supervisory roles in the professional kitchen

A supervisor will typically undertake the following eleven quality control tasks within a kitchen environment:

ISTOCK / © KELLY CLINE

A chef supervisor demonstrating a task with a member of the team

1   Plan, organise and supervise the work of the chefs within your section.

2   Set and communicate targets stating the quality points that are to be achieved and the time frame considered necessary to establish work schedules.

3   Supervise all food preparation tasks throughout the day and monitor the quality of ingredients, dishes and produce.

4   Ensure that the production of dishes is to customer requirements – including during service – and meets all time constraints and deadlines.

5   Check and order supplies as required by the section or kitchen.

6   Assist in planning menus with the line manager or head chef.

7   Keep quality records in line with health and safety regulations.

8   Make quality reports in line with the organisation's requirements.

9   Monitor the behaviour of the team and solves problems that may arise.

10 Contribute to individual and team development, identify training requirements and undertake training sessions in the preparation of dishes and certain everyday tasks.

11 Perform other related duties as assigned by the operational management.

It is generally accepted that a good supervisor is also a strong leader. The term 'leadership' refers to the search for precision in the delivery of services within the hospitality industry.

The diverse nature of the hospitality industry ensures that it is very unlikely that a task is carried out by a single person; there is usually at least one other helping to prepare, serve, clear or manage. This allows the opportunity for a leader to emerge and help steer the group towards achieving their goal.

The characteristics of leadership

When identifying a good leader or assessing your own performance there are several key characteristics worth considering:

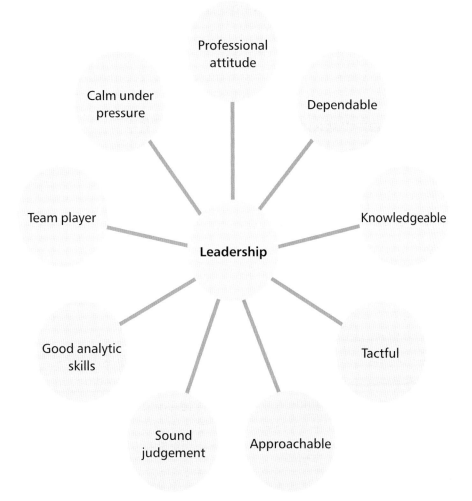

Leadership is a skill that requires practice and dedication; motivating a team is a major factor alongside ensuring that the team stays focused on the common goal.

A leader should be:

- Challenging – ensuring that you look for opportunities to improve performance.
- Inspirational – motivating individuals and empowering the team at all levels.
- Leading by example – setting guidelines and working in a professional and inspirational way.
- Open to discussion – sharing best practice and discussing improvements in a controlled professional manner.

Leadership is often defined in two ways: *transactional* and *transformational* leadership. These definitions were developed over years of research and evaluation. A leader meets certain criteria which are then assigned to either category.

A transactional leader

This refers to the way in which a leader achieves their goals by using behaviour, incentives and rewards to motivate their team. The term 'transaction' is the same as in a business transaction where one person receives an exchange or payment for goods or services offered. Below is an example of how the transactional cycle works:

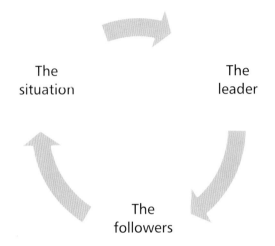

The situation

The leader

The followers

Using the cycle above as a guide we can see how a sous chef may offer an incentive, such as additional time off, for tighter wastage control of ingredients in a kitchen – this shows the leader offering an incentive to the follower in the situation.

A transformational leader

A transformational leader has the ability to assess, develop and eventually change the behaviour and mindset of the team over a long period of time. This type of leadership is highly sought after as it enables the business to achieve a common goal amongst all team members to exceed their own expectations and deliver a first class service.

A successful leader will work with the team to ensure motivation, encouragement and make individual team members feel respected in their day-to-day work. The three factors essential to becoming a transformational leader are illustrated below:

A transformational leader

Be charismatic

Be able to stimulate staff intellectually

Show consideration for individuals

The demands of leadership

A leader has to be able to cope with pressure from all directions and ensure that they always remain composed and self-confident. There are two aspects of a leader's responsibility which they must come to terms with very quickly:

1 Meeting set targets and achieving goals

2 Maintaining and developing positive working relationships.

Unfortunately, the two are not always easy to achieve together as the target may require increasing a person's work load. In the hospitality industry there are many essential and consequential factors that a leader must manage such as:

▓ The owner's requirements

▓ Customer needs and expectations

▓ Employees

▓ Competitors

▓ The head office

▓ Market fluctuations, e.g. cost, business considerations and market.

The qualities that are required of a good leader are varied. In order to help meet the increasing demands placed on leadership the qualities outlined below are requisite:

1 Confidence in your own ability and that of your team

2 The ability to demonstrate a logical approach to all tasks

3 Forward thinking

4 A good understanding of behaviour concepts

5 A visual awareness and the ability to connect with people

6 A politically correct attitude at all times

7 High motivation

8 An aim to improve the business and the team whenever possible.

A sous chef leading the team during a tasting session before service

Leadership styles

You can regard leadership styles in one of two ways.

1 Ask 'what is my leadership style?'. This is to focus on what you enjoy, what you may possibly be good at and what strengths and weaknesses you have.

2 Ask 'what leadership style is most suitable for the person, team or organisation that I am leading?'. This is to focus on the needs of the situation, on the criteria for success and on your approach that will bring about the maximum impact.

Modern leadership demands both. You need to recognise your own strengths and exploit them, but you also need to have an ability to adapt your style to different situations in order to achieve the maximum effectiveness. Rather than completely using their own preferred style, excellent leaders are able to adopt different approaches to suit the various needs of differing circumstances.

The leadership styles listed in the table below are based on Steve Myers' *MTR-i* (Management Team Role Indicator) model that defines types of leadership. This model assumes that a modern leader will:

■ Develop the flexibility to be able to use any of the styles

■ Recognise the different demands of each situation

■ Adapt appropriately, by using the styles that will give optimal achievement.

The 'Type' column below is based on the *MTR-i* team role model. It identifies what type or style of contribution is being made to the team. *MTR-i* team roles change from situation to situation, in accordance with the demands of the environment.

TYPE	DESCRIPTION	WHEN TO USE	WHEN NOT TO USE
Coach	People-oriented, motivator, builds personal relationships, likeable, interpersonal skills, cares for others	Commitment from others is critical, or in sensitive situations	Decisions need to be forced through, conflict is being avoided
Campaigner	Value-driven, has passion for key issues, focuses on important themes, champions the cause	The group has lost its sense of identity, or it is doing too many unimportant things	There is a problem that needs to be solved with dispassionate objectivity (e.g. technical issues)
Explorer	Tries things that are new, introduces change, looks for unexpected outcomes, creates new opportunities, experiments	The group is 'stuck in a rut', or the status quo needs to be challenged	There are already too many initiatives under way and some stability is needed
Innovator	Develops long-term vision, produces radical ideas, foresees the future, anticipates what is outside current knowledge	Radical change is needed, change is a long-term activity	There are immediate dangers, the group may not survive in the short term
Sculptor	Takes action, produces results, leads from the front, sets an example, does what is asked of others	There is some lethargy, or lack of achievement has destroyed motivation	The group is being too expedient, current success may ebb in the future
Curator	Observes, listens, clarifies goals, establishes realistic expectations, makes aims crystal clear	The direction is vague or expectations have not been articulated	There are already too many goals or too much information *continued*

TYPE	DESCRIPTION	WHEN TO USE	WHEN NOT TO USE
Conductor	Organises, makes plans, sets measurable goals, coordinates the work of different people, manages resources	There is chaos/lack of organisation, or there are no measures of achievement	There are so many processes that creativity has been stifled
Scientist	Analyses, uses models, produces explanations, compares other situations, engages in intellectual debate	The situation is complex or driven by technical solutions	People's feelings are paramount, or the group goes round in circular arguments

This table of leadership styles can be used to increase the effectiveness of a leader. The key to success is developing an external awareness of what is required, and the internal flexibility to be able to access each style as appropriate.

There are other models that explore management and leadership styles in an effective way that may help the candidate develop their own style to suit the needs of the team or situation. Kurt Lewin (in 1939) led a group of researchers in identifying different styles of leadership. This early study has been very influential and has established three major leadership styles that are widely used in businesses, government and the military today: authoritarian (autocratic), participative (democratic) and delegative (free rein).

Authoritarian (autocratic)

This style is used when leaders inform their employees about what they want done and how they want it accomplished without first obtaining the advice of their team. Two appropriate situations in which to use this style are when you have all the information available to solve the problem, or if you are short on time and your employees are well motivated.

Some chefs or leaders are inclined to think of this style as a vehicle for yelling, using demeaning language and leading by threats or by abusing their power. This is not the authoritarian style; rather it is an abusive, unprofessional style that will lead to a lack of team motivation. It has no place in a leader's repertoire.

The authoritarian style should normally only be used on rare occasions. If you have the time and want to gain more commitment and motivation from your employees, then you should use the participative style.

A chef using the 'authoritarian' leadership style

Participative (democratic)

This style involves the leader including one or more team members in the decision making process (i.e. determining what to do and how to do it). However, the leader maintains the final decision making authority.

A chef using the 'participative' leadership style

A chef using the 'delegative' leadership style

Using this style is not a sign of weakness; rather it is a sign of strength that your team will respect.

This is normally used when you have part of the information, and your team members have other parts. (Note that a leader is not expected to know everything – this is why you employ knowledgeable and capable team members.) Using this style is of mutual benefit because it allows individuals to become part of the team and allows the leader to make better decisions.

Delegative (free rein)

In this style, the leader allows the team or individuals to make the decisions. However, the leader is still responsible for the decisions that are made. This is used when employees are able to analyse the circumstances and determine what needs to be done and how to do it. A leader must recognise that they cannot do everything. A good leader must set priorities and delegate certain tasks.

This is not a style to use in order that you can blame others when things go wrong; rather this is a style to be used when you fully trust and have confidence in the people in your team. Do not be afraid to use it, however, it must be used astutely. This is also known as 'laissez-faire' style, which means the non-interference in the affairs of others.

A good leader uses all three styles, depending on what forces are involved between the followers (team members), the leader and the situation. Some examples include:

- Using an authoritarian style on a new employee, such as a trainee chef, who is just learning the job. The leader is competent and a good coach. The employee is motivated to learn a new skill. The situation is a new environment for the employee.

- Using a participative style with a team of chefs who know their job. The leader knows the problem, but does not have all the information. The chefs know their jobs and want to become part of the team.

- Using a delegative style with a chef who knows more about the job than you. The chef needs to take ownership of their job. Also, the situation might call for you to be at other places, doing other things.

- Using all three styles – telling your team that a procedure is not working correctly and a new one must be established (*authoritarian*). Asking for their ideas and input on creating a new procedure (*participative*). Delegating tasks in order to implement the new procedure (*delegative*).

The characteristics of a good team

How people behave and perform as members of a group or team is as important as their behaviour or performance as individuals. Harmonious working relationships and good teamwork help make for a high level of staff morale and work performance. Successful teamwork is an essential element of management practice such as the use of empowerment. Teamwork is important in any organisation but may be especially significant in the hospitality industry where there is a direct impact on customer satisfaction. Effective teamwork will improve organisational competitiveness by:

- Improving productivity
- Improving quality and encouraging innovation
- Taking advantage of the opportunities provided by technological advances
- Improving employee motivation and commitment.

A good team makes all the difference to any business. Team building can at times be a daunting task but it can be achieved with good leadership skills. Setting targets and ensuring the team understands their individual roles and responsibilities will help to build a strong team. Team building activities help a group achieve more and it also helps individuals to bond better. So, what are the characteristics of a good team? Which are the various qualities one should look for in a good team member? Listed below are some of the specific characteristics that are required for a good team.

- Everyone participates actively and positively in meetings and projects.
- Team goals are understood by everyone.
- Individual members have thought hard about creative solutions to the problem.
- Members are carefully listened to and receive thoughtful feedback.
- Everyone takes initiative to get things done.
- Each teammate trusts the judgment of the others.
- The team is willing to take risks.
- Everyone is supportive of the project and of others.
- There is plenty of communication between team members.
- Team decisions are made using organized, logical methods.
- Full team acceptance is expected as decisions are made.
- Dissenting opinions are recorded, and may be revisited if future situations dictate.
- Team goals are given realistic time frames.
- Everyone is focused on the ultimate goal of the project, while also working on the underlying details.

Team development

Participating in team development programmes bring the following benefits:

Team benefits

- Increased confidence within the team
- Improved levels of trust between individual members of staff
- Improved effectiveness of teams, within and beyond their own professional settings
- Enhanced shared leadership skills and effectiveness
- Building capacity for improved team working throughout the organisation
- Developing a team vision for improving practice
- Immediate results can be applied to your team.

Personal benefits

- Interacting and learning with outside specialists in a range of fields
- Gaining confidence to try things out in your team
- Being challenged and stretched to work collaboratively
- Developing professional relationships
- Developing your problem solving skills
- Building local networks that allow teams to share knowledge together.

Individual team development over a set period with mentoring and support processes in place will be helpful in identifying strengths and gaps in an individual team member's range of skills. The appropriateness of any personal development target being set is crucial to the whole process. Agreeing targets that are too basic means that the individual will not be working to their full potential, while setting targets that are too ambitious means that undue pressure will be put on the individual.

A simple test as to the appropriateness of a specific development to the team or individual is to review how 'SMART' it is, that is, to check the agreed target against the following criteria:

- Is the target **specific** enough – is everyone involved clear about what exactly needs to be achieved?
- Is the target **measurable** – can you actually demonstrate that a change has taken place?
- Is the target **achievable** – does the target take into account the existing levels of skill, with some sense of progress that is still possible, given the level of skills at present?

- Is the target **relevant** – is it an area the individual can actually have a direct impact on?
- Is the target **time-based** – does everyone involved know when the target has to be achieved by?

The training requirements of your team

A development plan looks at the personal and professional development of an individual. As we have just seen, the main aim is to ensure that an individual is improving their learning and performance through forward planning and setting specific goals which can be appropriately measured.

As a supervisor your role would be to support your colleagues by helping them in designing their development plan, and also ensuring that they are aware of the different learning opportunities available to them. It is also important that any learning activity undertaken is constantly reviewed and monitored to check your staff member's progress.

In implementing the individual training needs of the members of your team one key aspect that supervisors and managers need to be aware of is the equal opportunities legislation that applies to training and development. Regardless of the level of knowledge and skill that your employees have, all of them should be treated equally and be given the same opportunities to develop themselves further.

Once it has been decided which is the most cost effective and beneficial way to carry out the training, it has then to be decided how to carry out the training itself. There is a variety of different training methods or learning activities that could be used to help employees develop their knowledge, skills and attitude. Some of them are trainer centred, some are learner centred, and some can be a mixture of both.

Trainer centred

This gives the trainer control over the pace and content of the learning. The trainer will decide which exercises to use, structures the session and draws out key learning points, perhaps through a lecture or presentation.

Learner centred

This method gives the learner complete control. The learner might use self study texts, questionnaires, learning logs or E-learning.

Trainer and learner centred

Coaching is an example of this method. It is a process which will involve both the trainer and the learner. Using strong questioning techniques the trainer will draw out the answers and raise awareness in the learner.

 ACTIVITY

Commonly used training methods

On the following page is a table with the most commonly used training methods – make a note in the last column stating whether you think it is trainer centred, learner centred or if both methods are involved.

Training methods chart

METHOD	DESCRIPTION	USUAL OUTCOME	TRAINER, LEARNER CENTRED OR BOTH
Lectures and presentations	Trainer delivers prepared exposition, preferably using visual aids	Knowledge – fact and opinions	
Briefing groups	Short exposition by trainer, followed by questions and discussion	Knowledge – fact and opinions	
Discussion groups	Participative discussion led by one of the learners on a specified topic	Some knowledge – facts and opinions, attitudes and interpersonal skills	
Plenary discussion	Session following practical or other activity, usually led by the trainer, to pull out key learning points and/or relate theory to practice	Reinforcement and reflection – depending on task under review	
Demonstrations	Trainer shows learners how to do a task, e.g. operate a machine	Knowledge – how to, preparation for skills training	
Practical	Learners operate under trainer's supervision and receive feedback	Psychomotor or interpersonal skills	
Role-play	Learners put themselves in someone else's shoes for the purpose of practical exercise	Changing attitudes, interpersonal skills	
Video/DVD	Sound and vision	Knowledge	
Case studies	Write up of an incident or situation with questions for analysis and/or discussion	Analytical and decision making skills	
Business games/ computer simulations	Board or computer games or evolving case studies which allow participants to see the consequences of their decisions	Analytical and decision making skills	
Incident method	Learners are given last item in a sequence of events and asked to reconstruct circumstances through questioning trainer	Analytical and questioning skills	
In-tray exercises	Learners are given a series of memos, and other papers or electronic communications to be prioritised and dealt with	Prioritising, planning, organising, delegating and other managerial skills	

METHOD	DESCRIPTION	USUAL OUTCOME	TRAINER, LEARNER CENTRED OR BOTH
Group/individual projects	Investigation and report, usually with recommendations on issues or concern	Knowledge – facts and opinions; investigative, analytical and problem solving skills	
Books, manuals and self study texts	Written descriptions, analyses or instructions, sometimes with checklist and self test questions	Knowledge – facts and opinions	
E-learning	Electronic, internet based media which present learner with information and/or situations and questions and provide feedback on responses	Knowledge – facts and opinions; investigative, analytical and problem solving skills	
Embedded E-learning	Computer 'trains' operator step-by-step as tasks are carried out	Knowledge and skills but varying extent of actual learning	
Learning log	Diary or journal used by learner to reflect on work or learning events and draw out and record learning points	All types	
Team tasks	Practical indoor or outdoor exercises or simulations	Planning, organising, team and interpersonal skills	
Coaching	Learner takes responsibility for own learning and uses trainer as coach to raise awareness	All types	

Assessment of knowledge and understanding

The following projects, activities and assessments are directly linked to the essential knowledge and understanding outlined in this chapter.

1 Discuss the benefits of creating a team that work well together and the importance of communication in the workplace.

2 List the five main points that should be taken into consideration when sourcing a new supplier and why these are important.

i) _____

ii) _____

iii) _____

iv) _____

v) _____

3 What are the different ways in which training can be carried out?

4 What is the difference between trainer centred and learner centred activities?

5 Why is it important for your team members to write a development plan?

Research Task

The benefits of learning and the development of the team have been outlined in this chapter. Your task is to research an organisation in the hospitality industry (this could be your workplace), to find out what learning opportunities are available to their staff and the different ways in which they are utilised to assist with staff development.

2

Supervising food safety in catering (Unit 302)

LEARNING OUTCOMES

This chapter introduces the important subject of food safety in catering and key supervisory responsibilities.

The chapter takes account of the latest approach to food safety and consumer protection and is set at level three formal training as described in the UK industry guides to good hygiene practice. This will ensure compliance of the Food Safety Act 1990, the Food Hygiene (England, Scotland, Wales, Northern Ireland) Regulations 2005.

The chapter introduces candidates to the importance of food safety in catering and supervisory responsibilities. Food business operators are responsible for identifying the training and instruction needs of food handlers and for determining how these needs are met. The measures put in place should ensure that all food handlers have sufficient knowledge and competence to handle food safely. This training relates to the nature of food handlers' duties, the types of foodstuff handled and associated food hazards, and the risks to food safety presented by food operations for which the food handler is responsible.

There are **four** principal outcomes to this chapter. At the end of this chapter the candidate will be able to:

- Ensure compliance with legislation
- Apply and monitor good hygiene practice
- Implement food safety management procedures
- Receive and store food safely

The legality of the information contained within this chapter is current and relevant at the time of printing; however, the acts are routinely and annually analysed and reformed as appropriate. Care should be taken to ensure that all information is checked against government guidelines.

Further information can be sourced from the following website: http://www.food.gov.uk

INTRODUCTION

The chef must be particularly conscious of the need for hygiene: many commodities have to be handled and prepared for the customer without any type of heat treatment. High standards of hygiene are essential to prevent food poisoning, food spoilage, loss of productivity, pest infestation and potential criminal prosecution for malpractice.

Food hygiene implies more than just the sanitation of work areas. It includes all practices, precautions and legal responsibilities involved in the following:

1 Protecting food from risk of contamination

2 Preventing organisms from multiplying to an extent which would pose a health risk to customers and employees

3 Destroying any harmful bacteria in food by thorough heat treatment or other techniques.

PERSONAL HYGIENE

Good hygiene systems must be followed by all food handlers. Regular hand washing is a requirement of the chef, and in all aspects of a chefs' working day. The following procedure should be followed:

1 Use an approved hand washing detergent, which should be provided by the employer, preferably in liquid form and from a dispenser

2 Use hot water and an approved drying system

3 Apply an alcohol-based hand disinfectant for maximum disinfection.

Two students fully dressed in chef's uniforms

Hand washing must be undertaken:

■ Before commencing work (to wash away general bacteria)

■ After using the toilet or contact with faeces

■ After breaks

■ Between touching raw food and cooked food

■ Before handling raw food

■ After disposing of waste

■ After cleaning the workspace

HEALTH & SAFETY

Plastic disposable spoons should be used to taste food during preparation and cooking and then disposed of immediately. Use a new spoon for each tasting.

- After any first aid or dressing changes
- After touching face, nose, mouth or blowing your nose
- Hand washing and sanitation should take place at every possible opportunity.

Tasting food whilst cooking

Whilst it is good practice for a chef to constantly taste food during cooking, you must use a spoon that is washed between tastings. A disposable plastic spoon that is discarded after tasting is best practice. The practice of tasting food from the fingers is tantamount to spitting in the food and must be prohibited. The mouth is likely to harbour *Staphylococci* and so food handlers should not chew gum, eat sweets, spit or touch their mouth or nose whilst working.

A chef tasting food with a plastic spoon

Hair

Hair should be washed regularly and kept covered. It should be tied up if shoulder length and placed inside a hairnet. To maintain food hygiene standards many types of hat are now available from suppliers, most of which are disposable. They also present a professional image in serving and kitchen areas that are visible to the public and customers.

Hair tied back with a hairnet and hat

Cuts, boils and septic wounds

Food handlers should always cover cuts, grazes, boils and septic wounds with the appropriate dressing or with brightly coloured blue waterproof plasters. Cuts on fingers may need extra protection with waterproof fingerstalls or latex disposable gloves.

Chef with short hair and a chef hat

Smoking

This is prohibited where food is being prepared because:

- There is a danger of contaminating food with *Staphylococci* from the fingers which may have touched the lips and the saliva on the cigarette end.
- It encourages coughing.

A skullcap

Jewellery and cosmetics

Food handlers and chefs should not wear watches, rings, earrings or other piercings because they can harbour dirt and bacteria. Plain wedding bands are permitted, but these can still harbour significant levels of bacteria. Strong-smelling perfume may cause food to be tainted and make-up should be used minimally.

A chef hat

A chef jacket

Non-slip safety shoes

An apron

Chef neckerchief

Chef trousers

IMAGES COURTESY OF RUSSUMS.CO.UK

Protective clothing

Every person handling food must wear protective clothing. It should be lightweight, washable and strong. White clothing has the advantage of showing up dirt easily. It is important that chefs wear the following protective garments in the kitchen environment:

1 Chef hat or skullcap

2 Chef jacket – double breasted

3 Apron – long and made from heavy cotton

4 Non-slip safety shoes

5 Trousers – comfortable fit and preferably cotton

6 Chef neckerchief – coloured appropriately (if required).

Protective clothing is worn to protect the food from risk of contamination and to help protect the chef from spillages of any kind. Protective clothing should not be worn outside of food premises, including travelling to and from work.

A CLEAN AND HYGIENIC WORK AREA

The use of premises which are clean and can be correctly maintained is essential for the preparation, cooking and service of food. **Cross-contamination** risks should be minimised by the provision of separate preparation areas for the various raw and cooked foods. The table describes the various fittings and fixtures that need to be considered in a kitchen before the main equipment is planned:

FIXTURES AND FITTINGS	RECOMMENDATIONS
Ceilings	White in colour to reflect the light. Smooth-textured, without cracks or peeled paint/plaster. Usually panelled to hide the ventilation system.
Floors	Should have a durable, non-slip and non-permeable material. They can be tiled but polyurethane screeds are now used extensively in food processing areas. This type of screed is fast to install, offers good levels of chemical resistance even to the most aggressive acids and fats, and can be installed to withstand steam cleaning. It is a slip-resistant surface (equally important), designed to give a textured finish.
Lighting	Good lighting is essential to avoid eye strain. Natural light is best but where artificial lighting is used some thought should be given to the type used.
Ventilation	The requirements of a high-performance kitchen ventilation system for the modern kitchen. The extracted air should be free from grease and odours, and be discharged up single or multiple chimney stacks. A canopy system should be built around the existing structure of the kitchen to cover at least all cookery areas. The incorporation of a balancing system to ensure equal extract along the whole cook line is very important.

FIXTURES AND FITTINGS	RECOMMENDATIONS
Ventilation *Continued*	Replacement air is introduced into the kitchen through low-velocity diffusers mounted in the front face of the canopy and spot cooling nozzles can also provide a cooler air temperature in the kitchen. These are a potential source of dirt, grease and dust and should be cleaned on a very regular basis.
Walls	Ceramic wall tiles were considered the best surface for areas where liquids splash a wall surface, potentially overcoming a damp or hygiene problem. Many such areas still exist in industrial and commercial hygiene-sensitive areas. Their durability, long-term appearance and cost of maintenance can be questionable and today there is a viable alternative to consider. Modern alternatives to ceramic wall tiles include PVC wall cladding systems, resin wall coatings and screed mortars. They offer a hygienic finish capable of withstanding heavy-impact use.

EQUIPMENT

Work surfaces and equipment for the preparation, cooking and service of food should be impervious and easy to clean. Equipment should be constructed from materials which are non-toxic, corrosion resistant, smooth and free from cracks. Apparatus such as a **bain-marie** should be able to store hot food for up to two hours at an ambient temperature of 63°C and regular temperature checks should be taken. The surfaces should be easy to clean even when hot and should allow the food to be presented in an attractive manner.

Worktops and chopping boards

It is very important to keep all worktops and chopping boards clean because they touch the food your customers are going to eat. If they are not properly clean, bacteria could spread to food and make your customers ill.

- Always wash worktops before you start preparing food.
- Wipe up any spilt food immediately.
- Always wash worktops thoroughly after they have been touched by raw meat, including poultry, or raw eggs.
- Never put ready-to-eat food, such as tomatoes or fruit, on a worktop or chopping board that has been touched by raw meat, unless you have washed it thoroughly first.

If you have a dishwasher, this is a very effective way to clean plastic chopping boards. Dishwashers can wash at a very high temperature, which kills bacteria. Otherwise, wash chopping boards thoroughly with hot water and detergent. Sanitise boards on a regular basis using an appropriate sanitising substance.

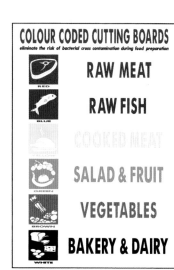

IMAGE COURTESY OF RUSSUMS.CO.UK

Coloured high-density chopping boards

Ideally, it is standard practice to have separate chopping boards for raw meat and for other foods. A standardised system of coloured boards and knife handles which help to minimise cross-contamination are widely available. They should be as follows:

- Red – raw meat and poultry
- Yellow – cooked meat and poultry
- Blue – raw fish (in this book, white and wooden backgrounds may be used for photographic purposes)
- Brown – vegetables
- Green – fruit and salads
- White – dairy and pastry items.

These boards must be cleaned between use, ideally with sanitiser and clean cotton, non-woven fabric or specialised paper cleaning cloths. They should be soaked over night in a sterilising solution on a regular basis. The boards are stored in racks and should not be touching each other.

If boards become damaged they should be discarded. Bacteria can multiply in cracks and blemishes, and be the cause of contamination.

Kitchen cloths

Dirty, damp cloths are the perfect breeding ground for bacteria. It is very important to wash kitchen cloths and other cleaning cloths, sponges and abrasive materials regularly and leave them to dry before using them again.

Ideally, try to keep different cloths for different jobs. For example, use one cloth to wipe worktops and another to wash dishes. This helps to stop bacteria spreading.

The safest option is the use of disposable kitchen towels to wipe worktops and chopping boards. This is because you throw the kitchen towel away after using it once, so it is less likely to spread bacteria than cloths you use again.

Tea towels can also spread bacteria, so it's important to wash them regularly and be careful how you use them. Remember, if you wipe your hands on a tea towel after you have touched raw meat, this will spread bacteria to the towel. Then, if you use the tea towel to dry a plate, the bacteria will spread to the plate.

Knives, spoons and other utensils

It is important to keep knives, wooden spoons, spatulas, tongs and other utensils clean to help stop bacteria spreading to food. It is especially important to wash them thoroughly after using them with raw meat, otherwise they can spread bacteria to other food.

Once again, a dishwasher is a very effective way to clean knives and other utensils because dishwashers can wash at a very high temperature, which kills bacteria. Otherwise, wash them thoroughly with hot water and detergents.

SAFE FOOD STORAGE

An HACCP food management system will also examine the point of food storage. It should cover the receiving of goods where the core temperatures and condition of the delivery is thoroughly checked. Fresh meat that has been delivered should have a core temperature of a maximum of 8°C. All fresh produce should be delivered in unbroken, clean packaging and in clean delivery vehicles that are refrigerated. If you suspect a delivery has not met the requirements of your HACCP it should be refused and returned immediately to the supplier. A goods inwards sheet showing the company, invoice number, core temperature, any problems and how they were dealt with allows received goods to be monitored.

After the commodity has been received it needs to be correctly stored. Raw meat and fish should be stored and covered in separate refrigerators at 4°C. If there is not enough capacity for two separate refrigeration systems, *cooked products must be stored above fresh meat*. Fish should be stored as low in the refrigerator as possible. This is the coldest part of the refrigerator and a layer of crushed ice will help to keep the temperature down. This method eliminates cross-contamination from storage and optimises quality. All foods should be labelled with the date of delivery/production, a description of the contents and the recommended use by date.

 CHEF'S TIP

As a result of changes in European food hygiene regulations on 1 January 2006, the Food Standards Agency has issued new guidance on temperature control legislation in England, Wales and Northern Ireland. The guidance contains advice on the types of foods that are required to be held under temperature control and on the circumstances in which some flexibility from the temperature control requirements is allowed. The guidance is intended to complement best practices in the food industry, which might involve, for example, keeping foods at chill temperatures below the legal maximum and thereby providing additional assurances of food safety.

VIDEO CLIP
Receipt and storage of produce

An example of a Goods Received Checklist.

Chef's name _____

Production area _____

Goods Received Checklist

Date	Time	Supplier	Order correct	Delivery note/ Invoice number	Fault (Identify product)	Action	Temperature reading	Signature

THE CHEF'S RESPONSIBILITIES FOR FOOD SAFETY

The professional chef is responsible for ensuring that food safety and the legislation that surrounds are strictly enforced at all times.

A chef's role in the kitchen is not only to produce high quality food but also to ensure that the customer is kept happy and safe. Food safety is defined as the safeguarding of food from 'farm to fork'. This means ensuring that the produce is fit to eat, that it is stored, prepared and cooked to a constant high level; and that the administrative tasks are completed as required, such as keeping fridge temperature records.

One of the most important skills a chef can acquire in the kitchen is organisation; this will facilitate cleaning, cooking, storage and record-taking. This skill will be developed with experience and will ensure that a highly motivated, professional kitchen is maintained at all times.

Daily activities that need to be completed are:

- Fridge and freezer temperature monitoring
- Received food temperature monitoring
- Cold and hot hold temperature monitoring
- Core temperature monitoring
- Disinfection of all contact areas.

Weekly activities that need to be completed are:

- Deep cleaning of the kitchen
- Checking, signing and collation of all records
- Updating of record files (files are to be kept for a minimum of three months).

It has been shown that an organised, clean and safe working environment will produce higher quality produce and make for a happier environment to work in. An enjoyable working environment will also help to reduce staff absence and reinforce team spirit.

CHEF'S TIP

A laminated chart situated in the kitchen listing routine tasks such as fridge temperature monitoring is a simple way to ensure the tasks are completed.

HEALTH & SAFETY

When unpacking a delivery, always ensure the product packaging is undamaged to avoid possible personal injury from broken goods.

TYPES OF BACTERIA THAT CAUSE FOOD POISONING

Salmonella

There are approximately over 2000 types of Salmonella; the most common varieties are *Salmonella enteriditis* and *Salmonella typhimurium.* These organisms survive in the intestine and can cause food poisoning by releasing a toxin on the death of the cell. The primary source of salmonella is the intestinal tract of animals and poultry. It will therefore be found in:

A well laid-out store room

■ Human and animal excreta

■ Excreta from rats, mice, flies and cockroaches

■ Raw meat and poultry

■ Some animal feed.

Staphylococcus aureus

About 40–50 per cent of adults carry this organism in their nose, mouth, throat, ears and hands. If present in food, *Staphylococcus aureus* will produce a toxin which may survive boiling for 30 minutes or more. The majority of outbreaks are caused by poor hygiene practices which result in direct contamination of the food from sneezing or uncovered septic cuts and abrasions. Frequently, the cooked food has been handled whilst still slightly warm, and these storage conditions have encouraged the organism to produce its toxin.

Clostridium perfringens

This is commonly found in human and animal faeces and is present in raw meat and poultry. This organism forms spores which may survive boiling temperatures for several hours. Outbreaks can involve stews and large joints of meat which have been allowed to cool down slowly in a warm kitchen and either eaten cold or inadequately reheated the following day.

Bacillus cereus

This is a spore-forming organism. The spores survive normal cooking and rapid growth will occur if the food has not been cooled quickly and refrigerated.

This bacteria will induce nausea and vomiting within five hours of ingestion.

Food storage label

VIDEO CLIP
Control of pests
and infestations

Food temperature safety guide

LEGISLATION AFFECTING ALL FOOD HANDLERS

The law

The law states that all catering businesses are required to produce food that is safe to eat, and that proprietors must be able to demonstrate what they have done to ensure they are serving safe food – and have this written down.

The law explained

CHEF'S TIP

The HACCP system relies on staff adhering to the rules and regulations. Ensure that all staff are aware of their responsibility at all times.

Due diligence is the main legal defence endorsed by the Food Safety Act 1990. It provides the best protection to companies that need to demonstrate in court that all reasonable precautions have been taken to avoid the sale of unsafe food.

The first step for food manufacturers developing a HACCP system is to set up a team, whose members must be adequately trained in HACCP principles and their application. This team will also decide who should be responsible for implementing the system.

The next stage is to carefully identify each step in the preparation of each dish, starting with the purchase of the ingredients and ending with sale to the customer, and to formulate these steps into a flowchart, such as that below. Each element of the flowchart would then need to be broken down and additional detail added, such as transport in a clean vehicle with temperature controls.

Each step then needs to be carefully analysed to identify what could go wrong and result in a safety hazard to the customer. Such hazards include bacteria, foreign bodies and chemical contaminants.

In addition, where **vegetarian, vegan** or allergen-free food is prepared alongside other food, it is important to undertake a risk assessment to identify, segregate or manage any allergens or ingredients that could cause harm or discomfort to customers.

The next stage is to identify what can be done to control potential hazards.

Controls may include:

- Separation of raw and cooked foods to avoid cross-contamination
- Personal hygiene rules to avoid contamination by bacteria
- Correct cooking times and temperatures to destroy harmful bacteria.

For every step where a potential hazard has been identified, it will be necessary to consider whether or not the customer will be harmed if nothing is done. That will dictate which steps are critical control points.

The next stage is to set standards, or critical limits, for the controls. These will specify the conditions that must be met to ensure that the food will be safe. Checks should be carried out at predetermined times and records kept to show that the controls are working.

If monitoring shows that critical limits are not being met, a designated person must take corrective action. They must also record what action has been taken.

Whenever a recipe is altered, a new dish added to the menu, a new activity introduced or the structure of the kitchen changed, the HACCP system must be reviewed. But even if no changes take place in the kitchen, the HACCP system should be reviewed at least once a year.

 CHEF'S TIP

Any produce that may cause an allergic reaction should be stored in a sealed container and only used as required.

VIDEO CLIP
An EHO visit to a professional kitchen

Food allergies and intolerances

It is critical to be aware of the issues of food allergies and intolerance when preparing, cooking and serving certain foods:

■ An allergy to food is the hypersensitivity of food constituents. The immune system reacts to a particular food, believing it is not safe to eat. In severe circumstances this can cause a life-threatening reaction.

■ An intolerance to food does not involve the immune system and is generally not life threatening. However, it can still make people ill and it may affect their long-term health.

The following are examples that the chef needs to be aware of:

■ *Lactose intolerance* – a condition in which the body lacks the enzyme lactase and so cannot process lactose. Lactose is present in milk and dairy products.

■ *Coeliac disease* – an intolerance to gluten, a protein substance present in wheat, rye, barley and oat products.

■ *Peanuts and tree nuts* – peanuts in particular can cause extreme reactions and even death. It is impossible for the chef to guarantee a nut-free diet to the guest.

■ *Eggs* – intolerance to the proteins in egg whites or yolks, or sometimes both.

■ *Fish* – fish allergies are more common in children than adults; even the smell can bring on a reaction in a sensitive person. Common fish known to cause symptoms are cod, salmon, trout, herring, bass, swordfish, halibut and tuna.

■ *Shellfish* – reactions to the ingestion of shellfish can be severe, even at the level of inhalation of cooking vapours. Great care should be taken to avoid cross-contamination between shellfish products and all other foodstuffs that might be in contact with the diner. Shellfish commonly known to cause allergic reactions include shrimp, crab, crayfish, lobster, oysters, clams, scallops, mussels, squid and snails. People allergic to shrimp often suffer from respiratory allergy. Crab is also a potent allergen. Shrimp, lobster and crawfish contain common major allergens, making cross-reactivity between shrimp and crab, and lobster and crawfish possible.

HAZARDS

 CHEF'S TIP

Charts allow people to absorb information quickly and easily. When displayed in appropriate areas of a kitchen they help to ensure that best practices are used.

The two diagrams on the following page outline the different types of hazards and the consequences associated with them.

The factors which can cause food poisoning include:

■ Biological contamination

■ Physical contamination

■ Chemical contamination.

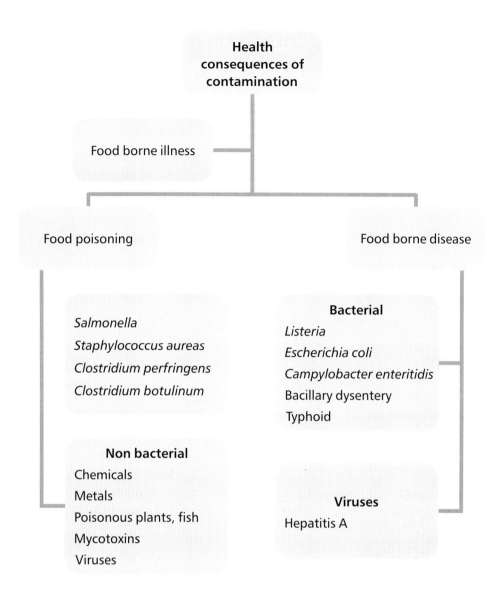

Health consequences of contamination

Food borne illness

Food poisoning

Food borne disease

Bacterial
Salmonella
Staphylococcus aureas
Clostridium perfringens
Clostridium botulinum

Bacterial
Listeria
Escherichia coli
Campylobacter enteritidis
Bacillary dysentery
Typhoid

Non bacterial
Chemicals
Metals
Poisonous plants, fish
Mycotoxins
Viruses

Viruses
Hepatitis A

Biological contamination is caused when ideal conditions, such as warmth, food, moisture and time, are afforded to **pathogens**. Poor personal hygiene practices, cross-contamination, storage, chilling and cooking can all lead to food poisoning. Food poisoning is caused when pathogenic micro-organisms, **bacteria** in particular, are present in sufficient amounts to make

VIDEO CLIP
Core temperatures

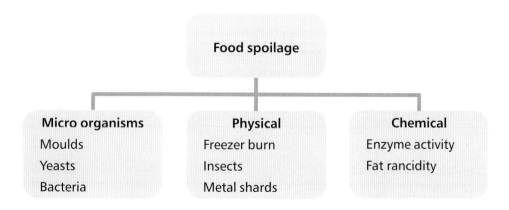

Food spoilage

Micro organisms
Moulds
Yeasts
Bacteria

Physical
Freezer burn
Insects
Metal shards

Chemical
Enzyme activity
Fat rancidity

VIDEO CLIP
Colour coded
chopping boards

the body ill. Different pathogens affect the body in different ways, and the end result can be diarrhoea, vomiting, dehydration and even death.

Physical contamination is caused when an objectionable substance is present in food, such as glass found in a beef stew. Physical contamination can produce symptoms in the same way as bacterial poisoning.

Chemical contamination occurs when a chemical such as sanitiser, bleach or washing-up liquid comes into contact with food and is ingested by a person. The usual reaction is vomiting, which should be avoided if possible because any injury received during swallowing may be worsened by vomiting.

Food-borne illness is mainly associated with poor handling of foodstuffs. This is why chefs and food handlers undergo such thorough training.

Food poisoning and food-borne disease are separate hazards and there are various differences between the two.

Food-borne diseases:

▓ Incubate for a longer period of time

▓ Require a smaller amount to make somebody ill

▓ Are transported on food but do not use it to multiply

▓ Can be spread by items other than food

▓ Can enter the bloodstream

▓ Symptoms may or may not include vomiting or diarrhoea.

CHEF'S TIP

A monthly test of all staff (which is then recorded) will give reassurance to the chefs, management and Environmental Health Officer that every effort is being made to ensure that best practices are used and that a due diligence defence is being built should the need arise.

CONTROLS

Food safety needs to be addressed by ensuring that adequate controls are in place. Controls range from those which require regular adjustment to those which cannot be altered, such as design and construction of premises. All control measures should be built into the organisation's framework and continually monitored by the senior personnel responsible for their implementation.

Controls come in many forms, from spot checks of staff uniforms to advanced training and HACCP.

Staff should be regularly tested on their knowledge and on the effectiveness of the monitoring systems used in the organisation. A kitchen is only as effective as its weakest member of staff; if a chef is unable to take temperatures, cook correctly or follow standard hygiene practices then an incident is likely to occur.

Food storage and temperatures

Raw meat, poultry and game and charcuterie – 4°C or below. Store away from cooked meat and cooked meat products to avoid any risk of cross-contamination.

Cooked meat – 4°C or below. Keep away from raw meat and meat products.

Uncooked fish – 4°C or below. Keep in separate compartments or in plastic fish trays with lids if possible, and away from other foods which may become tainted.

Frozen food – –18°C or below. Thaw only immediately prior to using the commodity.

Fish (smoked or cured) – 8°C. Keep in chilled storage away from other foods, which may become tainted.

Fruit (fresh and dried). Store in a cool, dry, well-ventilated area, away from other food, at least 15cm from the ground. Discard at the first sign of mould growth. Do not overstock.

Pasta, rice and cereals – Store in self-closing tightly lidded containers in dry cool storeroom or cupboard.

Eggs – Refrigerate at 8°C or below. Use strictly in rotation and ensure the shells are clean.

Fats, butter, dairy and non-dairy spreads – 8°C or below. Keep covered and away from highly flavoured food, which may taint.

Milk and cream – 8°C or below. In a separate dairy refrigerator that is used for no other purpose and in strict rotation.

Canned and bottled goods – Cool, dry, well-ventilated storage area. Blown, rusty or split tins must not be used.

Root vegetables – Store in sacks or nets as delivered in cool, well-ventilated area.

Leaf and green vegetables – 8°C. Use on day of delivery.

Freezers, whether upright or chest freezers, should be maintained at a maximum temperature of –18°C. All food should be covered to prevent **freezer burn** and labelled with the date of production and a use by date.

Ambient stores should be clean and well ventilated, with mesh over windows and doors to help with pest control. All foodstuffs must be stored away from the floor and be rotated on a first in and first out basis.

Glass fronted fridge

PREPARING, COOKING AND STORING FOOD SAFELY

Frozen food should be defrosted in a refrigerator and treated as fresh food with the same use by date. All root vegetables must be washed prior to peeling and then rewashed after peeling. Leaf vegetables such as cabbage and spinach should be washed in several changes of cold water to allow soil and grit to go to the bottom of the sink. Ideally a separate preparation area should be facilitated to help prevent cross-contamination.

Chilling food not for immediate use should ideally be achieved in blast chillers where the core temperature is brought down from 70°C to 4°C in 90 minutes or less. With these temperature ranges both pathogenic and bacterial growth is inhibited although not completely stopped.

Digital food thermometer

If food that has been cooked is not for immediate consumption, or is to be frozen, it should be well covered with cling film or ideally vacuum packed to create an airtight barrier and prevent freezer burn. Storage should be within manufacturer's guidelines and the foods must be clearly labelled as previously mentioned.

 CHEF'S TIP

The correct measurement of temperature should be monitored by the use of an accurate digital food thermometer. The probe is inserted into the centre of meat joints or placed onto the surface of other ingredients to give a temperature reading within a few seconds. Alcohol-based sanitiser wipes should be used to clean the stainless steel probe after every use to prevent cross-contamination.

AREAS WHERE HAZARDS MIGHT OCCUR

STEP	HAZARD	CONTROL
Receipt of goods	▥ Contaminated high-risk foods ▥ Damaged or decomposed goods ▥ Incorrect specifications ▥ Growth of pathogens between the time of receipt and storage	▥ All deliveries inspected and checked by a staff member ▥ Appropriate labelling ▥ Prompt and correct storage
Storage	▥ Contamination of high-risk foods ▥ Contamination through poor handling ▥ Contamination by pests ▥ Spoilage of food by decomposition	▥ Correct usage of refrigeration regimes ▥ Foods must be suitably stored in the correct packaging or receptacles ▥ Materials that are in direct contact with food must be of food-grade quality ▥ A contract for a pest control service must be in place ▥ Correct stock rotation ▥ Out of date and unfit food stuffs must be segregated from other foods and removed from the premises
Preparation	▥ Contamination of high-risk foods ▥ Contamination through poor handling ▥ Growth of pathogens and toxins	▥ Keep raw and cooked foods separate ▥ Use pasteurised eggs for raw and lightly cooked egg dishes ▥ All food contact surfaces must be fit for purpose ▥ Food handlers must be trained in hygienic food handling techniques ▥ Keep the exposure of fresh foods at ambient temperatures to a minimum ▥ Label all food that is to be used more than one day in advance of production with its description and use by date
Cooking	▥ Survival of pathogens and spores	▥ Cook all foods to the minimum recommended temperature
Chilling	▥ Growth of pathogens, spores = toxin production ▥ Contamination	▥ Cool foods as quickly as possible, to 8°C in 90 minutes ▥ Keep food that is chilling loosely covered ▥ Use only clean equipment

STEP	HAZARD	CONTROL
Hot hold	■ Growth of pathogens and toxin production ■ Contamination by staff and customers, especially in self-service operations	■ Maintain food at 63°C and discard after 2 hours ■ Keep containers covered when not in service ■ Use sneeze screens ■ Supervise self-service
Cold hold	■ Growth of pathogens and toxin production ■ Contamination by staff and customers especially in self-service operations	■ Keep food at 5°C and discard after 4 hours ■ Keep containers covered when not in service ■ Use sneeze screens ■ Supervise self-service

How to produce a HACCP (Hazard Analysis Critical Control Point) plan using the twelve step formula

1 Assemble the team responsible for HACCP

Initially you must assemble a team that is comprised of multi-ability individuals; they should have managerial, technical and specialist knowledge of the particular area involved. It is important to select a team that is familiar with the environment but people that do not spend every day working in that particular zone, as they become blinkered to the areas requiring attention.

■ The team should be aware of all hazards.

■ The team should have a good understanding of how hazards are controlled.

■ Identify any training required within the team prior to commencing the HACCP plan.

■ Visit the government website (http://www.food.gov.uk). The food standards agency publishes practical guidance on all matters regarding food safety and the relevant industry.

2 Describe the product

In a professional organisation all products with full descriptions need to be documented and all relevant information compiled.

■ Raw materials

■ Storage conditions

■ Processing

■ Ingredients and products

■ Packaging

■ Shelf life, best before and use by dates

■ Hygiene risks.

3 Identify intended use

Having produced the above information several questions then need to be answered such as:

▓ What is the shelf life of the product?

▓ Can the food product be traced back to the farm?

▓ Are there any special requirements for production or consumption?

▓ Does the product require ambient, refrigeration or freezing temperatures?

4 Construct a flow diagram

The flow diagram should be drawn up by the HACCP team and should cover all stages of the operation from supply to consumption. See the example below for a cooked roast chicken

Purchase
↓
Delivery
↓
Frozen storage
↓
Defrost
↓
Refrigerated storage
↓
Preparation
↓
Cook
↓
Blast chill
↓
Package/label/code
↓
Refrigerated storage
↓
Refrigerated distribution

5 Confirmation of flow diagram

This process is important and must be completed at all stages of the process, this ensures that the HACCP plan is accurate and follows all specifications.

If there are any differences at this stage that are not identified and confirmed they may cause potential problems in the future.

6 Hazard analysis and control measures

This forms the most complex stage of the process. Each hazard must:

▓ Identify all hazards that may occur at each stage

■ Decide which hazards need to be eradicated or reduced to a safe level prior to production

■ Consider how likely each hazard is to occur

■ Decide what control measures need to be implemented.

7 Determine the critical control points

A CCP is a step or point in a process where a control can be applied.

It is essential to reduce or remove any hazards within the process, if it is not controlled then this may cause harm to the consumer.

The points, which are indicated on the flow chart, if not controlled could cause serious food poisoning or even death.

8 Establish critical control limits

The limits need to be checked on a regular basis to ensure the parameters do not fall into a dangerous zone. For example, a cooked chicken must reach 70°C for 2 minutes and hot held above 63°C. These limits are to reduce the dangers of microbiological food poisoning.

9 Establish a monitoring system for each control point

This process involved monitoring points along a food chain to ensure there are no breaks in the chain and at no time does the process become a hazard.

There is no individual check for a CCP but a series that ensures safety is always maintained and hazards are reduced to a safe level.

10 Establish corrective actions

A full documented CCP will ensure that any deviation from the plan will result in a correct action being undertaken.

For example, if the cooked chicken does not reach 70°C for 2 minutes the checks in place will ensure the food is either cooked until the core temperature is achieved and maintained or the product is thrown away. This process ensures that no break in the chain occurs and the food maintains safe to eat.

11 Establish verification procedures

Verification is achieved once the work methods are operational; this process ensures that all checks, CCPs and corrective actions are being followed. Only during operation can verification be achieved as this highlights areas that require attention and ones that are working perfectly.

It is recommended that this process is completed at least every six months to ensure that the processes are working and the food is safe for the consumer.

12 Establish documentation and record keeping

Documentation and record keeping are essential as they provide due diligence in case a food related incident occurs.

Documentation and record keeping examples are:

■ A detailed hazard analysis report
■ Records of regular monitoring
■ Records of procedures.

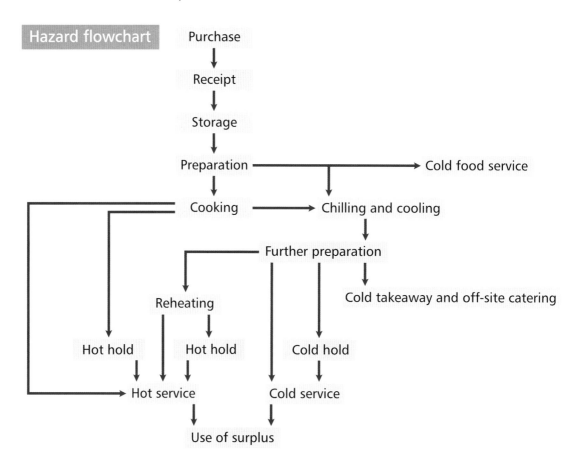

Hazard flowchart

General hazard controls to consider

■ Regular servicing of equipment
■ Use of a temperature probe to check on stored food
■ Use of a temperature probe to check on food storage equipment
■ Investigation of all complaints of suspected food-borne illnesses
■ Regular inspections by a health and safety officer
■ Frequent self inspections
■ Comprehensive cleaning programmes
■ Adequate staff training in food handling and hygiene practices.

In every professional kitchen, a working system that controls the purchase and use of all ingredients needs to be maintained. It should detail the work flow to prevent hazards from occurring during the storage, preparation, cooking and service of food.

Assessment of knowledge and understanding

You have now learned about the health and hygiene responsibilities of everyone in the workplace. This will enable you to ensure your own work areas, food preparation, cookery and service actions reduce risks in health.

To test your level of knowledge and understanding, answer the following short questions. These will help to prepare you for your summative (final) assessment.

1 State the food safety hazards that wearing jewellery can cause.

2 Identify who health hazards are reported to.

3 Identify the importance of reporting illnesses quickly and the significance of stomach illnesses.

4 State three reasons why work surfaces and chopping boards should be clean and hygienic.

i) _____ ii) _____

iii) _____

5 Explain the reason for regular maintenance checks.

6 Explain the importance of storing food at the correct temperature.

7 Describe the term 'stock rotation'.

Research Task A

Carry out a HACCP assessment on the following products. Consider the hazard, the critical control point and the action to be taken.

(a) Fresh raw poultry _____

(b) Fresh fruit and vegetables _____

Research Task B

The HACCP assessment criteria have been outlined in this chapter. Your task is to produce a personalised HACCP plan for a restaurant or hotel (this could be your workplace), to find out what systems could be improved and developed. The plan should focus on high risk areas such as delivery, storage, preparation and cooking.

3
Practical gastronomy (Unit 303)

LEARNING OUTCOMES

The aim of this chapter is to enable the candidate to develop the necessary knowledge and understanding of the principles of the dining experience. It covers the influences on gastronomy, including that of culture, religion, geographical location, the transportation of commodities, and science and technology.

The candidate will need to evaluate the factors that contribute to the dining experience and how customer needs can differ.

There are **two** principal outcomes to this chapter. At the end of this chapter the candidate will be able to:

■ Explain the influences on eating and drinking cultures
■ Investigate the supply and use of commodities

INTRODUCTION

Gastronomy is the study of the relationship between food and culture. There are numerous areas studied in this chapter, including culture, location, the human body and religion. For many people food and gastronomy are a way of life regardless of whether this relates to a simple family roast or a twelve course tasting menu in a three Michelin starred restaurant.

In this modern day full of technological advances geography is no longer a barrier to the consumer or the chef; exotic ingredients and dishes from all over the world are now common place and their ready availability has reduced the cost.

Key economic issues such as sustainability and food air miles – have become a focal point which many people are striving to improve.

Cultural and religious beliefs have played a large part in the development of gastronomy. A dining experience from India, Asia, Africa, modern Britain or America is readily accessible to all and helps develop a range of exciting styles of cooking and service.

A contemporary presentation of salmon tartare

One of the newest and most exciting areas of gastronomy is the use of technology; whether it is the use of an immersion circulator, liquid nitrogen or a vacuum machine, new cooking, serving and entertainment possibilities are changing the way food is thought of.

The health issues surrounding diners have played an enormous part in the way food is designed and cooked for consumers. The days of thick gelatinous sauces and high fat meals served regularly are gone. In their place are light lower fat dishes that form part of a balanced diet.

Gastronomy has become a very talked about subject with celebrity chefs, food programmes, cooking shows, competitions and kitchen alchemists unlocking the secrets of the professional kitchen and enticing a new breed of gastronome into the mix.

Geography

The term geography when used within the context of gastronomy refers to terrain, lakes, rivers, the sea, soil and the climate.

Examples of naturally sourced products making the most of locally skilled workers include clotted cream from Devon, crabs from Cromer, Gloucester old spot pigs and Jersey Royal potatoes. By using sustainable local produce not only is there less environmental impact but there is a reduction in air miles, which offsets the carbon footprint.

The increase in global temperature ascribed to climate change has enabled a variety of new species to grow which in turn has made the production of certain food stuffs, such as increased grape production, a new line of olive groves and an increased interest in small holding farms which are self sufficient and produce items for local restaurants, accessible in the United Kingdom.

To view a food map of the United Kingdom visit the Virtual Kitchen website at www.virtualkitchen.co.uk

A small holding pig farm producing organic meat

Small holding farmers

The local community

The environment

The cycle, illustrated above, continues to flow as each point supports the other, ensuring good value, community spirit and a sustainable, well maintained environment for future years.

Transport and transportation

Distribution lorries

As mentioned above, the importance of reducing food air miles has never been so imperative, not only is it the responsibility of everyone associated with the industry but it has become a prerequisite for the majority of diners.

Reducing food orders into weekly slots instead of daily ones is one option available, another is sourcing local produce. By purchasing seasonal produce the chef eradicates the requirement to source abroad for out of season items and thereby reduces the carbon footprint.

There are numerous modes of transport available to suppliers, ranging from the worst carbon versions such as:

- Air transport
- Lorries
- Vans

to the carbon low–neutral versions such as:

- Boats
- Trains
- Locally sourced
- Hand delivered
- Farmers markets.

A farmers market

The following websites give information regarding food miles:

http://www.climatechoices.org.uk/pages/food3.htm
http://www.bbc.co.uk/bloom/guides/foodmiles.shtml

Local producers and even suppliers are now offering the consumer a choice of produce with information as to food miles attached. This allows the chef/purchaser to make an informed decision.

Science and technology

This can be the most exciting and yet worrying of all the areas of gastronomy. The use of equipment such as immersion circulators and water baths can reduce the wastage of food and improve the flavour and texture of tougher cuts.

Specialist ingredient companies have been introduced to provide a natural enhancement to dishes such as carrageenan which is formed from seaweed or Gellan which is created from a bacterial fermentation. These items to name a few can be used to produce hot gels, heat stable foams and liquid centre encapsulations.

Visit the website – www.msk-ingredients.com

The use of Agar

Food chemistry has become a much talked about subject. Understanding how proteins unravel and then form a mesh when eggs are cooked allows a chef to create new dishes. The creation of a soft poached Scotch quail egg using controlled water temperatures, liquid nitrogen and a stop watch has changed how chefs look at food and the boundaries by which they were restricted.

The improvement in the knowledge of science has, however, brought about some unnatural occurrences such as shorter ripening times, less fat in livestock, GM (genetically modified) foods, intensive farming and an increased shelf life.

These advancements may have a future detrimental effect on the well-being of the human race and the way we grow and harvest crops. There is, however, a drive among many to grow organic food and nurture the land to reap future harvests.

Considerations when choosing suppliers

It can be a very challenging and lengthy process when trying to find a suitable supplier to provide produce, but once a solid working relationship has been established it is vital to the successful running of a kitchen.

Most chefs and businesses will source their products from wholesalers, with those that supply specialist commodities usually being recommended by word of mouth from other kitchens. A good reputation can surpass a good supplier and the latter is invaluable in obtaining your required produce.

There are two main types of buying methods. They are commonly referred to as 'informal' buying, which means that an agreement between supplier and purchaser will be verbal, and 'formal' buying, which means that a written agreement will be put in place and is usually undertaken by means of a computerised system of ordering.

When considering which supplier to employ you should take the following factors into consideration:

Quality: You should never buy from a supplier before sampling the produce that they have to offer, even more so with a large wholesaler as you may be required to sign a contract agreeing to purchase their goods for a minimum period of time or at a minimum delivery cost. You should always establish work principles and delivery times with the supplier. Food produce must always be fresh, labelled clearly, properly contained and stored in accordance with health and safety regulations. The supplier should also be aware of the origins of the produce and have the relevant paperwork available.

Quantity: Especially with smaller and local suppliers, you will need to establish the volume of goods that they regularly have available. If this is not determined first, then you run the risk of not having enough stock when specifically required. With equipment items you run the risk of a supplier not being able to replace goods within a reasonable timescale if they do not have a good stock.

Variety: A good variety of produce should be easily made available and with most suppliers specialising in such items as cheeses/dairy, fish, meat, fruit and vegetables, you may well require a separate supplier for each. With technology advancing rapidly, as far as possible, it should be ensured that a supplier has a wide variety of equipment available such as an immersion circulator (this is an expensive and complicated piece of equipment) and that they are aware of technological advances and new products that may be of interest. For any specialist supplier, they should have a good supply of general products as well as specialist items.

Cost: Supplier costs must be calculated carefully prior to instruction/agreement. It should be ensured that any carriage charges are made clear, whether VAT is included in the prices or if this needs to be added, if any ordering charge or minimum order amount applies and if there are any other additional costs that you need to be aware of.

Reliability: Of high importance, any supplier utilised must be reliable. Without them being able to deliver the produce to you, as regularly as you require and in a correct state, then a kitchen will not be able to run smoothly and you could be left without goods and unable to prepare a menu or certain dishes. Fresh produce should be of the highest quality. A professional supplier relies on good feedback and word of mouth to maintain and improve their business. When purchasing any electrical items it is advisable to ask about customer 'after-care', as there may be additional maintenance/ servicing/repair costs that need to be taken into consideration, as well as timescales for emergency call-outs, for example how long it would take to have a piece of equipment repaired if it broke?

When using a supplier on a regular basis, especially for non-specialist items, it is a good idea to negotiate prices, especially on large orders. If you intend to use a supplier regularly and can establish special rates for common items or large quantities of items, you will both benefit through saving money and cost efficiency.

It is imperative that a supplier is given any order requests as soon as practicable so that they have as much time as possible to source produce. By communicating regularly with a supplier you can be kept up to date with details of any special offers and/or specialist goods available and discuss any other matters such as when a particular staff member is absent who the next point of contact would be.

Factors that make a good dining experience

When dining out there are numerous factors that influence our enjoyment. These vary from the delivery and presentation of food to our perception of value for money.

Below is a chart outlining the key areas associated with a 'good' dining experience:

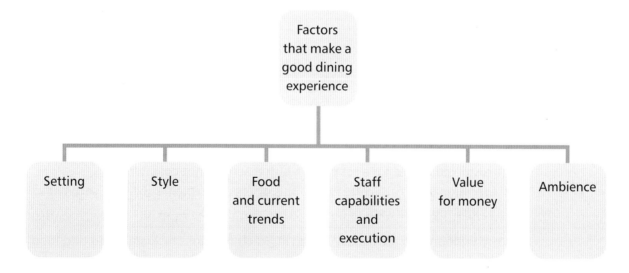

Of course not all restaurants operate in the same format. For example, a three Michelin starred restaurant's standards are considerably higher than those of a canteen operation. The key to an enjoyable experience is to adjust expectations to match the environment the customer is in. A customer has the right to expect a good level of customer care involving attentiveness, attention to detail, value for money and staff friendliness.

BAEVSKIY DMITRY

Attentive service

JOE BIAFORE

A tapas dish served as a snack during the day

Other factors such as style and ambience are not always in place; for example, a local restaurant may not have the soft furnishings or the striking tableware of a high end restaurant but will have friendly staff that work hard so the customer enjoys their dining experience.

Meal types

Traditionally meal types are broken down into the following categories:

- Breakfast
- Lunch
- Afternoon tea
- Dinner.

These have stood the test of time for centuries; however, modern day menus and meals have changed vastly. With the introduction of varied cultural and religious influences, meal times may occur late into the evening, take the form of a buffet or tapas.

Breakfast meals usually consist of the following items:

- Cereals/porridge and yoghurts
- Fruit juices, fresh and preserved fruit
- Egg dishes
- Smoked fish
- Fried meats such as sausage, bacon, black pudding and kidney dishes
- Cold meats
- Sauté potatoes
- Selection of breads and morning goods such as croissants and Danish pastries
- Preserves
- Tea/coffee/hot chocolate.

Lunch meals may take the form of a Table D'hôte, a set menu with a restricted choice for a set price, a buffet serving hot/cold items or occasionally an à la carte menu. This offers complete flexibility as each choice is individually priced.

Afternoon teas are usually served in hotels for those residents requiring food and drink during the afternoon.

Below is an example of an afternoon tea menu:

TRADITIONAL AFTERNOON TEA

Smoked Salmon Sandwiches

Ham Sandwiches

Chicken Sandwiches

Cucumber Sandwiches

Mature Cheddar Cheese Sandwiches

Egg Mayonnaise and Cress Bridge Roll

Freshly Baked Raisin and Apple Scones with

Devonshire Clotted Cream and Strawberry Preserve

Assortment of Afternoon Tea Pastries

Ritz Chocolate Cake

Traditional Afternoon Tea £38 per Person

Champagne Afternoon Tea £49 per Person

Including a glass of Champagne

Celebration Afternoon Tea

Including a birthday cake £49 Per Person

Including a birthday cake and a glass of Champagne £58 Per Person

---

Dinner is usually à la carte as mentioned above or a tasting menu offered by some establishments. This latter menu is a chance for the guest to sample a larger selection of dishes offering smaller portions for a set price. Wine is also offered with each course for a supplement. Below is an example of a tasting menu:

Selection of canapés

Home Smoked Mackerel with Fennel Confit, Avocado, Fresh Crab, Bramley Apple and Sesame Seeds

Marinated Scallops with Brandade Mousse, Cauliflower and Truffle Salad, Lemon Oil and Baby Wood Sorrel

Pan-Fried Foie Gras with Balsamic Gel, Roasted Chantenay Carrots and Pistachio Powder

Pan-Fried Icelandic Cod with an Emulsion of Brown Shrimps, Romanesco and Pinenuts, Broccoli Velouté and Sea Purslane

Roasted Saddle of Fallow Venison, Baked Beetroot, Fresh Walnuts, Pomme Soufflé, Date and Port Sauce

Cheese Selection

Mango and Lime Velouté, Chilli Coconut Foam and Thai Basil

Bitter Sweet Chocolate Tart, Stout Ice Cream and Macadamia Nut Cream

Coffee and Petits Fours

Social, cultural and religious influences on gastronomy

Social influences

Members of a **social group** depend on each other, share a common culture, and influence each other's behaviours and values. A person's membership in a particular peer, work, or community group impacts food behaviours. For example, a young person at a restaurant may eat certain foods when accompanied by friends and other foods when accompanied by their spouse or family members.

Religious influences

Different Religious beliefs may vary from very relaxed to highly restrictive where gastronomy is concerned. This will affect a follower's food choices and behaviours. For example, in some religions specific foods are prohibited, such as pork among Jewish and Muslim faiths. Alcohol is also banned by some faiths so care must be taken to be prescriptive when producing menus.

Cultural influences

Each culture has their own speciality foods and preparation methods. Britain, France, China, Japan, Mexico, Pan Asia, Italy and India are examples of cultural areas known for their gastronomy.

Within each culture there is an etiquette that is followed when eating and drinking. This will vary depending on the country, background and cultural ties of each person.

Media and individuals influence

The use of the media to promote gastronomy over the last few years has been immense. Celebrity chefs cooking on television, competitions, back to basic cooking programmes and the government campaign encouraging people to eat five fruit and vegetables a day has created intense interest in this area.

There has been a huge advancement in high level catering colleges offering bespoke courses and specialist skills, providing 'the experience' into the trade that customers expect and deserve.

MONKEY BUSINESS IMAGES

A well organised brigade of chefs

Dining experiences

The dining experience will always depend upon the venue selected. This should not, however, detract from the positive feelings a guest should leave with, chief among which are:

■ Satisfaction
■ Value for money

■ Attentiveness

■ Welcome.

These factors should remain constant and ensure the guest returns again.

This chart shows the different areas of exposure that a customer could expect within the gastronomic world.

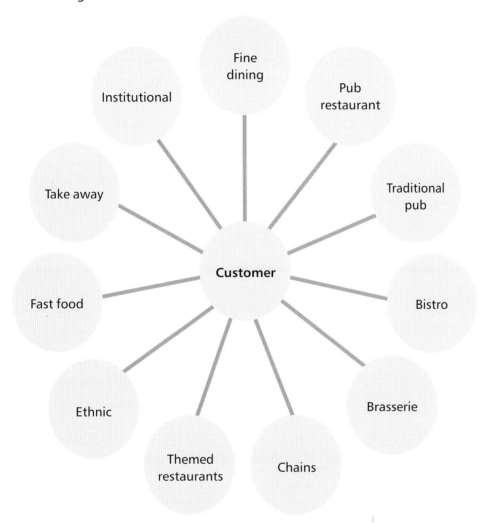

Lifestyle changes

The modern day climate has seen a move towards ready meals and fast food at one end with the media and government trying to encourage a more wholesome approach to the topic at the other.

The introduction of healthy eating initiatives has seen many people return to the kitchen to produce healthy meals for the family and increase their fruit and vegetable consumption.

The price of meals offered by many top restaurants has opened the door to many who have begun to find a real appreciation for quality produce, techniques and settings. The interest has led to a huge surge in the market for gastronomy and food in general.

Assessment of knowledge and understanding

The following projects, activities and assessments are directly linked to the essential knowledge and understanding outlined in this chapter.

1 Discuss the benefits of sourcing local suppliers and interacting with them as a community.

_____

_____

2 List the 10 types of establishment that are associated with gastronomy.

i)_____   ii)_____

iii)_____   iv)_____

v)_____   vi)_____

vii)_____   viii)_____

ix)_____   x)_____

3 What are the main influences on gastronomy?

_____

_____

4 Explain how technology and science can both benefit and potentially harm gastronomy.

_____

_____

5 What types of meal are there and give examples for each?

_____

_____

Research Task

Gastronomy has been discussed as a whole within this chapter. Highlight one particular area that is of significant interest to you and research how to develop it for the future, for example:

■ Science and technology – look at new techniques of cooking and food presentation.

■ Look at potential problems and faults that may occur.

■ Develop a dining experience that mirrors these ideas.

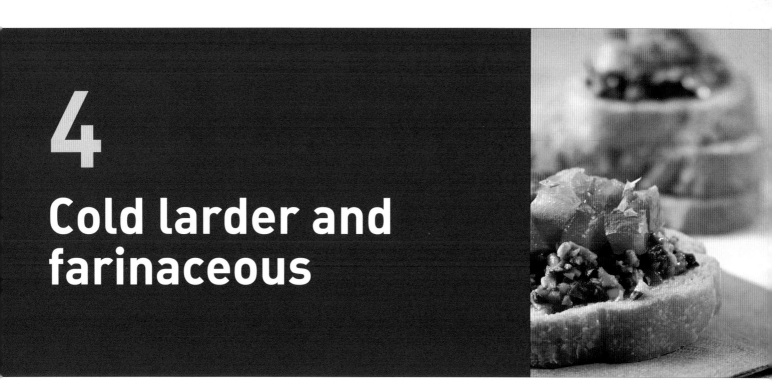

4
Cold larder and farinaceous

LEARNING OUTCOMES

The aim of this chapter is to enable the candidate to develop skills and implement gathered knowledge in the preparation, cookery and presentation principles of different cold starters, salads, pasta and canapés. This includes the appropriate use of materials, ingredients and equipment.

At the end of this chapter the candidate will be able to:

■ Identify a range of commodities and their uses in cold larder work

■ Understand the use of relative ingredients, selecting and stating the quality points of various commodities and cold dishes

■ Prepare, cook and present a range of cold dishes

■ Identify the correct storage procedures and holding temperatures for canapés, salads and cold starters

■ Select the required tools and equipment for preparing and cooking cold dishes

■ Identify each pasta variety and finished dish

■ Understand the use of relative ingredients in pasta cookery

■ Prepare and cook each type of pasta variety

■ Be competent at preparing and cooking a range of pasta-based dishes

INTRODUCTION TO THE CHEF GARDE MANGER

The **chef de garde manger** is a mixed position within the professional kitchen. *Garde manger* is a French term which translates as 'keeping to eat'. Historically, the title was given to a chef whose job was to take charge of raw food and keep it fit to eat. This chef had to be skilled in the science of food preservation and preparation and in the art of food presentation.

The role of the modern chef garde manger, or larder chef, has evolved in response to changes in dining trends and in technology in the kitchen. This chef is still responsible for the production and preservation of cold soups, salads, **canapés**, **charcuterie** products, cheeses, condiments and **buffets**, but now they are also likely to present centrepieces in fat, carved fruits and vegetables and create ornate decorative dishes using poultry, game, fish, shellfish and meat.

VIDEO CLIP
Canapés: prawn with lemon dressing and pâté en croute

CHEF'S TIP

Always try to keep dishes simple when using top-quality fresh ingredients. Using a maximum of five different food components will prevent the dish from becoming too complicated.

THE BEGINNING OF A MEAL

Certain words have been used to describe an element, dish or type of course in the culinary arts. Every once in a while, words used to describe a course or dish can mislead the customer. This can be the case with **amuse bouches**, appetisers and hors d'oeuvres. Each term is associated with small, delicate portions of food and so it can easily be assumed that they are all the same type of dish.

- *Amuse bouches* (sometimes called amuse gueules) – these are little savoury nibbles, to be eaten within two bites and offered just for fun as 'mouth amusements' before the starter course is served. They can be presented hot or cold.

- *Appetisers* – these are small portions of food that are the first food to be served at the table. They are part of the planned menu, served before the starter or a main course. Some chefs use this small appetiser as something to titillate the appetite. Pre-dessert appetisers are even served in many high-class modern restaurants.

- *Hors d'oeuvres* – this term, which translates literally as 'outside the works', was borrowed by French chefs to refer to delicate, small portions of food served separately (or apart) from the main meal. Usually served as a starter on its own.

Many different terms are used internationally for starters or hors d'oeuvres, and most countries have some form of starter course or small presentation of food to indulge the appetite. The following are examples of various countries' approaches to small food dishes, either to be served at the beginning of a meal or as the meal itself:

- *Antipasti* (Italy) – small salads, cooked vegetables, fungi, fish dishes, eggs or cured meats, simply decorated.
- *Antojitos* (Mexico) – small servings of spiced vegetables and pulses with tortilla bases, such as tacos, quesadillas and enchiladas.
- *Chat* (India) – small portions of food eaten at all times of the day.
- *Dim sum* (China) – meaning 'touch the heart', dim sum was originally a Cantonese custom linked to the Chinese tradition of yum cha (drinking tea); served in traditional Chinese tea houses.
- *Meze* (Greece) – can be as simple as a small bowl of olives, or more complicated, such as stuffed marinated vine leaves; served with a pre-dinner drink.
- *Tapas* (Spain) – the tradition of tapas was to serve a slice of ham, cheese or bread over a glass of sherry at roadside inns, and because this custom spurred the sales of alcoholic beverages, tapas became well established; there are many different varieties, with every region having its own speciality tapas.

Meze

Tapas

HORS D'OEUVRES

When choosing the menu, the hors d'oeuvres are carefully selected to complement the following courses. The selection of hors d'oeuvres on a menu needs to offer a complete range to cater for all diets (e.g. vegetarian or vegan diets or religious restrictions).

Hors d'oeuvres can be served as a starter or as a main course. An extended selection can be served as a buffet. This is similar to the Russian zakuskis, which are usually a collection of small hors d'oeuvres presented on a separate table for guests to help themselves to before the main meal commences.

A single hors d'oeuvre is a simple cold dish with one main ingredient and an accompanying garnish. Hors d'oeuvre varies contain a selection of main ingredients; each will contain small quantities of a range of products. The idea for plated combinations of themed ingredients, or assiettes, originated from this.

There are three main types of hors d'oeuvres:

1 *Hors d'oeuvre* **chaud** – hot items, can be vegetable-based, meat, game, fish, egg, dairy, soufflé or tartlet
2 *Hors d'oeuvre singular* – single-food items, served only with certain dressings and in one piece or one portion, for example avocado pears, caviar, stuffed eggs, langoustine, melon, **pâté** or diverse fruit cocktails
3 *Hors d'oeuvre variés* – selection of items consisting of multiple ingredients. They can be cut into small dice, strips, cubes or pieces, include pickled, marinated or seasoned ingredients and be served with additional fresh herbs, dressings, vinaigrettes or mayonnaise-based sauces.

CHEF'S TIP

The chef garde manger requires many specialised pieces of equipment and tools to complete this diverse work. The main tools and equipment that will be used are:

- Canale knife

- Turning knife

- Tomato knife

- Small and medium palette knives

- Parisienne cutters (large and small)

COMMODITIES

Cold red and white meat products

All cuts of meat should be purchased as fresh as possible, and chefs should receive each product and evaluate its quality before using. The chef garde manger should be capable of noting the warning signs when meat is lacking in quality; such as excessive odour, slimy to the touch, incorrect weight, incorrect delivery temperature, dull rather than bright colouring, poor marbling in certain cuts and tough texture.

Storage and hygiene must be thoroughly considered when preparing and cooking meat products. Being high in protein, meats carry a considerable risk of bacterial cross-contamination. Care must be taken to ensure meats are not served undercooked.

The cold state of prepared and cooked meat should be monitored carefully. Red meats have a high fat content, which may begin to solidify and congeal within the presented dish after a period of time.

Pork has a number of uses within the garde manger. Its high fat content makes it a good source of moisture within pâtés, terrines and stuffing or **farce**.

Veal is a very lean meat, similar to beef, and so is lacking in natural fats. Veal tends to be mixed with pork when making terrines, pâtés or raised pies so that the fat from the pork will keep the dish moist.

Cold poultry products

Poultry is the most versatile of all the meats within the garde manger. It is an easy commodity to work with and there is little wastage; all parts of a bird can be used to make items such as **mousses**, **ballotines** and **galantines**. The winglets can be turned into small canapé items, such as chicken cherries. It is an inexpensive commodity and can be very cost effective to serve.

Foie gras is a commodity much prized by chefs throughout the world and is considered a universal delicacy. It is the enlarged liver from a goose or duck that has been force fed and fattened for a period of up to five months. These speciality poultry do not exercise and are overfed, which results in a substantial fatty liver. The following quality checks should be carried out when purchasing foie gras:

- A light yellow to amber colour
- Firm to the touch, but should give slightly under thumb pressure and the mark should remain visible
- The fewer blemishes apparent, the higher the grade.

When preparing foie gras for cold dishes (such as for mousses, terrines, **parfaits** and **forcemeats**) the liver must be cleaned and have all the veins removed before cooking. As little damage as possible should be done to the liver during preparation.

Cold game products

Most game items have a prominent flavour and are relatively simple to use within the garde manger. The flavour and tenderness of game begins to improve as it ages. The technique of aging game is to hang the carcass for between 7 and 14 days (depending on the type of game) at a temperature of 1–3°C. This allows the enzymes in the meat to break down the complex proteins in the carcass.

After the aging process the flavour and tenderness can be further enhanced by **marinating**. This should, however, never be done to mask or overpower the natural flavours of the meat. The acids contained in a **marinade**, such as vinegar, citric juices and alcohol, will break down proteins in the meat, making it tenderer. However, the meat should not stay in a marinade for too long. The most common dishes for game products are game pies, terrines and pâtés.

VIDEO CLIP
Preparation of duck liver, orange and hazlenut paste

Cured and smoked meats

Curing is the addition of salt, sugar or nitrate to any protein to preserve, flavour and colour the meat. The salt penetrates the flesh and dehydrates the meat by a process called osmosis. This results in a lower moisture content, which inhibits the growth and reproduction of bacteria.

The basic curing methods can be applied to meat products in many different ways:

- *Dry curing* – the curing ingredients are applied directly onto the meat. This is the slowest method, and is used in curing hams, bacon, salt beef and other small cuts of meat.
- *Dry sugar curing* – sugar and nitrate are added to salt, which is then directly applied to the surface of the meat. The meat is always cured in a refrigerator. This method can be used for poultry, game and smaller cuts of meat.
- *Brine curing (pickling)* – the meat is cured with a **brine** made from salt and nitrate, and sometimes sugar. The meat is soaked for a specific time in a refrigerator. Large cuts of meat are cured in this way, such as ham and turkey.

Smoking is another method of preserving meats. It also adds flavour and colour to the meat, and can be used for other commodities such as fish. The process for smoking meats is the same as for curing, followed by washing and smoking.

There are two methods of smoking food, cold and hot smoking:

1 *Cold smoking* – a controlled flow of smoke at about 35°C is blown over the commodity for about 5–6 hours. This creates a lightly smoked and slightly drier product.

Cured meats and dried sausages hanging for purchase

Cold smoked salmon hanging for purchase

2 *Hot smoking* – the smoking temperature is higher at 70–80°C and the heat of the smoke will cook the product as it is being smoked. This usually produces a stronger, smokier flavour.

Smoking times will vary for different types of produce, being anything from 20 minutes to several days. The most commonly used woods for smoking are beech, oak and chestnut, with additional flavours such as juniper, sage and rosemary used for aromatic flavourings. Further flavours that can be used include hickory, scented teas (such as jasmine), fir wood and pine needles.

Technique for hot smoking

Placing tea leaves into the bottom of a tray

Placing a cooling rack over the tray

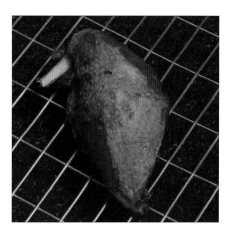

Laying the food items to be smoked onto the rack

Covering with foil and placing onto a stove top

Lifting the foil to reveal the item being smoked

Vegetables and fruit

A fruit and vegetable stall at a local market

These are widely used within the garde manger due to the variety of different methods in which they can be cooked and presented.

A wide range of salad greens are available for use in the kitchen and freshness is the key when purchasing. A good salad green is one that has retained its moisture, crispness and colour and is free of bruising.

Good quality bulbs, roots, tubers and young vegetables are easier than ever to source and are increasingly popular for use in simple salads. Baby fruits and vegetables are visually appealing food items and require little preparation.

Eggs

The common hen's egg is not the only type of egg to be used in the preparation of salads and cold dishes. Many menus opt for duck or quail eggs, which can transform a simple salad into a diverse culinary experience.

Eggs can be served boiled or poached to accompany salads and cold dishes, and are a valuable source of protein and vital nutrients.

Farinaceous products

Farinaceous ingredients – starchy products high in **carbohydrate**, such as polenta, couscous, noodles, bulgur wheat, pearl barley and pastas – are ideal ingredients for salads.

Chefs are rediscovering traditional recipes from around the world, such as tabbouleh and Moroccan couscous.

Fish

Fish is a diverse commodity, and it is generally a light and flavoursome option within a menu. Smoked salmon, fish terrines and gravadlax are standard starter dish concepts.

The same health and safety precautions that apply to meat also apply to fish. Fish should not be stored for longer than three days and smoked products and raw products should be kept in separate refrigerators.

Dairy-based products

Dairy products, such as fresh milk, different creams, crème fraîche, fromage frais, yoghurt and cheeses, are important commodities in the garde manger. The use of cheese as a course on a menu is increasing in popularity.

When creating a cheese selection for a menu, at least three types of cheese should be offered: a hard cheese, a blue-veined cheese and a soft cheese, either with a downy rind or with a washed rind. (A washed rind cheese is one that has had its rind soaked or rubbed with brine or alcohol, whereas a downy rind cheese has been left to ripen and develop a white dappled rind.)

To prevent cheeses from drying out they should be wrapped in cheesecloth or waxed paper, depending on the variety, which allow the cheese to 'breath'. All types should be stored in a refrigerator, ideally being removed approximately one hour prior to serving. By serving cheese at **ambient temperature**, the customer will be able to fully appreciate the texture, flavour and smell of each cheese.

Fungi

Mushrooms have a broad range of characteristics and different flavours. Although they have a high water content, their nutritional content is greater than that of green vegetables, although not as high as root vegetables.

CHEF'S TIP

When sourcing eggs be sure to pick those with a Red Lion stamp. This means that the farm where the egg was produced has been inspected and the eggs are protected against infection from Salmonella.

Quail's eggs

VIDEO CLIP
Using fish: mixed fish salad with crispy croutons

Smoked mackerel

CHEF'S TIP

If choosing a selection of cheeses for a board to present to customers, the chef should consider:
– whether the cheeses are in season, because they will then be at their finest
– how long they have been matured; the more mature, the stronger and more prominent the taste
– the use of cheeses produced locally by a farmers or artisan cheese makers.

British and continental cheeses

Varieties of mushrooms

The three main mushroom classifications are:

1 Field or wild mushrooms

2 Cultivated mushrooms

3 Exotic mushrooms.

Fresh hand-picked wild mushrooms are expensive, which will immediately add to the selling price of a dish. Prices for hand-picked mushrooms will also fluctuate due to their availability and seasonality.

One of the most popular ingredients with chefs is the truffle. Prices for both black and white truffles can be very high, with white truffle prices reaching high into the thousands of pounds per kilogram at certain times of the year. Usually originating in Italy, white truffles are used to favour oils or are used in cooking a range of dishes, such as risottos.

Rice

Rice is a versatile product to cook and present, and is used as a starchy carbohydrate accompaniment to a number of meat, poultry and fish dishes.

Sushi is essentially cold cooked rice dressed with vinegar, shaped into bite-sized portions, decorated with raw or cooked fish, egg or vegetables and wrapped in seaweed. The vinegar rice used in sushi is slightly harder than plain boiled rice because it is cooked in less water. Quick cooling of the cooked rice while tossing it is the key to producing good, shiny sushi rice.

Pulses

Pulses are beans, lentils and chickpeas, all of which have excellent nutritional benefits and are valuable sources of protein. Pulses are economical ingredients and can be used to make a variety of salads.

Tinned, cooked pulses are liable to be more expensive than dried pulses, but are much easier to use as they do not require **soaking**. Pulses can be used as a main ingredient for salads.

CHEF'S TIP

Cooking pulses in a flavoured or spiced liquid can greatly enhance and complement the flavours of the dish.

SALADS

Salads are extremely versatile dishes and can consist of raw, cooked, cold or warm ingredients. Salads will usually be dressed and seasoned (unless requested otherwise by a customer), and can be served as an accompaniment, side dish or main course.

Many different contemporary styles of salad from around the world are used in modern menus. The main categories of salads are listed below:

CHEF'S TIP

There are many different salad items, such as lettuce, spinach, herbs, spicy greens, bitter leaves and microsalads. They can be used in different combinations to add a depth of flavour and varying textures.

■ *Simple salads* - the basis of a **simple salad** is the use of one main ingredient and an accompanying dressing or garnish. These salads can be either raw or cooked and can be made up of vegetables, fruits, meats, fish or shellfish, but they are always served cold and with a cold dressing such as vinaigrette. An example is a tomato salad.

- *Compound salads* – the aim of a **compound salad** is to combine multiple contrasting ingredients, differing in texture, flavour and colour, but still utilising items that are complementary to each other. A classic example is à la grecque (meaning cooking in a Greek style), which is cooked and served in a vinegar and oil solution with aromatic spices. Salad components can include meat, fish and vegetables.

- *Combination salads* – these are made up of several different types of ingredients which have been prepared separately but presented together on one plate. Crucially, the ingredients are not blended together. These are substantial salads and are usually featured on menus as main courses.

- *American salads* – originating in the USA, these salads are usually served as an accompaniment to a hot dish, such as roast turkey. In North America, salads are traditionally served during a banquet instead of sauces or cooked vegetables. An example is orange and watercress salad with a walnut vinaigrette, served to accompany roasted duck.

- *Salad tiède* - *tiède* means warm, therefore these salads will typically consist of a hot ingredient accompanied by cold items. **Salad tiède** is generally served as a starter or a main course.

When designing a salad, the chef garde manger must carefully consider the various factors that contribute to a salad's success:

- *Appearance* – the salad should not only be pleasing and colourful, but also be in keeping with the style of the menu.

- *Appropriateness* – this is quite a broad issue and often not fully considered. For example, it may not be appropriate to serve certain foods to people of specific religions or ethnic backgrounds or with particular medical conditions. Repeating ingredients used elsewhere in a menu will unbalance the eating experience.

- *Flavour* – if a food item lacks flavour it should not be considered; salads should always be appealing to the appetite. Salads are frequently used as palette cleansers or as a bridge in a menu between other foods or courses.

- *Texture* – variety and contrasts in texture add interest and value to most dishes.

- *Nutritional value* – customers are becoming increasingly concerned about health and nutrition. It is both good business and socially responsible to address this issue by making reasonable changes to ingredients or cooking methods where appropriate.

- *Portion size* – this is relative to the entire meal. Chefs should consider what is an appropriate quantity to serve. Salad ingredients should not be too large or too small to make a pleasing presentation.

- *Cost* – it is important to assess and evaluate the cost contribution and margin for profit for all salad and commodity items.

 CHEF'S TIP

Ensure that you prepare the cold element of a salad tiède in plenty of time before the hot ingredients are required so that the dish can be served at the correct temperature, giving the right balance of hot and cold temperatures on the plate.

 CHEF'S TIP

Do not dress a salad with a vinaigrette or dressing too early as this will break down the structure and texture of leaves and herbs.

A terrine presented alongside cold tuna and salmon

TERRINES

These meat, poultry, fish, vegetable or game products are named after the mould in which they are produced. Terrines can be produced in a variety of shapes and sizes, and can be presented as cold mousses, pâtés or parfaits, jellied and layered, or by cold pressing.

Terrines usually consist of more than one type of food product. The ingredients are used in varying proportions and are prepared in different ways, depending on the effect the chef garde manger wishes to create. The terrine mould will usually be lined with bacon, seaweed, vegetables or fat, which helps to hold the terrine together.

Lining a terrine with cling film

Lining a terrine with bacon

Lining a terrine with seaweed

VIDEO CLIP
Preparation of foie gras, artichoke and herb terrine

Placing vegetables into terrine

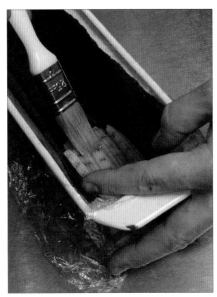

Brushing with aspic to set vegetables

Building next layer

PÂTÉS AND PARFAITS

These products can be made of **offal**, meat, poultry, fish, vegetables or game and are rich in flavour. Pâtés can be coarse textured or fine pastes, whereas parfaits have the consistency of whipped cream or butter.

There are two methods for preparing parfaits:

1 Prepared then cooked

2 Cooked then prepared.

The classical prepared then cooked method is to add cooked shallots, flambéed with alcohol, to melted clarified butter. Egg yolks and blended livers are added to the mixture and butter and cream are slowly mixed in. The mixture is then passed through a sieve, seasoned well and poured into a prepared terrine mould. It is then placed in a bain marie and cooked in an oven until the core temperature reaches 68°C.

CHEF'S TIP

Keep a container of hot water and a clean cloth when slicing products such as terrines and pâtés; a hot, clean knife will slice cleanly and produce neat slices.

Preparation of a pâté

Sautéing onions and herbs

Combining minced meat with onions and beating together

Adding eggs and cream to the base mixture

Blending in a food processor to a course mixture

Seasoning the pâté mixture

Covering the mixture with streaky bacon and plastic film

The second method varies in that the ingredients are cooked prior to preparation. Extra butter is used in this method to counteract the lack of protein structure and to achieve the same effect as the classical parfait. Shallots are cooked in butter with livers to a medium cooked point, alcohol is then added and flambéed. The shallots and livers are left to cool, then blended together with a small amount of cream until a smooth texture is achieved. The mixture is then passed through a sieve, and softened (but not clarified) butter is folded in. It is then seasoned and poured into the terrine mould and refrigerated until set.

MOUSSES

Mousses are lighter in texture than pâtés and are not as rich in flavour, which makes them a little more versatile.

A basic raw mousseline recipe for meat, poultry or fish uses 500g of fresh protein to approximately 900ml of chilled double cream, four egg yolks and two whole eggs. The protein needs to be **minced** twice and passed through a sieve, to break down the protein structure, and then chilled over ice. Using a blender, the protein is combined with the eggs and seasoning, which are added slowly until a smooth texture is achieved. The chilled double cream is incorporated into the mixture slowly to prevent the mousseline from splitting. The mousseline can then be poached, steamed or baked, or used in terrines that are to be cooked.

Cooked mousses differ by using a meat, fish, poultry or vegetable base that has already undergone cooking and gelatine or agar-agar is used to set the mixture. The base ingredient is blended until smooth while the gelatine or agar-agar is melted. The setting agent is then beaten into the base mixture, which is seasoned as required. Cream, lightly whipped to a soft peak, is gently folded into the mixture to form a light mousse, which can be **piped**, formed into **quenelles** or layered into a terrine mould, before being allowed to set in a refrigerator.

PASTA COMPOSITION

Pasta is a generic term used to describe many products made from semolina and/or flour that has been milled from the hardest of all wheat, durum wheat. The name 'durum' comes from the Latin word *durus*, meaning 'hard'.

The key to creating a good pasta dough is to use the strongest flour, which has the highest gluten content. Gluten is essential for creating the elasticity required to form a pliable dough. The amount of water the dough can absorb depends on the quality of the protein and starch. The size of the semolina also plays a key role in this process: too small will result in sticky dough, too large and the dough will be dry, resulting in white spots in the finished product.

Durum wheat's hardness makes it the wheat of choice for producing pasta. When most wheat is milled, the heart of the wheat kernel (endosperm) breaks down into a fine, powdery flour, but the endosperm of durum is hard enough to hold together. The result is the granular product called semolina. Durum wheat kernels are amber-coloured and larger than those of other wheat varieties. Also unique to durum wheat is the fact that its endosperm is not creamy white but yellow, which gives pasta its distinctive colour.

00 flour is now used extensively within the catering trade for making pasta. It is an Italian wheat flour which has a very low extraction rate (this is the amount of whole wheat extracted from the grain during the milling process) and low ash content. Italian flours are classified by ash content, which measures the mineral content of flour.

> ASH
>
> The ash content of flour is determined by burning a given quantity of the flour under prescribed conditions and then measuring the residue. The mineral content varies, depending on many factors such as the variety of wheat, the terrain, the fertilisation and the climate. The greater portion of minerals found in a kernel of wheat is contained in the germ and in the **husk** (the bran), and the least amount is in the endosperm. As a consequence, if flour contains a greater number of bran particles, it will have an elevated ash content. The determination of the ash content serves to estimate the degree of the endosperm separation from the bran during milling, i.e. the grade of flour. Generally, flours thought to be of higher quality are more refined and produce less ash. 00 flour also has a low protein content.

Wheat kernel

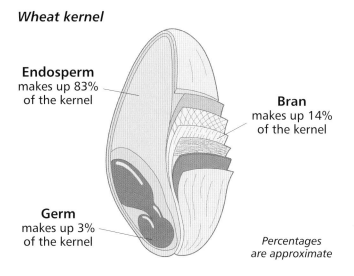

Endosperm
makes up 83%
of the kernel

Bran
makes up 14%
of the kernel

Germ
makes up 3%
of the kernel

*Percentages
are approximate*

VIDEO CLIP
Making fresh pasta dough

Different flavoured pastas

Pasta being put through a pasta machine

Pasta hanging to dry

Pasta shapes and flavours

When making pasta dough you should use only the best and freshest ingredients; this will ensure the end product will be of the highest quality in both appearance and flavour.

The traditional way of making pasta dough is to prepare the mixture on a large unvarnished wooden table, which keeps the temperature and humidity constant. The method, still used in classical training, is to create a mound of flour with a well in the centre for the eggs, oil and salt, bring in the flour slowly to form the dough and then **knead**.

The modern method, now widely used, is to place all the ingredients into a food processor and blend for 10–20 seconds until a loose ball is formed.

Whichever method is used, the dough should feel just firm and not sticky. Depending on the size of the eggs used, extra flour may be required to bring the dough together. Knowing the correct feel to the dough will come with experience, and once mastered will allow you to produce perfect paste every time.

The finished dough should be wrapped in cling film and rested for a minimum of 30 minutes (overnight if possible), which will allow the gluten to relax and so prevent shrinkage when the dough is rolled out.

The dough can be rolled out with a rolling pin or using a pasta machine, with the latter allowing large quantities to be rolled out to exact thicknesses and at greater speed.

A–Z OF PASTAS

There are over 500 varieties of pasta, all with different designs and shapes. Here is a selection:

- *Angolotti* – small, crescent-shaped dumplings, usually stuffed with meat
- *Bucatini* – slightly thicker and hollow version of spaghetti
- *Cannelloni* – large, short tubes, stuffed with an appropriate filling and baked
- *Capellini* – 'angel hair', the thinnest of all pastas, like spaghetti
- *Cappelletti* – 'little hats', small peaked-hat shapes stuffed with chicken, pork, mortadella and cheese
- *Conchiglie* – small, round shells, either ridged or smooth, the cavity is ideal for stuffing or sauce
- *Farfalle* – small bow-tie shapes
- *Fettuccine* – like tagliatelle but a bit narrower and thicker
- *Fusilli* – spiral-shaped pasta twists
- *Lasagne* – the broadest pasta, around 5–8cm wide, either ridged or smooth
- *Linguini* – flat spaghetti

1. Linguini being made: roll out the dough until a number 2 thickness is achieved

2. Trim the pasta to achieve a neat edge

3. Put the trimmed pasta through the fine attachment

4. Finished linguini

■ *Macaroni* – short hollow pasta, sometimes with an elbow to form an angle

■ *Orecchiette* – 'little ears', small ear-shaped pasta

■ *Pansotti* – triangular ravioli

■ *Papardelle* – broad egg noodles, sometimes with wavy edges

■ *Patina* – the term used to describe all the tiny pasta shapes used in soups

■ *Penne* – tubular pasta, ridged or smooth, about 4–5cm long, cut on the angle

■ *Ravioli* – flat stuffed pasta shapes

1. Ravioli being made: cut out neat circles of pasta dough

2. Spoon filling onto half of the discs, leaving the others to use as lids

3. Brush the base with water

4. Lay the lid over the filling

5. Squeeze the discs together and then cut a neat disc with a cutter

6. Finished ravioli

- *Rigatoni* – ridged tubular macaroni, 5cm long
- *Spaghetti* – thin, solid strings of pasta (vermicelli in southern Italy)
- *Tagliatelle* – long, thin egg noodles, about 6mm wide

3 Finished tagliatelle

VIDEO CLIP
Cutting tagliatelle

1 Tagliatelle being made: roll out the dough until number 2 is achieved

2 Put the trimmed pasta through the medium attachment

- *Tortelli/tortellini* – small, ring-shaped pasta dumplings, stuffed (tortellini are half the size of tortelli).

1 Tortellini being made: brush the pasta disc with water

2 Fold over and form a seal by squeezing the pasta together

3 Stand the pasta up and squeeze the tips together

VIDEO CLIP
Producing various tortellini

4 Gently fold back the edges

5 Finished tortellini

RECIPES

Gravadlax with beetroot dressing and chilli taco

INGREDIENTS	4 PORTIONS	10 PORTIONS
Salmon fillet (skin on, trimmed and pin boned)	300g	800g
Sugar	150g	425g
Good-quality salt	180g	500g
Orange juice and zest	1 each	3 each
Dill	½ bunch	1½ bunches
Plain flour	200g	500g
Lard	10g	25g
Good-quality salt	10g	25g
Saffron water	To soften	To soften
Ground chilli flakes	1tsp	1tbsp
Assorted leaves	50g	125g
Cooked baby beetroot	50g	125g
Olive oil	4tbsp	10tbsp

Method of work

1 Finely chop the dill. Mix the sugar, salt and chopped dill together. Slash the salmon skin and rub the salt mixture on both sides, then leave for at least 24 hours, wrapped in plastic film in a refrigerator.

2 Take the flour, lard and second amount of salt and mix well, then slowly add enough saffron water to form a soft paste (pasta dough consistency).

3 Sprinkle in the chilli and knead well, then wrap in plastic film and chill for at least 30 minutes.

4 Roll the paste using a pasta machine until the desired thickness is achieved.

5 Cut out desired shapes, lay onto a lightly oiled tray and **bake** at 50°C until dry.

6 Remove the salmon from the cure and wash off, pat dry and place onto a chopping board.

7 **Slice** the salmon, going from tail to head, into neat pieces then roll into rosettes.

8 To serve, lay a leaf on the plate, top with the rosette of salmon and garnish with a chilli taco.

9 **Blend** the beetroot with a little olive oil until a smooth dressing is achieved.

10 **Drizzle** the beetroot and oil mixture around.

Duck liver and orange quenelles, with caramelised oranges

INGREDIENTS	4 PORTIONS	10 PORTIONS
Shallots	60g	150g
Garlic	1–2 cloves	3–4 cloves
Duck livers (cleaned and trimmed)	200g	500g
Olive oil	30ml	80ml
Butter	80g	200g
Orange segments	12	30
Orange liquor (such as Grand Marnier)	60ml	150ml
Sugar	40g	100g
Good-quality salt and pepper	To taste	To taste
Cayenne taco (see recipe on p. 63)	4	10
Chives	8	20
Salad leaves	as required	as required

Method of work

1 Finely chop the shallots and garlic. In a frying pan, fry off in the olive oil until tender and without colour.

2 Melt the butter in a small saucepan.

3 In a separate hot pan, season and sear the duck livers. When rare, flambé with the orange liquor.

4 Place the shallots and duck livers in a blender and blend until a smooth paste. Slowly add the melted butter and the cream. Season as required.

5 Chill the mixture slightly until pliable then quenelle onto a lined tray. Cover and chill until required.

6 Boil the sugar with a little water until a light caramel is formed, add the orange segments, remove from the heat and allow to cool.

7 To serve, place three quenelles of parfait on the plate and garnish with a **pluche** of salad, caramelised orange, chives and cayenne taco.

Carpaccio of beef with rocket and horseradish cream

INGREDIENTS	4 PORTIONS	10 PORTIONS
Beef fillet	100g	250g
Olive oil	40ml	100ml
Horseradish cream	2tbsp	5tbsp
Double cream	50ml	125ml
Lemon juice and zest	½ lemon	1½ lemons
Rocket	60g	150g
Shaved Parmesan cheese	40g	100g
Reduced sherry vinegar	4tbsp	10tbsp
Good-quality salt and ground white pepper	To taste	To taste

Method of work

1 Heat a frying pan, add a little oil and roll the trimmed beef fillet until seared on the outside.
2 Season the fillet and then wrap in cling film.
3 Allow to cool, then freeze overnight.
4 Remove the beef, unwrap a little, then using a sharp knife or slicing machine shave thin slices and arrange on a plate.
5 Lightly **whip** the cream to soft peaks and **fold in** the horseradish, lemon juice and zest.
6 Spoon the cream around the plate.
7 Drizzle around the oil and drops of reduced sherry vinegar.
8 Finally, season the beef with salt and pepper and garnish with rocket and Parmesan cheese.

Warm crab cakes with tomato dressing

INGREDIENTS	4 PORTIONS	10 PORTIONS
White crab meat	100g	250g
Breadcrumbs	100g	250g
Mayonnaise	40ml	100ml
Finely chopped spring onion	1tbsp	3tbsp
Cayenne taco (see recipe on p. 63)	4 spirals	10 spirals
Assorted lettuce leaves	50g	125g
Tomato concassé	100g	250g
Finely chopped shallots	1tbsp	2½tbsp
Olive oil	3tbsp	8tbsp
Sugar	1tsp	3tsp
Red wine vinegar	1tbsp	2½tbsp
Good-quality salt and ground white pepper	To taste	To taste

Method of work

1 Mix the picked crab meat, mayonnaise, spring onion and half the breadcrumbs, season well, then mould into small cakes.
2 Roll the cakes in the remaining breadcrumbs until no crabmeat is showing.
3 Sweat the tomato, shallots, sugar and oil until very soft, then add the vinegar, season and blend until smooth.
4 **Deep fry** the crab cakes until a golden brown colour is achieved.
5 To serve, dress the leaves and arrange on the plate, add the crab cake and cayenne taco and spoon the tomato dressing around.

Rabbit terrine with plum chutney and garlic tomatoes

INGREDIENTS	4 PORTIONS	10 PORTIONS
Flesh from whole rabbit	½	1
Chicken breast	1	2
Pork trimmings	80g	200g
Brandy	½ measure	1 Measure
Thyme	4 sprigs	8 sprigs
Bay leaf	½	1
Double cream	100ml	250ml
Parma ham	8 slices	20 slices
Liver and kidney (from the rabbit)		
Chilled egg whites	1	2
Mace	Pinch	Pinch
Plum chutney (plums cooked in sugar, cinnamon, red wine, red chilli and redcurrant jelly, reduced to taste)	4 small spoons	10 small spoons
Good-quality salt and ground white pepper	To taste	To taste
Cherry tomato (heated in oil and garlic then cooled)	4	10
Thyme	2 sprigs	4 sprigs
Bay leaf	½	1
Mixed lettuce leaves	50g	125g
Cayenne taco (see recipe on p. 63)	4	10

Method of work

1 Marinate the rabbit, chicken and pork in brandy, thyme and bay leaf overnight.

2 Set aside the rabbit fillets. Mince the rabbit (including liver and kidneys), chicken and pork, once through a medium mincer and twice through a fine mincer. Then pass through a sieve. Blast chill to get very cold.

3 When the mince is cold, **beat** with the double cream in a robot coupe. Season with salt, pepper and mace and quickly add the chilled egg whites.

4 **Poach** a little to test for holding consistency and taste.

5 Line a small terrine mould with oil and two layers of cling film. Line with the Parma ham.

6 Place the rabbit mix in the terrine mould and layer in the slices of rabbit flesh from the fillet. Smooth down and fold over the Parma ham. Cover with foil.

7 **Steam** for 25–30 minutes at 100°C in a steamer.

8 Remove and chill until required.

9 To serve, slice the terrine carefully with a warm wet knife and position on the plate with the cayenne taco, add the garlic-infused cherry tomato, a plum chutney and some dressed mixed lettuce leaves.

Duck liver pâté with Belgian endive, herb oil and foie gras

INGREDIENTS	4 PORTIONS	10 PORTIONS
Duck livers	100g	250g
Port wine reduction	25ml	60ml
Shallots finely chopped	1	3
Garlic finely chopped	2 cloves	6 cloves
Pork fat finely diced	30g	75g
Fresh breadcrumbs	4tbsp	10tbsp
Liquid whole egg	20ml	50ml
Belgian endive	12 leaves	30 leaves
Foie gras fine dice	20g	50g
Chives	8	20
Cherry tomato	4	10
Herb oil	2tbsp	5tbsp
Ground white pepper	To taste	To taste
Good quality salt	To taste	To taste

Method of work

1 In a food processor blend the livers, egg, reduction, breadcrumbs, shallots and garlic until a course paste is formed.
2 Fold in the foie gras, season and taste raw. Place into a terrine mould lined with cling film.
3 Cover with foil and steam at 100°C for 25 to 30 minutes, until just set.
4 Remove and chill over night.
5 When required, quenelle onto a plate, garnish with Belgian endive, chives and cherry tomato.
6 Spoon around the herb oil.

Raw, lime marinated tuna with Dijon dressing and leaves

INGREDIENTS	4 PORTIONS	10 PORTIONS
Tuna loin	100g	250g
Lime juice	½ lime	1½ limes
Olive oil	50ml	125ml
Dijon mustard	1tbsp	2½tbsp
White wine vinegar	25ml	70ml
Saffron taco (see recipe on p. 63)	12 each	30 each
Mixed fine leaves	60g	160g
Sea salt	Pinch	Pinch
Chervil	Sprigs	Sprigs
Good-quality salt and ground white pepper	To taste	To taste

Method of work

1 Thinly slice the tuna then brush with lime juice and sea salt (this must be served within 4 minutes).

2 Prepare the Dijon dressing: combine the mustard with 1 part vinegar to 3 parts oil and season.

3 Dress the leaves with a little dressing.

4 Arrange the tuna on the plate, add the leaves, saffron tacos and chervil, then spoon a little Dijon dressing around the plate.

Smoked lamb's tongue with curly endive, blackened red peppers and red wine reduction

INGREDIENTS	4 PORTIONS	10 PORTIONS
Lamb's tongue	200g	500g
Tea bags (jasmine)	4	10
Long grain rice	80g	200g
Granulated sugar	50g	125g
Thyme	Sprigs	Sprigs
Curly endive	80g	200g
Red peppers	1	3
Olive oil	100ml	250ml
Red wine vinegar	50ml	125ml
Red wine	50ml	125ml
Redcurrant jelly	50g	125ml
Cherry tomatoes	4	10
Good-quality salt and ground white pepper	To taste	To taste

Method of work

1 Empty the contents of the tea bags into a roasting tray and add the sugar, rice and thyme. Place into an oven at 200°C until smoking.

2 Place a cooling rack onto the tray and lay on the tongue, cover with foil and return to the oven for 4 minutes.

3 Remove and allow to cool.

4 Brush the peppers with oil and hold over a naked flame until blackened.

5 Place the peppers into a bag, seal and wait 5 minutes.

6 Remove the peppers, peel and quarter, and remove the seeds.

7 **Julienne** the peppers and mix with a little seasoning and a splash of red wine vinegar.

8 Heat the red wine, remaining vinegar and redcurrant jelly until reduced by half, add the tomatoes and chill until ready to use.

9 Arrange the peppers, leaves, tomato and tongue on the plate, finish with a little reduction.

Asian pigeon breast with fine potato salad, oven dried tomatoes and lightly spiced yoghurt

INGREDIENTS	4 PORTIONS	10 PORTIONS
Pigeon breasts	4	10
Tandoori paste	2tbsp	5tbsp
Lime juice	½ lime	2 limes
New potatoes (blanched, peeled and diced)	80g	200g
Basic vinaigrette	2tbsp	5tbsp
Plum tomatoes (1/6 dried overnight in a cool oven)	4 pieces	10 pieces
Cherry tomatoes	4	10
Greek yoghurt	2tbsp	5tbsp
Ground cumin	1tsp	3tsp
Ground cayenne	1tsp	3tsp
Lemon juice	½ lemon	1½ lemons
Cayenne taco (see recipe on p. 63)	4	10
Good-quality salt and ground white pepper	To taste	To taste

Method of work

1 Marinate the pigeon in tandoori paste, lime juice and seasoning for 30 minutes.

2 Place the pigeon on a tray in a hot oven and bake for 8 minutes.

3 Take the potatoes, season and add vinaigrette.

4 Mix the yoghurt with lemon juice, cumin and cayenne

5 To assemble, spoon the potato salad onto the plate. Slice the pigeon around, add the tomatoes and spoon the yoghurt on to the plate.

6 Finish with the cayenne taco for added height.

Quail egg and kedgeree potato cake with wild leaves and citrus oil

INGREDIENTS	4 PORTIONS	10 PORTIONS
Quail eggs	6	15
Natural smoked haddock	80g	200g
Fresh milk	100ml	250ml
Clouté	½	1
Braised rice	50g	125g
Grated potato	100g	250g
Curry powder	To taste	To taste
Pasteurised egg	To bind	To bind
Fresh white breadcrumbs	2tbsp	5tbsp
Wild lettuce leaves	50g	125g
Lemons	½	1
Limes	½	1
Olive oil	50ml	125ml
Good-quality salt and ground white pepper	To taste	To taste

Method of work

1 Boil the quail eggs, **refresh** and peel.
2 Poach the haddock in milk infused with the clouté until just cooked.
3 Remove the haddock, **flake** into a bowl with the breadcrumbs, rice, potato, curry powder and enough egg to bind.
4 Form small cakes and pan fry until golden.
5 Place the lemon and the lime into the olive oil and bring to the boil. Simmer for 10 minutes, then pass and cool quickly.
6 Assemble by placing halved eggs around the plate, cakes in the middle, dressed leaves on top and citrus oil around.

Smoked salmon and king prawn terrine with a light cucumber, pepper and lemon salad

INGREDIENTS	4 PORTIONS	10 PORTIONS
Smoked salmon	300g	1 kg
King prawns (cooked)	8	20
Double cream	150ml	450ml
Horseradish cream	To taste	To taste
Lemon juice and zest	½ lemon	1½ lemons
Cayenne pepper	Pinch	Pinch
Gelatine	2 leaves dissolved	5 leaves dissolved
Diced cucumber	50g	125g
Diced yellow peppers	50g	125g
Microleaf salad	35g	85g
Sun-blushed tomatoes	8	20
Cayenne taco (see recipe on p. 63)	4	10
Good-quality salt and ground white pepper	To taste	To taste

Method of work

1 Line a small terrine mould with cling film, then lay in thin slices of smoked salmon and chill.

2 Blend the remaining salmon with the horseradish cream, half the lemon juice and zest and cayenne.

3 Remove and place into a cold bowl.

4 Whip the cream until soft peaks are formed then fold into the salmon.

5 Fold in the dissolved gelatine (ensuring it is at room temperature – no hotter).

6 Spoon a little salmon mousse into the mould, then add half the king prawns.

7 Top up with mousse. Slice the remaining king prawn and add to the terrine.

8 Finish with mousse and fold over the salmon.

9 Chill for at least 1 hour.

10 Remove from the mould and roll in extra cling film; this will help the terrine keep its shape when slicing.

11 To assemble, slice the terrine and lay on the plate, arrange the microleaves and sun-blushed tomatoes.

12 Combine the remaining lemon with the diced cucumber and pepper and arrange in a small spoon. Finish with a cayenne taco.

Oriental duck salad with apple, sesame and roasted cashews

INGREDIENTS	4 PORTIONS	10 PORTIONS
Duck breast	2	5
Honey	2tbsp	5tbsp
Soy sauce	1tsp	2½tsp
Hoi sin	1tsp	2½tsp
Julienne of apple	60g	150g
Toasted sesame seeds	1tsp	2½tsp
Coriander	20g	50g
Roasted cashew nuts	2tbsp	5tbsp
Oyster sauce	40ml	100ml
Water	40ml	100ml
Red chillies	1	2½
Spring onions	1	2½
Garlic chopped	2 cloves	5 cloves
Ginger grated	1tsp	2½tsp
Good-quality salt and ground white pepper	To taste	To taste

Method of work

1 Score the duck breasts and rub with honey, soy sauce and hoi sin. Leave to marinate for 2 hours.

2 Pan fry the duck until pink, then allow to cool slightly.

3 Mix the apple with the sesame seeds and coriander.

4 Boil the oyster sauce, water, chillies, spring onions, garlic and ginger for 1 minute, then pass and chill.

5 To assemble, slice the duck and lay on the plate with the apple salad and roasted cashews. Serve oyster sauce in a small spoon.

Egg pasta dough

 CHEF'S TIP

When making fresh pasta dough, numerous flavours can be incorporated, such as pesto, tomato or spinach. Care must be taken to adjust the recipe to ensure the same firm consistency is achieved in the finished product.

INGREDIENTS	4 PORTIONS	10 PORTIONS
OO grade flour	110g	225g
Eggs	1	2
Egg yolks	1½	3
Olive oil	8ml	15ml

Method of work

1 Place flour on to a clean work surface and make a well.
2 In a medium bowl beat the egg yolks and whole eggs together with the olive oil.
3 Slowly add the egg mixture to the flour, stirring in stages, until a paste is formed.
4 Knead the dough until a smooth texture is achieved.
5 Place the dough in a refrigerator to rest for at least 30 minutes before rolling out.

Sun-dried tomato pasta dough

INGREDIENTS	4 PORTIONS	10 PORTIONS
OO grade flour	110g	225g
Eggs	1	2
Egg yolks	1½	3
Olive oil	8ml	15ml
Sun-dried tomato paste	15g	30g

Method of work

1 Place the flour on to a clean work surface and make a well.
2 In a medium bowl beat the egg yolks and whole eggs together with the olive oil and tomato paste.
3 Slowly add the egg mixture to the flour, stirring in stages, until a paste is formed.
4 Knead the dough until a smooth texture is achieved.
5 Place the dough in a refrigerator to rest for at least 30 minutes before rolling out.

Saffron pasta dough

INGREDIENTS	4 PORTIONS	10 PORTIONS
OO grade flour	110g	225g
Eggs	1	2
Egg yolks	1½	3
Olive oil	8ml	15ml
Saffron strands	2g	5g

Method of work

1 Place the flour on to a clean work surface and make a well.
2 Warm the olive oil in a small saucepan and infuse the saffron strands, then leave to cool.
3 In a medium bowl beat the egg yolks and whole eggs together with the saffron-infused oil.
4 Slowly add the mixture to the flour, stirring in stages, until the mixture becomes a paste.
5 Knead the dough until the paste is a smooth texture and yellow in colour. If needed, infuse more oil and saffron then add, introducing more flour to dry the paste.
6 Place the dough in a refrigerator to rest for at least 30 minutes before rolling out.

Spinach pasta dough

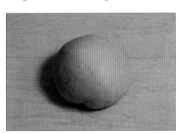

INGREDIENTS	4 PORTIONS	10 PORTIONS
OO grade flour	110g	225g
Eggs	1	2
Egg yolks	1½	3
Olive oil	8ml	15ml
Spinach	70g	150g

Method of work

1 Place the flour on to a clean work surface and make a well.
2 Warm a small saucepan and wilt down the spinach with a small amount of water then allow to cool. Place the spinach into a blender and blend until a smooth paste is achieved.
3 Remove from the blender and spoon into a muslin cloth, then squeeze into a clean saucepan until all the chlorophyll has been extracted.
4 Reduce the liquid until it is a concentrate then chill.
5 In a medium bowl beat the egg yolks and whole eggs together with the chlorophyll.
6 Slowly add the mixture into the flour, stirring in stages, until a dough is achieved.
7 Knead the dough until a smooth texture is achieved and it is a subtle green colour. More flour can be added to the dough if it is too wet.
8 Place the dough in a refrigerator and allow to rest for at least 30 minutes before rolling out.

Squid ink pasta dough

INGREDIENTS	4 PORTIONS	10 PORTIONS
OO grade flour	110g	225g
Eggs	1	2
Egg yolks	1½	3
Olive oil	8ml	15ml
Squid ink	2tbsp	5tbsp

Method of work

1 Place flour on to a clean work surface and make a well.
2 In a medium bowl beat the egg yolks and whole eggs together with the olive oil.
3 Slowly add the mixture to the flour, stirring in stages, until a paste is formed.
4 Knead the dough with the squid ink (remember to wear gloves for this recipe) until a smooth texture is achieved and it is a subtle black colour.
5 Place the dough in a refrigerator to rest for at least 30 minutes before rolling out.

Tomato linguini with black pudding and roasted butternut squash with an olive oil infused with lemon thyme

INGREDIENTS	4 PORTIONS	10 PORTIONS
Tomato pasta dough	400g	1kg
Black pudding	100g	250g
Butternut squash	100g	250g
Extra virgin olive oil	50ml	125ml
Lemon thyme	¼ bunch	½ bunch
Chives	Sprigs	Sprigs
Good-quality salt and white pepper	To taste	To taste

Method of work

1 Roll out the pasta until thin then cut into thin strips (see making linguini, page 61).
2 Heat the oil with the lemon thyme and leave to infuse for a minimum of 20 minutes (best overnight).
3 Peel, deseed, dice and roast the squash until **caramelised**.
4 Cut the black pudding into dice and fry quickly in oil then mix with the butternut squash.
5 Blanch the pasta in boiling salted water until **al dente**, then drain and mix with the black pudding mix.
6 Place the pasta into a bowl, drizzle with the remaining oil and garnish with sprigs of chives.

📖 **CHEF'S TIP**

Ensure there is at least double the amount of water to pasta when cooking as this prevents the pasta coagulating.

Ricotta and wild sorrel tortellini with a pistachio pesto and garlic foam

INGREDIENTS	4 PORTIONS	10 PORTIONS
Plain pasta dough	400g	1kg
Ricotta cheese	200g	500g
Pistachio nuts	50g	125g
Parmesan cheese	50g	125g
Olive oil	70ml	175ml
Basil leaves	¼ bunch	½ bunch
Wild sorrel	70g	175g
Garlic	4 cloves	10 cloves
Fresh full fat milk	50ml	125ml
Good-quality salt and white pepper	To taste	To taste

Method of work

1 Mix the ricotta with the chopped blanched sorrel leaves, season well.

2 Roll out the pasta into thin sheets and cut out into circles approximately 5cm in diameter.

3 Brush the pasta circles with water and spoon the ricotta into the middle.

4 Fold the pasta over and pinch the points together (see making tortellini, page 62).

5 Make the pesto using half the oil, lightly toasted pistachios, basil and Parmesan by placing all the ingredients in a liquidiser and pulsing until almost smooth (the consistency should be slightly thicker than a sauce).

6 **Blanch** the garlic in boiling water for 2 minutes, place the garlic into the milk and bring to the boil; remove the pan from the heat and liquidise.

7 Blanch the pasta in boiling salted water, drain and mix in a bowl with the pesto.

8 Pulse the garlic mixture until a foam appears, spoon over the tortellini and serve.

CHEF'S TIP

When rolling and storing pasta, use semolina and not flour to prevent it sticking together; this will ensure the strands or sheets are separate and prevent the cooking liquid becoming cloudy and thick with gluten.

Saffron papadelle with mussel and Pernod sauce, sautéed leeks and a selection of wild mushrooms

INGREDIENTS	4 PORTIONS	10 PORTIONS
Saffron pasta dough	400g	1kg
Mussels	200g	500g
Pernod	25ml	60ml
Double cream	150ml	375ml
Diced onion	75g	180g
Baby leeks	50g	125g
Assorted wild mushrooms	50g	125g
Mussel or fish stock	75ml	180ml
Good-quality salt and white pepper	To taste	To taste

Method of work

1 Roll pasta and cut into papadelle then cook in boiling salted water for 2 minutes, refresh in ice cold water and drain.
2 In a hot pan, sweat the onion then add the mussels and the Pernod, cover with a lid and cook for 1 minute.
3 Remove from the heat and pass the liquor.
4 Add the double cream, reduce and season.
5 Cut the leeks into diamonds then sauté with the trimmed wild mushrooms, season well.
6 Mix the sauce through the pasta and mussels and arrange in a bowl.
7 Finish with the leeks and wild mushrooms.

Open spinach lasagne of lobster with chervil, tomato and shellfish foam

INGREDIENTS	4 PORTIONS	10 PORTIONS
Spinach pasta dough	100g	250g
Whole cooked lobster	1	2½
Concassé of tomato	2tbsp	5tbsp
Chopped chervil	4tsp	10tsp
Wild garlic and red pepper vinaigrette	4tbsp	10tbsp
Shellfish shells	200g	500g
Brandy	30ml	75ml
Tomato purée	1tbsp	2½tbsp
Fish stock	100ml	250ml
Double cream	100ml	250ml
Butter	50g	125g
Good-quality salt and white pepper	To taste	To taste

Method of work

1 Sweat the shells in butter for 3 minutes.
2 Add the brandy and flambé.
3 Add the tomato purée and cook for 2 minutes.
4 Add the stock and allow to simmer for 25 minutes, until the liquor has reduced by half.
5 Add the cream and reduce until slightly thickened.
6 Pass, correct the seasoning and keep warm.
7 Roll the pasta dough into lasagne sheets and blanch in boiling salted water until al dente. Drain and pat dry.
8 Add to the shellfish sauce with half the lobster tail meat chopped, tomato concassé and chervil.
9 Arrange the mix into a bowl
10 Remove a little sauce and blend until a foam is achieved, then spoon over.
11 Finish with the red pepper dressing, remaining lobster tail and claw.

Spaghetti carbonara with a cep mushroom dressing, crispy streaky bacon and a Parmesan crisp

INGREDIENTS	4 PORTIONS	10 PORTIONS
Plain pasta dough	400g	1kg
Double cream	100g	250g
Fresh eggs	2	5
Parmesan cheese	100g	250g
Cep mushrooms (fresh or frozen)	100g	250g
Olive oil	50ml	125ml
Whole grain mustard	2tbsp	5tbsp
White wine vinegar	20ml	50ml
Streaky bacon	50g	125g
Grated Parmesan cheese	100g	250g
Good-quality salt and white pepper	To taste	To taste

Method of work

1. Roll out the pasta dough thinly and cut into spaghetti.
2. Cook in boiling salted water until al dente then refresh in ice water and drain.
3. Mix the egg, mustard, cream and cheese then slowly heat, stirring constantly until the sauce thickens.
4. Spread the grated Parmesan into circles on silicone paper about 7cm across then bake at 180°C for 7 minutes.
5. Once the cheese has slightly coloured, lay over a rolling pin and allow to bend.
6. Sauté the mushrooms in oil and add the vinegar, then season.
7. Mix the pasta with sauce then arrange in a bowl.
8. Finish with mushroom vinaigrette, crispy bacon and Parmesan crisp.

 CHEF'S TIP

Pasta once cooked can be bland and requires careful seasoning; this, however, must be balanced with the addition of sauce and/or garnish.

Spinach tagliatelle with seared lemon sole and vine-ripened tomato coulis and aged balsamic vinegar

INGREDIENTS	4 PORTIONS	10 PORTIONS
Saffron pasta dough	400g	1kg
Lemon sole	280g	700g
Olive oil	50ml	125ml
Vine-ripened tomatoes	200g	500g
Basil	¼ bunch	½ bunch
Shallots	4	10
Aged balsamic vinegar	20ml	50ml
Curry powder	pinch	pinch
Good-quality salt and white pepper	To taste	To taste

Method of work

1. Mix the oil, chopped shallots, basil stalks and chopped tomatoes and place on the heat. Simmer for 1 hour, remove from the heat and liquidise.
2. Roll out the pasta dough until thin then cut into tagliatelle.
3. Reduce the balsamic vinegar in a pan over a fierce heat until tacky, then cool.
4. Dust the lemon sole with curry powder and sear gently on both sides.
5. Blanch the pasta in boiling salted water then drain, mix with tomato coulis and place in a hot bowl.
6. Lay slices of lemon sole over the pasta with tomato coulis, basil and drops of balsamic glaze.

 CHEF'S TIP

Do not reboil the tomato coulis once cooked as it will split and unlike other sauces it will not emulsify again properly.

Chilli goat's cheese pansotti with tomato, lime and spring onion salsa

INGREDIENTS	4 PORTIONS	10 PORTIONS
Fresh egg pasta squares (7cm × 7cm)	12	30
Goat's cheese (chevre)	175g	400g
Coriander	¼ bunch	½ bunch
Green chillies	½	1½
Garlic	2 cloves	5 cloves
Parmesan	50g	125g
Olive oil	1tbsp	2½tbsp
Butter	40g	100g
Plum tomatoes	400g	1kg
Limes	1	2½
Spring onions	¼ bunch	½ bunch
Castor sugar	1tbsp	2½tbsp
Ginger	1tsp	2½tsp
Herb oil	1tbsp	2½tbsp
Good-quality salt and white pepper	To taste	To taste

Method of work

1 Combine the goat's cheese with the chopped coriander, chopped green chilli, Parmesan and half of the chopped garlic.
2 Wet the edges of the pasta squares and divide the goat's cheese mix between them all, fold one corner over to form triangles then seal the edges.
3 Brush the bottoms of each pasta shape with olive oil then place onto a steamer tray and steam for 5 minutes.
4 Melt the butter and sweat down the chopped tomato concassé with the remaining chopped garlic, chopped ginger and lime juice and zest.
5 Add the sugar to taste and the thinly sliced spring onions.
6 Arrange the pasta in a bowl, top with the salsa and finish with herb oil.

Truffled spaghetti with asparagus

INGREDIENTS	4 PORTIONS	10 PORTIONS
Fresh egg spaghetti	350g	875g
Asparagus	1 bunch	2½ bunches
Butter	50g	125g
White truffle oil	1tbsp	2½tbsp
Grated pecorino cheese	100g	250g
Black truffles	10g	25g
Rocket	100g	250g
Good-quality salt and white pepper	To taste	To taste

Method of work

1 Place the spaghetti into a large pan of boiling salted water and cook until al dente, refresh in ice water.
2 Peel the asparagus, quarter lengthways and cut into 4cm strips. Blanch in boiling salted water and refresh in ice water.
3 Reheat the spaghetti and asparagus in the butter then mix together with the rocket.
4 Arrange in a bowl, place the truffles and pecorino onto the pasta. Drizzle some truffle oil over and serve.

CHEF'S PROFILE

Name: MARTYN NAIL

Position: Executive chef

Establishment: Claridges

Main responsibilities: I oversee everything.

When did you realise that you wanted to pursue a career in the catering and hospitality industry?
I thought I liked cooking and so went on to college.

Training:
After finishing school, I attended Catering College at Highbury College of Technology. I passed my three year diploma in July 1986, achieving a distinction.

Experience:
I have only worked at Claridge's. It's a fascinating place, always throwing up new challenges. There's always something new to learn! In 2003 I was awarded a scholarship to Cornell University in New York. Whilst I was there I visited various restaurants and hotels (such as La Bernardin) which gave me new insights and was very inspiring. In January this year I also did a trip round New York, Las Vegas and San Francisco, exploring their restaurants. It was a great way to gain knowledge and understanding about America's dining concepts.

What do you find rewarding about your job?
Training, and seeing young people progress to be confident, capable chefs.

What do you find the most challenging about the job?
Ensuring that change is communicated well and clearly to achieve maximum buy-in.

What advice would you give to students just beginning their career?
Be patient even if you think what someone is trying to teach you is boring, one day it will be of use.

Who is your mentor or main inspiration?
Chef Jean-George Vongerichten. Not only is he incredibly talented, but is also a very nice man! He's just so approachable. Vong at The Berkeley hotel was an amazing place. It had amazing food and service.

What traits do you consider essential for anyone entering a career as a chef?
Passion, dedication and discipline.

Can you give one essential kitchen tip or technique that you use as a chef?
Treat all ingredients with respect. Cook them with the respect they deserve.

Claridge's grouse and foie gras pie with apricot and wild mushrooms

INGREDIENTS

Hot water pastry

Milk	400ml
Water	200ml
Lard	325g
Plain flour	1.300kg
Salt	2tsp
Egg wash	2 egg yolk equal amount of cold water

For filling

Grouse bones removed and flesh checked for shoot	5
Lobe of duck foie gras, pre-cooked	1
Mixed wild mushrooms	200g
Dried apricots	15
Leafs of gelatine	8
Ruby port	30ml
Madeira	15ml
Salt	10g
White pepper	
Thyme	2 sprigs

For lining the pie

Streaky bacon	500g
Consommé jelly	500ml
Chicken consommé	
Gelatine	10 leafs

Method of work

1 Heat the water, milk and lard to 85°C.
2 Put the flour and the salt in a well on a bench.
3 Gradually add the liquid to the flour and stir as you do it.
4 Work the ingredients lightly to form the pastry.
5 Wrap in cling film and chill.
6 Allow the pastry to come to room temperature then roll to 0.4cm.
7 Cut the pastry to desired shape to line mould, reserving some to form the lid.
8 Line the greased mould with pastry, being sure to overlap the edges and pressing tight in to the tin and leaving a 3cm border of pastry out of the edge of the tin.
9 Line the pastry with streaky bacon.
10 Add all the ingredients for the filling in a bowl and mix in the seasoning. Allow to stand for 1 hour.
11 Arrange the filling in the pie to form a mosaic.
12 Close over the bacon and bring up the overlapping pastry border.
13 Now prepare your lid and make one or two steam holes, egg wash and decorate.
14 Brush the top of the overlap with the egg wash and apply the lid to the pie.
15 Allow to rest for at least half an hour before cooking.
16 Cook at 210°C until golden (approximately 15 minutes) then cover with foil and continue to cook at 210°C until you get a core temperature of 55°C. Allow to rest at room temperature for 25–30 minutes then cool in a fridge for 1 hour until the pastry sets.
17 Soften the gelatine in cold water.
18 Bring the consommé to the boil, add the gelatine and allow to cool.
19 Pour the prepared jelly through the steam hole. Allow this to set in the fridge for 20 minutes before topping up with the jelly again. Repeat this until the jelly reaches the top of the steam hole.
20 Allow to rest for at least 24 hours before de-moulding and slicing.

CHEF'S PROFILE

Name: **ANGELA HARTNETT**

Current job role and main responsibilities: I am Chef Patron of my own London restaurant and I oversee all the food and beverage operations.

When did you realise that you wanted to pursue a career in the catering and hospitality industry?
I always wanted to run my own restaurant from an early age. My grandparents owned a fish and chip shop.

Experience:
1 Midsummer House, Cambridge
2 Gordon Ramsay, Aubergine
3 Marcus Wareing, Petrus
4 Gordon Ramsay, Holdings

What do you find rewarding about your job?
I love teaching young cooks and get pleasure from seeing the customers when they have enjoyed dining with us.

What do you find the most challenging about the job?
Finding good staff and retaining them.

What advice would you give to students just beginning their career?
Choose a path you enjoy and are passionate about.

Who is your mentor or main inspiration?
My family and their love of food. Also Gordon Ramsay and Nadia Santini.

What traits do you consider essential for anyone entering a career as a chef?
- Understanding the source of your produce
- People management skills
- Common sense
- Organisation

A brief personal profile:
- Chef de Partie, Aubergine
- Sous Chef, Petrus Restaurant
- Executive Chef, Hilton Creek Dubai
- Chef Patron, Connaught Hotel
- Won Hotel Restaurant of the Year
- Won BMW Newcomer of the Year

Can you give one essential kitchen tip or technique that you use as a chef?
Taste everything.

Pumpkin tortelli

INGREDIENTS	4–6 PORTIONS
Fresh pumpkin (seeded and cut into wedges)	2kg
Freshly grated Parmesan	100g
Chopped mustard fruits	100g
Pasta dough	
Amaretti biscuits (crushed)	2–3
Good-quality salt and freshly ground black pepper	To taste
Sage butter	
Vegetable stock	200ml
Butter	100g
Fresh sage	12 leaves

Start this recipe the day before you want to eat it.

Method of work

1 Preheat an oven to 180°C.

2 Arrange the pumpkin wedges in a roasting tin and sprinkle with rock salt.

3 Cover the tin with foil and cook in the oven for 45–50 minutes or until tender when pierced with the point of a knife.

4 Remove from the oven. Leave until cool enough to handle, then scrape the pumpkin flesh from the skin.

5 Place the flesh in a muslin cloth or a fine sieve and hang overnight above a bowl in a cool place to drain off all the excess liquid.

6 Place the pumpkin in a food processor and blend until smooth. Add the Parmesan and mustard fruits and season. Pulse blend to combine.

7 Roll out and cut up the pasta dough. Place teaspoons of filling at 2cm intervals along each strip of pasta, then fold into parcels about 3cm square.

8 At this stage you can par-cook them to use later. Bring a large pan of salted water to the boil and blanch the tortelli for 30 seconds. Drain and plunge immediately into iced water. Remove and place on a lightly oiled baking sheet. Drizzle with a little olive oil and then cover with plastic film. The tortelli can be refrigerated for up to 24 hours.

9 Place the stock and butter in a pan and bring to the boil over a medium heat, whisking vigorously to prevent the mixture from splitting. Add the sage leaves and a little seasoning just before serving.

10 Bring a large pan of salted water to the boil. Add the tortelli and cook for 3 minutes. Drain and serve, drizzled with the sage butter and with the amaretti crumbs sprinkled on top.

5
Advanced soups and sauces

LEARNING OUTCOMES

The aim of this chapter is to enable the candidate to develop the skills and knowledge required for the preparation and cookery of stocks, soups and sauces and dressings.

At the end of this chapter the candidate will be able to:

- Identify each sauce, stock and dressing variety and finished product
- Understand the use of relative ingredients in stock, sauce and dressing cookery
- State the quality points of various stock, sauce and dressing commodities and end products
- Prepare and cook each type of stock, sauce and dressing variety
- Identify the storage procedures for stocks, sauces and dressings
- Be competent at preparing and cooking a range of stocks, sauces and dressings

INTRODUCTION

Sauces

A sauce is most accurately described as a flavoured liquid, which in essence is a base that has been thickened. A **stock** is generally regarded as the base for many sauces and is an extremely important component.

The thickenings used for sauces vary greatly, depending on the base ingredient.

For instance, hollandaise is thickened by adding **clarified butter** to egg yolks, mayonnaise by adding oil to egg yolks, **beurre blanc** with whisked butter, and cream sauces are reduced with double cream.

Modern sauces are lightened by using less fat to take into account society's healthier lifestyles. However, **cream**, **jus** and butter are still used to complement many dishes.

A sauce performs an important role in a dish: it complements, enhances and creates an attractive finish to the dish. The sauce's appearance should be glossy and its consistency correct, and it should have a defined flavour but never overpower the flavour of the main ingredient of the dish. The potential of a sauce to highlight a dish is often overlooked, and the seasoning will perform a pivotal role: a bland sauce will ruin a perfectly cooked meal.

There are several basic techniques for making sauces.

Deglazing

This is the process of allowing the caramelised pan or tray juices and sediment to be released into added liquid, which may be water, stock, wine or other liquid-based commodities.

Any excess fat is drained off first, then the liquid is added while stirring rigorously over a hot stove. The liquid is reduced and a good jus or stock added. A small amount of butter can also be added to finish the sauce. The liquid is then passed through muslin cloth and a fine **chinois** to create a smooth consistency.

Skimming

This process is one of the most important a chef must master. A well skimmed sauce or stock will have clarity and clear flavour, which will be ruined if left unattended. The use of a perforated spoon or small ladle to remove the scum and foam that develops at the surface of a cooking liquid will prevent the stock or sauce from becoming cloudy and bitter.

Any excess traces of fat or oil can be removed by dragging dish papers across the top of the liquid until it is crystal clear. A brown stock can be chilled until it gelatinises and the fat can then be removed from the surface before using.

HEALTH & SAFETY

Many sauces contain dairy produce and so the base ingredients should be kept below 8°C (4°C is best practice) until required.

VIDEO CLIP
Complex sauces used at competition level

Deglazing a pan

It is important to skim stock

Passing a stock

Reducing a liquid

Whisking butter into a sauce

Straining and passing

Forcing a liquid or **purée** through a drum sieve, conical strainer, chinois or muslin cloth will ensure the finished sauce is smooth and emulsified. The use of muslin cloth when passing a jus is essential to remove excess sediment (this process is generally repeated at least twice to ensure a crystal-clear finish).

Reducing

By reducing a liquid over a fierce heat a more intensified flavour is achieved. However, the volume of liquid is reduced, which must be taken into account when preparing a dish and for portion control. Over reducing a liquid can result in the appearance of a bitter flavour.

Whisking and blending

These processes rely on rapid movement to **emulsify** products such as creams, eggs and purées, giving them a light, smooth and delicate flavour and appearance. This is caused by the increased aeration within the sauce.

Egg-yolk based emulsified sauces, such as hollandaise sauce, require the eggs to be beaten over a bain marie, which cooks the egg yolks but prevents them from curdling. The vigorous whisking during the cooking process increases the volume of the sauce.

THICKENING SAUCES

Roux

The most well-known of all thickening agents in the kitchen, the basic **roux** is a combination of equal quantities of melted butter and flour mixed together over heat until the mixture comes away from the sides of the pan.

Three types of roux are generally used in professional cookery. A white roux is generally used with the addition of boiled milk to achieve a béchamel sauce. A blond roux is achieved by cooking the mixture for slightly longer until a light sandy colour develops. White stock is then added to create a **velouté** sauce. The last is a brown roux, which uses flour browned in the oven. Brown stock (estouffade) can then be added to make a brown sauce (**espagnole**).

Beurre manié

Beurre manié is a combination of equal quantities of flour and butter made into a paste. This cold uncooked mix is whisked into hot liquid and cooked out until the desired thickness is achieved.

Breadcrumbs/rice

These are used in a raw state and added to a hot sauce. The cooking process makes their starch molecules burst and the starch content will then thicken the liquid.

Butter

Whisking or hand blending small cubes of chilled unsalted butter into a hot sauce will give a glossy rich texture. However, the sauce must not be reboiled as the butter within the sauce will split from the water content.

Powdered starch thickening agents

These come in numerous forms, such as cornflour, arrowroot and fecule. To use these products a little powder should be mixed with cold liquid until a paste is formed, this mix is then whisked into hot liquid which will instantly thicken. The paste must be smooth and gradually added otherwise lumps will form in the sauce.

Arrowroot becomes transparent once added to sauce and is therefore used when thickening hot fruit sauces when clarity is required.

Egg yolks and cream (liaison)

This mixture is achieved by whisking the egg yolks and cream with a small quantity of a hot sauce. It is then added to the remaining hot sauce. The resultant sauce must not be allowed to boil again as it will curdle. This sauce thickening agent is classically used when using velouté sauces; it will enrich the sauce and will only thicken it slightly.

EMULSIFIED SAUCES

This area of sauce-making requires the most skill. The keys to a good emulsified sauce are the order in which ingredients are added, the temperature, and the speed at which the ingredients are blended.

Emulsified sauces are produced by dispersing fats as small droplets in liquids they would not otherwise mix with. Various proteins are used to stabilise the emulsion formed by mixing the two principal ingredients. The most common emulsified sauces are mayonnaise, hollandaise and beurre blanc. However, many other water-based solutions can be emulsified with fats by using egg yolks, powdered lecithin, gelatine or agar-agar as a stabiliser. When egg yolk is used it is the lecithin protein it contains that acts as the stabiliser.

The fat is slowly added to the liquid (e.g. water, vinegar or lemon juice) and this is slowly whisked to form an emulsion. The two liquids will combine with the stabiliser, and if the conditions are right (correct temperature and constant manipulation) they will coagulate and form an emulsion.

All emulsified sauces are unstable and will separate if stored for too long or at the wrong temperature. There are methods to rescue a separated emulsification: putting a few drops of hot water in a bowl and whisking the curdled mix into it slowly can sometimes remedy the problem.

Temperature control can be a problem for hollandaise sauce. A mix that has separated due to being too cool can be brought back by whisking it into a little boiling water. A hot mix can be remedied in a similar fashion but instead using iced water.

BUTTER SAUCES

Three main types of butter sauce are used in the kitchen:

Hot butter sauces

▪ **Beurre noisette** – nut-brown butter, classically served with fish.

▪ **Beurre noir** – black butter, classically served with skate wings or veal brains.

Warm butter sauces

▪ *Beurre blanc* – white butter, classically served with vegetables, fish or white meats.

▪ *Hollandaise* – classically served with grilled meats, or made into a derivative such as mousseline or moutarde.

▪ *Béarnaise* – similar to hollandaise, but a reduction of shallots, pepper and tarragon is used to create the flavour of the sauce.

Cold butter sauces

▪ *Café de Paris butter* – contains a mix of fresh herbs and spices. Other condiments such as marjoram, mustard, dill, rosemary, tarragon, paprika, capers, chives, a little curry powder, parsley, shallots, garlic, anchovies and Worcestershire sauce is beaten into unsalted butter. The resulting compound butter is shaped into a cylinder and chilled. When served, a piece is sliced off and allowed to melt on top of, for example, grilled **entrecôte** steaks.

▪ *Parsley butter* – softened unsalted butter has a little lemon juice and chopped fresh parsley beaten into it. Seasoning and a little cayenne pepper are added and then chilled before use. This butter is sometimes also known as beurre Maître d'Hotel.

VELOUTÉ SAUCE

The velouté sauce is made in the same way as a béchamel sauce except that stock replaces the milk content and no clouté is used. A liaison is added to finish the sauce.

Variations of velouté are:

▪ *aurore* – addition of fresh tomato sauce

▪ *curry* – addition of curry paste

▪ *estragon* – addition of tarragon.

HEALTH & SAFETY

Warm sauces fall into the temperature danger zone and must be carefully controlled to prevent bacterial growth.

VIDEO CLIP
Tomato and basil beurre blanc

BROWN SAUCE (ESPAGNOLE)

Classically, a brown sauce is made by taking a brown roux and adding brown stock. This can then be mixed with the same quantity of brown stock and reduced by half to create a **demi glace**.

In modern professional cookery, a brown sauce or jus is made by browning meat trimmings and some aromatic vegetables before **deglazing** with wine and adding brown stock. This is then reduced, passed and seasoned, and the consistency checked before using.

Variations of brown sauce are:

- *bordelaise* – addition of red wine and bone marrow.
- *chasseur* – addition of mushrooms, white wine, shallots, fresh tarragon. and tomato **concassé**.
- *diable* – addition of chopped shallots, vinegar, Worcester sauce, cayenne pepper and peppercorns.

PURÉED AND BLENDED VEGETABLE SAUCES

These sauces are the most versatile as they can be used on all types of meat, fish, poultry, game and vegetarian dishes. The sauce base is made by puréeing or blending a cooked main ingredient (e.g. garlic, roasted red peppers) and then a stock, cream or butter is added to obtain a smooth, well-flavoured sauce. These sauces can be served hot, warm or cold.

FOAMS

This type of sauce has recently transformed modern high-class restaurant dishes. The base liquid, which may be cold or hot, is aerated by whisking, blending or by using a gas-charged siphon to create a frothy texture. The foam is then spooned onto the dish; but it should only be added at the last minute to ensure that the air remains in the sauce for the duration of the customer's eating experience. A heavy, well-flavoured sauce can be used to create a light delicate accompaniment that still keeps the taste required. Foams best suit cream, vegetable or fruit sauces as it is difficult to keep denser sauces aerated.

VIDEO CLIP
Producing foams using a bamix and espuma

When aerating a sauce, the size of the container needs to be double the volume of sauce being used. If a blender is used, it should be positioned so that its blades skim the surface of the sauce, which causes the bubbles/froth to develop. A siphon will inject gas directly into the liquid, and will expel the foam directly into the bowl, glass or plate being used to serve the dish.

A gelatinisation agent, such as gelatine or agar-agar, is sometimes used to stabilise the foam and create a stronger, foamier texture.

Olive oil flavoured with herbs and chillis

FLAVOURED OILS

The idea of using flavoured oils in sauces is being explored more and more. There are many different oils and flavours available, which makes them extremely versatile. They may be used sparingly to complement sauces and dishes, adding colour and texture, or they may be a main component.

Spices lend themselves exceptionally well to oil flavouring; they are first dry roasted and then added to good-quality oil, which is then allowed to **simmer** for at least an hour. Herbs can be finely chopped or puréed into oil, which allows the natural chlorophyll to turn the oil a green colour.

Oils such as white and black truffle are expensive and very pungent; a few drops added to dishes such as risottos are extremely effective. Flavoured oils can be stored for long periods of time if kept in airtight containers in cool, dry conditions.

COULIS

A **coulis** is made by very slowly warming through ingredients, such as plum tomatoes, shallots, oil, fresh basil and garlic, and then liquidising them into a fine sauce. The base ingredients form an emulsion, in which the oil is blended into the sauce. Because of the emulsification, this kind of sauce cannot be served hot and must be carefully monitored.

Fruit coulis are generally puréed fruits that have been combined with sugar in the form of stock syrup to adjust the consistency. A little lemon juice can be added to enhance the natural flavours of the fresh fruits.

VINAIGRETTES

Classically, a vinaigrette is an emulsion of three parts oil and one part vinegar, with the addition of a little mustard and various flavourings and seasonings. It is considered to be a typically French dressing, and is used mostly for salads and **hors d'oeuvres**.

Modern vinaigrettes use the lightest oils, flavoured vinegars and subtle mustards to complement each dish as required. They can be served cold or warm.

Split dressings

These dressings are technically vinaigrettes as they contain the same ingredients, however due to the fact that emulsification has not taken place they belong to their own classification.

MAYONNAISE

HEALTH & SAFETY

When making mayonnaise, use only pasteurised egg. This will reduce the risk of salmonella.

This is an emulsion of egg yolks, oil, mustard, vinegar and lemon juice. The egg yolks form the main structure as the lecithin protein they contain prevents the sauce from splitting. Mayonnaise is the basis of many classical dressings and sauces for the larder section.

Some derivatives of mayonnaise are:

■ Tartare sauce

■ Remoulade

■ Aïoli.

CREAM-BASED SAUCES

There are two main types of cream-based sauce:

◼ Cooked ◼ Uncooked.

The cooked versions are mentioned earlier; for example fish cream sauce, which is a reduction of fish stock, white wine, shallots and cream, reduced to a coating consistency. Other types of cream sauces can be produced from a basic velouté base by adding cream to the final stages of cooking.

Cold cream sauces can be whipped, thickened, flavoured or poured, and can be served as accompaniments with salads, cold meats and starters. Different types of cream base can be used, such as crème fraîche, soured cream, whipping cream and natural yoghurt.

PESTO

This is an Italian sauce that originates from Genoa but is today widely used throughout cuisine. The basic ingredients for **pesto** are a good-quality virgin olive oil, garlic, pine nuts, parmesan cheese and fresh basil. Sun-dried peppers and tomatoes can be added for a twist on this classic sauce.

PURÉE-BASED SAUCES

Purée-based sauces are usually cooked recipes containing vegetables or fruits and are blended and passed through a chinois. To produce a coarse purée, the main raw ingredient is blended and not passed.

SALSA

Salsa simply means 'sauce' in Spanish. Salsas can be served either warm or cold and are used either to add spice to a dish or to balance an already heavily spiced dish and 'cool' it down. They can be produced from fruit or vegetables, or a mix of both. Salsas are regarded more as a cross between a salad and a dressing, rather than strictly as a sauce.

REDUCED VINEGARS

Vinegars such as balsamic, cider or red wine reduce well and form a syrup-like consistency. Reduced vinegars can be presented onto a plate to give a sweet, slightly thick and syrupy appearance. They are used generally to add colour and decoration to a plate, in collaboration with other dressings and sauces.

STORAGE OF COLD SAUCES AND DRESSINGS

Sauces and dressings should be made on a daily basis to get the freshest flavour possible. If they need to be stored, they should be kept chilled and must be correctly labelled and dated during storage.

Some dressings and sauces are, however, better left to mature, such as Cumberland sauce. These should be kept chilled in a covered container.

Dressings that use oil as a main ingredient will begin to solidify when chilled. It will be necessary to allow such dressings to warm up to room temperature before use; this allows the dressing to become fluid again.

An alternative method of storage is to vacuum pack sauces into various sized portions. Some sauces can also be frozen and defrosted as required.

RECIPES

Hollandaise sauce

 CHEF'S TIP

Temperature is very important when making hollandaise sauce: if the liquid is too hot the egg will scramble, and if the butter is too hot or too cold the sauce will split.

INGREDIENTS	10 PORTIONS
White wine vinegar	2tbsp
Water	2tbsp
Crushed peppercorns	1tsp
Egg yolks	4
Clarified unsalted butter	250g
Lemon juice	½ lemon
Good-quality salt and ground white pepper	To taste

Method of work

1 Place the vinegar, water and peppercorns into a saucepan and place onto a medium heat. Reduce by one-third.

2 Strain the liquid through a fine chinois and allow to cool slightly.

3 Mix the egg yolks with the liquid and **whisk** over a bain marie until the ribbon stage is achieved.

4 Slowly trickle the warm clarified butter into the egg mixture, whisking constantly until the sauce has emulsified into a thick and glossy consistency.

5 Add the lemon juice and **correct** the seasoning. Keep warm until required for service.

Whisking the egg yolks and liquid over a bain marie

Drizzling the butter into the egg mix while whisking

Beurre blanc

INGREDIENTS	10 PORTIONS
Shallots, chopped	2 each
White wine vinegar	3tbsp
White wine	4tbsp
Water	2tbsp
Diced unsalted butter	200g
Lemon juice	½ lemon
Good-quality salt and white pepper	To taste

Method of work

1 Place the shallots, white wine vinegar, white wine and water in a pan and reduce by half.

2 Remove from the heat. Whisk in the **diced** cold butter until emulsified and the sauce thickens to the correct consistency.

3 Season well and add a little lemon juice.

Béarnaise sauce

INGREDIENTS	10 PORTIONS
White wine vinegar	2tbsp
Water	2tbsp
Fresh tarragon	2tsp
Crushed peppercorns	1tsp
Egg yolks	4
Clarified unsalted butter	250g
Lemon juice	½ lemon
Fresh chopped tarragon	2tsp
Fresh chopped chervil	2tsp
Good-quality salt and ground white pepper	To taste

Method of work

1 Place the vinegar, water, tarragon and peppercorns in a saucepan and reduce by one-third.

2 Strain the liquid and allow to cool slightly.

3 Mix the egg yolks with the reduced tarragon liquid and whisk over a bain marie until the ribbon stage is achieved.

4 Slowly pour the warm clarified butter into egg mix, whisking constantly until the sauce is thick and glossy.

5 Add the lemon juice and season.

6 Add the chopped chervil and tarragon to the sauce. Keep warm until required for service.

Velouté sauce (modern version)

CHEF'S TIP

This sauce relies on the ingredients for its distinctive delicate flavour, so only use good quality wine and stock

INGREDIENTS	10 PORTIONS
Parsley stalks	4tsp
Shallots, chopped	4 small
Unsalted butter	75g
White wine	100ml
White stock	350ml
Double cream	350ml
Good-quality salt and white pepper	To taste

Method of work

1. **Sweat** off the parsley stalks and shallots in the butter without any colour. Add the white wine and reduce by two-thirds.
2. Add the stock and reduce by a further two-thirds.
3. Add the double cream and simmer until reduced by half and the desired consistency has been achieved.
4. **Pass** through a fine chinois and correct the seasoning.

Veal jus

CHEF'S TIP

Good flavour and colour are achieved by browning the meat and vegetables: too little and the sauce will be too light, too much and the sauce will taste burnt.

INGREDIENTS	10 PORTIONS
Brown veal stock	900ml
Beef trimmings	200g
Garlic	1 clove
Fresh thyme	3tsp
Red wine	200ml
Mirepoix of vegetables (carrots, celery, onion and leek)	100g
Tomato purée	25g
Good-quality salt and white pepper	To taste

Method of work

1. Brown the beef trimmings with the garlic and thyme in a saucepan or in a roasting tray in the oven at a high temperature.
2. Add the **mirepoix** of vegetables and tomato purée and brown again.
3. Deglaze the pan with the red wine and remove all sediment from the bottom.
4. Add the stock and reduce by half. **Skim** continuously to remove the scum.
5. Pass through a chinois, correct the consistency and the seasoning.

Light chicken jus

INGREDIENTS	10 PORTIONS
Brown chicken stock	750ml
Chicken carcasses	400g
Shallots	5
Mushroom trimmings	10
Garlic	½ bulb
Bay leaf	1
White wine	200ml
Tomato purée	25g
Good-quality salt and white pepper	To taste

CHEF'S TIP

Remove as much fat from the chicken carcasses as possible. This will reduce the amount of fat released into the sauce and will cut down on skimming.

Method of work

1 Chop the chicken carcasses into small pieces. Colour in a hot pan with a little oil until golden brown in colour.
2 Add the chopped shallots, mushroom trimmings, garlic, bay leaf and tomato purée and continue to colour all the ingredients.
3 Add the wine and reduce until only a little liquid is remaining.
4 Add the stock and reduce by half, skimming continuously.
5 Pass through a chinois and muslin cloth, then thicken as required and correct the seasoning.

Bordelaise sauce

INGREDIENTS	10 PORTIONS
Veal jus/demi glace	450ml
Shallots	4
Vegetable oil	45ml
Red wine	200ml
Crushed peppercorns	1tsp
Bay leaf	1
Bone marrow	60g
Unsalted butter	40g
Good-quality salt and white pepper	To taste

CHEF'S TIP

The marrow can be kept frozen until required and then soaked. This will defrost the marrow and remove any unwanted blood deposits.

Method of work

1 Finely chop the shallots. Sweat in the oil with the peppercorns and bay leaf.
2 Add the red wine and reduce by half.
3 Add the jus. Bring to the boil and simmer, skimming occasionally.
4 Soak the beef bone marrow for 20 minutes in cold water, then clean and slice.
5 Add a knob of the butter to the jus and whisk in to give a good glaze.
6 Add the marrow to the sauce to warm through and serve.

Fresh tomato sauce

 CHEF'S TIP

This sauce is vibrant in colour and flavoursome. As an alternative, the tomatoes can be cut into concassé and the purée omitted. The same cooking procedure applies except do not blend to leave the chunky texture.

INGREDIENTS	10 PORTIONS
Unsalted butter	100g
Shallots, finely chopped	4
Fresh chopped thyme	1tsp
Bay leaf	1
Chopped garlic	4 cloves
Ripe plum tomatoes, chopped	800g
Tomato purée	25g
Caster sugar	75g
Tomato juice	150ml
Fresh basil stalks	3tsp
Good-quality salt and white pepper	To taste

Method of work

1 Sweat the shallots, thyme, bay leaf, and garlic in butter.
2 Add the chopped plum tomatoes, purée, caster sugar, tomato juice and basil stalks.
3 Simmer for 45 minutes.
4 Blend in a liquidiser until smooth and pass through a chinois.
5 Correct the seasoning and serve.

Court bouillon

 CHEF'S TIP

This stock is essential for fish cookery and can be made in advance, but it should not be kept for longer than four days.

INGREDIENTS	10 PORTIONS
Leeks	10
Celery	5 sticks
Carrot	5
Onion	5
Shallots	10
Fennel	2½
Garlic	2 cloves
Fresh bay leaf	1 leaf
Fresh parsley	Sprig
Peppercorns	12 each
Juice and zest of lemons	5 lemons
White wine	60ml

Method of work

1 Chop all vegetables and place in a saucepan with the herbs, cover with cold water and bring to the boil.
2 Add the remaining ingredients and simmer for 30 minutes.
3 Chill and store in a sealed container in a refrigerator until required.

Roasted yellow pepper sauce

 CHEF'S TIP

This sauce works with red or green peppers or tomatoes. For a more subtle taste, the vegetables can be blanched in vegetable stock instead of being roasted.

INGREDIENTS	10 PORTIONS
Yellow peppers	400g
Olive oil	30ml
Chopped garlic	2 cloves
Chopped onion	80g
Vegetable stock	250ml
Double cream	75ml
Good-quality salt and white pepper	To taste

Method of work

1 Pre-heat an oven to 180°C.
2 Deseed and chop the peppers roughly. Place in a bowl with the olive oil, chopped onions, chopped garlic and season well with salt and pepper.
3 Place onto a tray and **roast** for 20 minutes.
4 Remove the roasted vegetables from the oven and liquidise in a food blender, slowly adding the stock.
5 Pour into a saucepan and bring to the boil, add the cream and cook to the required consistency.
6 Pass through a chinois, correct the seasoning and serve.

Champagne and dill cream foam

 CHEF'S TIP

Foams are excellent for giving flavour but with a very light taste. The key to a good foam is milk, which allows the sauce to froth and hold volume for long enough to serve.

INGREDIENTS	10 PORTIONS
Shellfish sauce (see recipe on p. 98)	250ml
Champagne	100ml
Fresh chopped dill	3tsp
Full fat milk	75ml

Method of work

1 Bring the sauce to the boil and add the champagne, milk and dill.
2 Place a small amount into a tall jug or container. Using a hand blender, aerate until foam begins to appear.*
3 Spoon the foam over a finished dish at the last minute of service.

*Alternatively, place into a siphon and charge with a gas cartridge. Keep the siphon warm in a bain marie of hot water at 80°C for service. Shoot the foam through the siphon when required and serve.

Milk and chopped dill added to the sauce

Aerating using a hand blender

Shellfish sauce

 CHEF'S TIP

Ensure the alcohol is burned away completely or the finished sauce will have a bitter flavour.

INGREDIENTS	10 PORTIONS
Lobster/crab/langoustine shells	450g
Garlic	3 cloves
Mirepoix of vegetables (carrots, onions, leek and celery)	100g
Tomato concassé	150g
Brandy	125ml
Fish stock	250ml
Double cream	150ml
White wine	100ml
Diced butter	50g
Fresh dill	2tsp
Fresh tarragon	1tsp
Good-quality salt and white pepper	To taste

Method of work

1. Roast the seafood shells with the garlic and mirepoix of vegetables until golden brown in colour.
2. Deglaze the pan with brandy and **flambé**.
3. Add the tomato concassé and fish stock and bring to the boil.
4. Skim constantly and simmer for 40 minutes until reduced by half.
5. Add the double cream and continue to reduce.
6. Pass the sauce through a chinois into a clean saucepan. Bring the sauce to the boil to reduce again and adjust the seasoning.
7. Add the wine. Add the cubes of butter, whisking continuously.
8. Add chopped fresh herbs to finish.

Roasting the shells

Vegetable nage

 CHEF'S TIP

This stock really needs 24 hours to sit, to allow the vegetables to infuse the liquor. There is no quick way of making this; but the end product is worth the effort.

INGREDIENTS	10 PORTIONS
Onions	80g
Carrots	80g
Celery	50g
Leek	50g
Garlic	3 cloves
Lemon juice	½ lemon
White peppercorns	¼tsp
Star anise	1
Water	500ml
White wine	50ml
Fresh tarragon, basil, coriander, thyme and parsley	Sprig of each

Method of work

1 Slice all the vegetables and place into a saucepan with the lemon juice, garlic, peppercorns, star anise and water.
2 Bring to the boil and simmer for 10 minutes.
3 Remove from heat. Add the wine with all the fresh herbs.
4 Cool and refrigerate for a minimum of 24 hours before using as required.

Sliced vegetables, lemon juice, peppercorns, star anise and water placed in a pot

Adding the wine and all the herbs

Sweet curry sauce

INGREDIENTS	10 PORTIONS
Unsalted butter	30g
Diced onion	40g
Diced pineapple	400g
Diced banana	50g
Diced apple	50g
White flour	30g
Madras curry paste	30g
Grated coconut	1tbsp
Chicken stock	500ml
Bouquet garni	1 small

Method of work

1 Sweat the onions in the butter, stir in fruit and cook for approximately 5 minutes.

2 Add in the flour, curry paste and coconut. Cook out for 5 minutes, stirring continuously to prevent burning. Add the chicken stock and bouquet garni.

3 Bring to the boil and simmer for 45 minutes. Check the seasoning and serve.

Sprinkling in the flour, curry paste and coconut

Mussel stock

INGREDIENTS	10 PORTIONS
Fresh cleaned mussels	750g
Water	300ml
White wine	100ml
Shallots	50g
Celery	40g
Fresh parsley and thyme	Sprig of each

Method of work

1 Place the water, white wine, chopped shallots, sliced celery, parsley and thyme into a saucepan and bring to the boil.

2 Add the mussels, cover with a lid and boil for 3–4 minutes.

3 Remove the mussels and use if required for another dish.

4 Leave the stock to stand for 5 minutes to let any grit sink to the bottom. Strain through muslin cloth. Use as required.

Savoury sabayon

INGREDIENTS	10 PORTIONS
Egg yolks	6
Warm water	4tbsp
Lemon juice	2 lemons
Salt	4g
White wine	240ml
Chives, chopped	4tsp

Method of work

1 Whisk the egg yolks and water over a bain marie until the ribbon stage is achieved.
2 Slowly add the lemon juice and warmed white wine.
3 Continue to aerate until the mixture doubles in size.
4 Season well and add the chopped chives.
5 This sauce can be used as a **glaze** under or over meat, fish or poultry dishes.

Saffron fish sauce

INGREDIENTS	10 PORTIONS
Fish stock	500ml
White wine	250ml
Noilly Prat	200ml
Finely chopped shallots	100g
Double cream	400ml
Saffron	1tsp
Diced unsalted butter	70g

Method of work

1 Bring the stock, white wine, chopped shallots and Noilly Prat to the boil and reduce by half.
2 Add the cream and bring back to the boil. Reduce until the sauce has thickened to the required consistency.
3 Remove from the heat and add the saffron, allowing 5 minutes to infuse into the sauce.
4 While the sauce is still warm, whisk in the butter a little at a time on the side of the stove.
5 Strain the sauce through a fine chinois. Reheat without boiling and serve as required.

Reducing stock with white wine, shallots and Noilly Prat

Adding the cream

Adding the saffron

A pureé soup

A cream soup

A broth

A consommé

A bisque

A chowder

SOUP CLASSIFICATION

Soups can be categorised as follows:

■ *Purée* – a soup named after or thickened by its main ingredient, such as mushroom, potato and leek or tomato.

■ *Cream* – a purée soup with the addition of cream, thin béchamel or crème fraîche. Cream of mushroom, cream of potato and leek, cream of tomato and cream of vegetable are all variations. It is essential that these soups have a smooth consistency and have been passed.

■ *Velouté* – a soup to which a **liaison** of cream and egg yolk has been added.

■ *Broth* – a soup that is composed of a strongly flavoured stock and a named garnish, such as mutton. This type of soup is not passed, and the vegetables are cut in varying shapes according to the recipe's requirement. Examples are mutton broth and Scotch broth. Potages also come under this type of soup.

■ **Consommé** – clear soups that are prepared from stock flavoured with various meats and vegetables. They are clarified and should be clear when finished. **Bouillons** also come under this category, but they are not clarified to the same level. Examples are consommé julienne, consommé Celestine and consommé royale.

■ *Bisque* – taken from the French term *bi cuit* (biscuit), bisque is a soup made from crustaceans and is traditionally served with water biscuits. It is thickened with rice and the shell of the crustacean used and finished with cream. Examples are lobster and prawn bisque.

■ *Chowder* – this is generally a seafood soup, usually based on molluscs but can have added smoked white fish. It is usually associated with New England, and the most popular version is clam chowder. The term may also describe a buttery, hearty soup made with corn and chicken. The term 'chowder' may derive from the French word for a large caldron, *chaudiere*, in which Breton fishermen threw their catch to make a communal fish stew. Examples are clam, cockle or chicken and sweetcorn chowder.

■ *Foreign* – also known as miscellaneous soups, these are all soups of a traditional, modern and national nature that do not fall into any other category. There are many examples, such as: the simple Jewish chicken soup; the gumbos made from okra, chicken, seafood or meat in the American south; India has many types of lentil soups; Middle Eastern Muslims break their Ramadan fast with harira, made from lentils, chickpeas and lamb; Japan is famous for soups based on **miso** (fermented soybean paste); Eastern Europe possesses goulash (a beef and paprika stew that started life as soup) and borsch (beetroot and meat soup); Spanish gazpacho is always in vogue; the Greeks have avgolemono, an egg and lemon soup; Italy has numerous bean and pasta soups, such as

VIDEO CLIP
Preparation of gazpacho

minestrone; and Scotland is renowned for cullen skink (smoked haddock soup) and Scotch broth (mutton and barley soup).

■ *Chilled* – nearly all soups that are served hot can also be served chilled. However, when chilled the intensity of flavour is reduced. They may therefore need a stronger base or a more intense seasoning.

The skills required to create an outstanding soup are the same as those needed to make a delicate sauce. The modern chef has a wide variety of ingredients at their disposal to meet the requirements of today's more perceptive customers. The balance of flavours, seasoning, consistency, texture and temperature needs to be understood to create a well-flavoured and satisfying soup.

VELOUTÉS

The quality points of this type of soup are that they should have a delicate flavour and have a velvety, smooth texture. This will be attributed in part to the use of well-flavoured stocks, careful simmering and the addition of a liaison of egg yolks and cream. Once the liaison is added the soup needs to be reheated very carefully and must never be allowed to reboil.

 CHEF'S TIP

It is imperative that unblemished, fresh ingredients are used when making soups. Always check that the ingredients meet with the dish requirements by using correct **mise en place** methods and weighing each ingredient prior to preparation.

Basic velouté recipe

INGREDIENTS	MAKES 1 LITRE
Butter	60g
Flour	60g
White stock	1250ml
Egg yolks	2
Cream	100ml
Good-quality salt and white pepper	To taste

Method of work

1 Prepare a blond roux with the butter and the flour.
2 Mix in the boiling white stock gradually using a wooden spoon. Avoid lumps by adding a little at a time and bring to the boil whilst continuously stirring.
3 Bring back to the boil, skim and season and leave to simmer for 45 minutes.
4 Pass through a fine chinois into a clean pan and reboil.
5 Whisk together the egg yolks and cream and add one third of the soup, whisking quickly. Add to the remaining soup and continuously stir until the liaison is fully combined and has slightly thickened to velouté. Correct the seasoning and add any garnish before serving.

GARNISHES AND ACCOMPANIMENTS

Most soups are accompanied by bread, usually in the form of bread rolls or sliced **baguettes**. However, **croûtons**, sippets and toasted flutes may also be served at the table. Today, croûtons are often quite rustic is style, with large pieces of bread drizzled with olive oil and baked in the oven until crisp.

- Croûtons – small cubes of white crustless bread (1cm × 1cm) that are pan fried in clarified butter. The butter is heated in a pan and the diced bread added; the pan is constantly shaken so that the croûtons colour evenly. The croûtons are spooned out onto kitchen paper and patted dry.
- *Sippets* – triangles of bread cut from the corners of pan loaves, thinly sliced and toasted in an oven. To add flavour, garlic can be rubbed onto the bread before turning over to toast the other side.
- *Croûtes de flûte* (toasted flutes) – slices taken from a thin baguette. They can either be toasted on both sides or brushed in melted butter and crisped in the oven.
- *Diablotins* – thin round slices of toasted bread, topped with grated cheese and browned in the oven. Can be coated with reduced béchamel.
- *Melba toast* – **melba toast** is toasted bread that is cut between the toasted surfaces whilst still hot. The uncooked side is rubbed on a service cloth to remove the rough bread and then also toasted.
- *Cheese straws* – puff pastry strips the have cheese added at the last turn. They are twisted and baked until crisp.

Croûtons, sippets and croûtes de flûte

Brunoise

Julienne

Paysanne

Vegetable garnishes

Used as a light garnish for consommés, broths or purée-based soups. Careful cutting into neat, even and standardised shapes is important to the finished result.

- *Brunoise* – cut equal amounts of carrot, turnip, leek and celery into 2mm dice, for consommés and slightly larger for broths
- *Julienne* – cut equal amounts of carrot, turnip, leek and celery into thin strips up to 35mm in length
- *Paysanne* – cut equal amounts of turnips, carrots, swede, potato, leek and celery into 1cm squares.

SERVING TEMPERATURES AND QUANTITIES

Hot soups should be served very hot and any accompanying garnishes should be added when serving. The Food Hygiene (England) Regulations 2006 state that hot food needs to be kept at or above 63°C in order to control the growth of pathogenic micro-organisms and the formation of toxins. The soup should not be kept for service or on display for sale for a period of more than two hours.

Cold soups should be served chilled at below 8°C and not at room temperature.

When calculating the amount of soup required for a given number of portions, take into account the following points:

- Portion size is dependent on the size and style of the menu and the number of courses that follow
- The recipe method must be followed correctly
- Each ingredient must be accurately measured
- No more than 200–250ml per portion should be served.

RECIPES

Basic clear consommé

Clockwise: fish, game, chicken and beef consommé

CHEF'S TIP

Make sure the raft of clarification stays floating. If it starts to sink, raise the temperature. This will help to combat cloudiness.

VIDEO CLIP
Preparation of consommés Celestine

INGREDIENTS	4 PORTIONS	10 PORTIONS
Minced flesh (e.g. beef, fish, poultry, game)	200g	1kg
Carrot	40g	100g
Onion	40g	100g
Celery	40g	100g
Leek	40g	100g
Bay leaves	1	2
Thyme	1 sprig	2 sprig
Peppercorns	4	10
Good-quality salt	Pinch	5g
Cold stock (e.g. beef fish, poultry, game)	200ml	500ml
Hot stock (e.g. beef fish, poultry, game)	1 litre	2.5 litres
Egg whites	1	2–3

Method of work

1 Peel and chop all of the vegetables into a **macédoine**.
2 Thoroughly mix all of the minced flesh, vegetables, herbs, seasoning, egg whites and cold stock (this is called the clarification) together and allow to stand for 30 minutes.
3 Mix well with the hot stock and bring to the boil as quickly as possible. Keep the bottom of the pan clear by using a spatula, but avoid disturbing the clarif.
4 Allow to simmer gently for 2–3 hours.
5 Strain through a dampened muslin cloth and adjust the seasoning with salt only.
6 Serve in a warm consommé cup, plain or with a named garnish.

Tomato consommé *Consommé madrilène*

INGREDIENTS	4 PORTIONS	10 PORTIONS
Basic beef consommé clarification	4 portions	10 portions
Very ripe tomatoes	4	10
Tomato concassé	120g	300g
Extra celery	100g	250g
Shredded sorrel	1tbsp	1–3tbsp

CHEF'S TIP

Tomatoes are over 90 per cent water, therefore it important to squeeze as much out as possible. You can still use the juice in the consommé as long as it is clarified along with the stock.

Method of work

1 Squash the tomatoes and squeeze the water into the clarification.

2 Add the tomato flesh and celery to the clarification and proceed as for basic consommé.

3 Serve hot or cold, garnished with the evenly cut tomato concassé and shredded sorrel.

Consommé with poached quail's eggs *Consommé Colbert*

INGREDIENTS	4 PORTIONS	10 PORTIONS
Chicken consommé	1.25 litres	3 litres
Quail's eggs	12	30
Fine julienne of carrot celery, leek and turnip	160g	400g
Butter	20g	50g
Chives	To garnish	To garnish

CHEF'S TIP

Hen's eggs are the classical choice for this soup, but the easy availability of quail's eggs means they are now preferable.

Method of work

1 Cook the vegetables in the butter in a covered pan until just cooked and drain on dish paper.

2 Poach the eggs in a little of the consommé, taking care to keep the yolks runny. Refresh and keep for service.

3 Place the vegetable garnish and three eggs per portion in the bottom of the consommé cup.

4 Pour the very hot consommé onto the eggs and vegetables.

5 Allow to stand for 1 minute before service to allow the eggs to heat through.

6 Serve with some chopped chives.

Consommé with chicken quenelle

 VIDEO CLIP
Preparation of chicken and herb quenelles

INGREDIENTS	4 PORTIONS	10 PORTIONS
Chicken consommé	1.25 litres	3 litres
Chicken breast meat	100g	250g
Double cream	40ml	100ml
Egg whites	1	2
Good-quality salt and white pepper	To taste	To taste
Chives	To garnish	To garnish

Method of work

1. Mince the chicken through a fine plate three times, making sure that the flesh is chilled between each mincing.
2. In a metal bowl over ice, beat in the cream to make a fine forcemeat of chicken.
3. Season and test a small piece in simmering stock. Adjust the seasoning if necessary.
4. Make small quenelles of chicken forcemeat and poach in a little of the consommé.
5. Serve the remaining consommé with chicken quenelles and garnish with chopped chives.

Petite marmite

INGREDIENTS	4 PORTIONS	10 PORTIONS
Basic consommé	1.5 litre	3.5 litre
Diced lean rump beef	80g	200g
Chicken wings	4	10
Carrots	80g	200g
Leek	80g	200g
Turnip	80g	200g
Celery	80g	200g
Savoy cabbage	50g	125g
Bone marrow	8 slices	20 slices
Baguettes	12 slices	30 slices

Method of work

1. Blanch and refresh the beef, add to the consommé and simmer very gently for 1 hour.
2. Trim the wings and blanch in boiling water, add to the consommé and simmer for 20 minutes.
3. Turn the carrots and cut the celery into diamonds, add to the consommé.
4. Add the shaped turnips, cut leeks and cabbage and continue to simmer.
5. Dip the slices of bread into the fat from the soup and toast in the oven.
6. **Degrease** the soup and correct the seasoning.
7. Add the sliced marrow to the soup and poach for 2–3 minutes.
8. Decant into either a single or individual earthenware dishes and serve accompanied by the toasted flutes.

Consommé with turned vegetables and flutes
Croûte au pot

INGREDIENTS	4 PORTIONS	10 PORTIONS
Consommé	1 litre	2.5 litres
Carrot, turnip, courgette	160g	400g
Flutes	¼ loaf (4 thin slices)	½ loaf (10 thin slices)
Goose/duck fat	20g	50g

Method of work

1 Shape the vegetables into small barrel shapes and cook in seasoned boiling water or stock.
2 Brush the flutes with melted fat, season and bake in the oven until crisp.
3 Serve the soup with the vegetables as a garnish and the baked flutes separately.

 CHEF'S TIP

Croûte au pot was originally served from a petit marmite. However, by today's tastes the vegetables would be considered to be overcooked.

Chilled consommé and garnishes

INGREDIENTS	4 PORTIONS	10 PORTIONS
Consommé	1 litre	2.5 litres
Named garnish	200g	500g

Chilled consommés are normally placed in the refrigerator one or two hours before service. Their sometimes gelatinous appearance is due to the concentration of protein. The addition of 10g of leaf gelatine per litre of consommé will set it to the required consistency. Various flavours can be added to base consommés:

■ *Consommé Madrilène en Gelée* – consommé flavoured with celery, tomato and pimentos, garnished with tomato julienne, shredded fresh sorrel and cooked vermicelli pasta

■ *Consommé à l'essence d'estragon en Gelée* – chicken consommé infused with fresh tarragon leaves after the clarification process

■ *Consommé Madeira en Gelée* – beef consommé flavoured with Madeira

CHEF'S TIP

Instead of using gelatine, the addition of an alternative setting gel such as agar-agar can be used.

Clear chicken soup with egg

INGREDIENTS	4 PORTIONS	10 PORTIONS
Dried shitake mushrooms	4	10
Chicken stock	1 litre	2.5 litre
Chopped onion	80g	200g
Poached eggs	4	10
Fresh chervil	4 pinches	10 pinches
Dark soy sauce	1tbsp	2tbsp
Chilli sauce	1tsp	1tbsp
Good-quality salt and pepper	To taste	To taste

 CHEF'S TIP

The onions are boiled to give a slightly acidic background to the flavours. The mushrooms can be left in to give a more rustic broth.

Method of work

1. Boil the mushrooms in water for 5 minutes. Drain, remove the hard stalks and cut the caps into julienne. Reserve for garnish.
2. Simmer the chopped onions in the stock for 15 minutes, drain and discard the onions.
3. Add the soy sauce, chilli sauce and mushrooms.
4. Bring to the boil, correct the seasoning and strain through muslin cloth. Reboil.
5. Add the eggs and allow to simmer for 1 minute to poach them.
6. Serve with one egg per portion and the fresh chervil.

Chilled almond and garlic soup

INGREDIENTS	4 PORTIONS	10 PORTIONS
Crushed garlic	4 cloves	10 cloves
Ground almonds	80g	200g
Fresh breadcrumbs	50g	125g
Olive oil	80ml	200ml
White wine vinegar	20ml	50ml
Grape juice	500ml	1.25 litres
Skinned grapes	200g	500g
Water	200ml	500ml
Sliced toasted almonds	20g	50g
Good-quality salt and mill pepper	To taste	To taste

Method of work

1. Purée the almonds, garlic and breadcrumbs in a food processor.
2. Add the oil to make a paste.
3. Add the vinegar and then the grape juice and water.
4. **Season to taste**.
5. Quarter the grapes and mix with the chilled soup.
6. Serve with toasted almonds.

 CHEF'S TIP

This is a traditional wedding soup of the city of Cordoba in Spain.

Bortsch

CHEF'S TIP

The overriding flavour and colour of bortsch should be beetroot, whether it is a consommé or a more rustic purée.

INGREDIENTS	4 PORTIONS	10 PORTIONS
Duck stock	1.25 litres	3 litres
Minced duck meat	100g	250g
Minced shin of beef	100g	250g
Duck carcass	1	2–3
Egg whites	1	3
Parsley stalks	4	10
Celery	80g	200g
Fennel	40g	100g
Marjoram	1tsp	1tbsp
Grated beetroot	200g	500g
Carrot	80g	200g
Onion	80g	200g
Leek	80g	200g
Smoked duck	100g	250g
Diced rump beef	80g	200g
Beetroot julienne	40g	100g
Shortcrust pastry tartlet cases	4	10
Duck fine forcemeat	80g	200g
Double cream	100ml	250ml
Lemon juice	½ lemon	1 lemon

Method of work

1 Make a consommé using the vegetables, herbs, egg whites, minced beef and duck (see recipe for basic consommé on page 115).

2 Cook and purée the beetroot, add to the consommé and pass through a fine sieve.

3 Garnish with a julienne of cooked beef, smoked duck, beetroot and leek julienne

4 Serve with tartlets filled and baked with a fine forcemeat of duck and cream soured with the lemon juice.

Hot and sour soup

INGREDIENTS	4 PORTIONS	10 PORTIONS
Finely shredded pork or chicken	160g	400g
Grated fresh ginger	20g	50g
Minced garlic	40g	100g
Chopped spring onion	80g	200g
Sherry	40ml	100ml
Clear chicken bouillon	1 litre	2.5 litres
Drained straw mushrooms	200g	500g
Bamboo shoots	200g	500g
Diced firm tofu	200g	500g
Cider vinegar	40ml	100ml
White pepper	To taste	To taste
Dark soy sauce	To taste	To taste
Red chilli pepper	½	1
Eggs	1	2
Sesame oil	25ml	50ml

Method of work

1   Heat the sesame oil. Add the meat and **sauté** until cooked.
2   Drain and set aside.
3   Sweat the garlic and ginger, add the sherry and stock.
4   Add the bamboo shoots, mushrooms, onions and tofu and bring to the boil.
5   Flavour soup with the vinegar (which gives the sour taste) and the white pepper (which gives the hot taste).
6   Add enough of the soy sauce to give a brown colour, then season with salt.
7   Cut the chilli pepper into thin slices.
8   Bring the soup back to the boil and add in the sliced chilli pepper.
9   Simmer for 3 minutes.
10 Slowly and evenly pour in the lightly beaten eggs. Do not stir again until the egg comes to the surface.
11 Add a small amount of the sesame oil for extra flavour and colour.
12 Reheat and serve garnished with chives.

 CHEF'S TIP

Cayenne or hot chilli powder can also be used to create the hot flavour.

Japanese noodle soup

INGREDIENTS	4 PORTIONS	10 PORTIONS
Chicken consommé	1 litre	2.5 litres
Miso	40ml	100ml
Soba or egg noodles (cooked)	200g	500g
Sake	40ml	100ml
Rice vinegar	20ml	50ml
Japanese soy sauce	40ml	100ml
Sliced asparagus	120g	300g
Sliced shitake mushrooms	80g	200g
Julienne of carrot	80g	200g
Sliced spring onions	40g	100g
Chopped chilli	1	2–3
Good-quality salt and pepper	To taste	To taste

CHEF'S TIP

Miso is made from fermented soya and comes in the form of a paste.

Method of work

1. Dissolve the **miso** in the boiling consommé.
2. Add the soy sauce, vinegar and sake and cook until the alcohol has evaporated.
3. Add the vegetables and simmer for 3 minutes. Correct the seasoning.
4. Divide the noodles and pour on the soup. Serve immediately.

Bisque

Bisques are named after the crustaceans used as the main ingredient. With lobster and crab, do not use the claws as they will not get passed through a chinois.

INGREDIENTS	4 PORTIONS	10 PORTIONS
Named crustacean, shells and flesh	300g	750g
Butter	60g	150g
Carrots	40g	100g
Onion	40g	100g
Celery	20g	50g
Leek	40g	100g
Bouquet garni	1 small	1 medium
Brandy	20ml	50ml
Fish stock	800ml	2 litres
Dry white wine	80ml	200ml
Tomato purée	20g	50g
Cayenne pepper (approx.)	Pinch	3g
Rice flour	60g	150g
Unsalted butter	40g	100g
Double cream	40ml	100ml

VIDEO CLIP
Preparation of lobster bisque

Method of work

1 Peel, wash, dice and sweat the vegetables in the butter.
2 Add the shells and flesh and cook at a higher temperature for 2–3 minutes.
3 Raise the heat and add the brandy. Shake the pan and flambé until the flames disappear (this burns off the alcohol).
4 Add the rice flour, tomato purée and cayenne pepper.
5 Add the stock and wine and simmer (skimming when necessary) for 20 minutes.
6 Remove the crustacea and cool slightly.
7 Remove the flesh and pound the shell using a pestle and mortar until smooth. Reserve some of the flesh for garnish.
8 Return the flesh and shell to the bisque and simmer for a further 20 minutes.
9 Purée the soup and pass through a chinois into a clean pan. Adjust the seasoning and consistency.
10 Reboil and add the unsalted butter and cream.
11 Serve with crushed water biscuits, and garnish with the reserved flesh.

Iced mussel soup

CHEF'S TIP

Sauté the mussel garnish in a little green herb oil just before service to give a warm and cold sensation for your guests.

INGREDIENTS	4 PORTIONS	10 PORTIONS
Mussels	1kg	2.5kg
White wine	80ml	200ml
Crushed garlic	1 clove	2–3 cloves
Red pepper	1	2–3
Cucumber (medium sized)	1	2–3
Sliced radish	100g	250g
Button mushrooms	200g	500g
Peeled broad beans	400g	1kg
Peeled tomatoes	300g	750g
Lemon juice	½ lemon	1 lemon
Tabasco sauce	To taste	To taste
Good-quality salt and mill pepper	To taste	To taste

Method of work

1 Steam the mussels in the wine and garlic.
2 Remove the flesh and keep the juices.
3 **Grill** the pepper to loosen the skin and deseed.
4 Peel and chop the cucumber, sprinkle with salt and allow to sit in a colander for 10 minutes.
5 Keep some red pepper, mussels and broad beans to one side for garnish.
6 Purée all the ingredients in a food processor, adding water to correct the consistency. Pass through a fine chinois.
7 Chill in the refrigerator for several hours.
8 Serve garnished with a dice of red pepper, mussels, beans and a fresh herb of your choice.

Chicken velouté with tongue and mushrooms
Velouté Agnes Sorel 1

INGREDIENTS	4 PORTIONS	10 PORTIONS
Chicken velouté (see recipe on p. 113)	1 litre	2.5 litres
Button mushrooms	80g	200g
Cooked ox tongue	80g	200g
Cooked chicken breast	80g	200g

Method of work

1 Cut the chicken, mushrooms and tongue into a fine julienne.
2 Sauté the mushroom and add the tongue and chicken to heat through.
3 Add to the soup just before service.

Pumpkin velouté with toasted pumpkin seeds

INGREDIENT	4 PORTIONS	10 PORTIONS
Pumpkin flesh	200g	500g
Onion	50g	250g
White of leek	50g	250g
Celery	50g	250g
Butter	40g	100g
White vegetable stock	1 litre	2.5 litres
Bouquet garni	Small	Medium
Double cream	40ml	100ml
Egg yolk	1	2–3
Good-quality salt and pepper	To taste	To taste

Method of work

1 Peel, de-seed and chop the pumpkin.
2 Sweat the vegetables in the butter with the chopped pumpkin.
3 Add the stock and bouquet garni. Simmer until all the ingredients are fully cooked.
4 Purée and pass through a fine chinois.
5 Adjust the seasoning and consistency.
6 Whisk the yolks and cream in a bowl until mixed.
7 Add a little of the soup and add the liaison back to the soup.
8 Serve with toasted pumpkin seeds.

 CHEF'S TIP

This soup can be made from other squashes, such as butternut, but still garnish with roasted pumpkin seeds.

Fish velouté with quenelles and mussels

INGREDIENTS	4 PORTIONS	10 PORTIONS
Fish velouté	1 litre	2.5 litres
Mussels	1kg	2.5kg
White wine	40ml	100ml
Fine fish forcemeat	80g	200g

Method of work

1 Steam the mussels in the wine.
2 Remove the mussel meat and strain the juices into a clean pan.
3 Make small quenelles with the forcemeat and poach in the mussel juices.
4 Add the quenelles and mussels to the soup just before service.

CHEF'S TIP

Reduce the mussel juice to enrich the soup, but take care not to over-reduce as the liquor can go from cooked to burnt in an instant. When prepared in smaller quantities there will not be enough mussel juice, so add fish stock and season well.

Chicken velouté with parsley and chicken dumplings

INGREDIENTS	4 PORTIONS	10 PORTIONS
Chicken velouté	1 litre	2.5 litres
Parsley purée	20g	50g
Double cream	20ml	100ml
Chicken stock	200ml	1 litre
Fine chicken forcemeat	80g	200g
Good-quality salt and pepper	To taste	To taste

Method of work

1 Mix the parsley purée and add to the double cream to make a loose purée and season well. Heat carefully in a small saucepan and keep hot for service.
2 Season the forcemeat well. Form quenelles using two teaspoons. Place each quenelle in simmering stock and poach until cooked.
3 Heat the velouté and serve with the parsley purée and chicken quenelles.

 CHEF'S TIP

This is a visually striking soup, but you can use other purées such as carrot or black bean.

Assessment of knowledge and understanding

You have now learned about the use of the different varieties of soup and how to produce different soups applying an array of commodities and preparation techniques.

To test your level of knowledge and understanding, answer the following short questions. These will help to prepare you for your summative (final) assessment.

Quality identifications

1 List three examples of velouté.

i)_____ ii)_____ iii)_____

2 List three examples of consommé.

i)_____ ii)_____ iii)_____

3 List the two most important aspects to check before serving every soup.

i)_____ ii)_____

Materials and storage

1 List three pieces of equipment that can be used to pass a soup.

i)_____ ii)_____ iii)_____

2 Give two reasons why the weighing and measuring of ingredients is so important.

i)_____ ii)_____

Preparation

1 Explain the term 'clarification' in relation to consommé.

_____

2 Describe the process of making a royale.

_____

3 List four different accompaniments for soup.

i)_____ ii)_____

iii)_____ iv)_____

Cooking

1 Explain why you should never boil a velouté soup.

_____

2 State three factors in relation to portion control which should be considered when preparing and serving soup.

i)_____ ii)_____ iii)_____

3 Explain what happens if the sabayon overheats when making a hollandaise sauce.

_____

Health and safety

1 List two safety points when passing a hot soup through a chinois.

i)_____ ii)_____

2 State two healthy options when making soups.

i)_____ ii)_____

Name: SHANE OSBORN

Position: Chef/Co-owner

Establishment: Pied à Terre

Current job role and main responsibilities: Cooking hands-on at Pied à Terre.

When did you realise that you wanted to pursue a career in the catering and hospitality industry?
I started in catering when I was 13 as my mother was a caterer. It was my first part-time job.

Training: I started a four-year apprenticeship in 1985 at the age of 15.

Experience:
- Le Bateau Ivre in France (two Michelin stars)
- L' Oranger
- The Square
- Pied à Terre, under Tom Aikens.

What do you find rewarding about your job?
Every day is a school day. Working with people who are passionate about their job.

What advice would you give to students just beginning their career?
Aim for the top. Always try to do better the next day, and don't ever give in.

Who is your mentor or main inspiration?
I thrive on the need to improve myself – to better myself and the food I cook every day.

What traits do you consider essential for anyone entering a career as a chef?
Stamina and determination.

Can you give one essential kitchen tip or technique that you use as a chef?
Learn how to season!

Name: **PAUL RANKIN**

Current job role and main responsibilities: Paul Rankin runs a successful restaurant business, the Rankin Group.

When did you realise that you wanted to pursue a career in the catering and hospitality industry? Paul first became interested in cooking when he was travelling the globe in his twenties. It was on these travels that he met his Canadian wife Jeanne in Greece. The couple returned to Canada where Paul started working as a waiter and instantly fell in love with the excitement of the restaurant world.

Experience:

1   After travelling through India, Australia, Singapore, Malaysia, Thailand, Hong Kong and China, Paul and Jeanne returned to work for 3 years under the expert guidance of Albert Roux.
2   Following a period as Head Chef in a Californian Restaurant, Paul and Jeanne returned to Belfast in 1989 to open their first restaurant – Roscoff – and soon had been credited with Northern Ireland's first Michelin Star.
3   Almost two decades on since first opening Roscoff, Paul now boasts two of the best restaurants in the country with the new Roscoff and the funkier and more casual Cayenne. In addition, Paul runs a host of premium cafes and has trained a legacy of star chefs who are ensuring that Ireland continues to boast a world class reputation for cuisine.

Achievements:

*   Paul's TV career took off soon after with three series of the popular 'Gourmet Ireland' - a showcase for Irish produce and the country's artisan producers.
*   Paul's TV career is still flourishing and this summer he has been busy filming for numerous new shows about to hit the screens. From 'The People's Cookbook' with Anthony Worrell Thompson, a new series and new format of 'Ready Steady Cook' to 'Local Food Heroes' with Gary Rhodes. In addition, he has just appeared in 'Take on the Takeaway' and has been working on a brand new series called 'Food Poker' which starts on BBC2 this autumn.
*   To date, Paul and Jeanne have written five books and contributed to countless others. *Gourmet Ireland I & II* accompanied the television series. *Hot Food* and *Ideal Home Cooking* followed with the fifth title, *New Irish Cookery*, a compendium of over 140 mouth-watering recipes with an authentic spirit that reflects their shared passion for cooking with fresh and tasty Irish ingredients. *The People's Cookbook* has also just been released following the very successful TV series.

Red lentil and ham soup

INGREDIENTS	SERVES 8
1 ham shank about 900g (about 2lb) **or 500g piece of ham or bacon, or a ham bone**	
Large onion, finely chopped	1
Stick celery, finely diced	1
Medium carrot, grated	1
Large potato, peeled and cut into 1cm dice	1
Red lentils, washed and drained	200g
Chopped fresh parsley to garnish	
Optional	
Serve with floury potatoes	

Method of work

1 Place the ham shanks in a large pot with about 3½ litres of cold water.

2 Bring to the boil, skim off any scum which rises to the surface. Simmer for 2½–3 hours or until the meat is very tender. (This will not take as long if you are using a piece of ham or bacon.)

3 45 minutes before the end of the cooking time, add the vegetables and the lentils. Skim the soup as it comes back to the boil. The soup is ready when the lentils are cooked, but it will taste much better if it is left to stand for 4–5 hours, or over night. Season to taste.

4 To serve, remove the ham and either save it for another use or chop, or flake the meat into small pieces and return to the soup. Ladle into warmed soup bowls and sprinkle with parsley. Serve the potatoes on the side.

6

Advanced skills and techniques in producing vegetable and vegetarian dishes (Unit 304)

LEARNING OUTCOMES

The aim of this chapter is to enable the candidate to develop the necessary advanced skills knowledge and understanding of the principles in preparing and cooking vegetables to dish specifications. The emphasis in this chapter is on developing precision, speed and control in existing skills and perfecting more refined and advanced techniques.

INTRODUCTION

The large number of different types and varieties of vegetables enables the chef to give great depth and variety to their menu and to the diet of the customer.

A thorough understanding of the various qualities of each group of vegetables and the characteristics of each type within those groups enables the professional chef to create vegetable dishes that exploit those qualities to their own advantage. This understanding gives the diner a true gastronomic journey through a menu.

VIDEO CLIP
Covent Garden
vegetable market

BRASSICAS (BRASSICAEA)

Brassicas, also known as flower heads, are part of the mustard and cabbage family. The main edible parts of these plants develop above the ground. Some varieties are grown for their roots (swede, turnip; see root vegetables).

VEGETABLE	CHARACTERISTICS	QUALITY POINTS	STORAGE	MAIN COOKERY METHODS
Broccoli	Varieties include calabrese (tight green flower heads) and spouting (longer stems and looser head)	Heads should be fresh and aromatic. Avoid wilted or yellowing heads	Refrigerate for 2–3 days	Boil, steam, stir fry
Brussels sprouts	Closely related to cabbage and named after is original place of cultivation. It has a nuttier flavour than cabbage and is most seasonal around the Christmas period	Tight heads with the leaves wrapped around and with no wilting. The cut end should not be overly discoloured	Refrigerate for 4–5 days	Boil, steam, sauté, stir fry
Cauliflower	Closely related to broccoli, it is characterised by its tight thick white flower	Look out for frost damage – looks almost black. The plant should feel heavier than it looks. The leaves should be tight to the flower	Keep in a cool place for 2–3 days	Boil, steam, stir fry, raw, pickle
Cabbage	There are several varieties in use: white, red, green, savoy, spring greens. The younger leaves at the centre of the head are usually used	White and red should be very firm with no obvious discolouration. Loose leaf varieties should have a large heart and no wilting of the outer leaves	White and red: up to 14 days in a refrigerator. Leafier varieties: in a cool place for 2–3 days	Steam, boil, stir fry, pickle, ferment
Chinese leaves	Also known as Chinese cabbage, it has the same uses as pak choi. It gives a delicate flavour of cabbage	The leaves are pale green with no discolouration and are packed tightly together in a long cylindrical shape	Refrigerate for 4–5 days	Stir fry, salads
Kale/curly kale	A winter leaf that does not form a head. The leaves grow along a thick stem	Bright green leaves with no discolouration. Should feel firm to the touch and have no limp leaves	Refrigerate for 4–5 days	Boil, steam
Pak choi/bok choi	A common vegetable used in Chinese cuisine. It has a peppery flavour and lends itself to fast cooking	There should be no blemishes on the stalks and the leaves should be strong dark green colour	Refrigerate for 1–2 days	Stir fry, white can be braised

IMAGES COURTESY OF THINKVEGETABLES.CO.UK

BULBS (ALLIUMS)

Bulbs are perennial bulbous plants that have a characteristic pungent flavour and aroma. In culinary terms they are the most important flavour enhancer next to salt and are used in the cuisines of almost every country worldwide. They vary in intensity from variety to variety. The pungency can be tempered with long slow cooking or through an understanding of the qualities of each variety.

VEGETABLE	CHARACTERISTICS	QUALITY POINTS	STORAGE	MAIN COOKERY METHODS
Garlic	Garlic is bulb that has its own unique flavour which changes if it is crushed or chopped. It benefits from cooking, but can be eaten raw when it has a pungent peppery flavour. The stalk can be eaten early in the season. Usually, the smaller the bulb, the more pungent the flavour	Papery skin, with the cloves tight together. There should be no sprouting and the should feel firm and heavy	In a cool, dry, dark place up to 2 weeks	fry, roast
Leeks	The leek does not form a bulbous base. It has a long cylindrical shape with tightly wrapped leaf sheaths. It is used as used as ingredient, and in its own right as a main ingredient. The fibrous and tough green tops are usually used in stocks	The main part of the leek should be white or pale green with little dark green. Bend the leak to check that there is no woody centre (a sure sign that the vegetable had gone to seed, 'bolted'). Avoid buying if the leafy parts have started to yellow. Should feel firm and heavy	1 week in a cool dark place, but can be refrigerated	Braise, and as an ingredient in other dishes
Onions	There are many types of onion, almost all have a papery outer skin and a layered moist interior. The main types are red and white, which have a milder and more delicate flavour than the yellow. There is also the small button and pickling onions	Should feel firm and heavy, the skin should be dry and with no mould growing, and there should be no sprouting	Onions can be stored for many months in a dry dark place if they are hung on strings. If in bags store in a cool dark place	Braise, fry

VEGETABLE	CHARACTERISTICS	QUALITY POINTS	STORAGE	MAIN COOKERY METHODS
Shallot	A small mildly flavoured onion that has a place of its own in the culinary world. Most commonly available varieties are banana, brown English and the pink shallot. They are mainly used as ingredients in other dishes and impart a mild onion flavour that does not overpower other flavours	Should feel firm and heavy, the skin should be dry and papery and with no mould growing, and there should be no sprouting	2–3 months in a cool dark and dry place. Avoid refrigeration if possible	Ingredient in other dishes
Spring onions	Also known as scallions (Ireland), gibbons (Wales) and cibies (Scotland), these are early-maturing varieties of onion that are harvested before the formation of a bulb. Some varieties do go on to form a small edible bulb	Colour ranging from white at the base to deep green at the top. They should feel firm to the touch, with no wilting or discolouration	Refrigerate for 1–2 days	Raw, stir fry

FUNGI/MUSHROOMS

Historically, fungi have been used as food in a variety of ways. Mushrooms are used in cookery, yeast is used in baking and mycelial fungi are used for making soy sauce and tempeh. Fungi have no green parts and do not need sunshine to grow, they digest their foods externally, absorbing nutrients into their cells.

Mushrooms are the above ground fruiting (spore producing) bodies of a fungus. There are both cultivated and wild varieties of mushroom. If you are buying wild mushrooms be sure that they are from a reputable source as there are many poisonous varieties that take an expert's eye to distinguish. In culinary terms, mushrooms add a huge variety of flavours and textures to any cuisine.

VEGETABLE	CHARACTERISTICS	QUALITY POINTS	STORAGE	MAIN COOKERY METHODS
Cèpes	Known as porcini in Italy, cepes are highly prized, with a rich nutty flavour. Small cepes are held in high regard	Should be firm and feel heavy. Avoid slimy textures	Refrigerate in paper bags for 1–2 days. Can be dried or bottled for extended storage	Sauté

VEGETABLE	CHARACTERISTICS	QUALITY POINTS	STORAGE	MAIN COOKERY METHODS
Chestnut mushrooms	Similar to a white mushroom but with a brown cap and a deeper flavour	No blemishes, firm and dry to the touch and feel heavy	Refrigerate in paper bags for 1–2 days.	Sauté and as an ingredient in other dishes
Chicken of the woods	A large meaty mushroom found on the side of woodland trees (mostly oak). It has a lemony chicken flavour	Use small and immature, or use the tender outer edges of the mushroom	Use within 1 day, or freeze	Any dish that applies to chicken
Giant puffball	A very large white fungus that has a white firm interior	The exterior should be white and firm. It should sound hollow when tapped and have a meaty aroma	Refrigerate for 1 day	Can be sliced and fried or used as white mushrooms
Morels	A highly prize mushroom that appears in the spring. It has a rough exterior with many nooks and crannies and a deep aromatic flavour. They can accompany rich dishes and still be detected.	Check for insects. Morels should be quite spongy with an intense aroma and not slimy	Refrigerate in paper bags for 1–2 days. Dry very well for extended storage	Stuffed, sauté
Oyster mushrooms	Oyster mushrooms grow on trees but are easily cultivated. They have a pleasant deep flavour. Their texture when cooked is soft but this does not detract from the flavour	The mushroom has a pronounced cap and the gills and stem should be the same colour. Should feel heavy and not slimy	Refrigerate in paper bags for 1–2 days. Dry very well for extended storage	Stir fry, sauté
Shiitake	Shiitake are delicately textured mushrooms that are harvested from hardwood trees. They come in a range of colours and are quite meaty in flavour and have a slippery texture after cooking	Should not feel too slippery to the touch. Must be correctly delivered in paper-lined boxes with little sign of disturbance and no sign of bruising	Refrigerate for 1–2 days	Stir fry, sauté

VEGETABLE	CHARACTERISTICS	QUALITY POINTS	STORAGE	MAIN COOKERY METHODS
White mushrooms	The most common of the cultivated mushrooms. They are sold as closed-cup and button mushrooms or as flat open mushrooms. Each type has a pleasant and delicate flavour that can carry and enhance the flavours of other ingredients	Button or closed-cup mushrooms should be white with no blemishes, firm to the touch and feel heavy. Flat mushrooms should have dark gills and a pinkish edge. They also should be firm and heavy	Refrigerate in paper bags for 1–2 days	Sauté, grill, deep and stir fry. Can also be used as a stuffing and as a vegetarian sauté dish, e.g. stroganoff

IMAGES COURTESY OF THINKVEGETABLES.CO.UK

TUBERS

TUBERS

A tuber is a special type of root that acts as the plant's food store and is grown entirely underground. It is generally the only part of the plant used, indeed in the case of potatoes (which is a member of the tomato family) the fruit of the plant is poisonous.

Tubers are the staple food sources of many cultures. Their ease of cultivation, storage properties and versatility make them very important in the diets of these cultures. The potato in particular has many varieties and uses, which are listed in a separate usage chart.

Potatoes are available in many varieties, and most growers produce potatoes that they know will sell and which have distinctive uses.

The main categories of potato are:

▪ *Early or second early* – which includes new potatoes. These potatoes are either grown to mature early in the season or are main crop potatoes that are picked before full maturity. These have the advantage of high nutritional values and require simple cookery methods that lend themselves to the delicate flavours. Their disadvantage is a comparatively short storage time.

▪ *Main crop* – these potatoes are allowed to come to full maturity and are robust enough for extended storage, which makes them such an important staple food for so many people.

Each type of potato has a unique eating quality, which can be categorised into waxy or floury. This refers to the texture of the cooked potato. As a general rule, waxy potatoes are suitable for salads and boiling whole and floury potatoes are suitable for baking, for chips and for mashing.

VEGETABLE	CHARACTERISTICS	QUALITY POINTS	STORAGE	MAIN COOKERY METHODS
Jerusalem artichokes	Jerusalem artichokes are neither artichokes nor from Jerusalem. They are the tuberous roots of a plant from the sunflower family.	Firm to the touch, moist flesh, not too knobbly	In a dark cool place for 8–10 days	Boil
Potatoes	See potato chart on the next page.			
Sweet potatoes	Yellow to deep orange in colour (a source of carotene; vitamin A). Historically it was more important than the potato until the popularity of the potato came to the fore. It is the staple food of central America, the Caribbean and the tropical south.	Firm flesh, no sign of woodiness and free from blemishes	In a cool dark place for up to 3 weeks	Fry, boil, roast bake
Yams	All edible yams have to be cooked to destroy dioscorine, a bitter and toxic substance found in raw yams. They are the staple food of western Africa and the Pacific islands. The average size is that of a small marrow.	Should have a coarse brown skin, which should be firm and unbroken. The flesh should be moist and creamy	In a cool dark place for up to 4 weeks	Boil, fry, roast

POTATO VARIETY	WAXY	FLOURY	CHARACTERISTICS	EARLY	MAIN CROP	MAIN COOKERY METHODS
Anna		✓	Uniform shape, white skin and flesh		✓	Bake, boil, mash
Anya	✓		A small variety, nutty flavour, pink skin	√2nd	✓	Boil, salads

POTATO VARIETY	WAXY	FLOURY	CHARACTERISTICS	EARLY	MAIN CROP	MAIN COOKERY METHODS
Avalanche		✓	White skin, creamy flesh	✓	✓	Bake boil
Cara		✓	White or pink skin, creamy moist flesh		✓	All methods
Carlingford	✓		White skin, oval, good new potato	✓		Bake, boil, mash
Desiree		✓	Pink skin, soft yellow flesh		✓	All methods
Estima		✓	White skin, moist white flesh	✓2nd		All methods
Golden Wonder		✓	Brown skin, white flesh, improves with storage	✓		Crisps especially, and all other methods
Jersey Royal	✓		Kidney shaped, pale yellow flesh, excellent new potato	✓	✓	Salads, boil
Kerr Pinks		✓	Pink skin, white flesh	✓	✓	All methods
King Edward		✓	White and pink skin, pale yellow flesh		✓	All methods
Maris Bard	✓		Creamy flesh, white skin	✓		Not suitable for boiling but good for all other methods
Maris Piper		✓	Cream skin and flesh, most popular in fish and chip shops	✓	✓	Chips especially, and all other methods
Pentland Dell	✓	✓	Pale skin and flesh, even sized	✓	✓	Bake, chip, roast
Picasso	✓		Small, pale skin and flesh	✓	✓	Boil, salads
Pink fir apple	✓		Long knobbly, Excellent nutty flavour		✓	Boil, salads. Best cooked in skin and peeled later
Record		✓	White skin, creamy yellow flesh	✓	✓	All methods
Red Rooster		✓	Red skin, creamy yellow flesh	✓	✓	All methods
Vitelotte	✓		Also known as Truffe de Chine, a purple potato with dark knobbly skin	✓		Boil, salads
Wilja		✓	Oval shape, pale skin and flesh	✓2nd		All methods

ROOTS

Edible root serve the same purpose of any other root in that they take up water and nutrients to nourish the plant. They may or may not be entirely covered with soil. For the chef, they provide flavour, texture, colour and valuable nutrition.

VEGETABLE	CHARACTERISTICS	QUALITY POINTS	STORAGE	MAIN COOKERY METHODS
Beetroot	A deep purple root that has a sweet earthy flavour. It is high in potassium. The leaves can be cooked like spinach	Firm to the touch. Even size and shape. The leaves should be intact and there should be a fresh earthy aroma	In a dark cool place for up to 4 weeks	Steam, boil, pickle, salad, roast, soups
Carrots	Carrots are the most popular vegetable after potatoes. They can lift a dish with a splash of colour and a sweetness of flavour	Main crop carrots should have no blemishes, cracks or heavy soil deposits. Young carrots should be thin and with fresh foliage	Refrigerate for 5–10 days	Buttered, glacé, Vichy, purée, baby, soup
Celeriac	Also known as turnip rooted celery. The plant is grown for its root rather than its stems. It has a faint aroma and taste of celery	Firm, should feel heavy, no blemishes other than the grooves on the skin	In a dark cool place for 10–14 days	Boil, buttered, creamed
Horseradish	Horseradish is a root grown for its powerful flavour and is usually grated to mix with cream for sauces	Should feel heavy. The skin should not be too woody and the flesh should be slightly moist	In a dark cool place for 10–14 days	Grated
Mouli/daikon radish	A long white radish that has a mild flavour and is used extensively in Chinese cuisine	The leaves should be still intact and green, the skin should be smooth and free of blemishes	Refrigerate for 10–12 days	Mainly stir fry

VEGETABLE	CHARACTERISTICS	QUALITY POINTS	STORAGE	MAIN COOKERY METHODS
Parsnips	A relation of carrots, parsnips have a very sweet flavour that is evocative of winter and Christmas	Choose medium-sized roots as the fully matured vegetable can be woody, unless it has been subjected to a frost. Should feel firm with no blemishes or shoots	10 days in a well-ventilated room	Boil, roast, creamed, fry, soups
Radishes	Radishes are pungent and peppery roots, usually a bright red colour that livens up summer salads	Should be free from blemishes	Refrigerate for 2–3 days	Grated
Salsify/ scorzonera	These roots are closely related; salsify is light in colour and scorzonera is much darker. Both have a white flesh that oxidises very quickly. They should be stored in acidulated water after peeling	Should be firm to the touch, have their tops intact and snap easily	Refrigerate for 7–10 days	Boil, deep and shallow fry
Swedes	Similar to turnips, the matured roots of a member of the cabbage family. Raw, the flavour is slightly peppery, and cooked a sweet flavour is produced	Not too large, should feel heavy and firm to the touch. Should not be split as this is a symptom of a poor watering regime in the summer months	In a cool dark place for 2–3 weeks	Boil, buttered, fry, glacé, purée, soups
Turnips	A root of the cabbage family. The flesh is white and the skin is white to purple. A mild peppery flavour. The leaves can be cooked as turnip tops	The leaves should be intact and the flesh should be firm and not spongy	In a cool dry place for up to 10 days	Boil, buttered, fry, roast, soups

IMAGES COURTESY OF THINKVEGETABLES.CO.UK

LEAVES

These vegetables, as the name suggests, are mostly leaf and green in colour. They grow using photosynthesis, which is a process that uses water and sunlight to produce natural sugar and oxygen. Some varieties may also belong to other vegetable groups, such as cabbage.

VEGETABLE	CHARACTERISTICS	QUALITY POINTS	STORAGE	MAIN COOKERY METHODS
Chicory	Chicory can be either white or red. Because of its characteristic bitterness it is not always conducive to the northern European palate. If it is sweetened with honey or sugar it can be very pleasant	The leaves should be tight and blemish free. There should be no wilting	Refrigerate for 2–3 days	Raw for salad, braise
Cress	Delicate leaves with a faint peppery flavour	Fresh vibrant colour and no wilting of the stems	Refrigerate for 2 days	Salad
Lettuce	There are many types of lettuce. They are usually used in salads to give bulk and freshness. Some have a peppery taste, such as rocket or dandelion, and some have more delicate flavours, such as Iceberg, butterhead and frisee. It is up to the chef to mix varieties and use each type to their best advantage	The leaves should be vibrant, crisp and have no discolouration or wilting	Refrigerate for 2 days	Salad, braise
Pousse	This is a baby form of spinach. It has a light delicate flavour that is pleasing to the palate	The leaves should be crisp with a small stem	Refrigerate for 2–3 days	Boil, sauté, creamed, purée, salad
Spinach	A robust leaf that is the mainstay of many dishes. It should have the stem removed before cookery.	The leaves should be blemish free, crisp and deep green	Refrigerate for 2–3 days	Boil, sauté, creamed, purée
Swiss chard	Similar to spinach, this leaf should have the stem removed with a knife	The leaves should be blemish free, crisp and a deep green or mottled red	Refrigerate for 2–3 days	Sauté, boil
Watercress	A traditional garnish to roast meats in the English style. The peppery properties are an ideal accompaniment	Bright and deep green leaves with no bruising. Delivery should be in iced boxes	24 hrs in a cold refrigerator	Garnishes, soups

IMAGES COURTESY OF THINKVEGETABLES.CO.UK

STEMS

These vegetables are rooted and grow out of the ground. They can also have usable leaves but are generally grown for their stems.

VEGETABLE	CHARACTERISTICS	QUALITY POINTS	STORAGE	MAIN COOKERY METHODS
Asparagus	A very luxurious stem that comes in green and white varieties. Should be simply cooked to let its flavour come through	The tips should be compact, the stalks should not be limp or damaged. Avoid any woodiness	Refrigerate for 2–3 days	Poach, soups
Celery	Celery is at the heart of many dishes because of its distinct flavour and texture	The leaves should be fresh and bright, the stalks should be blemish free and firm	Refrigerate for 4–5 days	Braise, boil, raw and as ingredient in other dishes
Kohlrabi	A member of the cabbage family, there are two varieties: green and purple. The bulbous stem is eaten rather than the leaves	Look for small young vegetables with no blemishes and firm to the touch	In a cool place for 10–12 days	Boil
Sea kale	A rare vegetable that can be bitter if picked incorrectly. It should be buried with sand to keep the stalks white	Long slender stalks with fresh leaves at the top. Free from blemishes and firm to the touch	Refrigerate for 2–3 days	Boil, buttered, fry

VEGETABLE FRUITS AND SQUASHES

These vegetables are the fruits of the plants. They usually grow from a stem and have seeds, and can be dry or juicy on the inside.

VEGETABLE	CHARACTERISTICS	QUALITY POINTS	STORAGE	MAIN COOKERY METHODS
Aubergines	An aqueous vegetable that can be a little bitter and sponge-like when cooked. Salting for 30-40 minutes helps to remove this bitterness and reduces the amount of fat that is taken in	It should feel firm and have a fresh aroma and the skin should have a waxy feel	Refrigerate for 2–3 days	Fry, grill, bake, stuffed
Courgettes	A small variety of the marrow family. Best flavours are obtained from medium-sized courgettes during the summer months	Deep green or yellow in colour, firm to the touch. No wrinkles or blemishes	Refrigerate for 4–5 days	Fry, stuffed, provençale
Cucumbers	An aqueous vegetable that is light and delicate in flavour. It refreshes the palate and is very low in calories. The skin and seeds should be removed as they have a tendency to cause indigestion	Should not be too thick or knobbly, but should feel heavy and have a pleasing aroma. The flesh should be firm and very juicy.	Refrigerate for 3–5 days	Salads
Marrows	A large aqueous vegetable that can be rather bland but has a slightly sweet background flavour	Small vegetables with firm blemish-free skin, should feel heavier than looks	Refrigerate for 2–3 days	Fry, stuffed, provençale
Peppers	Members of the capsicum family, which includes the chilli peppers. The colour can indicate the sweetness: green and black are the sharpest while red, yellow and orange are sweetest	The skin should be shiny, waxy and not wrinkled. The flesh should be crisp	Refrigerate for 4–5 days	Grill, sauté, stuffed, soups, raw
Tomatoes	A red fleshed fruit that comes in many varieties. Tomatoes are at their best in the summer months. With modern production they are available all year round, but the flavour is best when they are in season. The stronger flavour and characteristic aroma of vine-ripened tomatoes come from the vine and not the tomato.	Firm red flesh with no blemishes or cracks in the skin. Break one open to see the flesh, which should be juicy and sweet	Refrigerate for 3–5 days	Grill, blanch, stuffed

PODS AND SEEDS

These are the seed-bearing pods and seeds of plants, especially those from the pea and bean family (legumes), usually grown as bushes and vines. They epitomise the summer, even though they are now available all year round.

VEGETABLE	CHARACTERISTICS	QUALITY POINTS	STORAGE	MAIN COOKERY METHODS
Broad beans	A large bean that is best eaten when just picked, or peeled and cooked if stored for short period of time	Should be as fresh as possible. The outer pod should feel strong and crisp. The beans should have a skin that is easily peeled	Refrigerate for 1–2 days after picking, after that frozen broad beans have a superior quality	Boil, stew, soups
Butter beans	A large bean that is best eaten when just picked	Should be as fresh as possible. The outer pod should feel strong and crisp	Refrigerate for 1–2 days after picking, after that frozen beans have a superior quality	Boil, stew, soups
French/dwarf bean	Long thin pods that are sweet to the taste	Bright green and sweet tasting, not limp	Use on day of purchase	Boil, buttered
Okra	This pod contains rows of seeds and becomes slimy when cooked. Popular with Cajun and Caribbean cuisines	Should be bright green and not fibrous and have no signs of bruising	Refrigerate for 2–3 days	Boil, fry, buttered, soups
Peas	Fresh peas are wonderful to eat. Unfortunately it is very difficult to get them fresh as they deteriorate very quickly after picking. Frozen peas are usually the only alternative	Fresh pods should be bright green. If they are shrivelled in any way, insist on a tasting. If they are not tender and sweet, resort to the frozen alternative	Use on the day of purchase. Peas freeze very well when just picked. Use frozen petit pois	Boil, buttered
Runner beans	Coarser than green beans, these are only really available in the summer. The pod is the main part that is eaten	Should not be too large and should snap easily	Refrigerate for 2–3 days. Freeze very well	Boil, buttered

VEGETABLE	CHARACTERISTICS	QUALITY POINTS	STORAGE	MAIN COOKERY METHODS
Sugar snaps/ mange tout	Immature peas that are picked for their pods rather than the peas	Bright green and sweet tasting, not limp	Use on day of purchase	Boil, buttered
Sweetcorn	A variety of maize, which has been the staple food of the Americas for many hundreds of years. The plant is very easy to grow and harvest. Sweetcorn is grown chiefly for human consumption, but varieties are grown for animal consumption and flour production	Sweetcorn starts to deteriorate after picking: the sugars begin to turn to starch. Press a kernel: the juice should run clear. The outer leaves should be tight to the cob and the threadlike fronds should be a dark brown	Ideally use on the day of purchase but can be refrigerated for 2–3 days. Freezes and cans very well	Boil, fry, buttered, soups

VEGETARIAN DIET

A vegetarian is someone living on a diet of grains, pulses, nuts, seeds, vegetables and fruits with or without the use of dairy products and eggs.

A vegetarian does not eat any meat, poultry, game, fish, shellfish or crustacea, or slaughter by-products.

The Types of Vegetarian

■ **Lacto-ovo-vegetarian** – eats both dairy products and eggs. This is the most common type of vegetarian diet.

■ **Lacto-vegetarian** – eats dairy products but not eggs.

■ **Vegan** – does not eat dairy products, eggs, or any other animal product.

Potential problems for vegetarians

Many foods contain ingredients derived from the slaughter of animals for example:

■ Gelatine is made from animal ligaments, tendons, bones etc. which have been boiled in water.

■ It is often found in confectionery, low fat spreads and desserts, and other dairy products.

■ The term animal fat refers to carcass fat and may be present in a wide range of foods, including biscuits, cakes and margarines.

- Suet and lard are types of animal fats. Certain food additives (E numbers) may be derived from animal sources.
- Cheese is often made with rennet extracted from the stomach lining of slaughtered calves.
- Vegetarian cheese is made with rennet from a microbial source.

There is an association that supports and promotes vegetarianism. The Vegetarian Society offers guidance not only to its people who have chosen to become a vegetarian but to businesses offering ideas and good working practice ideas.

Many vegetarians that eat eggs will eat only free-range eggs. This is due to moral objections to the battery farming of hens. Many organisations now only endorse products containing eggs if they are certified as free-range.

Practices in catering

Vegetarians dining out will expect work surfaces and chopping boards, utensils and all other kitchen equipment and facilities to be either kept separate from those used for non-vegetarian food preparation, or cleaned thoroughly before vegetarian food preparation.

Caterers should also ensure that fryers, grills and griddles used for preparing non-vegetarian products are thoroughly cleaned. Fryers must be filled with fresh, uncontaminated oil before vegetarian food is cooked.

It is recommended that caterers keep a separate set of utensils for the preparation and serving of vegetarian meals.

Protein

Vegetarians obtain protein from:

- Nuts: hazels, brazils, almonds, cashews, walnuts, pine kernels etc.
- Seeds: sesame, pumpkin, sunflower, linseeds.
- Pulses: peas, beans, lentils, peanuts.
- Grains/cereals: wheat (in bread, flour, pasta etc.), barley, rye, oats, millet, maize (sweetcorn), rice.
- Soya products: tofu, tempeh, textured vegetable protein, vegetarian burgers, soya milk.
- Dairy products: milk, cheese, yoghurt (butter and cream are very poor sources of protein).
- Free range eggs.

It is essential to balance the amino acids in a vegetarian diet. Amino acids are the units from which proteins are made and there are 20 different types in all. We can make many of them in our bodies by converting other amino acids, but eight cannot be made, they have to be provided in the diet and so they are called essential amino acids.

Single plant foods do not contain all the essential amino acids we need in the right proportions, but when we mix plant foods together, any deficiency in one is cancelled out by any excess in the other. We mix protein foods all the time, whether we are meat-eaters or vegetarians. It is a normal part of the human way of eating. A few examples are beans on toast, muesli, or rice and peas. Adding dairy products or eggs also adds the missing amino acids, for example macaroni cheese, quiche and porridge.

It is now known that the body has a pool of amino acids so that if one meal is deficient, it can be made up from the body's own stores. Therefore, we don't have to worry about complementing amino acids all the time, as long as our diet is generally varied and well-balanced. Even those foods not considered high in protein are adding some amino acids to this pool.

Carbohydrate

Carbohydrate is our main and most important source of energy and most of it is provided by plant foods. There are three main types: simple sugars, complex carbohydrates or starches and dietary fibre.

The sugars or simple carbohydrates can be found in fruit, milk and ordinary table sugar. Refined sources of sugar are best avoided as they provide energy without any associated fibre, vitamins or minerals and they are also the main cause of dental decay.

Complex carbohydrates are found in cereals/grains (bread, rice, pasta, oats, barley, millet, buckwheat, rye) and some root vegetables, such as potatoes and parsnips. A healthy diet should contain plenty of these starchy foods as a high intake of complex carbohydrate is now known to benefit health. The unrefined carbohydrates, like wholemeal bread and brown rice are best of all because they contain essential dietary fibre and B vitamins.

The exact amount of carbohydrate that you need depends upon your appetite and also your level of activity. Contrary to previous belief a slimming diet should not be low in carbohydrates. In fact starchy foods are very filling relative to the number of calories that they contain.

Dietary fibre

Dietary fibre or non-starch polysaccharide, as it is now termed, refers to the indigestible part of a carbohydrate food. Fibre can be found in unrefined or wholegrain cereals, fruit (fresh and dried) and vegetables. A good intake of dietary fibre can prevent many digestive problems and protect against diseases like colon cancer and diverticular disease.

Fats and oils

Too much fat is bad for us, but a little is necessary to keep our tissues in good repair, for the manufacture of hormones and to act as a carrier for some vitamins. Like proteins, fats are made of smaller units, called fatty acids. Two of these fatty acids, linoleic and linolenic acids, are termed essential as they must be provided in the diet. This is no problem as they are widely found in plant foods.

Fats can be either saturated or unsaturated (mono-unsaturated or poly-unsaturated). A high intake of saturated fat can lead to a raised blood cholesterol level and this has been linked to heart disease. Vegetable fats tend to be more unsaturated and this is one of the benefits of a vegetarian diet. Mono-unsaturated fats, such as olive oil or peanut oil, are best used for frying as the poly-unsaturated fats, like sunflower or safflower oil are unstable at high temperatures. Animal fats (including butter and cheese) tend to be more saturated than vegetable fats, with the exception of palm oil and coconut oil.

Vitamins

Vitamin is the name for several unrelated nutrients that the body cannot synthesise either at all, or in sufficient quantities. The one thing they have in common is that only small quantities are needed in the diet. The main vegetarian sources are listed below:

- **Vitamin A** (or beta carotene) – red, orange or yellow vegetables like carrots and tomatoes, leafy green vegetables and fruits like apricots and peaches. It is added to most margarines.
- **B vitamins** – this group of vitamins includes B1, B2, B3, B6 and B12. All the B vitamins except B12 occur in yeasts, whole cereals (especially wheat germ), nuts, seeds, pulses and green vegetables.
- **Vitamin B12** – this is the only B vitamin that may cause some difficulty as it is not present in plant foods. Only very tiny amounts of B12 are needed and vegetarians usually get this from dairy produce and free range eggs. It is sensible for vegans and vegetarians who consume few animal foods to incorporate some B12 fortified foods in their diet. Vitamin B12 is added to yeast extracts, soya milks, vegetarian burgers and some breakfast cereals.
- **Vitamin C** – fresh fruit, salad vegetables, all leafy green vegetables and potatoes.
- **Vitamin D** – this vitamin is not found in plant foods but humans can make their own when skin is exposed to sunlight. It is also added to most margarines and is present in milk, cheese and butter. These sources are usually adequate for healthy adults. The very young, the very old and anyone confined indoors would be wise to take a vitamin D supplement especially if they consume very few dairy products.

- **Vitamin E** – vegetable oil, wholegrain cereals and eggs.
- **Vitamin K** – Fresh vegetables, cereals and bacterial synthesis in the intestine.

Minerals

Minerals perform a variety of jobs in the body. Details of the some of the most important minerals are listed below:

- **Calcium** – important for healthy bones and teeth. Found in dairy produce, leafy green vegetables, bread, tap water in hard water areas, nuts and seeds (especially sesame seeds), dried fruits and cheese. Vitamin D helps calcium to be absorbed.

- **Iron** – needed for red blood cells. Found in leafy green vegetables, wholemeal bread, molasses, eggs, dried fruits (especially apricots and figs), lentils and pulses. Vegetable sources of iron are not as easily absorbed as animal sources, but a good intake of vitamin C will enhance absorption.

- **Zinc** – plays a major role in many enzyme reactions and the immune system. Found in green vegetables, cheese, sesame and pumpkin seeds, lentils and wholegrain cereals.

- **Iodine** – present in vegetables, but the quantity depends on how rich the soil is in iodine. Dairy products also have plenty of iodine. Sea vegetables are a good source of iodine for vegans.

RECIPES
Baby onion tart tatin

INGREDIENTS	4 PORTIONS	10 PORTIONS
Baby onions	200g	500g
Butter	80g	200g
Puff pastry	200g	500g
Good-quality salt and white pepper	To taste	To taste

Method of work

1 Cut the onions in half and caramelise in a pan with the butter.
2 Season to taste and allow to cool slightly.
3 Roll the pastry until it is larger than the pan.
4 Place the pastry on top of the onions and fold the edges between the sides of the pan and the onions.
5 Place the pan in a hot oven and bake until the pastry is thoroughly cooked.
6 Place a plate on top of the pan and turn the pan upside down so the tart falls onto the plate. Serve either individually or sliced.

 CHEF'S TIP

To reduce cholesterol, use sunflower oil flavoured with a little sesame seed oil.

CHEF'S TIP

For individual portions use blini pans.

Cauliflower gratin

INGREDIENTS	4 PORTIONS	10 PORTIONS
Cauliflower	300g	750g
Butter	50g	125g
Mornay sauce	8tbsp	20tbsp
Grated Gruyère cheese	50g	125g
Good-quality salt and white pepper	To taste	To taste

Method of work

1 Remove the green leaves from the cauliflower and cut the florets away from the stem.
2 Boil the cauliflower in salted water until slightly under-done. Refresh under running water.
3 Drain well in a colander and then on absorbent paper.
4 Butter the inside of a gratin dish. Season the dish and the cauliflower.
5 Add the cauliflower to the dish, coat with the Mornay sauce and sprinkle the top with the grated cheese.
6 Bake in a hot oven until the top is thoroughly coloured.

 CHEF'S TIP

To reduce the fat, make the Mornay with semi-skimmed or skimmed milk.

CHEF'S TIP

Mix the Gruyère with grated Parmesan to create a more intense flavour.

Celeriac and potato croquette

INGREDIENTS	4 PORTIONS	10 PORTIONS
Celeriac	200g	500g
Potatoes	200g	200g
Egg yolks	2	5
Grated nutmeg	To taste	To taste
Butter	40g	75g
Good-quality salt and white pepper	To taste	To taste
Flour, egg wash, fresh breadcrumbs	To pané	To pané

Method of work

1 Peel and boil the celeriac until almost tender. Cool and grate on the rough side of the grater.
2 Peel and boil the potatoes. Drain the water and allow residual water to evaporate. Pass the potatoes through a ricer.
3 Add the butter, egg yolk and seasonings.
4 Add the grated celeriac and form into croquettes, 5cm × 2cm.
5 Chill the croquettes and then pané.
6 Deep fry until golden brown, ensuring an internal temperature of 75°C.

CHEF'S TIP

Use a dry variety of potato such as Desiree or Maris Piper to get a pleasant finish to the croquettes.

CHEF'S TIP

Reduce or remove the butter content to lower the calories.

Creamed broccoli Pithivier

INGREDIENTS	4 PORTIONS	10 PORTIONS
Broccoli florets	400g	1kg
Vegetable stock	100ml	250ml
Butter	50g	125g
Double cream	80ml	200ml
Puff pastry	200g	500g
Good-quality salt and white pepper	To taste	To taste
Egg wash		

Method of work

1 Blanch and refresh the broccoli, drain well.
2 Boil and reduce the stock by two-thirds, add the cream and reduce to a sauce consistency.
3 Add the butter and shake the pan until the sauce has thickened, adjust the seasoning and allow to cool.
4 Season the broccoli and mix in the now almost set sauce.
5 Roll the pastry and cut into two circles per portion, one slightly bigger than the other.
6 Divide the mixture evenly and place on the smaller of the pastry circles. Brush the pastry edges with water.
7 Place the larger pastry circles on top and crimp the edges. Brush with egg wash. Cut a spiral pattern in the top and bake in a hot oven until the pastry is fully cooked. Serve immediately.

CHEF'S TIP

If the Pithivier browns too quickly reduce the oven temperature to 130°C and continue to cook.

CHEF'S TIP

Cream sauce is used in this recipe because it has a neutral flavour and so allows the broccoli flavour to come through. However, a béchamel sauce will achieve a similar finish but with less fat.

Leek and wild mushroom ragout with toasted pine nuts

INGREDIENTS	4 PORTIONS	10 PORTIONS
Leeks	200g	500g
Wild mushroom	200g	500g
Shallots	50g	125g
Garlic	1 clove	2–3 cloves
Olive oil	50g	125g
Lemon juice and zest	1 lemon	2½ lemons
Cooked tomato concassé	100g	500g
Chopped fresh parsley	4tbsp	10tbsp
Pine nuts	50g	125g
Good-quality salt and mill pepper	To taste	To taste

CHEF'S TIP

Most varieties of mushroom can be used in this dish, but avoid mushrooms with a very high water content.

CHEF'S TIP

Increase the nutritional value of this dish by adding cooked beans, such borlotti beans.

Method of work

1   Wash and slice the leeks, chop the shallots and crush the garlic. Sweat in the olive oil and allow to stew until tender.
2   Remove the mixture and raise the heat in the pan. Sauté the mushrooms and season to taste.
3   Add the zest of the lemon and allow to cook for 1 minute.
4   Add the lemon juice to the mushrooms and allow the acid to evaporate.
5   Add the cooked leeks and tomato concassé. Bring to the boil, and season to taste.
6   Toast the pine nuts in a dry pan or grill under the salamander.
7   Serve the ragout sprinkled with the pine nuts and chopped parsley.

Mushroom soufflé

INGREDIENTS	4 PORTIONS	10 PORTIONS
Button mushrooms (fried and puréed)	200ml	500ml
Thick béchamel	100ml	500ml
Egg yolks	2	5
Egg whites	2	5
Butter	50g	125g
Good-quality salt and white pepper	To taste	To taste

Method of work

1   Combine the mushrooms and béchamel and correct the seasoning.
2   Mix in the egg yolks.
3   Whisk the whites to form stiff peaks.
4   Add three-quarters of the whites and mix into the mushrooms.
5   Fold in the remainder of the whites.
6   Grease the soufflé dishes and fill to two-thirds.
7   Bake at 180°C until well risen and the interior is still soft.
8   Serve immediately.

CHEF'S TIP

Dust the interior of the soufflé dish with flour to give a straighter rise.

Roasted vegetable ratatouille

CHEF'S TIP

Use over-ripe tomatoes to give a deep red colour, or alternatively add a little tomato purée.

CHEF'S TIP

Reduce the fat content by simply tossing all the vegetables in half the oil and roasting them together in the oven.

VIDEO CLIP
Ratatouille

INGREDIENTS	4 PORTIONS	10 PORTIONS
Aubergine macédoine	200g	500g
Courgette macédoine	200g	500g
Onion macédoine	200g	500g
Assorted pepper macédoine	200g	500g
White wine	50ml	125ml
Tomato concassé	200g	500g
Chopped onion	50g	125g
Crushed garlic	1 clove	2–3 cloves
Olive oil	50ml	125ml
Bay leaf	2	5
Thyme	2 sprigs	5 sprigs
Good-quality salt and mill pepper	To taste	To taste

Method of work

1 Heat the oil in a pan and add the chopped onion and garlic, allow to colour slightly.

2 Roast the pepper, onion, courgette and aubergine macédoine in a hot oven until golden brown at the edges and add to the onions.

3 Add the wine and allow to reduce.

4 Add the tomatoes then add the thyme and bay leaf tied together and season.

5 Simmer for 20 minutes, check the seasoning and serve.

Royale of carrots with garlic oil

CHEF'S TIP

Other root vegetables can be prepared as royals.

CHEF'S TIP

To reduce the fat content double the béchamel and remove the cream.

INGREDIENTS	4 PORTIONS	10 PORTIONS
Carrots	200g	500g
Sugar	Pinch	Pinch
Butter	50g	125g
Béchamel	50ml	125ml
Double cream	50ml	125ml
Egg yolks	4	10
Garlic oil	1tbsp	2½tbsp
Good-quality salt and mill pepper	To taste	To taste

Method of work

1 Cook the carrots in salted water with the butter and sugar.

2 Purée until smooth and combine with the cream, béchamel and egg yolks.

3 Season to taste and pour into buttered moulds.

4 Cook in the oven in a bain marie until set (approximately 20 minutes).

5 Serve drizzled with the garlic oil.

Sautéed Brussels sprouts with oak-smoked bacon and chestnuts

CHEF'S TIP

Lay the sprouts on a clean cloth after blanching to remove as much moisture as possible.

CHEF'S TIP

To reduce fat content use a julienne of lean bacon.

INGREDIENTS	4 PORTIONS	10 PORTIONS
Brussels sprouts	400g	1kg
Chopped onions	100g	250g
Oak-smoked bacon lardons	50g	125g
Chestnuts	50g	125g
Olive oil	50ml	125ml
Good-quality salt and mill pepper	To taste	To taste

Method of work

1 Prepare, blanch and refresh the Brussels sprouts.

2 Roast the chestnuts in a hot oven. Allow to cool and then peel.

3 Heat half the oil in a pan and sweat the onions. Add the bacon and cook without colour.

4 Heat the remainder of the oil in a separate pan and add the sprouts. Sauté on a high heat until the sprouts begin to colour, then add the chestnuts and the cooked onions and lardons and allow them to colour also.

5 Season to taste and serve.

Fried rice with oriental vegetables

CHEF'S TIP

For a different finish add a little oyster sauce.

INGREDIENTS	4 PORTIONS	10 PORTIONS
Boiled long grain rice	400g	1kg
Sliced red onions	80g	200g
Sliced spring onions	40g	100g
Grated ginger	20g	50g
Crushed garlic	1 clove	2–3 cloves
Julienne of mouli	80g	200g
Sliced pepper	80g	200g
Soy sauce	20ml	50ml
Sesame seed oil	10ml	25ml
Vegetable oil	20ml	50ml
Good-quality salt and pepper	To taste	To taste

Method of work

1 Heat the oils in a wok and add the garlic and ginger allow to cook for 1 minute.

2 Add the onions and peppers.

3 Add the mouli and spring onions and stir fry for 1 minute.

4 Add the rice and **stir fry** until hot.

5 Add the soy sauce, stir, season and serve.

Braised butternut squash with Quorn

INGREDIENTS	4 PORTIONS	10 PORTIONS
Butternut squash	400g	1kg
Chopped onion	100g	250g
Canned tomatoes	200g	500g
Crushed garlic	1 clove	2–3 cloves
Quorn mince	100g	250g
Olive oil	40ml	100ml
Vegetable stock	100ml	250ml
Good-quality salt and pepper	To taste	To taste

 CHEF'S TIP

If you find the tomatoes to be too acidic, add a small amount of sugar and vinegar reduced to a caramel (gastrique).

Method of work

1 Halve the squash, remove the seeds and scoop out the flesh.
2 Place the flesh of the squash in an ovenproof dish, add the stock, season and braise in the oven for 15–20 minutes.
3 Heat the oil and sweat the onion and garlic, add the Quorn and cook for 1 minute.
4 Add the tomatoes and season to taste.
5 Correct the consistency of the sauce with the cooking liquor from the braised squash.
6 Strain the squash, correct the seasoning and combine with the Quorn mixture. Serve immediately.

Spinach subric

INGREDIENTS	4 PORTIONS	10 PORTIONS
Spinach	200g	500g
Thick béchamel	50ml	125ml
Egg yolks	1	2–3
Double cream	1tsp	1tbsp
Nutmeg	To taste	To taste
Clarified butter	40g	80g
Good-quality salt and pepper	To taste	To taste

 CHEF'S TIP

Other cooked vegetables can be used for this dish. Just keep the same ratio of ingredients.

 CHEF'S TIP

To reduce fat content use vegetable oil instead of butter

Method of work

1 Blanch and refresh the spinach.
2 Combine all the ingredients.
3 Allow to cool.
4 Divide into portions and fry in clarified butter until brown on each side.
5 Serve very hot.

Bacon and cream cheese stuffed mushrooms

CHEF'S TIP

Mix the breadcrumbs with grated Parmesan for extra flavour.

CHEF'S TIP

Use low fat cream cheese and lean bacon for a healthier option.

INGREDIENTS	4 PORTIONS	10 PORTIONS
Flat mushrooms	4	10
Pancetta lardons	100g	250g
Chopped onion	80g	200g
Cream cheese	100g	150g
Breadcrumbs	50g	125g
Mill pepper	To taste	To taste

Method of work

1 Sauté the lardons to release the fat.
2 Sweat the onion and the chopped stems of the mushrooms in the bacon fat until tender. Drain off the excess fat.
3 Crumble the bacon, onion and mushroom stems and mix with softened cream cheese.
4 Stuff each mushroom and bake at 180°C for 10–15 minutes.
5 Sprinkle with fresh breadcrumbs and season with the milled pepper.
6 Finish under the salamander until tops are just golden.

Petit pois à la Française with pancetta crisps

CHEF'S TIP

If the sauce is too thin add some beurre manié to thicken.

CHEF'S TIP

To reduce the fat content use grilled back bacon that has been shredded.

INGREDIENTS	4 PORTIONS	10 PORTIONS
Fresh or frozen peas	400g	1kg
Button onions	100g	500g
Iceberg lettuce	100g	500g
Vegetable stock	1 litre	2.5 litres
Sliced pancetta	4 rashers	10 rashers
Flour	20g	50g
Lemon juice	½ lemon	1 lemon
Good-quality salt and pepper	To taste	To taste

Method of work

1 Blanch the button onions and shred the lettuce.
2 Cut the pancetta rashers in half at an angle. Press between two baking sheets and put in the oven to crisp.
3 Add the flour and lemon juice to the stock, mix thoroughly and bring to the boil.
4 Add the peas, onions and lettuce. Cook for 5 minutes.
5 Adjust the seasoning and consistency and serve topped with the pancetta crisps.

Braised globe artichoke stuffed with tomato and garlic fondue, glazed courgettes, crispy aubergine and herb beurre blanc

Bill Hill

INGREDIENTS	4 PORTIONS	10 PORTIONS
Medium globe artichokes	4	10
Black olives cut into thumb nail pieces	12	30
Blanc liquor	To cover	To cover
Diced tomato flesh, skinned with seeds removed	400g	1kg
Unsalted butter	25g	60g
Cloves crushed garlic	2	5
Chopped shallot	50g	120g
Small bouquet garni	1	2
Red wine vinegar	20ml	50ml
Tomato purée	1 tsp	2 tsp
Sugar	To taste	To taste
Seasoning	To taste	To taste
Pieces of turned courgette	400g	1kg
Unsalted butter	5g	15g
Water	50ml	120ml
Seasoning	To taste	To taste
Aubergine	1	2
Corn flour	50g	120g

Method of work

1 Turn and cook artichokes in a blanc, then remove the choke and reserve.

2 Sweat the shallots and garlic in butter until soft, deglaze with vinegar. Add purée and cook out for 2 minutes and add tomato flesh and bouquet garni. Season and cook slowly until the liquid has evaporated.

3 Adjust with sugar and season.

4 Place courgettes in a small pan with butter, water and a pinch of salt and pepper. Cover with a lid and place on a high heat. Cook until the water has evaporated.

5 Glaze with the butter.

6 Peel aubergine and remove any excess flesh. Then cut into julienne.

7 Coat in corn flour and deep fry at 150°C until crispy. Drain on absorbent paper.

8 For 200ml of herb beurre blanc (see page 93) with the addition of 1tbs chopped herbs (parsley, tarragon, chervil and chives) for every 4 portions.

9 Reheat artichokes in blanc, and stuff with hot tomato fondue.

10 Place in centre of bowl and pour beurre blanc around. Place the courgettes and black olives around the artichoke and top with crispy aubergine.

Rösti potatoes with a spinach stuffing

INGREDIENTS	4 PORTIONS	10 PORTIONS
Medium potatoes	4	10
Cooked spinach	100g	250g
Butter and oil	To fry	To fry
Grated nutmeg	To taste	To taste
Good-quality salt and pepper	To taste	To taste

CHEF'S TIP

Use a floury potato to give a white interior to the rösti.

CHEF'S TIP

Alternatively, brush the röstis with olive oil and bake them in a hot oven.

Method of work

1 Peel the potatoes and boil for ten minutes (the time may vary depending on the size of the potatoes). The potatoes should remain hard; it is important not to boil them for too long.

2 Allow the potatoes to cool slightly then wrap in plastic film and refrigerate for at least 1 hour. Grate the potatoes (they should be quite sticky), season to taste and divide into individual balls.

3 Chop the spinach and season with salt, pepper and freshly grated nutmeg.

4 Press the spinach into the potatoes and form them into neat patties so that the spinach is completely enclosed.

5 Fry in the butter and oil for 5–10 minutes on each side or until golden brown.

Pommes Anna with truffles

INGREDIENTS	4 PORTIONS	10 PORTIONS
Peeled potatoes	100g	250g
Truffle trimmings	40g	100g
Butter	80g	200g
Good-quality salt and mill pepper	To taste	To taste

CHEF'S TIP

This potato dish can be prepared using ramekin dishes for individual portions.

CHEF'S TIP

To reduce the cholesterol content replace the butter with olive oil.

Method of work

1 Slice the potatoes on a mandolin set at approximately 2mm. Do not place the slices in water.

2 Line the base of an Anna mould with silicone paper.

3 Heavily butter the sides of the mould and season the sides and base.

4 Arrange the potatoes in circles, adding a few pieces of truffle and seasoning to each layer, until the mould is full.

5 Cover with another disk of paper and bake at 170°C until the centre is cooked and the edges are golden brown.

6 Half way through the cooking time remove the paper lid.

7 Loosen the edges and turn out onto a dish for service.

Potato bake with sour cream

INGREDIENTS	4 PORTIONS	10 PORTIONS
Medium potatoes	8	20
Chopped celery	100g	250g
Chopped onion	100g	250g
Butter	80g	200g
Sour cream	80ml	200ml
Sugar	5g	25g
Rubbed thyme	1tbsp	2–3tbsp
Chopped basil	1tsp	1tbsp
Good-quality salt and pepper	To taste	To taste

CHEF'S TIP

Grated cheese can be added to the main dish and sprinkled on prior to gratinating.

CHEF'S TIP

Use thick béchamel to lower the fat content and omit the sugar to reduce the calories.

Method of work

1 Boil the potatoes in salted water until tender.
2 Sweat the onions and celery in half the butter.
3 Heat the sour cream and remaining butter.
4 Mash the potatoes and combine the vegetables, herbs, sugar and seasoning.
5 Place into an ovenproof dish or individual ravier dishes and bake at 175°C until browned. Serve immediately.

Saffron-infused potatoes with saffron cream

INGREDIENTS	4 PORTIONS	10 PORTIONS
Maris Piper potatoes	20	50
Saffron	1g	2–3g
Double cream	100ml	250ml
Vegetable stock	200ml	500ml
Butter	40g	100g
Good-quality salt and white pepper	To taste	To taste

CHEF'S TIP

Deep fry the skins until crispy and serve with a sour cream dip as a bar snack.

CHEF'S TIP

To lower the fat content use thin béchamel to replace the double cream and butter.

Method of work

1 Shape the potatoes with a turning knife until a neat barrel shape is formed (keep the peeled skins).
2 Place half the saffron into salted water. Add the potatoes and bring slowly to the boil, poach the potatoes until just done.
3 Meanwhile, boil and reduce the stock by three-quarters. Add the cream and saffron until a sauce consistency has been achieved. **Monter au beurre** the cream with the butter.
4 Very gently fold the potatoes into the cream and serve.

Spiced potatoes Kashmiri style

INGREDIENTS	4 PORTIONS	10 PORTIONS
Small Maris Piper potatoes (boiled)	600g	1.5kg
Clarified butter	40g	100g
Fennel seeds	1tsp	1tbsp
Mild curry powder	20g	50g
Thick natural yoghurt	160ml	400ml
Garam masala	¼tsp	½–¾tsp
Chopped coriander	1tsp	1tbsp
Green chilli	1	2–3
Good-quality salt	To taste	To taste

 CHEF'S TIP

The chillies are usually added at the end of cooking, but they can be omitted to give a less fiery finish.

 CHEF'S TIP

Use olive oil in place of butter to reduce the cholesterol content.

Method of work

1 Peel the potatoes and fry in the clarified butter until golden brown. When they are well coloured, remove with a perforated spoon and keep to one side.
2 Lower the heat and add the fennel seeds and curry powder. Allow the flavours to develop for 2 minutes.
3 Return the potatoes to the pan and add the yoghurt.
4 Add the garam masala, chopped coriander leaves and the chopped and deseeded chilli and season with salt.
5 Serve as an accompaniment to curried meats.

Baked potatoes with wild mushrooms

INGREDIENTS	4 PORTIONS	10 PORTIONS
Medium sized baking potatoes	4	10
Butter	100g	250g
Mixed wild mushrooms	100g	250g
Double cream	100ml	250ml
Noilly Prat	40ml	100ml
Chopped shallots	40g	100g
Chopped garlic	1 clove	2–3 cloves
Chopped tarragon	1tsp	1tbsp
Salt and pepper	To taste	To taste

 CHEF'S TIP

Use a floury potato such as Desiree or Maris Piper.

 CHEF'S TIP

Omit the alcohol and substitute thin béchamel or yoghurt for the cream to reduce the calories and cholesterol.

Method of work

1 Place the potatoes on a baking sheet with a layer of salt and cook until the centres are tender.
2 Meanwhile, sweat the shallots and garlic for a few minutes. Add the mushrooms and raise the heat to allow the mushrooms to sauté.
3 Add the Noilly Prat and flambé the mushrooms.
4 Add the cream and allow to come to the boil. Add the tarragon.
5 Season the mixture and serve with the baked potatoes.

Assessment of knowledge and understanding

You have now learned about the use of the different types of vegetables and how to prepare and cook different vegetable dishes.

To test your level of knowledge and understanding, answer the following short questions. These will help to prepare you for your summative (final) assessment.

Quality identifications

1 List four categories of vegetables.

i) _____   ii) _____

iii) _____   iv) _____

2 List two examples of each category.

i) _____   ii) _____

3 List two quality points you should look for when receiving each type.

i) _____   ii) _____

Vegetarians

1 List three types of vegetarians and explain what food they cannot eat.

i) _____   ii) _____

iii) _____

2 Identify five of the vitamins and minerals naturally occuring during a vegetarian diet to ensure good health is maintained.

i) _____   ii) _____

iii) _____   iv) _____

v) _____

Materials and storage

1 Explain the recommended storage method for mushrooms.

_____

2 State three factors in relation to portion control that should be taken into consideration when cooking pommes Anna.

i) _____   ii) _____

iii) _____

Preparation

1 Explain the terms 'blanch' and 'refresh' in relation to cooking green vegetables.

_____

_____

2 Describe the method of preparation for petit pois à la Française.

_____

_____

Cooking

1 Explain what a 'subric' is.

_____

_____

2 Explain the reason for not washing the starch from the potatoes in pommes Anna.

_____

_____

Health and safety

1 State two healthy options when finishing vegetable dishes.

i) _____ ii) _____

2 State why it is important to consider using sunflower oil instead of butter when preparing vegetable dishes.

_____

_____

CHEF'S PROFILE

Name: **Paul Gayler**

Position: Executive Chef de Cuisine

Establishment: The Lanesborough (London)

Current job role and main responsibilities: Responsible for all food and for ensuring exacting standards.

When did you realise that you wanted to pursue a career in the catering and hospitality industry?
At the age of 12. I began to help my parents with the running of an outside catering company and decided that was what I wanted to do as a career.

Training:
I did a two year course at Thurrock Tech, followed by work in France and in leading establishments in London.

Experience:
1   Crillon Paris
2   Royal Garden Hotel, London
3   Dorchester
4   Inigo Jones Restaurant
5   Halkin Hotel
6   Lanesborough

What do you find rewarding about your job?
Its diversity – no two days are the same. It also provides a chance to express yourself.

What do you find most challenging about the job?
Maintaining standards, 7 days a week, 24 hours a day, 52 weeks in a year – under constant pressure.

What advice would you give to students just beginning their career?
Keep focused on your objectives, know where you want to be and what you want to achieve as a goal. Set your target and go for it.

Who is your mentor or main inspiration?
The chefs I have worked with: Remy Fougere (Royal Garden), who is a great classical chef, and Anton Mosimann (Dorchester) for his insight into the modern cuisine of the 1980s.

What traits do you consider essential for anyone entering a career as a chef?
Do it because you want to – not because it sounds interesting and trendy! Long and unsociable hours and hard work are what to expect in a bustling hospitality business, but you can make it rewarding.

Can you give one essential kitchen tip that you use as a chef?
Keep your knives sharp and you will find the job easier! Blunt knives make things harder, and are far more dangerous as well.

Pan-fried potato and fruit terrine

This unusual terrine goes particularly well with slices of baked gammon or with game. It is best made a day or two before you need it – not only does this enhance the flavour but it also makes it easier to slice before frying.

INGREDIENTS	8–10 PORTIONS
Streaky bacon rashers (rind removed)	450g
Olive oil	4tbsp
Onion (finely chopped)	1
Waxy potatoes	675g
Mixed dried fruit, such as prunes, apples and apricots (cut into 2cm dice)	125g
Eggs	3
Double cream	100ml
Potato flour (or arrowroot)	2 tablespoons
Beaufort or Gruyère cheese (cut into 1cm cubes)	150g (5oz)
Freshly grated nutmeg	To taste
Unsalted butter	25g (1oz)
Salt and freshly-ground black pepper	To taste

Method of work

1 Preheat an oven to 180°C.

2 Stretch the bacon rashers by running the back of a knife along each one, then use then to line a 900g loaf tin or terrine dish. Overlap them slightly and let them overhang the top of the tin.

3 Heat the olive oil in a frying pan, add the onion and sauté until golden. Transfer to a plate and leave to cool.

4 Peel the potatoes and grate them coarsely. Put them in a tea towel and squeeze out excess liquid, then put them in a large bowl.

5 Add the onion, dried fruit, eggs, cream, potato flour and finally the cheese. Mix well and season with nutmeg, salt and pepper.

6 Pack the mixture into the bacon-lined tin and fold the overlapping bacon over the top.

7 Cover with a piece of lightly greased foil, place in the oven and cook for about 1½ hours, until soft when tested with a skewer. Leave to cool, then place in the refrigerator to set firm.

8 To serve, turn the terrine out and cut into slices 2cm thick. Fry in the butter until golden and slightly crisp.

7

Advanced skills and techniques in producing meat dishes (Unit 305)

LEARNING OUTCOMES

The aim of this chapter is to enable the candidate to develop the essential advanced skills, knowledge and understanding of the principles in preparing and producing a variety of meat dishes. This covers the development of more refined and advanced techniques, including information on materials, ingredients and equipment. The emphasis in this chapter is on developing existing skills and knowledge to reflect more advanced techniques.

There are **two** principal outcomes to this chapter. At the end of this chapter the candidate will be able to:

■ Prepare meat, cuts, joints and associated products
■ Produce meat dishes, associated products and garnishes

INTRODUCTION

Meat can be defined as skeletal muscle of an animal reared for the table, the most common meats being beef, pork and lamb. Other types of meat include goat, mutton, veal and venison.

The proteins that make up the muscle are myosin and actin, which are found as long thin molecules in the muscle fibres. These molecules bind together to form complex molecules called acto-myosin. Approximately 15–20 per cent of lean meat is made up of protein, with the remainder of the bulk being 75 per cent water and 5–10 per cent fats and connective tissues. The quality of meat – its colour, texture and flavour – are determined by the arrangement of the muscle fibres, connective tissues and fat.

Connective tissues are those that physically bind all the tissues in the body – they literally connect individual tissues to each other. One of the main types of connective tissue is **collagen**, which breaks down into gelatin when cooked slowly over a long period of time. Muscles that undertake a lot of work (such as leg muscles) have dense fibres and a higher proportion of collagen. Muscles such as the loin have long slender fibres and less collagen. These meats can be cooked much more quickly.

Fat tissue is a form of connective tissue, where some of the cells take on the role of energy storage. Fat is found in three different areas of meat:

- Under the skin layer, to help provide insulation to the cold
- Around important organs, such as the kidney, for protection
- In connective tissues

Modern methods of farming tend to produce animals that have little fat. However, the intramuscular fat in meat (marbling) is important for achieving a soft texture. The fat renders (melts) and lubricates the muscle fibres during the cooking process, helping to give flavour and to tenderise the meat.

Meat obtains its colour from two sources:

- *Haemoglobin* – the red pigment in blood that transports oxygen around the body
- *Myoglobin* – a reddish brown protein that stores oxygen in the muscle

Myoglobin temporarily stores oxygen within the muscle in readiness for action or exercise. Age affects the amount of myoglobin present, which accounts for beef being darker than veal and mutton darker than lamb. Pork is pale because of the early slaughter weight of the animals and their lack of exercise.

When an animal is first slaughtered its blood will be oxygenated (oxymyoglobin) – if the meat is sliced shortly after slaughter the cut surface will be bright red. The blood will then become deoxygenated (metmyoglobin) and change to a burgundy colour. This reaction can take a very short time and it should be noted that it does not mean that the meat is bad. This effect can be prevented by creating a barrier using plastic film or a vacuum pouch.

ORGANIC PRODUCTION

Economics have forced modern suppliers to produce mild, tender meat, which has become the public's usual expectation. However, small producers are now rearing traditional breeds to produce more mature and flavoursome

CHEF'S TIP

Muscle fibres are the part of the muscle that moves. The basic texture of the meat is determined from the mass and thickness of these fibres, which produce the 'grain' of meat.

CHEF'S TIP

Rabbits, chickens and turkeys have predominantly white meat because they do not use their muscles as frequently as cattle or lamb. Their muscles therefore consist predominantly of white fibres, although their leg muscles are a mixture of half white and half red fibres.

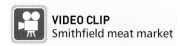
VIDEO CLIP
Smithfield meat market

CHEF'S TIP

Well flavoured meat comes from animals that have led a full and active life. However, exercise increases the size and strength of the muscle fibres and so the meat will be tougher.

meat for customers who require a high-quality product. The rise of organic farming, with its greater emphasis on animal welfare, has improved distribution and supplies of better quality meat. Generally, organic meat is produced locally and is traceable - the full process it has gone through before it reaches the customer can be tracked. Certain standards must be met before meat can be labelled as organic:

- All meat must be produced to the Soil Association's standards
- All produce must be sourced either directly from the supplier's farms or from selected local organic producers who adhere to the same Soil Association standards
- The highest animal welfare standards must be observed at all times
- All meat must be butchered professionally, on site if possible
- All produce must be completely traceable
- Minimal transport of live animals, to reduce stress of animals before slaughter

Organic beef as an example

There can be huge differences in the amounts of time that non-organic cattle spend grazing. The most intensive systems involve keeping bull calves indoors or in yards. Bull calves are used because they grow quickly. They are fed on high levels of concentrated feeds and silage and are fattened up as quickly as possible. The animals are confined in large numbers, which can increase the risk of infectious diseases.

By contrast, less-intensive systems allow the calves – castrated bulls and heifers (female cows) – to remain with their mothers. The whole herd is allowed to graze for one or two summers and may be brought indoors during the winter.

All beef in the UK is either produced from herds that use specific beef breeds, such as Aberdeen Angus, South Devon or Hereford, or from dairy herds where a bull from a beef breed is crossed with the cows. Organic producers are encouraged to choose breeds that suit the conditions on their farms.

An organic beef system allows cows and their calves to graze in pasture for most of their lives. They can be finished in well-bedded spacious yards, provided this period does not exceed a fifth of their lifetime. Organic cattle do not have to be housed during the winter, but if they are kept outside, there must be shelter, food and water. At least 60 per cent of the diet must consist of grass, hay or silage. Intestinal worms are a common problem in all cattle. They can be avoided on organic farms by rotating the pastures (moving the cattle between fields) and also by allowing the calves to pick up natural immunity from their mothers.

Black Aberdeen Angus

The beef labelling scheme ensures that any information put onto packs of beef can be verified.

TRACEABILITY

Traceability is designed to give the chef and the customer the ultimate guarantee of safety and quality of food. Information can now be communicated through labelling that allows the customer to directly trace a piece of meat back to a particular country of origin, locality/area, farm, breed, abattoir and supplier; effectively giving the history from farm to plate. The label can also include further information, such as the date of slaughter, place of butchery, age and sex of the animal, production method (e.g. organic, grass-fed) and meat maturation time.

SOURCING THE PRODUCT

There are important animal welfare and food safety issues to address which are closely connected to the overall quality and price of meat. Pork, beef, lamb and mutton cost more to produce where farmers have improved the living conditions for their animals, for example by providing them with high-quality feed. Consumers are taking a higher level of interest in animal welfare issues and also in the quality of the product that you prepare, cook and serve. It is possible to purchase quality meat on a restricted budget by following these basic rules:

- Consider cost effective cuts from better quality meat. By using the less well known cuts of meat, the chef will have to be innovative and skilled in the preparation and presentation of these cuts.
- Reduce waste by specifying exactly and correctly from your supplier what you want and how you want it butchered. Alternatively, buy meat on the carcass and butcher it yourself to further restrict wastage and to ensure that you utilise as much of the carcass as possible. By butchering your own meat, you will reduce labour costs from your meat supplier.
- Use vegetables, carbohydrates, stuffing and farces to add complexity and value to your dish.

The best way to secure a consistent supply of good quality meat is to build up a long term relationship with your butcher or meat supplier. They should be fully aware of the nature of your business so that they understand your needs and become an extended part of your team.

As a chef you should always take the opportunity to visit their operation too and visit their farms to understand the animal welfare standards of the meat that you purchase. You should be aware of your meat's provenance and history and also look to see if your meat has quality approvals from agencies such as BPEX, EBLEX and Freedom Foods.

Certification Mark

STORAGE AND PRESERVATION OF MEAT

Bacteria and moulds can multiply and grow very quickly on meat and so it will rot very quickly if it is not carefully stored. There are several methods of preservation that improve the storage life of meat.

- *Canning* – this was originally done by sealing a square tin can with solder and heating it until the meat was sterilised. Canning continues today but in a much refined form.
- *Dehydrating* – meat is cut into strips and hung to dry. This method is most popular in countries that have a dry climate.
- *Smoking* – meat and fish were originally hung in chimneys to dry. As well as having a drying effect, wood smoke contains compounds that have preserving and flavouring qualities.
- *Dry curing* – until the invention of canning, salting was the most important method of preservation. The meat would be smothered in salt for up to 2 months. It would then last for many more months.
- *Wet curing (picking)* – a heavy salt solution has the same effect as dry curing. The brine can be soaked into the flesh to speed the process and increase the water content.
- *Sealing* – meats have been sealed into containers for many hundreds of years. This has the effect of preventing air getting to the meat and so slows the growth of bacteria. Some meats are sealed in fats, such as confit of duck or potted tongue, which can then be cooked in the same fat. Even today, the vacuum pack system relies upon air being excluded. Care should be taken when using this method. Excluding the air affects bacteria that need air to flourish (aerobic) but it does not affect bacteria that do not need air (anaerobic). The smell of decomposing flesh is a safety marker – the smell tells you that the meat is not fit for consumption.
- *Refrigeration* – meat is kept covered at a temperature range of 1–4°C. This is a method of short-term preservation.
- *Freezing* – frozen meat is kept at a minimum of –18°C. When meat is frozen quickly the ice crystals that are formed will be much smaller, leading to less cell damage and less water forming during the defrosting process. Care should be taken when storing frozen meat. Freezer burn occurs if the food is not completely covered during the freezing process.

Traditional or seam butchery?

There are two main categories of butchery:

- The traditional butchery style has until recently been to cut the carcass of meat following the bone structure. This gives muscles with different characteristics in one cut resulting in a variety of eating qualities and textures, some will be better than others and require a different cooking time.

■ Seam butchery is now increasingly used in the UK. This manner of butchery cuts the carcass according to muscle position, following natural 'seams' of meat.

The advantages of seam butchery over the traditional method are that it produces less wastage and creates a more consistent cooking and eating quality for the meat because cuts include just one continuous muscle rather than one or more with different structures.

BEEF (*BOEUF*)

Beef is the edible meat of domestic cattle. Most beef comes from castrated males killed at 18 months of age. Heifers can also be used for beef if they are not required for breeding.

The carcases are allowed to cool naturally after slaughter and left to hang for up to 42 days. The **hanging** process (or **ageing**) creates a slow chemical change during which the meat becomes progressively more flavourful. Enzymes found in the muscle will generate flavour by breaking down other cells, turning large flavourless molecules into smaller well-flavoured deposits. Some chefs ask for longer ageing, but no appreciable difference is experienced after 28–30 days.

BSE (bovine spongiform encephalitis), also known as mad cow disease, caused the death of millions of cattle. This was brought about by feeding cattle with by-products derived from sheep that had a brain disease called scrapie. A form of the disease known as variant CJD was also passed to humans. This disease has an extremely long incubation period and so it is not known how long it will take to eradicate. BSE appears to have been eliminated in the UK thanks to the culling of infected herds and changes in feeding practices.

A butcher cutting a carcass

MICHAEL PEARDY

BEEF (*BOEUF*)

VIDEO CLIP
Preparation of beef sirloin

VIDEO CLIP
Preparation of beef fillet

QUALITY POINTS

■ The muscle should be red with slight marbling. This is a clear indicator that the animal was well nourished

■ The fat should be creamy in colour and brittle. If the fat on the outside of the meat (subcutaneous fat) is thin and soft to the touch the animal was probably force-fed or killed too young. There will be a resultant lack of flavour

■ There should be a pleasant aroma that shows no signs of rancidity. Beef and its fat start to decay after a short period at ambient temperature, even after just a few hours, and gives off a characteristic rotting odour.

■ The lean meat should not feel sticky to the touch. The surface of the meat is metabolised by bacteria and mould which causes discolouration and by-products that give a sticky feel to the flesh

Common breeds used in farming

- ▦ Aberdeen Angus
- ▦ Devon
- ▦ Herefordshire
- ▦ Holstein
- ▦ Cross breed of Limousin and Holstein.

Main beef-producing area

The main beef producing areas in Great Britain

Beef is almost always butchered into quarters and then broken down into primary cuts.

Beef hindquarter

Average weight 85–90kg

HINDQUARTER OF BEEF

JOINT	FRENCH	USE	AVERAGE WEIGHT
1 Fillet	Le filet	This is the leanest and most tender piece of beef and lends itself to grilling, roasting, frying and pot roasting	3–3.5kg
2 Sirloin	L'aloyau	A lean piece of meat that is good for frying, roasting and grilling. Care should be taken to remove any sinew from the back prior to roasting and remove any piece of the rump that remains	12–14kg
3 Wing rib	Les côtes d'aloyau	There are three wing ribs on each side of beef. Can be roasted as a piece or chined and cut into cutlets	5–6kg
4 Thin flank	La bavette d'aloyau	Also known as skirt, this is coarse meat with about 50% fat. It is good for sausages or mincing	8–10kg
5 Rump	Culotte	Frying, roasting, braising. There are several muscles on this joint that give different textural experiences when eating	10kg
6 Topside	La tranche tendre	Braising, stewing, slow roasting at low temperatures. This piece is used in the sandwich industry and by upmarket delicatessens	9–10kg
7 Thick flank	Tranche graisse	A large piece of lean meat that lends itself to being braised as a piece as it can disintegrate if used in small pieces in stews	10–11kg
8 Silverside	Gîte à la noix	Silverside is very coarse and requires long slow cooking. Good for pickling and boiling	12–14kg
9 Shin	La jambe le jarret	Because of the amount of collagen present, the shin makes excellent consommé	6–7kg
10 Kidney	Rognon	Pies, puddings	1–2kg
11 Fat (suet)	Graisse de rognon	Suet pastry, rendering	5–6kg

Beef forequarter

Average weight 75–80kg

BREAKDOWN ON A FOREQUARTER OF BEEF

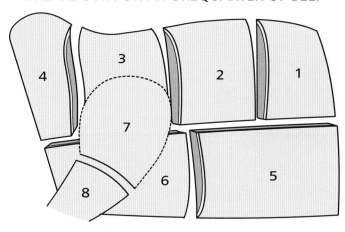

JOINT	FRENCH	USE	AVERAGE WEIGHT
1 Fore rib	Le côte première	The fore rib is the prime roasting joint from the side of beef. It has the best collagen to lean ratio, making it the most succulent. It can also be denuded of fat to give rib-eye steaks, suitable for grilling and frying	6.5kg
2 Middle rib	Le côte découverte	This is a flavoursome joint that can be used for braising in a single piece or for second-class roasting	8.5kg
3 Chuck rib	Le côte du collier	The high content of connective tissue in this joint means it benefits from stewing or braising. Be careful to remove all gristle and sinew	13kg
4 Sticking piece	Le collier-cou	Lean and high in flavour. Ideal for stewing and mincing	7kg
5 Plate	Le plat de côte	Remove all fat and use for stewing, mincing	8.5kg
6 Brisket	La poitrine	Brining and boiling brings out the best in brisket, although it can be boiled without brining	16kg
7 Leg of mutton cut (LMC beef)	L'épaule macreuse	When properly butchered, LMC beef is very lean and makes excellent braising steaks and paupiettes and is good for stewing and mincing	7-9kg
8 Shank	Jambe de devant	Very lean and high in collagen. Remove any gristle and mince for a consommé clarification mix	5kg

Alternative beef cuts

Blade fillet steak

Blade fillet steak

This cut is not very well known and is often left attached to the chuck and used for braising steak. This is such a shame as it is very tender with its own unique flavour.

The meat is located between the shoulder blade and the chuck. It is removed using the seam cutting method, which selects and removes individual muscles. When all connective tissue and gristle is removed, a tender and succulent piece of meat is left.

This cut will surprise many chefs because of its tender and juicy characteristics.

If handled well the tenderness could be mistaken for beef fillet and is ideal as an alternative to the popular cut but with a more intense flavour.

Cooking advice: the underblade pavé eats best rare to medium-rare as even the best steak will toughen with over cooking.

Flat iron steak

Flat iron steak

The flat iron steak is another little known, extremely tender and succulent steak from the forequarter. Some butchers claim, if this is matured and cut correctly, it can be as tender as rump or sirloin. This steak is becoming very popular in America for its tenderness. With its own character and flavour it has a very short grain and often contains some fat marbling.

This muscle is attached to the shoulder blade and is often used for braising steak as it contains a thick centre gristle. However using the seam cutting technique all gristle is removed which separates the meat into two sections. These are scored for effect and cut into steaks.

Cooking advice: flat iron steak is best cooked rare to medium-rare as over-cooking will toughen even the best steak.

Beef bavette steak

Beef bavette steak

This is an underrated cut of meat, often used for dice or even mince in the UK. However, when trimmed and well prepared, this cut is used for steaks in other parts of the world.

It is very popular with some chefs who regard the bavette more for its flavour and juiciness rather than its tenderness. The grain of the meat is coarse and loose and requires a little chewing, but this only brings out more flavour and texture which makes it stand apart from many other steaks.

The cut comes from the flank area, trimmed of all fat and gristle and only the lean meat is used.

Tip: the bavette is best pre-cut and fanned out on the plate for better presentation. This will also make it easier for the customer to eat.

Cooking advice: the bavette eats best rare to medium-rare, as over cooking will make this steak tough.

Important tips when cooking these alternative cuts

▓ All of these alternative steak cuts must be matured for a minimum of 14 days on the bone or in vacuum bags to optimise eating quality. It is recommended not to mature the body skirt, skirt diaphragm and flank skirt on the bone but in vacuum bags to enhance keeping quality.

▓ It is important to rest these steaks after cooking for 2–3 minutes prior to serving. This will enhance the tenderness and juiciness and it also stops the juices running out when cutting or slicing the steak for presentation.

▓ After grilling, whilst resting, place a small amount of butter on the steak to create a nice glaze and enhance the flavour.

▓ Always season the steak with salt and pepper and baste with cooking oil prior to cooking.

▓ It is also very important to provide your customers with sharp steak knives. Blunt knives will tear the steaks and might make it difficult to eat.

■ Make sure your meat is approved by the EBLEX Quality Standard Mark scheme to ensure all the meat comes from a quality assured supply chain, as most consumers want to know about the provenance of the meat served.

VEAL (*VEAU*)

Veal is the meat from beef calves, usually male calves from dairy herds. It has generally not been an important part of British cuisine, but it is very popular in Italy, Spain, France, Austria and Germany. There are moral arguments about the way that veal is reared.

Veal calves should be fed exclusively on milk – there should be a milky aroma from the kidneys and fat. The calves are slaughtered at between 2½ and 4 months. Because veal is very young it is low in myoglobin, which accounts for its pale colour.

The fat content is also minimal, and therefore the use of ingredients such as cream adds to the eating experience. Care should be taken not to over-cook veal, especially the parts that are grilled and roasted, as they can become dry and tough – they should be just cooked (à **point**) or slightly under-cooked.

VIDEO CLIP
Preparation of veal cushion

Side of veal

BREAKDOWN ON A SIDE OF VEAL

QUALITY POINTS

■ The fat is white, pleasant to smell and with a faint hint of milk. The subcutaneous fat should only have any thickness around the rump. It should be dry and not greasy

■ The muscles should not feel sticky to the touch. This is a sure sign of poor storage and the carcass being left at ambient temperature or poorly transported

■ The flesh is very lean and a very pale pink colour, except when a rose colour is specifically ordered. There should be no marbling as the animal should not have had a long enough life to produce intramuscular fat

JOINT	FRENCH	USE	AVERAGE WEIGHT
1 Scrag	Le cou	A flavourless joint that makes excellent stock. Can also be used for mince to make porjarski or for blanquettes	1.25kg
2 Neck	Collet	The neck can be prepared for stews or fricassée. If minced it can be used for fine forcemeats	3kg
3 Neck end	Côte découverte	Used for stewing. Bone and remove sinew before cutting into 2.5cm cubes	2kg
4 Best end	Le carré	The best end is a prime cut that is suitable for roasting, pot roasting, cutlets and frying	2–3kg
5 Loin	La longe	This is a lean joint, good for roasting. It can be cut into chops or steaks, but its lack of marbling precludes successful grilling. Braising is a good option	4kg
6 Rump	Le quasi or cul de veau	Used for escalope of veal or for sauté dishes. The rump can be roasted or braised as steaks. The trimmings can be used for stewing	2kg
7 Leg	Cuisseau	The leg can be cut into the following joints: Cushion (noix) Under-cushion (sous-noix) Thick flank (noix pâtissière) Each can be used for pot roasting, frying or grilling. The cushion is the main joint from which escalopes are taken	6–8kg
8 Knuckle/ shank	Le jarret	Mince, stews, first-class stocks and osso bucco ('bone with a hole', an Italian dish of braised shank)	2kg
9 Shoulder	L'épaule	The shoulder can be stuffed and roasted or used for braised dishes	3–5kg
10 Breast	La poitrine	The breast can be removed and braised or stewed, but care should be taken not to over-cook the joint. Using a fatty stuffing or barding the joint helps to prevent it drying out when roasting	2–3kg

LAMB AND MUTTON (*AGNEAU* AND *MOUTON*)

Lamb is the meat from young sheep and has a characteristic and delicate flavour. The flavour develops, becoming much deeper, as the lamb develops. Mutton is the meat from the adult sheep.

- *Spring lamb* – lamb in its first 6 months, but usually slaughtered at 3–4 months.
- *Lamb* – lamb up to 1 year old or when the lamb grows its first pair of permanent teeth.
- *Hoggett* –1 to 2 years old; technically this is mutton but without the developed flavour.
- *Mutton* – over 2 years old, and with a strong and well-developed flavour.

In the UK, the sheep industry is located so that particular breeds occupy specific environments to which they are adapted. The sheep of these environments are connected by the movement of lambs and older animals from higher to lower ground.

The hills

Hardy hill and mountain sheep are largely kept as pure breeds. Lambs not required to maintain flock numbers are transferred to the lowlands as store lambs to be fattened.

VIDEO CLIP
Preparation of lamb best end

The uplands

In upland areas there are again specific breeds. These and older draft mountain ewes are crossed with the longwool breeds.

VIDEO CLIP
Preparation of lamb shoulder

The lowlands

In the lowlands, the sheep are crossed with lowland sires to produce lambs that can be fattened on summer grass. Slower growing lambs join those that have arrived from the hills and upland areas to be fattened on root crops over the autumn and winter months.

QUALITY POINTS

- The lean flesh should be a dull red colour with a close grain
- The fat should be evenly distributed, dry to the touch and flaky in texture. The amount of fat is determined by the age and feeding of the animal
- The smell of lamb is pleasing and characteristic to the animal. This can be lost if the very lean parts of the lamb are denuded of all connective tissue and fat
- Lamb bones should be porous, as they are yet to mature and become dense, and have a small degree of blood present

Main sheep areas

The main lowland sheep areas in Great Britain

It is important to keep lamb and mutton cold when cutting the meat as the fat becomes greasy and knife handles become slippery to use.

Side of lamb/mutton

Average weight 18–21kg

BREAKDOWN OF A SIDE OF LAMB/MUTTON

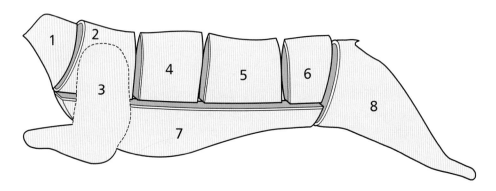

JOINT	FRENCH	USES	AVERAGE WEIGHT
1 Scrag	Le cou	Stewing and for broths This is the toughest part of the lamb and is traditionally cooked on the bone in Irish stew	1kg
2 Middle neck	Côte découverte	Stewing when the neck fillet is removed or grilling as uncovered cutlets. Be sure to remove all traces of **elastin**	2kg
3 Shoulder	L'épaule	Roasting, stuff with forcemeat and roast slowly. Can also be served as a half shoulder braised in a rich sauce, or diced for stewing	2 × 2.5kg
4 Best end	Le carré	The best end can be prepared into racks for roasting, or into cutlets, noisettes or rosettes for grilling and frying	2kg
5 Saddle	La selle	The saddle can be roasted on the bone or boned and stuffed. The loins can be removed and cut into rosettes and noisettes for frying and grilling. Fillet mignon also comes from the saddle, as do the cannons	3.5kg
6 Rump/ chump	Le quasi	A rump of lamb will yield four pieces for braising or roasting	2kg
7 Breast	La poitrine	The breast can be boned and rolled for slow roasting, or steamed and pressed to make epigrams	2kg
8 Leg	Le gigot	The leg can be used for roasting and the shank can be used for braising. The leg can also be broken down into its various muscle groups for frying and grilling. Mutton leg can also be used for boiling	2 × 2.5kg

The preparation of lamb into cutlets

1 Prepare the lamb by sawing at the bottom of the ribs until the chine bone is released.

2 Cut away the flesh from the chine bone to leave two pieces.

3 Make an incision just above the lean eye of the meat. Remove the flesh making sure to stay close to the bone.

4 Remove the bark.

5 Scrape each bone and then push the flesh from each bone from the side.

Removing the chine bone using a heavy knife

Cutting away the flesh at the top of the bones

Removing the bark

Scraping the bones

Pushing the flesh

Peeling the meat away from the bones

Trimming and removing the elastin

Cutting the cutlets

VIDEO CLIP
Preparation of pork loin for roasting

VIDEO CLIP
Preparation of pork belly

PORK (*PORC*)

Pork is the fresh meat of the domestic pig. Pigs are easy to breed and make slaughter weight in usually 6 months. Pork is widely used across the world, except within the Jewish and Muslim communities.

In the past it was recommended that pork should always be over-cooked to eliminate trichinosis (the larvae of a worm that can be passed to humans from under-cooked pork). However, with modern rearing, storage and preparation techniques, trichinosis has been practically eradicated, although care should be taken to cook the meat to 70–75°C. Pork is usually supplied butchered into sides.

New breeds of pig developed for the table have a high yield of flesh and a low proportion of fat, examples are Landrace and Duroc. Traditional breeds such as the Tamworth and Gloucester Old Spot have a greater covering of fat and much more tender flesh because they are generally reared free-range and are allowed to forage for food, especially acorns and apples.

Main pig production areas

The main pig production areas in Great Britain

QUALITY POINTS

- Pale pink flesh with a fine texture. Marbling can occur with organic and free-range pork. A smaller portion of free-range pork will satisfy the appetite compared with battery-reared pork

- Skin should be free of bristle and not wet to the touch. When the pig is slaughtered it is dipped and scalded, this loosens the hairs and allows them to be scraped off. Pork is the only meat where the skin is also eaten

- There should be a covering of fat, but it should not be excessive. A layer of 1–2cm of subcutaneous fat is sufficient, although contemporary preferences are for a thinner layer

- The bones should be small and pink. In older animals the bones are white and more dense

- If you are purchasing a whole pig make sure that the tail is intact. If pigs become distressed they try to bite each others' tails. Some breeders will dock their young pigs' tails

Side of pork

Average weight (excluding head) 16–18kg

BREAKDOWN OF A SIDE OF PORK

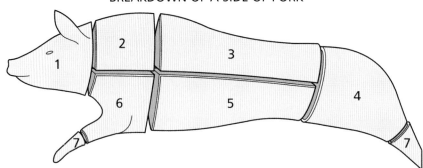

JOINT	FRENCH	USES	AVERAGE WEIGHT
1 Head	La tête	The head can be boned and stuffed, or it can be boiled and the flesh pressed for brawn. The cheeks can be braised. The head can also be boiled and presented with chaud-froid as a centrepiece for a buffet	4kg
2 Spare rib	L'échine	With the gristle removed, used for sausages, pork pies, slow roasting	2kg
3 Loin	La longe	Chops and cutlets are obtained from the loin, as is the fillet. All are suitable for frying and grilling. The loin can also be boned and rolled for roasting	5kg
4 Leg	Le cuissot	On or off the bone, pork leg is suitable for roasting. The legs can be dissected into individual muscles for cutting into steaks or stir frying. The leg can also be cured for ham, either a wet or dry cure can be used	4kg
5 Belly	La poitrine	Braised belly of pork is very popular. When boned and chopped it makes good emulsion sausages	3kg
6 Shoulder	L'épaule	With fat and gristle removed, the shoulder can be used to make sausages and forcemeats and can be diced for stews	3kg
7 Trotters	Le pied	The trotters should be blanched and then refreshed. They can be used to make gelatinous stock, stuffed and braised, or the meat can be picked off and added to brawn	0.5kg

BACON

Bacon is the cured side of a baconer pig (a pig that is allowed to grow bigger than a porker pig, usually a hybrid of Landrace and Tamworth). The meat is cured by either the wet cure or dry cure method. Dry cure is superior as it causes less shrinkage; the sides are strewn with salt and cured for 14 days. The pinkness comes from the addition of nitrate and the reaction of salt-tolerant bacteria. The cured bacon, referred to as green bacon, can be smoked or sold unsmoked.

QUALITY POINTS

- The lean muscle should be pink, firm and not sticky to the touch. Smoked bacon should feel dry to the touch

- The fat should be white and not excessive. With dry cured bacon the rind is usually left on and the fat should be dry to the touch. Vacuum packed bacon can be quite wet to the touch but can be dried with absorbent paper

- The rind must be free from wrinkles and not sticky. Wrinkles and stickiness indicate that the bacon has been poorly stored and is past its sell-by date

Bacon has been a staple of British society for many hundreds of years and was originally used as a way to store meat. Although the invention of refrigeration has made meat storage much easier, bacon continues to be produced because of its flavour. Bacon is still produced for the British market in many other parts of the world, the biggest producer being Denmark.

Side of bacon

Average weight 28–30kg

JOINT	USES	AVERAGE WEIGHT
1 Gammon	Boiled gammon is usually served cold, but it can be glazed, baked and served hot. Can also be sliced to make gammon steaks and grilled or fried	7–8kg
2 Back	Rashers of bacon and bacon steaks for grilling and frying	9–10kg
3 Collar	The collar can be tied for boiling or diced for pies and fricassées	4–5kg
4 Hock	The hock should always be boiled, but can also be roasted afterwards and served with mustard	4–5kg
5 Belly	Streaky bacon is taken from the belly and can be grilled or fried	4–5kg

BREAKDOWN OF A SIDE OF BACON

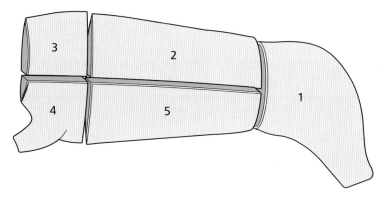

BEEF RECIPES

Beef Wellington

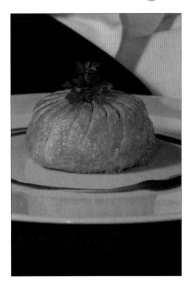

INGREDIENTS	4 PORTIONS	10 PORTIONS
Centre cut fillet of beef	600g	1.5kg
Vegetable oil	50g	100g
Chestnut mushrooms	300g	750g
Finely chopped shallots	50g	125g
Dry white wine	20ml	50ml
Butter	50g	125g
Foie gras	200g	500g
Puff pastry	500g	1kg
Egg whites	1	2-3
Chopped truffle trimmings	50g	100g
Madeira sauce	200ml	500ml
Good-quality salt and white pepper	To taste	To taste
Egg wash	1 egg	2 eggs
Herb pancakes		
Fresh eggs	4	8
Soft flour	150g	300g
Fresh milk	200ml	400ml
Chopped fresh chives and parsley	2tbsp	4tbsp
Vegetable oil for frying		

Method of work

1 Preheat an oven to 200°C.

2 Tie the fillet of beef to retain its shape, season well and seal in a hot pan with a little fat. Allow to cool completely. Reserve the pan juices. Lightly re-season the beef fillet and reserve in the refrigerator.

3 Finely chop or mince the mushrooms and cook with the shallots in the butter in a saucepan. Add the white wine and continue to cook until the wine has evaporated and the mixture is dry (**duxelle**). Season to taste and allow to cool completely.

4 To make the herb pancakes, beat the eggs and flour in a bowl until smooth. Slowly add the milk to create a thin consistency and then add the chopped herbs and seasoning.

5 Heat a little oil in a pancake pan and cook thin pancakes (one per portion) in the usual way.

6 Remove the beef fillet from the refrigerator and cut into the required portions. Cut away any remaining string.

7 Mix half of the truffles with the pâté and spread over each pancake, then add a layer of the duxelle. Place the sealed beef fillet on top and fold the pancake over to encase the fillet. Trim away any excess pancake. Wrap in plastic film and chill for 1 hour.

8 Roll out the puff pastry until it is large enough to wrap around the fillet of beef. Leave to rest for 15 minutes.

VIDEO CLIP
How to tie knots in butchery

CHEF'S TIP

Truffles are very expensive. A more economical method is to add a little truffle oil to the duxelle. Another cheaper alternative is to use chicken liver pâté in place of the foie gras. The beef is wrapped in herb pancakes to give extra protection from over-cooking the meat and to retaining the juices produced during the cooking process.

9 Discard the plastic film and place the pancake-wrapped beef fillet onto the pastry and roll the pastry around the beef, encasing it completely. Seal well to prevent any leakage during cooking.

10 Place on a baking sheet seam-side down and brush with **egg wash**.

11 Chill thoroughly for at least 1 hour and egg wash again. Score curved lines in the top of the pastry using the tip of a sharp knife.

12 Place in an oven for 20–25 minutes. Reduce the heat to 130°C until the required degree of cooking is achieved.

13 Allow to rest in a warm place for at least 5 minutes before serving.

14 Heat the pan juices and deglaze with some red wine. Add the Madeira sauce and strain through a fine chinois into a clean pan. Check the consistency and seasoning.

15 Add the remainder of the truffles and heat for 2–3 minutes.

16 Place each individual beef Wellington onto a serving plate and serve with the sauce.

Sealing the fillet

Portioning the fillet

Wrapping the fillet in the herb pancake

Tournedos Rossini

INGREDIENTS	4 PORTIONS	10 PORTIONS
Centre cut fillet of beef	600g	1.5kg
Foie gras	160g	400g
Thin slice of truffle (soaked in brandy)	4 slices	10 slices
Madeira sauce	200ml	500ml
Butter	40g	100g
Madeira wine	35ml	75ml
Thick sliced white bread (cut into a disc to the size of the fillet)	4 slices	10 slices
Fresh chervil	4 sprigs	10 sprigs
Good-quality salt and white pepper	To taste	To taste

Method of work

1 Completely remove any fat or connective tissue from the fillet and wrap tightly in plastic film. Place into a refrigerator and chill for a minimum of 3 hours. This allows the meat to set into a round shape.

2 Remove from the refrigerator and slice into the required tournedos steaks at approximately 150g per portion.

3 Remove the foie gras from the refrigerator for 5 minutes prior to slicing and cut into the required number of **collops**. Return to the refrigerator until required.

4 Heat the butter in a shallow pan until it starts to foam. Place the fillets into the pan and cook on both sides to the required core temperature.

5 Season the fillets, remove from the pan and keep warm.

6 Add the Madeira wine to the pan and deglaze with the cooked juices from the meat. Add the Madeira sauce and bring to the boil. Simmer for up to 4 minutes.

7 Strain the sauce into a clean pan, reheat and check the seasoning and consistency.

8 Sear the foie gras in a hot dry shallow pan until the collops are golden brown on each side. Place one on top of each fillet and keep warm.

9 Place the bread slices in the pan to fry quickly on both sides using the residue of the foie gras. Also warm through the truffle slices.

10 To serve, arrange the bread slice in the centre of each plate. Place the tournedos with the foie gras and sliced truffle on top with a **cordon** of Madeira sauce around it. Finish with a sprig of the fresh chervil.

Rolling the fillet in cling film

Cutting the fillet into 150g steaks

Cooking fillet of beef

Tournedos are cut from the centre of the beef fillet and are usually sautéed in butter with a named garnish or sauce.

Cooking the foie gras

Arranging the dish

Garnishes for alternative tournedos dishes

NAME	GARNISH
Alsacienne	Toss lardons in hot fat with sauerkraut. Dress on a fried croûton with the garnish
Béarnaise	Serve with watercress and béarnaise sauce (see recipe on p. 93)
Choron	Serve with sauce choron (tomato flavoured sauce Béarnaise), garnished with artichoke bottoms filled with peas and noisette potatoes
Duroc	Coat with chasseur sauce and serve with tomato concassé and noisette potatoes
Forestière	Serve on a croûton with sautéed wild mushrooms and lardons accompanied by Parmentier potatoes. Can be served with a red wine sauce
Helder	Serve with sauce Béarnaise, piped on top with cooked tomato concassé in the centre with a jus lie and Parisienne potatoes
Rivoli	Set on Anna potatoes with truffle sauce

Steak and smoked oyster pudding

INGREDIENTS	4 PORTIONS	10 PORTIONS
Suet pastry		
Soft flour	290g	600g
Baking powder	10g	20g
Beef suet	150g	310g
Cold water	75ml	150ml
Good-quality salt	To taste	To taste
Filling		
Chuck steak	400g	800g
Tinned smoked oysters	125g	250g
Thinly sliced onion	70g	140g
Fresh thyme	6 sprigs	12 sprigs
Garlic	1 clove	2 cloves
Seasoned soft flour	4tbsp	8tbsp
Worcestershire sauce	To taste	To taste
Beaten egg yolk	1	2
Stout gravy		
Finely chopped shallots	100g	200g
Garlic	1 clove	2 cloves
Fresh thyme	1 sprig	2 sprigs
Bay leaf	½ leaf	1 leaf
Crushed black peppercorns	5	10
Stout beer	600ml	1.2 litres
Red wine	400ml	800ml
Beef stock	2 litres	4 litres
Good-quality salt and white pepper	To taste	To taste
Parsley purée		
Fresh flat leaf parsley sprigs	300g	600g
Double cream	150ml	300ml
Good-quality salt and white pepper	To taste	To taste

Method of work

1 To make the parsley purée, take the washed, picked flat leaf parsley and blanch in plenty of boiling water for 3 minutes. Drain immediately in a colander.

2 While the parsley is still hot, squeeze out as much water as possible. Place the drained parsley into a food processor and blend, gradually adding the double cream.

3 When the cream has been completely added, remove the purée as quickly as possible and place in an airtight plastic bag. Keep in the refrigerator until required.

4   To make the suet pastry, sieve the flour, salt and the baking powder together. Add the beef suet and mix in the cold water a little at a time. This pastry should not be too sticky, so there may be a little water left over depending on the quality of flour used. Knead until a smooth and elastic pastry is formed. Wrap in plastic film and refrigerate until required.

5   Cut the chuck steak into small (1.5cm) cubes and reserve any meat trimmings for the sauce. Mix the cubed beef in a bowl with the drained smoked oysters, onion, thyme, garlic and flour.

6   Line dariole moulds with plastic film, overhanging by a few centimetres. Pin out the suet paste and cut one 18cm disc and one 6cm disc per portion. Leave to rest in a refrigerator, covered, for 5 minutes.

7   Line each mould with the larger disc of pastry, pushing well into the base of the mould. Leave a 1cm overhang of pastry around the edge.

8   Divide the filling between the moulds and pour in some cold water, to come three-quarters of the way up the mould. Sprinkle with a few drops of the Worcestershire sauce.

9   Brush inside each pastry mould with the beaten egg yolk and place the smaller disc on top. Fold over the overhanging pastry and pinch inwards to seal the top. Wrap each mould tightly with plastic film twice.

10 Place the puddings into the steamer and steam for 2 hours.

11 To make the stout gravy, place the shallots, garlic, herbs, peppercorns and salt in a pan with the left over meat trimmings and carefully sweat for 10 minutes. Remove the lid and increase the heat to begin to caramelise the ingredients.

12 Add the red wine and reduce by three-quarters. Add the stout and reduce in the same way. Add the stock and reduce to the required consistency. Pass through a fine chinois and correct the seasoning.

13 To serve, unwrap the puddings and turn out onto serving plates. Take the required quantity of the parsley purée and heat as quickly as possible in a small, dry shallow pan, seasoning to taste. Serve the stout sauce around the pudding and drizzle a small amount over the pudding also. Using a dessert spoon, create a quenelle of the parsley purée to sit on the top of each pudding.

Slow cooked fillet of beef with braised red cabbage and a smoked onion soubise sauce

INGREDIENTS	4 PORTIONS	10 PORTIONS
Beef fillet (trimmed and cut from the centre)	1 × 750g	2 × 900g
Sunflower oil	50ml	100ml
Braised Red Cabbage		
Red cabbage (with the central stem removed)	½ cabbage	1 cabbage
Red wine vinegar	50ml	100ml
Balsamic vinegar	45ml	80ml
Red wine	300ml	600ml
Demerara sugar	300g	500g
Star anise	2	5
Bay leaves	4	10
Whole cloves	3	8
Black peppercorns	10	25
Cinnamon stick	½	1
Good-quality salt	For salting	For salting
Smoked onion soubise		
Onions	2	4
Garlic	½ clove	1 clove
Fresh thyme	1 sprig	2 sprigs
White vegetable stock	200ml	400ml
Double cream	100ml	200ml
Oak wood chips	75g	150g
Good-quality salt and white Pepper	To taste	To taste

Method of work

1 Preheat an oven to 56–59°C.

2 Take the centre-cut fillet of beef and quickly seal in the sunflower oil in a pan until lightly brown all over. Allow to cool.

3 Wrap well in plastic film to help maintain the shape of the beef fillet, place on a baking tray and place in the oven for a minimum of 1½ hours.

4 To finish the beef, remove from the oven and carefully cut away the plastic film. Heat some sunflower oil in a hot pan and brown for 2 minutes on all sides.

5 For the smoked onion soubise, cover the base of a baking tray with oak chips sprinkled with a little water and place a perforated tray or wire rack on top. Slice the onions and garlic thinly and arrange in a small tray, place the tray on top of the oak chips. Place on a medium heat until it begins to smoke, then cover with foil and leave on the heat for five minutes. Remove from the heat and allow to cool.

6 Sweat the smoked onion and garlic with the thyme until golden. Add the stock and reduce by half.

7 Add the cream and bring back to the boil. Pour the contents of the pan into a food blender to liquidise to a smooth consistency. Pass through a fine sieve into a saucepan and correct the seasoning. Set aside for service.

8 Salt the sliced red cabbage in a colander for 2–3 hours to help bring out the colour. Rinse in cold water and pat dry with a clean kitchen cloth.

9 Place the vinegars, wine and sugar in a pan and bring to the boil. Place the broken cinnamon stick, star anise, peppercorns, cloves and bay leaves in a small muslin cloth and tie into a little bag. Add the cabbage and the muslin bag and slowly braise, covering the pan with a lid until the cabbage has cooked completely.

10 Remove the muslin bag and strain the cabbage in a colander while still hot.

11 To serve, spoon the cabbage into the centre of a serving plate. Slice the beef fillet and arrange slices on top of the cabbage. Quickly blend and aerate the smoked onion soubise with a stick blender and spoon onto the plate to accompany the beef. Garnish as required. Accompaniments such as fondant potatoes and a red wine beef jus can also be served.

Daube of beef provençale with a garlic mash

INGREDIENTS	4 PORTIONS	10 PORTIONS
Daube of beef		
Chuck steak	4 × 150g	10 × 150g
White wine	50ml	125ml
Cognac	25ml	70ml
Crushed garlic	1 clove	2 cloves
Fresh parsley stalks	8	20
White flour	To dust	To dust
Sunflower oil	50ml	100ml
Pancetta lardons	100g	250g
Black olives	20	50
Carrot	100g	250g
Onion	2100g	50g
Bouquet garni	Small	Medium
Tomato concassé	200g	500g
Sliced chestnut mushrooms	100g	250g
Dried orange peel	10g	25g
Lemon juice	½ lemon	1 lemon
Good-quality salt and white pepper	To taste	To taste
Garlic mash		
Maris Piper potatoes	750g	1.5kg
Unsalted butter	125g	250g
Garlic	2 cloves	4 cloves
Fresh cream	60ml	120ml
Good-quality salt and white pepper	To taste	To taste

CHEF'S TIP

Daube derives its name from the dish in which it was traditionally cooked (daubière). A paste of flour and water (repère) was used to give a tight seal around the top of a daubière.

Method of work

1   Trim and slice the beef into neat steaks and marinate for 10 hours in the wine, cognac, crushed garlic and parsley stalks.

2   Remove the steaks from the marinade and pat dry with a clean kitchen cloth. Dust the meat with the flour and season with salt and pepper and gently beat it in with the back of a heavy knife. Preheat an oven to 180°C.

3   Season each steak and seal in hot oil, then transfer to a braising pan.

4   Add the cleaned, peeled and chopped vegetables and sauté quickly in the hot fat until golden, then transfer to the braising pot with the beef.

5   Deglaze the pan with the marinade and add to the braising pan.

6   Add the remaining ingredients to the pan. Cover with a tight-fitting lid and place in the oven for 2–2½ hours.

7   When the beef is cooked, remove the beef steaks and cover with plastic film and retain for service. Discard the bouquet garni and orange peel.

8   Reduce the sauce to the required consistency and correct the seasoning.

9   Wash, peel and rewash the potatoes. Cut into a rough dice and cook in boiling salted water until tender. Drain in a colander.

10 Finely chop the garlic and sweat in a little of the butter.

11 Purée the potatoes with the sweated garlic, remaining butter and cream. Season to taste.

12 On a serving plate, pipe the garlic mash and place the **daube** of beef next to it. Spoon the sauce over and garnish as required.

Slicing the chuck steaks

Marinating the steaks

Beating flour into the steaks

Braised oxtail with black pudding and champ potatoes

INGREDIENTS	4 PORTIONS	10 PORTIONS
Trimmed oxtail	2	5
Black pudding	350g	900g
Mirepoix of carrot, onion, celery and leek	200g	500g
Chopped tomatoes	200g	400g
Fresh thyme	1 sprig	3 sprigs
Fresh bay leaf	1	3
Red wine	400ml	800ml
Brown beef stock	600ml	1.2 litres
Beef dripping or oil for frying	50g	100g
Good-quality salt and white pepper	To taste	To taste
Champ potatoes		
Maris Piper potatoes	750g	1.5kg
Unsalted butter	125g	250g
Fresh cream	60ml	120ml
Spring onions	4	10
Good-quality salt and white pepper	To taste	To taste
Garnish		
Tomato concassé	100g	300g
Fresh chopped parsley	1tbsp	3tbsp
Finely diced and blanched mirepoix of carrot, leek, celery and onion	200g	600g

Method of work

1 Preheat an oven to 220°C.

2 Using boning knife, remove excess fat from the tails and bone out the oxtail. Keep the meat whole and retain the bones.

3 Remove the black pudding from the skins and mince it down. Lay it along the centre of the meat. Taper the pudding in the opposite direction to the meat to give an even shape.

4 Roll and carefully tie the tails to give a neat cylindrical shape.

5 Seal the oxtail in a hot pan with the beef dripping and add the mirepoix of vegetables, chopped tomato, thyme and bay leaf. Continue to cook until the mirepoix is golden brown.

6 Brown the bones in the oven and add to the oxtail.

7 Place all the ingredients in a large braising pan or casserole with the red wine and the beef stock and cook in the oven for approximately 3 hours.

8 Remove the oxtails when cooked and strain the sauce through a fine chinois into a clean pan and skim. Reduce the sauce and correct the seasoning and consistency.

9 Wash, peel and rewash the potatoes. Cut into a rough dice and cook in boiling salted water until tender. Drain in a colander.

10 Finely chop the spring onions and sweat in a little of the butter.

11 Purée the potatoes with the remaining butter and cream. Season to taste and add the spring onions.

12 Heat the sauce and add the mirepoix garnish and tomato concassé. Serve the oxtails sliced onto the champ potato on a serving plate, using slices from each end of the tail to give a correct ratio of meat to stuffing.

13 Serve with the finished sauce and the chopped parsley.

Trimming and boning the oxtail

Spreading the black pudding onto the open oxtail

Tying the oxtail before sealing

Hot smoked fillet of beef with rocket salad

 CHEF'S TIP

This method can be used for preparing hot or cold beef. To preserve the beef, cure it for 24 hours and smoke to 70°C.

Method of work

1 Combine all the ingredients for the cure and mix together.

2 Trim the beef of all fat and connective tissue.

INGREDIENTS	4 PORTIONS	10 PORTIONS
The cure	Makes 500g	Makes 500g
Good-quality salt	250g	250g
Dark brown sugar	200g	200g
White pepper	10g	10g
Allspice	10g	10g
Ground mace	10g	10g
Crushed juniper berries	10g	10g
Pink salt	10g	10g
The dish		
Centre cut fillet of beef	500g	1.25kg
Hickory wood chips	75g	150g
Fresh rocket leaves	100g	500g
Extra virgin olive oil	20ml	50ml
Grated horseradish	25g	50g
Crème fraîche	200g	500g
Chopped chives	1tsp	1tbsp
Good-quality salt and black pepper	To taste	To taste

3 Place a layer of the cure mix on top of a sheet of plastic film, lay the beef on top and cover the beef with a generous layer of cure mix.

4 Roll the beef tightly in several layers of cling film.

5 Place the beef in a tray and lay another tray on top. Place a 1kg weight on top and leave in the refrigerator for 6–8 hours.

6 Remove from the refrigerator, unwrap and wash quickly in cold water. Pat dry with a paper towel and leave to stand in a well-ventilated room (this gives a sticky surface called a pellicle, which allows the smoke particles to attach to the surface of the meat).

7 Place the beef in a hot smoker set at 90°C for 1–2 hours until the core temperature of the beef reaches 65°C. Alternatively, preheat an oven to 90°C. Place the wood chips in the bottom of a roasting tray with a grill over the top. Heat the wood chips on a stove until they begin to smoke. Place the beef fillet on top and cover with foil before placing in the oven to cook.

8 Combine the olive oil, chopped fresh chives, grated horseradish and crème fraîche. Use half the dressing to dress the washed rocket leaves and season to taste.

9 Slice the beef very thinly and drizzle with the remaining dressing. Serve the beef with the rocket salad.

VEAL RECIPES
Braised cushion of veal *Fricandeau de veau*

INGREDIENTS	4 PORTIONS	10 PORTIONS
Cushion of veal	500g	1.5kg
Italian lardo (strips of fat)	200g	500g
Carrots	200g	500g
Button onions	200g	500g
Button mushrooms	200g	500g
Celery	200g	500g
White of leek	200g	500g
Bouquet garni	1 small	1 medium
Veal stock	1 litre	2.5 litres
Good-quality salt and white pepper	To taste	To taste
Noodle garnish		
Fettuccine	100g	250g
Olive oil	30ml	80ml
Fresh chopped parsley	1tbsp	3tbsp

CHEF'S TIP

The veal should be constantly basted to prevent it from drying out during cooking.

Method of work

1 Preheat an oven to 170°C.

2 Lard the veal with the lardo by inserting strips of fat into the joint using a **larding** needle. Trim and tie the joint with string.

3 Wash, peel and cut the vegetables into equal sizes and lightly fry in some fat. Transfer into the bottom of a heavy braising pan.

4 Place the joint into the hot fat to seal on all sides before placing on top of the bed of vegetables.

5 Add the veal stock and bouquet garni and season well.

6 Bring to the boil, skim, cover with a tight-fitting lid and place in the oven.

7 Baste every 10 minutes until the veal is cooked through, approximately 1 hour.

8 Remove the lid from the braising pot and continue cooking for a further 30 minutes so that the liquid begins to reduce. Baste frequently so that the stock forms a glaze and coats the veal and vegetables.

9 Remove the veal from the braising pot and leave to rest for 5 minutes. Pass the sauce through a fine sieve and retain the vegetables to serve as part of the overall dish. Correct the seasoning and consistency of the sauce.

10 Cook the fettuccine in plenty of boiling salted water. Drain well in a colander and return to the pan with the olive oil and the chopped parsley, toss carefully until all the ingredients are well combined. Correct the seasoning as required.

11 Remove the string from the veal and carve against the grain. Serve coated with the sauce and accompanied by the vegetables and fettuccine.

Lardo, or strips of fat, to be larded

Larding the veal

Veal kidneys in a Dijon mustard and tarragon sauce

INGREDIENTS	4 PORTIONS	10 PORTIONS
Veal kidneys (skinned, trimmed and sliced in half)	400g	1kg
Vegetable oil for frying		
Chopped shallots	80g	200g
Butter	50g	130g
Brandy	30ml	80ml
Dry white wine	50ml	125ml
Double cream	250ml	700ml
Dijon mustard	3tbsp	8tbsp
Fresh chopped tarragon	4tsp	10tsp
Good-quality salt and white pepper	To taste	To taste

Method of work

1 Heat the oil in a shallow pan. Season the kidneys lightly and sauté for 3–4 minutes. The kidneys should be slightly coloured on the outside but still pink inside.

2 Tip the kidneys into a colander to drain.

3 Add the butter and the shallots and sweat for a few minutes without colour. Add the dry white wine and reduce by half. Add the brandy and reduce by half again.

4 Pour in the cream, bring back to the boil and reduce to a sauce consistency. Remove from the heat and stir in the mustard and fresh tarragon and season to taste.

5 Add the kidneys and carefully reheat the sauce without boiling.

6 Serve with braised rice.

Veal pojarskis with foie gras and Smitaine sauce

INGREDIENTS	4 PORTIONS	10 PORTIONS
Minced lean veal	400g	1kg
Fresh milk	200ml	600ml
Unsalted butter	60g	125g
Double cream	100ml	250ml
White breadcrumbs	100g	250g
Grated nutmeg	To taste	To taste
Good-quality salt and white pepper	To taste	To taste
Smitaine sauce		
Finely chopped onion	50g	125g
Butter	25g	70g
Dry white wine	80ml	200ml
Lemon juice	¼ lemon	½ lemon
Soured cream	300ml	700ml
Garnish		
Foie gras	100g	250g
Baby spinach, washed and picked	400g	1kg
Fresh chervil	4 sprigs	10 sprigs
Veal jus	4tbsp	10tbsp

CHEF'S TIP

The bread and milk mixture is called 'bread panade' and is used as a binding agent in meat-based galettes.

Method of work

1 Ensure that the minced veal has been passed through the mincer twice to break the protein down.

2 Soak the breadcrumbs in the milk for a few minutes and then squeeze out any surplus milk.

3 Add the breadcrumbs to the veal and mix well. Season with salt, pepper and nutmeg. Work in the cold double cream, a little at a time, using a spoon. Mix thoroughly and beat well.

4 Divide the mixture into equal portion sizes and mould into round discs about 3.5cm thick. Use some flour to help mould the shapes.

5 Heat the butter in a shallow pan and carefully place the pojarskis to shallow fry. Fry until golden brown on both sides and thoroughly cooked (up to 15 minutes approximately). To check, press the pojarskis gently – the juices should run out clear and with no sign of blood, indicating they are cooked through. Retain in a warm place for service.

6 To make the Smitaine sauce, place the chopped onion in a saucepan with the butter and sweat without colour. Drain off the excess fat and add the white wine, reduce by two-thirds.

7 Add the lemon juice and then the soured cream. Continue to reduce the sauce to a coating consistency. Season well and pass through a fine sieve. Keep hot.

8 In a separate shallow pan quickly seal and cook the foie gras on both sides, season and retain for service. Place the washed spinach in the same pan. Season well and cover with a lid, place on the side of the stove until the spinach is wilted. Drain any excess moisture in a colander.

9 To serve, spoon the spinach into a stainless steel ring placed in the centre of a serving plate. Remove the ring, position the pojarski on the spinach and place a slice of foie gras on top. Spoon over the veal jus and then the Smitaine sauce. Garnish with the chervil.

Osso bucco

INGREDIENTS	4 PORTIONS	10 PORTIONS
Slices of veal knuckle (shank) on the bone	4 × 300g	10 × 300g
Olive oil	40ml	100ml
Flour for dusting	30g	70g
Diced onion	100g	250g
Diced celery	75g	150g
Diced carrot	75g	150g
Chopped garlic	2 cloves	5 cloves
Tomato concassé	500g	1250g
Tomato purée	100g	250g
Dry white wine	400ml	1 litre
Veal stock	400ml	1 litre
Dried lemon skin	25g	60g
Dried orange skin	25g	60g
Good-quality salt and white pepper	To taste	To taste
Gremolata		
Chopped flat leaf parsley	1tbsp	2tbsp
Grated lemon zest	1 lemon	2 lemons
Lemon juice	½ lemon	1 lemon
Olive oil	25ml	70ml
Crushed garlic	1 clove	2 cloves
Good-quality salt and white pepper	To taste	To taste

Method of work

1 Preheat an oven to 180°C.

2 Dust the osso bucco veal slices with the flour and season well. Heat the olive oil in a shallow pan and add the veal slices, colouring on both sides.

3 Add the chopped onion, carrots, celery and garlic and continue to cook, with a lid placed firmly on the pan, for 3 minutes.

4 Drain any excess fat and add the white wine to deglaze the pan. Add the veal stock and the lemon and orange skin plus the tomato purée and bring to the boil.

5 Place the lid on the pan and place into the oven for 1½ hours to cook.

6 Add the tomato concassé and correct the seasoning. Return to the oven for a further 15 minutes.

7 Make the gremolata by combining all the ingredients together.

8 Correct the seasoning and consistency of the osso bucco and serve with a separate risotto and drizzled with the gremolata dressing.

 CHEF'S TIP

Osso bucco is a classic dish from Milan that is served with risotto but it can also be served with plain boiled rice or a crisp green salad. It has many regional variations. The name 'osso bucco' means a bone with a hole, describing the veal marrow bone with the meat on the outside.

Braised veal cheeks with sweetbreads

INGREDIENTS	4 PORTIONS	10 PORTIONS
Veal cheeks		
Trimmed veal cheeks	4	10
Diced carrot	100g	200g
Diced onion	200g	400g
Chopped garlic	4 cloves	8 cloves
Chopped celery	80g	160g
Bay leaves	3	6
Fresh thyme	4 sprigs	10 sprigs
Veal stock	1 litre	2.5 litres
Black peppercorns	8	20
Good-quality salt	To taste	To taste
Veal sweetbreads		
Veal sweetbreads (trimmed, blanched and pressed)	400g	1kg
Vegetable oil	50ml	125ml
Chopped onion	50g	100g
Diced carrot	50g	100g
Veal stock	200ml	550ml
Good-quality salt and white pepper	To taste	To taste
Buttered savoy cabbage		
Savoy cabbage	½ cabbage	1 cabbage
Butter	75g	150g
Finely chopped onion	100g	220g
Lardons of bacon	50g	120g
Light chicken stock	75ml	150ml
Good-quality salt and white pepper	To taste	To taste

CHEF'S TIP

The veal cheeks can be braised the day before and simply reheated in veal stock to serve. This gives the cheeks time to set and so they will be easier to cut or carve.

Method of work

1 Preheat an oven to 180°C.

2 Trim, roll and tie the veal cheeks. Place all the ingredients into a pan with the veal cheeks. Slowly bring to the boil and cover with a lid. Pull to one side of the stove and slowly braise until the cheeks have cooked (approximately 3 hours).

3 For the veal sweetbreads, heat some of the oil in a shallow pan. Season the sweetbreads and quickly seal on both sides. Remove from the pan and add the carrots and onion to sweat for 2 minutes. Place the sweetbreads on top of the vegetables and add the veal stock. Cover with a buttered cartouche of silicone paper and place in the oven for approximately 40 minutes, basting occasionally with the cooking liquor.

4 Wash, trim, stalk and slice the cabbage into thin strips. Add the butter to a saucepan to melt before adding the cabbage and the chopped onion and bacon lardons. Sweat the cabbage and then add the stock and season with salt and white pepper. Continue to slowly cook on the stove until the stock has reduced.

5 Remove the veal cheeks and strain the cooking liquor into a saucepan. Reduce the liquid to a coating consistency, correct the seasoning and reserve. Remove the string and slice the veal cheeks.

6 Place the cabbage in the centre of a serving plate and set the veal cheek next to it. Remove the sweetbreads from the oven, carefully slice and arrange on the plate before finishing with the reduced veal jus.

LAMB RECIPES
Roast rack of lamb with parsnip purée and garlic jus

INGREDIENTS	4 PORTIONS	10 PORTIONS
Best ends of lamb (prepared into racks)	2	3
Double cream	100g	250g
Butter	300g	800g
Romano potatoes	500g	1.25kg
Parsnips	500g	1.25kg
Garlic	8 cloves	20 cloves
Fresh thyme	8 sprigs	20 cloves
Chopped shallots	200g	500g
Brown lamb stock	2 litres	4.5 litres
Plum tomatoes	100g	250g
Olive oil	50ml	100ml
Fresh sage	2tsp	5tsp
Fresh chervil	4 sprigs	10 sprigs
Good-quality salt and white pepper	To taste	To taste

Method of work

1 Preheat an oven to 200°C.

2 Place the prepared racks of lamb into a pan and brush with olive oil. Chop half of the fresh thyme and sprinkle on the lamb, season well.

3 Place in the oven to roast for about 16–20 minutes until pink.

4 Cut the potato into discs 3.5cm in diameter and approximately 3cm thick. Slowly cook in two-thirds of the butter and sage and take out just before it is cooked. Make a hole all the way through the centre with an apple corer and keep warm to one side.

5 For the parsnip purée, peel, wash and cut the parsnips into quarters lengthways and discard the hard centres. Dice into cubes. Boil in salted water, and drain in a colander when cooked. Place on a baking tray and put into the oven to dry out. Pass through a sieve and finish with the remaining butter, double cream and seasoning. Reserve in a warm place.

6 Meanwhile make a provençale garnish by sweating off half the finely chopped shallot, two cloves of garlic and the remaining thyme. Add the de-skinned and de-seeded chopped plum tomatoes. Fill the centre of each piece of potato with this mixture.

7 Reheat the stuffed potato garnish in the oven.

8 For the garlic jus, reduce the lamb stock with the remaining cloves of crushed garlic. Correct the consistency and seasoning and reserve for service.

9 To serve, place the potato garnish slightly off centre, to the left of the plate. Pipe the purée lengthwise, adjacent to the garnish. Slice the lamb into two pieces and sit upright, garnish with the fresh chervil. Finish with the garlic jus.

Roast stuffed saddle of lamb with rosemary jus

INGREDIENTS	4 PORTIONS	10 PORTIONS
Saddle of lamb (boned)	1	2
Minced chicken	150g	300g
Chopped fresh tarragon	2tbsp	4tbsp
Egg whites	1	2
Double cream	75ml	150ml
Lamb or pig caul (crepinette)	1 sheet	2 sheets
Carrots	100g	250g
Onion	100g	250g
Celery	100g	250g
Leek	100g	250g
Brown lamb stock	1 litre	2.5 litres
Rosemary leaves	3tbsp	8tbsp
Balsamic vinegar	3tsp	7tsp
Red wine	80ml	200ml
Good-quality salt and white pepper	To taste	To taste

Stuffing the lamb saddle between the cannons

Folding over the flaps of the saddle to encase the stuffing

Method of work

1 Season the lamb well.

2 Mix the chopped tarragon with the minced chicken and place into a food blender. Add the egg whites while blending the ingredients then slowly add the cold double cream. Season well.

3 Place some of this stuffing in the centre of the two attached cannons in the saddle. Lay one of the detached fillets on top of the stuffing and cover the fillet with some more of the stuffing. Repeat with the second fillet and cover with the remaining stuffing.

4 Lift up one of the belly flaps and fold it over so that the cannons sandwich the fillets and stuffing in the middle. Repeat with the other side. Season well.

5 Rinse half the caul in cold water and then carefully lay on a board. Lay the saddle on the centre of the caul and bring the sides up to enclose it. Rinse the rest of the caul and lay it flat on the board. Position the saddle on the nearest edge of the caul and roll it up. Tuck in the flaps at each end. The saddle can be tied or roasted as it is.

6 Preheat an oven to 220°C.

7 Wash, peel and rewash the vegetables, chop and place into the bottom of a roasting pan.

8 Place the saddle to sear in a pan with some hot oil. Transfer to the roasting tray and roast in the oven for 30 minutes.

9 Remove the roasted saddle of lamb and allow to rest on a wire rack in a warm place.

10 Place the roasting pan on a hot stove and brown the vegetables further.

11 Add the vinegar, wine and the fresh rosemary to deglaze. Continue to cook on the stove for a further 3–4 minutes.

12 Add the stock to the roasting pan and deglaze.

13 Strain into a saucepan and reduce to the required consistency. Correct the seasoning.

14 Carve the lamb in thick slices and serve with the rosemary jus.

Rump of lamb with a wild mushroom sausage and Madeira jus

INGREDIENTS	4 PORTIONS	10 PORTIONS
Lamb rumps (off the bone, trimmed)	4 × 160g	10 × 160g
Boned shoulder of lamb	300g	750g
Fresh, cleaned wild mushrooms	50g	140g
Eggs	2	4
Double cream	100ml	230ml
Finely chopped shallots	50g	120g
Fresh chopped coriander	25g	60g
Fresh chopped parsley	25g	60g
Convenience sausage skins		
Good-quality salt and white pepper	To taste	To taste
Mint pesto dressing		
Toasted pine nuts	25g	60g
Olive oil	150ml	340ml
Fresh garlic cloves	2 small	4 small
Fresh mint	50g	100g
Fresh basil	25g	50g
Good-quality salt	To taste	To taste
Fig and onion marmalade		
Red onions, thinly sliced	125g	300g
Clear honey	25g	50g
Red wine vinegar	2tbsp	5tbsp
Red wine	3tbsp	6tbsp
Dried figs	25g	60g
Madiera jus		
Finely chopped shallots	50g	100g
Finely chopped garlic	1 clove	2 cloves
Fresh thyme	1 sprig	2 sprigs
Bay leaf	¼ leaf	½ leaf
Balsamic vinegar	1tbsp	2tbsp
Madeira wine	200ml	400ml
Strong brown lamb stock	400ml	800ml
Olive oil	1tbsp	3tbsp
Good-quality salt and white pepper	To taste	To taste

Method of work

1 Preheat an oven to 180°C.

2 Place a large shallow pan to heat on the stove and add a little oil.

3 Season the rumps of lamb and place into the hot fat, flat side down, to seal. Sear until golden brown on all sides. Place each lamb rump onto a roasting tray and place into the oven for 13 minutes.

4 For the wild mushroom sausage, place the diced shoulder of lamb, chopped shallots and seasoning into a food blender. Blend together until the meat resembles a farce. Add the eggs and blend further. Slowly pour in the cream while still blending. Add the chopped coriander and parsley and briefly blend together. Check the consistency and the seasoning of the sausage paste. Mix in the prepared, roughly chopped assorted wild mushrooms.

5 Pipe into the soaked sausage skins to create one sausage of approximately 100g per portion. Leave to rest for approximately 20 minutes in the refrigerator. To cook, place under a salamander, turning every few minutes until cooked through.

6 For the mint pesto, put the pine nuts, olive oil, garlic, fresh basil and fresh mint into a food processor and blend until a paste has been formed. Leave to one side and gently warm prior to service.

7 For the Madeira jus, heat the oil in a sauteuse and add the shallots, garlic, thyme and bay leaf and cook for about 4 minutes, stirring frequently. Add the vinegar and continue to cook until the liquid has evaporated, then deglaze the pan with the Madeira.

8 Cook rapidly to reduce by about three-quarters. Add the stock, reduce the heat and simmer for 15 minutes, removing any scum that appears. Pass twice through a muslin-lined sieve and correct the seasoning and consistency.

9 For the fig and onion marmalade, place the sliced onions, honey, vinegar and wine in a pan. Bring to the boil and gently simmer until the onions are soft. Add the figs and cook very slowly to a marmalade consistency. Reserve warm for service.

10 To serve, remove the rumps of lamb from the oven. Immediately wrap them individually in plastic film and rest for five minutes. Spoon the red onion marmalade in the centre of a serving plate. Remove the rumps of lamb from the plastic film and strain any collected juices into the Madeira sauce. Carve the lamb and arrange next to the marmalade. After having grilled the sausages, cut each one in half on a slant and place on top of the marmalade. Run the mint pesto over the sausage and the Madeira jus around the plate.

Roast shoulder of lamb with minted pea purée, celeriac boulangère and a bramble jus

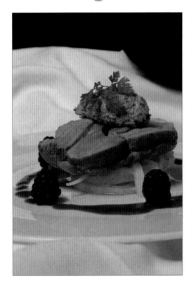

INGREDIENTS	4 PORTIONS	10 PORTIONS
Boned shoulder of lamb	1 × 2kg	2 × 2kg
Olive oil	4tbsp	8tbsp
Fresh rosemary	8 sprigs	16 sprigs
Garlic	4 cloves	8 cloves
Chopped shallots	100g	200g
Chestnut mushrooms	140g	280g
Chopped flat leaf parsley	50g	100g
Brioche crumbs	100g	200g
Butter	50g	100g
Good-quality salt and white pepper	To taste	To taste
Minted pea purée		
Finely chopped shallots	50g	150g
Fresh mint	4 stalks	10 stalks
Double cream	75ml	300ml
Garden peas (fresh or frozen)	400g	1kg
Good-quality salt and white pepper	To taste	To taste
Celeriac boulangère		
Celeriac	1.3kg	3kg
Sliced onions	200g	500g
Lamb stock	400ml	1 litre
Butter	150g	400g
Good-quality salt and white pepper	To taste	To taste
Bramble jus		
Strong lamb stock	450ml	1.2 litres
Finely chopped shallots	75g	200g
Pink peppercorns	10	26
Crème de cassis	75ml	200g
Blackberries	20	50
Red wine	75ml	200g
Unsalted butter	50g	125g
Good-quality salt and white pepper	To taste	To taste

Method of work

1   Preheat an oven to 200°C.

2   Trim the shoulder of lamb and process the trimmings in a blender until smooth. Gently fold in the chopped parsley. Season well. Sweat the shallots with the chopped chestnut mushrooms and, when cooled, add to the parsley mixture. Mix together the brioche crumbs and the softened butter.

3   Stuff the shoulder with the mixture and tie up. Rub with a little salt, pepper and olive oil. Make eight incisions in the shoulder, cut each clove of garlic in half and insert half a clove and a sprig of rosemary into each incision.

4   Heat a large roasting tray on the stove with a little of the oil and seal the prepared joint until brown on all sides. Remove from the pan and set aside.

5   For the celeriac boulangère, melt half of the butter in a shallow pan, add the sliced onions and cook without colour. Leave aside to cool down.

6   Slice the washed and peeled celeriac and place flat side down in a lightly buttered and seasoned baking dish. Place a layer of the cooked onions on top.

7   Repeat this process with a final layer of celeriac on top. Pour in the stock to just cover the celeriac and onions. Place slices of the remaining amount of butter on top with a final seasoning.

8   Position the shoulder of lamb on top of a wire rack and place this on top of the baking dish with the prepared celeriac boulangère.

9   Place in the oven for 30 minutes and then reduce the oven temperature to 150°C.

10 Baste every 15 minutes using the juices that drip into the celeriac. The lamb should be cooked after another 1 hour and 20 minutes. Remove the lamb and allow the joint to rest.

11 Finish baking the celeriac boulangère by turning the oven temperature back up to 200°C if required.

12 For the pea purée, cook the peas with the mint stalks in a little boiling water until tender, and refresh quickly to retain the colour.

13 Sweat the finely chopped shallots, adding the cream and seasoning.

14 Remove the mint stalks. When cooled slightly add the chopped mint and purée until smooth. Pass the mixture and reserve warm for service.

15 For the bramble jus, sweat the shallots then add the pink peppercorns and deglaze with the red wine and the crème de cassis. Reduce by half.

16 Add the stock and reduce to the correct consistency. Strain and correct the seasoning.

17 Poach the blackberries in the sauce gently for two minutes and remove for garnish. Whisk the butter into the jus and reserve warm for service.

18 To serve, arrange the celeriac boulangère onto the centre of a service plate. Carve the lamb to lay the slices on top.

19 Spoon the pea purée next to the lamb and serve the bramble jus with the blackberries around the plate.

Grilled rosettes of lamb paloise with gratin potatoes

INGREDIENTS	4 PORTIONS	10 PORTIONS
Prepared rosettes of lamb	12	30
Olive oil	4tbsp	8tbsp
Béarnaise sauce (made using chopped fresh mint in place of tarragon; see recipe on p. 93)	300ml	800ml
Fresh chopped mint	2tbsp	5tbsp
French beans	200g	500g
Parma ham	12 strips	30 strips
Unsalted butter	50g	120g
Good-quality salt and white pepper	To taste	To taste
Gratin potatoes		
Desiree potatoes	4	10
Double cream	250ml	700ml
Garlic	2 cloves	5 cloves

Method of work

1 Brush each rosette with oil and season well.

2 Wash, peel and rewash the potatoes. Slice each potato into three even slices. Using a plain pastry cutter, cut out circles of potato the same size as the rosettes.

3 Put the cream and crushed garlic into a pan. Bring to the boil and season. Place the potato discs into the cream and gently cook until soft.

4 Carefully remove the potatoes from the cream and place onto a baking tray, spoon a little of the cream over each potato and reserve.

5 Blanch the French beans and refresh in iced water. Evenly divide the beans between the portions required. Create three small bundles of the beans per portion and wrap each one in a strip of the Parma ham. Lay the bundles onto a tray and reserve.

6 Grill the rosettes until golden brown on the both sides and slightly pink in the centre.

7 Place the gratin potatoes in a preheated oven at 180°C while the lamb is cooking. Cook for approximately 6 minutes until lightly golden.

8 Warm the French beans in a small pan of simmering water, remove and brush with the melted butter.

9 To serve, place three gratin potatoes in a line on a service plate and lay a rosette on top of each. Then place a bundle of French beans on each rosette. Mix together the minted béarnaise sauce with the freshly chopped mint and spoon over each rosette. Finish with some fresh chervil.

 CHEF'S TIP

If required, remove the fat from the lamb rosette before grilling and slightly reduce the cooking time.

Cannon and faggot of lamb with Stilton dauphinoise

INGREDIENTS	4 PORTIONS	10 PORTIONS
Saddle of lamb	1 saddle	2½ saddles
Fresh rosemary	2 sprigs	5 sprigs
Sunflower oil	40ml	100ml
Lamb jus	300ml	850ml
Fresh thyme	2 sprigs	5 sprigs
Dry white wine	40ml	100ml
Lamb faggot		
Lamb liver	200g	600g
Lamb breast	100g	300g
Finely chopped onion	60g	180g
Butter	40g	80g
Fresh chopped parsley	2tbsp	6tbsp
Fresh chopped thyme	2tbsp	6tbsp
Garlic	1 clove	3 cloves
Whole egg	1 small egg	2 eggs
Wholemeal breadcrumbs	75g	225g
Pig's caul	4 sheets	10 sheets
Strong lamb stock	1 litre	2.5 litres
Good-quality salt and white pepper	To taste	To taste
Stilton dauphinoise		
Double cream	200ml	500ml
Fresh milk	100ml	275ml
Garlic	2 cloves	3 cloves
Desiree potatoes	3	6
Butter	25g	50g
Stilton cheese	100g	200g
Good-quality salt and white pepper	To taste	To taste

Method of work

1 For the lamb faggots, preheat an oven to 180°C. Finely chop the liver and breast of lamb and place in a saucepan with the chopped onion, garlic and the butter. Stew slowly for about 30 minutes with the lid on, do not colour the ingredients at this stage.

2 Strain off the fat and put the mixture into a bowl with the herbs and season well. Add the egg and combine all ingredients well.

3 Add enough breadcrumbs to make a mixture that will just hold together. Divide the faggot mixture into 60g pieces and wrap each in as little caul as possible to hold together. Shape into balls and put into an earthenware dish.

4 Pour the lamb stock over, enough to come half way up the faggots. Bake in the preheated oven for approximately 45 minutes until the faggots have a brown colouring. Reserve for service.

5 Remove the cannons from the saddle by cutting at the chine bone and following the bone with the knife until each cannon is released.

6 Carefully trim any silver membrane and fat. Remove the fillets and trim off any fat.

7 For the Stilton dauphinoise, place the cream, milk and garlic in a saucepan and bring to the boil. Remove from the heat and allow to cool.

8 Wash, peel and rewash the potatoes before slicing into 2mm thick slices. Butter an ovenproof dish and lightly season with the salt and pepper. Arrange the slices of potato over the base of the dish, slightly overlapping, and season each layer of potato.

9 Pour over the cream to cover the potatoes. Bake in an oven at 180°C for 30 minutes. Reduce the heat of the oven to 160°C and sprinkle the grated Stilton on top, cook for a further 15 minutes. Remove from the oven and set aside to rest.

10 Season and seal the cannons in hot oil in a shallow pan until browned on all sides. Place the cannons into the preheated oven for 6 minutes until the lamb is just pink inside, continually baste the cannon during the cooking process. Remove from the oven and allow the lamb to rest for 2–3 minutes.

11 Deglaze the shallow pan with the white wine and add the chopped fresh rosemary and thyme. Reduce by two-thirds and add the lamb jus. Bring back to the boil and adjust the consistency and seasoning, then pass through a fine chinois.

12 Cut the dauphinoise into rounds with a plain pastry cutter, one per portion, and set onto a service plate. Place a lamb faggot next the potato. Carve the cannons and place around the faggots. Serve with the rosemary jus.

 CHEF'S TIP

Dauphinoise potatoes were not traditionally made with cheese, however Emmental cheese is now usually used to add flavour.

Removing the cannons from the saddle

Removing the silver membrane

The prepared cannons ready for cooking

Fillet of lamb tapenade, mini shepherd's pie and garlic roasted root vegetables

INGREDIENTS	4 PORTIONS	10 PORTIONS
Prepared lamb fillets	2 × 400g	5 × 400g
Olive oil	40ml	100ml
Black olives	200g	500g
Anchovy fillets	50g	125g
Garlic	2 cloves	5 cloves
Pig's caul	4 sheets	10 sheets
Mini shepherd's pie		
Finely chopped onion	75g	225g
Finely diced carrot	50g	150g
Olive oil	40ml	100ml
Minced lamb	200g	600g
Lamb stock	100ml	350ml
Peas	50g	150g
Medium sized baked jacket potatoes	4	10
Butter	25g	100g
Fresh thyme	4 sprigs	10 sprigs
Garlic roasted root vegetables		
Carrot	1 large	3 large
Turnip	1 medium	2 medium
Swede	1 small	3 small
Celeriac	1 small	3 small
Button onions	16	40
Garlic	8 cloves	20 cloves
Olive oil	50ml	145ml
Rosemary and redcurrant jus		
Strong lamb stock	400ml	1 litre
Port	75ml	200ml
Chopped shallots	50g	145g
Redcurrants	40g	120g
Fresh chopped rosemary	1tbsp	2tbsp
Good-quality salt and white pepper	To taste	To taste

Trimming the fillets

Method of work

1 Bone the fillets and trim from fat and sinew. Preheat an oven to 180°C.

2 For the tapenade, put all the black olives and garlic in a pan with a little olive oil and sweat for 2 minutes. Place in a blender with the anchovy fillet and blend together with the seasoning to make a thick paste. Take it out and keep until required.

3 To prepare the lamb, lay the caul on a clean working surface and spread the tapenade evenly on the caul according to the width of the lamb fillets. Lay the lamb fillets on the caul and roll the caul around each fillet so that the tapenade is all around the lamb. Wrap the fillets in cling film as tightly as possible and put into a refrigerator for about 15 minutes.

4 Cook the fillets in a preheated steamer for approximately 12 minutes.

5 For the shepherd's pies, sweat the onion and carrot in a little olive oil. Add the minced lamb and season well. Add the lamb stock and peas and simmer for 5 minutes.

6 Spoon the potato out of their jackets and mash with the butter, chopped fresh thyme, salt and pepper. Grease small stainless steel rings (one per portion) and half fill with the minced lamb. Pipe the mashed potato on top and place into the oven for 15 minutes.

7 For the garlic roasted root vegetables, cut all the vegetables (except the onions) into 2cm cubes. Blanch each vegetable separately in boiling salted water. Place the olive oil in a sauteuse and heat on the stove, adding the blanched vegetables, garlic cloves and seasoning. Toss the vegetables for a few minutes before placing in the oven to roast for 15 minutes.

8 To make the sauce, reduce the lamb stock by half with the rosemary and in a separate pan reduce the port, redcurrants (washed and stalks removed) and chopped shallots by half. Add the rosemary stock and reduce until the correct consistency has been obtained. Pass through a fine chinois and correct the seasoning.

9 To serve, turn out the shepherd's pie at the top of the service plate and arrange a selection of the roasted vegetables at the bottom. Slice each lamb fillet and place slices on top of the vegetables. Pour the sauce around the plate and serve.

Cannon of lamb with basil mousse, pommes Anna, Provencal vegetables and tapenade sauce

INGREDIENTS	4 PORTIONS	10 PORTIONS
Cannon of lamb, trimmed to the eye	2	5
Crepinette	200g	500g
Diced chicken breast meat with the sinew and skin removed	125g	320g
Fresh sweet basil	1 bunch	3 bunches
Double cream	125ml	320ml
Sea salt	To taste	To taste
White pepper	To taste	To taste
Lemon juice	To taste	To taste
Gratin potatoes		
Desiree potatoes	4	10
Double cream	250ml	700ml
Garlic	2 cloves	5 cloves

Method of work

1. To prepare the chicken mousse, blend the chicken meat in a food blender and then pass it through a fine sieve. Take half of the fresh basil, blanch in boiling water for a few seconds and refresh in iced water, arrange on a clean kitchen cloth to drain and reserve to one side.

2. Beat in the double cream to the chicken meat whilst placing the bowl over ice to maintain the chilled temperature of the meat. The cream should be added slowly to prevent the mixture from splitting when cooked. Season well and chop the remaining fresh basil and fold into the mousse mixture.

3. Test the mousse for texture and seasoning by poaching a small quenelle in some water. Adjust the consistency and season if required and then place the mixture in a piping bag

4. Season and seal the lamb in hot oil in a pan and then chill quickly, when the lamb is cold pipe a 2cm layer of basil mousse on top of cannon.

5. Wrap the blanched basil leaves over the mousse and roll in the crepinette.

6. Heat some oil in a pan and carefully roll the cannon of lamb in warm oil and then place a knob of butter in pan. Place the cannon onto a small sheet of butter paper and roast in an oven at 180°C, basting occasionally until pink, and rest for a further 6 minutes.

INGREDIENTS FOR POMMES ANNA	4 PORTIONS	10 PORTIONS
Maris Piper potatoes	500g	1.2kg
Clarified butter	500g	1.2kg
Unsalted butter	10g	30g
Salt and white pepper	To taste	To taste

Method of work

1 Peel and carefully cut the potatoes into 2mm thick slices then cut into 1 inch discs, pat dry with kitchen paper. Do not place in water.

2 Warm the clarified butter to 80°C and place in the potatoes, gently heat until the potatoes are half cooked, this should take approximately 10 minutes, spoon out the potato slices and place onto grease proof paper.

3 Grease two 4-inch Anna moulds and chill them in a refrigerator.

4 Layer the half cooked potato slices in a rosette pattern in each mould, season well then repeat in the opposite direction with another layer. Repeat the process once more so that you have 3 layers in total.

5 Place the moulds on solid-top stove at a medium heat turning the potato occasionally until golden brown. Finally flip over and place 10g of unsalted butter in the centre and place in the oven for 5 minutes or until cooked all the way through.

6 Turn out and reserve for service.

INGREDIENTS FOR PROVENCAL VEGETABLES	4 PORTIONS	10 PORTIONS
Courgette, turned to 2.5cm size	1	3
Red pepper roasted peeled and cut into 2.5cm diamonds	½	1½
Yellow pepper roasted peeled and cut into 2.5cm diamonds	½	1½
Green pepper roasted peeled and cut into 2.5cm diamonds	½	1½
Baby aubergine, cut in half scored and roasted with olive oil, sea salt, bay leaf, thyme, garlic and black pepper, remove flavourings when cooked	2	6
Fresh plum tomatoes, blanched, peeled and cut in half. Deseed, toss in a little olive oil and place on a silicon mat upside down sprinkle chopped thyme, garlic and rosemary, a little sea salt, and dry in 100°C oven for 2–3 hours	2	6
Button onions, slowly cooked in a pan with a little oil until soft and glazed in their own caramelised juices	4	10
Black olives, stoned and cut into quarters	20g	50g
Lilliput capers	20g	50g
Olive oil		
Sea salt and black pepper		
Garlic	2 cloves	5 cloves

Method of work

1 Build up vegetables on top of aubergine and reheat though an oven at 160°C. Heat the olives and capers in olive oil and place on top of vegetables.

2 Garnish with deep fried basil leaf for service.

CHEF'S TIP

Lilliput capers are extra small and delicious; these tiny capers are packed with flavour. They are known as the highest quality available, and are indispensable as garnishes, tossed into salads, and is the basic ingredient for Pasta Puttanesque.

INGREDIENTS FOR THE TAPENADE SAUCE	4 PORTIONS	10 PORTIONS
Black Olives	100g	250g
Anchovies	20g	50g
Olive Oil	50ml	125ml
Garlic	1 clove	2 cloves

Method of work

1 Blend all the ingredients in a food processor until smooth. Check the consistency and seasoning. Warm the sauce for service.

To serve

Cut each cannon into 6 slices and place 3 slices per portion onto plate. Place the Pommes Anna and vegetables next to the lamb and spoon the sauce around.

Grilled lamb cutlet, lamb shoulder braised in Moroccan spices with courgettes, almond couscous and harissa jus

INGREDIENTS FOR LAMB CUTLET	4 PORTIONS	10 PORTIONS
Prepared and tied lamb cutlets	4	10
Olive oil	100ml	250ml
Crushed garlic	1 clove	3 cloves
Saffron	1 pinch	3 pinches
Freshly chopped rosemary	1g	3g
Fresh thyme	1 small sprig	3 sprigs
Fresh bay leaf – ripped	1	3

Method of work

1 Marinate all ingredients for 1 hour.
2 Remove lamb and wipe off excess oil, season with salt and pepper.
3 Quadrilage each side and cook until pink for about 2–3 minutes on each side.

INGREDIENTS FOR LAMB SHOULDER	4 PORTIONS	10 PORTIONS
Rolled and tied lamb shoulder	500g	1.25kg
Olive oil	50ml	125ml
Ground cumin	5g	12g
Ground coriander	2g	5g
Dried chilli flakes	1g	3g
Cinnamon stick	1	2
Crushed garlic	1 clove	2 cloves
Finely chopped onion	50g	125g
Chopped preserved lemon	1	2
Tomato purée	10g	25g
Cloves	3	8
Saffron	1 pinch	2 pinches
White pepper corns	6	16
Lamb stock	2 litres	5 litres
Salt and pepper		

Method of work

1   Brown the lamb in a hot pan using the olive oil. Remove and roll tightly in muslin cloth tying it at both ends.

2   In the same pan cook the onions and garlic until soft, add the spices and cook for a further five minutes.

3   Add tomato paste and cook out for 5 minutes, add the lamb stock and preserved lemons.

4   Place the lamb into the centre and bring to simmering point on the stove, cover with parchment and a lid.

5   Place in an oven, preheated to 150°C and braise for 2½–3 hours until tender.

6   Leave to cool slightly then remove from stock.

7   While the lamb is still warm cut into quarters, length ways and roll tightly in cling film to form a cylinder shape, place in a blast chiller until the meat has set.

8   Cut into 2.5cm discs and remove the cling film.

INGREDIENTS FOR HARISSA JUS	4 PORTIONS	10 PORTIONS
Braising liquor from lamb shoulder	Remainder from cooking process	Remainder from cooking process
Harissa paste	To taste	To taste
Salt	To taste	To taste
Pepper	To taste	To taste

Method of work

1   Pass liquor through muslin and reserve a third in a separate pan to reheat shoulder of lamb when required.

2   Reduce the remaining braising liquor to a coating consistency; add the Harissa to taste and season as required.

INGREDIENTS FOR ALMOND COUSCOUS	4 PORTIONS	10 PORTIONS
Pre-cooked couscous	100g	250g
Soaked golden raisins	25g	60g
Olive oil	50ml	125ml
Toasted almonds	25g	60g
Finely chopped shallots	10g	25g
Fresh, chopped coriander	1 small bunch	1 large bunch
Fresh, chopped mint	1 small bunch	1 large bunch
Lemon juice	To taste	To taste
Salt and pepper		

Method of work

1   Mix all ingredients together except the olive oil.
2   Reheat gently in a small pan with the olive oil.

INGREDIENTS FOR COURGETTES	4 PORTIONS	10 PORTIONS
Large green courgettes	2	5
Salt	2g	4g
Butter	10g	25g
Olive oil		

Method of work

1   Cut half of the courgettes lengthways into 5mm thick slices.
2   Brush with oil, season and chargill, reserve to one side.
3   Cut the other courgettes into 2.5cm lengths and then cut into quarters, turn into equal barrel shapes.
4   Place salt, butter and 2cm of water into a small sauce pan and bring to boil.
5   Add the turned courgettes and cover with a lid.
6   Cook rapidly for 2mins, remove from heat, drain excess liquid.

To finish

1   Place the shoulder on parchment paper into a small sauce pan adding the reserved cooking liquor.
2   Bring to boil and place into the oven at 180°C uncovered.
3   Baste every 2 minutes, for 10 minutes until a shiny glaze is reached.
4   Reheat the grilled courgette, place the couscous in an oiled 2.5cm metal ring, remove ring and wrap the courgette ribbon around.
5   Paint some glaze from the shoulder onto a service plate and place the couscous in the centre.
6   To the left; place the cutlet, to the right place the shoulder of lamb.
7   Sit the turned courgettes on top of the couscous.
8   Serve sauce separately.

PORK RECIPES

Honey glazed baked gammon with a peach compôte and piquant sauce

INGREDIENTS	4 PORTIONS	10 PORTIONS
Boned and rolled gammon joint	Allow 150g cooked gammon per portion	
Honey	100g	200g
Carrot	1 large	3 large
Onion	1 large	4 large
Bay leaves	3	6
Celery	2 large stalks	5 large stalks
White peppercorns	12	20
English mustard	20g	40g
Cloves	20	30
Peach compôte		
Fresh peaches (peeled and stone removed)	4	10
Sultanas	50g	100g
Ground cinnamon	½tsp	1tsp
Demerara sugar	50g	90g
Water	50ml	100ml
Piquant sauce		
Chopped shallots	25g	50g
White wine vinegar	40ml	75ml
White wine	40ml	75ml
Jus lie	400ml	800ml
Finely chopped gherkins	25g	50g
Finely chopped capers	15g	25g
Finely chopped fresh parsley	3tsp	1tbsp
Finely chopped fresh tarragon	1tsp	3tsp
Good-quality salt and white pepper	To taste	To taste

Method of work

1   Soak the prepared gammon joint for 24 hours in cold water in the refrigerator.

2   Preheat an oven to 185°C.

3   Remove the gammon joint and rinse in cold water. Place into a large saucepan and cover with cold water. Add the bay leaves, carrot, celery, white peppercorns and onion.

4   Bring to the boil and simmer. After 5 minutes skim the surface of impurities. Continue to simmer, allowing 1 hour per 1kg weight of meat plus an additional 30 minutes. To test if the gammon is cooked push a skewer or knife into the thickest part. There should be little resistance when the skewer is withdrawn.

5   Lift out the gammon and leave to cool for a few minutes.

6   Remove the rind and allow the joint to rest for 10 minutes, mix the mustard and honey and brush liberally over the gammon. Score the fat into diamonds using a sharp knife and push a clove into each diamond segment.

7   Place in a roasting dish and bake in the oven until deep golden brown. Baste the gammon with the pan juices from time to time.

8   For the peach compôte, cut the stoned and peeled peaches into large (3cm) dice and place in a saucepan with all the other ingredients. Slowly bring to the boil on a stove and turn the heat low to slowly cook the ingredients into a light compôte.

9   For the piquant sauce, place the shallots, white wine and vinegar into a small saucepan and reduce by two-thirds. Add the jus lie and reduce to a sauce consistency. Check the seasoning and add the gherkins, capers and herbs. Reserve for service.

10 Remove the gammon from the oven and dress on a platter for carving at the table, served with the sauce and compôte.

Fillet of pork with pea purée, herb noodles and sherry jus

INGREDIENTS	4 PORTIONS	10 PORTIONS
Butter	75g	150g
Trimmed pork fillet	2 × 300g	5 × 300g
Pea purée		
Finely chopped shallots	50g	150g
Fresh thyme	1 sprig	2 sprigs
Double cream	75ml	300ml
Garden peas (fresh or frozen)	400g	1kg
Good-quality salt and white pepper	To taste	To taste
Herb noodles		
Fresh noodle paste	350g	700g
Butter	50g	100g
Fresh chopped herbs (parsley, tarragon, chives and basil)	2tbsp	5tbsp
Sherry jus		
Olive oil	40ml	80ml
Finely chopped shallots	75g	150g
Chestnut mushrooms	75g	130g
Dry sherry	75ml	150ml
Madeira	50ml	100ml
Chicken stock	200ml	400ml
Veal jus	100ml	200ml

Method of work

1   Preheat an oven to 180°C.

2   Heat butter in a shallow pan, season the fillet and quickly brown on both sides. Place the pan into the oven to finish cooking for 15 minutes, basting the fillet continuously. Remove from the oven and rest for 5 minutes before finishing for service.

3   For the pea purée, cook the peas with thyme stalks in a little boiling water until tender. Refresh quickly to retain the colour.

4   Sweat the finely chopped shallots and add the cream and seasoning.

5   Purée the peas until smooth. Pass the mixture and reserve warm.

6   For the noodles, roll out the paste to a very thin rectangle using a pasta roller. Cut into 5mm wide strips and spread out onto a lightly floured tray and leave to dry for at least 30 minutes.

7   Place the noodles in a pan of boiling salted water and allow to simmer for 8 minutes. Drain in a colander. Melt the butter in a sauteuse, add the noodles and the herbs. Season well and toss until the herbs have fully mixed into the noodles. Reserve warm for service.

8   For the sherry jus, heat the oil in a saucepan and add the shallots and chestnut mushrooms and cook with a little colour. Add the sherry and Madeira and reduce by half. Add the chicken stock and veal jus and reduce by half again.

9   Pass through a fine chinois and correct the seasoning.

10 To serve, cut the fillet of pork on the slant into slices. Arrange slices on the plate, slightly overlapping each other. Garnish with the noodles placed to one side of the pork and the pea purée to the other. Spoon over the sherry jus.

Braised belly of pork with colcannon and cider sauce

INGREDIENTS	4 PORTIONS	10 PORTIONS
Pork belly	600g	1.5kg
Cider	320ml	800ml
Brown stock	160ml	400ml
Diced cooking apples	240g	600g
Demerara sugar	40g	100g
Butter	40g	100g
Diced onion	100g	250g
Mirepoix of carrot, celery and leek	200g	500g
Colcannon potatoes		
Maris Piper potatoes	250g	600g
Savoy cabbage	250g	600g
Leeks	100g	250g
Chives	2tbsp	4tbsp
Fresh milk	250ml	600ml
Butter	45g	100g
Good-quality salt and white pepper	To taste	To taste

Method of work

1 Remove the bone from the belly and singe any hairs with a flame.

2 Neatly trim the edges of the pork and then roll up the joint. Do not roll too tightly.

3 Starting in the centre, tie string around the joint. Repeat at 2.5cm intervals.

4 Preheat an oven to 180°C.

5 Season and sprinkle the belly of pork with the sugar. Heat a little oil in a hot pan (large enough to take the whole belly of pork) and place the belly of pork in the pan. Colour on each side until golden brown. Remove and set aside. Sweat the mirepoix and diced onion in the butter for 4 minutes without colour.

6 Place the mirepoix, diced cooking apples, pork, cider and stock in a covered pan and bring to the boil. Place in the oven and braise for 1½ hours. Check occasionally and add more stock or water as required.

7 Remove the lid and continue to cook for a further 1 hour, basting frequently.

8 Remove the pork and liquidise the cooking liquor. Pass through a fine chinois into a clean pan and correct the seasoning and consistency.

9 For the colcannon, shred the cabbage and cook quickly in boiling water. Drain in a colander. Cook and mash the potatoes. Slice the leeks and simmer in the milk until just cooked.

10 Mix in the potatoes, cabbage, chopped chives, butter and seasoning. Reserve for service.

11 Carve the pork belly, removing the string. Place slices onto a bed of colcannon potatoes and serve with a cordon of cider sauce.

Roast loin of pork with black pudding and apple, sage and onion foam

INGREDIENTS	4 PORTIONS	10 PORTIONS
Loin of pork joint	600g	1.5kg
Smoked pancetta	4 slices	10 slices
Butter	50g	100g
Braeburn apples	2	4
Chopped onion	50g	100g
Black pudding	200g	400g
Olive oil	25ml	50ml
Brown stock (beef, chicken or veal)	350ml	700ml
Good-quality salt and white pepper	To taste	To taste
Sage and onion foam		
Fresh sage leaves	1tbsp	2tbsp
Chopped onion	40g	80g
Garlic	1 clove	2 cloves
Chicken stock	200ml	400ml
Double cream	75ml	150ml

CHEF'S TIP

To achieve a successful crackling, ensure that there is a good layer of fat beneath the skin and that the skin has been evenly scored and well dried before roasting.

Method of work

1 Preheat an oven to 220°C.

2 Dry the pork skin with kitchen paper and leave to dry out for 20 minutes. Brush the skin lightly with the oil and season well with the salt and pepper.

3 Place into the preheated oven for 30 minutes and then reduce the temperature to 170°C. Occasionally baste the joint lightly. Allow 25 minutes per 500g of pork plus an extra 15 minutes cooking time.

4 For the sage and onion foam, sweat together the chopped onion, sage and garlic without colour. Add the chicken stock and reduce by half. Add the cream and bring back to the boil.

5 Place the mixture into a blender and liquidise until smooth. Pass through a fine sieve into a gas-charged canister and reserve at a temperature of 55°C. Charge the canister with the gas ready for service.

6 For the black pudding and apple, cut the apples into quarters and halve each quarter again. Discard the cores. Slice the black pudding into 5mm slices. Cut the pancetta into thin strips.

7 Warm the butter in a shallow pan until it begins to foam. Add the sliced black pudding and cook for 4 minutes. Remove the black pudding from the pan and reserve in a stainless steel bowl. Put the apple slices into the same pan and cook until a little colour has been achieved. Add the chopped onion and sliced pancetta and cook for a further 3 minutes. Finally, combine the black pudding with the apple mixture, season lightly and reserve warm for service.

8 When the pork is cooked, remove from the oven. Cover loosely with foil and rest for 20 minutes.

9 Allow the cooking juices and sediment from the pork to settle in the roasting tin, then drain off the fat without disturbing the sediment. Add the brown stock, bring to the boil and allow to simmer. Reduce to the correct consistency and season with a little salt if required. Pass through a fine chinois and skim off any remaining fat.

10 Using a sharp carving knife, remove the crackling from the loin of pork and cut the crackling into pieces. Carve the pork into slices. Serve each portion on a service plate with the crackling, black pudding and apple, sage and onion foam and the jus de rôti (roast gravy).

Pork and rabbit tourte with vegetable cream sauce

INGREDIENTS	4 PORTIONS	10 PORTIONS
Diced shoulder of pork	175g	350g
Skinned and boned rabbit	75g	150g
Smoked streaky bacon (rind removed)	25g	50g
Black pudding	50g	100g
Shredded suet	10g	20g
Brandy	50ml	100ml
Sherry	50ml	100ml
Fresh chopped thyme	½tbsp	1tbsp
Fresh chopped parsley	1tbsp	2tbsp
Fresh chopped sage	1tsp	2tsp
Puff pastry	250g	500g
Egg yolks (beaten for glaze with a drop of water)	1	2
Good-quality salt and white pepper	To taste	To taste
Vegetable cream sauce		
Carrot, leek, celery, red pepper cut into julienne	180g	350g
Fresh chopped chives	1tbsp	2tbsp
Dry white wine	50ml	100ml
Vegetable stock	125ml	250ml
Double cream	125ml	250ml
Good-quality salt and white pepper	To taste	To taste

Method of work

1   Cut the pork, rabbit, bacon and black pudding into small dice. Mix together in a plastic bowl with the suet. Add the brandy, sherry, herbs and seasoning. Cover with plastic film and leave to marinate in a refrigerator for 24 hours.

2   Drain off the marinade and place the ingredients into a blender. Blend into a farce or a finer texture. Test cook a small piece of the mixture in a frying pan to taste for seasoning.

3   Cut the puff pastry in half and pin out both pieces to approximately 3mm thick. Cut out 12cm discs (two per portion) and chill in a refrigerator for 1 hour.

4   Take approximately 100g of the meat mixture and roll to form a ball. Place in the centre of one puff pastry disc and brush around the edges with the beaten egg yolk. Cover with another disc of pastry and press the pastry discs together to form a seal. Trim the tourte with a 4cm plain cutter. Brush with the egg yolk mixture and chill in a refrigerator for 30 minutes. Brush once again with the egg glaze.

5   With the tip of a sharp knife, create curved shallow lines on the surface of the pastry. Preheat an oven to 180°c and bake the tourtes for 20–25 minutes, until the pastry is golden and well risen.

6   For the sauce, place the vegetable julienne into a saucepan with the white wine and slowly poach for a few minutes. Gradually reduce the wine before adding the stock. Reduce by half and add the cream. Bring to the boil and check the consistency and seasoning of the sauce. Add the chopped chives just before service.

7   Place a tourte into the centre of a service plate with the sauce spooned around.

Assessment of knowledge and understanding

You have now learned about the use of the different varieties of meat and how to prepare and cook different meat dishes.

To test your level of knowledge and understanding, answer the following short questions. These will help to prepare you for your summative (final) assessment.

Quality identifications

1 List three quality points you should check when receiving a veal delivery.

i) _____ ii) _____

iii) _____

2 State how marbling occurs in red meat and why it is important.

3 State why it is important to consider the traceability of meat products purchased from suppliers.

4 List four criteria for 'organic' products.

i) _____ ii) _____

iii) _____ iv) _____

Materials and storage

1 Explain the main benefit of hanging meat.

Preparation

1 Describe the method of preparation for a stuffed shoulder of lamb.

Cooking

1 Explain the reason for resting roasted meats prior to carving and serving.

2 Explain why meat should be browned or caramelised before being put into a stew.

Health and safety

1 List two safety points to observe when removing a heavy joint of meat from a hot roasting tray.

i) _____ ii) _____

2 Describe two safety procedures required when preparing a boned and rolled shoulder of pork.

i) _____ ii) _____

8

Advanced skills and techniques in producing poultry and game dishes (Unit 306)

LEARNING OUTCOMES

The aim of this chapter is to enable the candidate to develop the necessary advanced skills, knowledge and understanding of the principles in preparing and cooking poultry and game to dish specifications. The emphasis in this chapter is on developing precision, speed and control in existing skills and perfecting more refined and advanced techniques.

There are **two** outcomes to this chapter. At the end of this chapter the candidate will be able to:

■ Prepare poultry and game, cuts, joints and associated products
■ Produce poultry and game dishes, associated products and garnishes

INTRODUCTION

When we refer to poultry we describe birds specifically reared for the table. This includes chicken, guinea fowl, turkey, goose and duck.

Chicken (*poulet*)

Chickens are descendants from the pheasant family and originate from northern India and southern China.

From left to right – battery, organic and maize red chicken

In the UK, more than 90 per cent of chickens are battery reared. Because of intensive husbandry, the birds achieve slaughter weight at 6 weeks. The birds grow very quickly and live relatively short lives, and the meat is bland and can have a grainy texture.

Free range and especially **organic** chickens are allowed to forage in the open and have space to develop muscle and a stronger bone structure. The term 'free range' only means that the birds have access to an outdoor pen. There are several labelling systems in use for these birds, such as the Soil Association scheme. One British company has developed a system of labelling and rearing chickens similar to the French *Label Rouge*. 'Label Anglaise' shows that the chicken has been produced by farmers who use older breeds, such as Cornish Red and White Rock, and free range/organic methods of rearing:

- The diet consists of 70 per cent cereals, including maize
- No antibiotics, hormones or growth stimulators are used
- Slaughter after 81 days old.

The label is featured on menus and assures the customer that the chicken has been well reared and is flavoursome.

Corn-fed chickens are fed on a diet of maize or containing a proportion of maize. This does not guarantee any kind of quality assurance. The distinctive yellow colouring of the skin is often gained by the introduction of a yellow dye into the feed and not by the natural colour of the maize itself.

QUALITY POINTS

When buying chickens we should be able to identify the quality points associated with them:

- Clear skin with no blemishes and unbroken; the colour varies from breed to breed, but the most common battery-reared breeds – the hybrids, Ross and Cobb – have a pale creamy colour
- Flesh should be firm and pliable
- Not too much fat; check the abdominal cavity for excess
- No bruising, blood clots, ammonia sores on the legs or cuts
- The breastbone should be pliable (this is for younger birds that are destined to be grilled, roasted or sautéed)

PURCHASE SPECIFICATIONS

In general, older and larger birds will have a more pronounced flavour. However, organic poultry will ultimately have the best flavour, but it will be more expensive to purchase.

TYPE	AGE	AVERAGE WEIGHT
Poussin	Up to 6 weeks	250–400g
Spring chicken	6–8 weeks	1–1.25kg
Chicken	12–20 weeks	1–2kg
French Label Rouge	11.5 weeks	1–1.6kg
Capon (castrated male)	Up to 32 weeks	2–4kg
Boiling fowl	Up to 40 weeks	2–4kg

Bronze turkey

Turkey (*dinde*)

Turkeys are members of the pheasant family and were first domesticated by the Aztecs and Mexicans. They were introduced to Europe by the Spanish in the sixteenth century via Asia and became popular because of the delicate flavour of their meat. The term 'turkey' is thought to reflect the belief that they were imported from Turkey, at that time part of the vast Ottoman Empire.

The huge modern turkeys are mainly battery farmed. This practice originated in the late 1920s in British Columbia, when a breeder developed an 18kg bird with oversized leg muscles. This stock was used to perfect the more common Broad-breasted Bronze.

Once again, it is well worth spending time sourcing organic and free range birds, should budgets permit.

QUALITY POINTS

- Cock birds have a tendency to be drier and tougher than hens
- Bronze birds can have residual dark feather stubs; these can be removed with duck tweezers
- The flesh should be dry to the touch and without excess blemishes
- If the windpipe is still intact, it should be pliable and not rigid
- The breast should be plump in intensively reared birds and slightly leaner in the rarer organic varieties

Turkey is available in many weights, ranging from 4kg to 15kg. The Broad-breasted White turkey is the most common in today's marketplace and has a white, smooth and generally unblemished skin. Bronze turkeys are so called because of their distinctive plumage. Both Norfolk Black and Cambridge Bronze turkeys are worth looking out for as most of these birds are raised using traditional non-intensive farming methods. This means they take longer to mature, which contributes to a better overall flavour.

Duck (*canard*)

Duck is a web-footed water fowl, originally domesticated by the Chinese about 2000 years ago. It is highly appreciated for its rich moist meat. The common duck is the wild mallard, which is native to the northern hemisphere. The Barbary duck is a descendant of the Muscovy duck of Central and South America.

Norfolk duck

The type and breed of duck should be taken into account when purchasing. Barbary duck yields excellent suprême portions while Aylesbury is ideal for roasting. Gressingham duck has a good flavour due mainly to the fact that the birds are slaughtered at an older age. It is also smaller than the other ducks. Nantais duck is a traditional French breed that is becoming fewer in number.

Ducks are usually slaughtered from 6 to 16 weeks. Strictly speaking, the term 'duck' is applied to birds that are more than two months old; the younger birds are called 'ducklings'.

QUALITY POINTS

General

- Pale skinned and undamaged (except with wild varieties)
- Feet and bills should be brightly coloured
- Fresh pleasant smell
- Moist but not sticky
- Free from bruises, feathers and blemishes

Breeds

- Aylesbury – a small bird with white feathers and delicate flesh
- Gressingham – a cross between a domesticated duck and a mallard, a highly prized breed with a low fat content and rich flesh
- Norfolk – from the county of Norfolk, a domesticated fowl with similar attributes to Aylesbury
- Lincolnshire – as Norfolk, a common duck with similar attributes to Aylesbury
- Barbary – firm lean flesh with a strong flavour
- Nantais – small and slightly fatty with delicate flesh
- Rouennais – a larger duck than the Nantais, similar to the Aylesbury

Guinea fowl (*pintade*)

This is an excellent alternative to battery-farmed chicken in that the flesh is comparable to organic free range chicken. It can have a tendency to be dry so care must be taken when cooking. All recipes that apply to chicken also apply to guinea fowl. The meat has a more pronounced flavour and the birds are usually aged between 10 and 15 weeks before they are slaughtered.

Goose (*oie*)

Goose has a rich dark flesh with a copious covering of fat which means that it will very rarely dry out during cooking. They can weigh anything from 2.5kg to 12kg, depending on whether or not they were used for the production of foie gras. Goose should have the same quality points as duck. When not in season it can be purchased frozen. Geese are usually aged between 24 and 28 weeks at slaughter.

Poultry offal (giblets)

The giblets of poultry have many uses and can be essential in the preparation of many dishes. Although most poultry is purchased without giblets, they are still available from good suppliers. With correct storage and when used as fresh as possible they will enhance your repertoire of poultry dishes.

POULTRY OFFAL	USES
Livers	Garnishes, pâtés, terrines, stuffings, sautés; foie gras is the liver of specially fed ducks and geese
Cockscombs and kidneys	Classic garnishes such as favourite, Chevalière and Tivoli
Hearts	Stocks, consommés and salade Périgourdine
Necks	Stocks and consommés
Gizzards	Stocks, stews and pies
Winglets	Garnishes, boned and stuffed for braising

White meat and dark meat

The differences between white and dark meat are due to the work performed by the various muscles. Leg muscles contain more fat than breast meat, and even in intensive rearing they get used and exercised. The result is that they are more grainy and tougher in texture. The leg muscles use oxygen to burn fat to generate energy, and myoglobin – a reddish brown protein – stores the oxygen in the muscles. The extra myoglobin and fat in the legs accounts for the slightly stronger flavour and darker colour of the meat.

White meat from the breast and in battery-reared poultry is muscle that is seldom used. These muscles use glycogen – a form of sugar – as a source of energy. Glycogen does not need oxygen or fat, therefore there is a lack of myoglobin and very little fat in the breast meat.

THE STORAGE OF POULTRY

Poultry is a highly perishable commodity and so requires careful storage control. Fresh and chilled birds should be placed on clean trays in single layers, not stacked on top each other. The optimum storage temperature range is 1–5°C. Poultry should be used as quickly as possible, but at least within three days. Refrigeration leaves the poultry relatively unchanged from its fresh condition; both bacteria and meat enzymes become less active at lower temperatures thus slowing down spoilage.

The modern practice of vacuum packing butchered poultry and meat has the economic advantages of reduced storage space and a longer shelf life. It stores well because the raw protein does not have prolonged exposure to oxygen and therefore the fatty elements do not break down as quickly. Oxygen in the air and direct light will cause the flesh to become a dull colour and will slowly change the flavour.

The freezing of poultry greatly extends storage life because all biological processes are halted. Frozen poultry must be kept in a deep freeze until required and must be completely thawed before being cooked. Freezing immobilises the liquid/water content and therefore the meat will continue to be preserved so long as a temperature of –18°C is maintained. It is advised that 24 hours is allowed when defrosting poultry in a refrigerator. Wrapped poultry can be quickly defrosted in an iced water bath, which keeps the surface of the flesh safely cold.

HEALTH AND SAFETY

Salmonella and *E. coli* are always a cause for concern when dealing with poultry. All safety procedures must be adhered to, from the receiving of deliveries to the service of finished dishes.

Salmonella causes more serious food-borne diseases in Europe than any other microbe. It often has no effect on the animal carriers, but in humans it can be the cause of chronic infection and sickness. A particular strain of *E. coli*, named 0157:H7, can cause kidney failure, especially in children and the elderly.

To help prevent bacterial infection from poultry, it should always be assumed that all meat and poultry is infected with at least some bacteria. Measures must be taken to prevent cross-contamination; all hands, knives, chopping boards and workbenches used in preparation must be cleaned thoroughly with hot soapy water. *E. coli* is killed at 68°C. At this temperature the protein content in poultry and meat will denature and coagulate, any connective tissue will begin to dissolve and the flow of protein bound water (meat juices) will stop.

PREPARATION TECHNIQUES

It should be noted that the structures of the different types of poultry birds are very similar and therefore the various preparation techniques can be transferred between the different varieties.

Preparation of spatchcock and crapaudine

Spatchcock and crapaudine can be prepared from a single poussin, double poussin or a spring chicken. The cooking method used is grilling, which dictates the tenderness of the bird.

Spatchcock

Pluck any remaining feathers

Singe using a flame

Remove the wishbone

Using a poultry scissors, cut either side of the backbone between the hip joints and the shoulder joints

Open the bird up and place in onto a board

Skewer across each end, between each wing and then between each drumstick

Alternatively, skewer diagonally across the bird

Crapaudine

After plucking, singeing and removing the wishbone, cut under the breast but above the legs, almost to the neck of the bird

Pull open the bird and lay it onto a board

Press the bird onto the board

Force a skewer between each wing

Finally, force a skewer between each leg

VIDEO CLIP
Removing the breast from guinea fowl

VIDEO CLIP
Guinea fowl ballotine

VIDEO CLIP
Removing legs from a guinea fowl

VIDEO CLIP
Galentine of chicken

RECIPES

Spatchcock poussin Lyonnaise

INGREDIENTS	4 PORTIONS	10 PORTIONS
Poussin	4 × 300g	10 × 300g
Pommery grain mustard	150g	375g
Fresh breadcrumbs	400g	1kg
Unsalted butter	100g	250g
White chicken stock	100ml	250ml
Double cream	200ml	500ml
Tarragon	¼ bunch	½ bunch
Tomato concassé	50g	125g
Red onion	50g	125g
Good-quality salt and pepper	To taste	To taste

Method of work

1. Check that the poussin meets with quality standards. Spatchcock each poussin by splitting, flattening and securing with two skewers.
2. Season and **seal** in a hot pan.
3. Coat the poussin with half the mustard, leave for 30 minutes.
4. Melt the butter. Roll the poussin in breadcrumbs, sprinkle with the melted butter and grill until cooked.
5. Add the tarragon stalks to the stock and reduce by half. Add the double cream and remaining grain mustard then reduce by half again.
6. Pass through a chinois. Add chopped tarragon and correct the seasoning.
7. Mix the concassé with the finely chopped red onion, olive oil and seasoning and place on the chicken.
8. Serve sauce separately.

CHEF'S TIP

Care should be taken when grilling with breadcrumbs. Always ensure that the breadcrumbs are well soaked with butter to keep them moist. The majority of the butter will leave the breadcrumbs as they crisp up.

Royale of chicken purée

INGREDIENTS	4 PORTIONS	10 PORTIONS
White chicken meat	100g	250g
Béchamel sauce	50ml	125ml
Double cream	200ml	500ml
Egg yolks	6	15
White chicken stock	200ml	500ml
Tomato concassé	50g	125g
Chervil	¼ bunch	½ bunch
Tarragon	¼ bunch	½ bunch
Butter	50g	125g
Potato and parsley wafer	4	10
Good-quality salt and pepper	To taste	To taste

Method of work

1 Poach the white chicken meat then purée in a food processor.
2 Add the béchamel and half the double cream then pass through a drum sieve.
3 Bind with the yolks and season well. Place the mixture into buttered dariole moulds.
4 Place into a bain marie so the water comes half way up the sides of the dariole moulds and cook in the oven at 200°C for 15–20 minutes.
5 Reduce the chicken stock by half. Add the remainder of the cream and reduce by half again.
6 Pass the sauce and correct the seasoning. Add the tomato concassé, chopped tarragon and chervil.
7 Serve the royale on a heated plate with the sauce.
8 Arrange a potato and parsley wafer on top of the royale.

Chicken soufflé with thyme sauce

INGREDIENTS	4 PORTIONS	10 PORTIONS
Pot-roasted chicken	250g	625g
Thick chicken velouté	150ml	375ml
Egg yolks	3	8
Egg whites	3	8
Butter	100g	250g
Double cream	25ml	65ml
Light chicken jus	200ml	500ml
Chopped thyme	1tbsp	2½tbsp
Good-quality salt and pepper	To taste	To taste

Method of work

1 After pot roasting the chicken (with onion, carrot, celery, thyme and garlic with a splash of white wine at 180°C for 1 hour 15 minutes in a casserole with a tight-fitting lid), remove the chicken and strain the cooking liquor, which will be used to make the velouté.
2 Make a chicken velouté.
3 Remove the chicken skin and discard, remove all meat and place in a food processor until finely chopped.
4 Add the velouté and double cream, mixing well.
5 Add the yolks one by one and pass through a drum sieve using bowl scraper or wooden mushroom. Correct the seasoning.
6 Whisk the egg whites until stiff, then gently fold into the chicken mix.
7 Three-quarters fill buttered **ramekins** and bake in a hot oven, 200°C for 20 minutes.
8 Heat the chicken jus. Add the thyme and allow to infuse for 10-15 minutes. Remove the thyme.
9 Serve immediately with thyme chicken sauce.

Glazed duck breasts with sesame pak choy, crispy potato and enoki mushrooms

INGREDIENTS	4 PORTIONS	10 PORTIONS
Duck breasts	4 × 170g	10 × 170g
Honey	20ml	50ml
Soy sauce	4tbsp	10tbsp
Pak choy	400g	1kg
Sesame oil	2tbsp	5tbsp
Sesame seeds	1tbsp	3tbsp
Enoki mushrooms	100g	250g
Potatoes	400g	1kg
Good-quality salt and pepper	To taste	To taste

Method of work

1 Trim and **score** the duck breasts, **sear** skin-side down in a dry pan until coloured and the majority of fat has rendered down.

2 Pour away the fat, turn the duck over and drizzle with honey, place into a hot oven 180°C for 7 minutes, remove and rest.

3 Peel, grate and wash potatoes. Form into patties, season and deep fry until crisp.

4 Cut the pak choy into quarters and cook in sesame oil with the mushrooms, add the sesame seeds when nearly finished.

5 Arrange the pak choy and mushrooms on the plate and pour the liquid over.

6 Cut the duck in slices and lay on top, overlapping slightly.

7 Finish with crispy potatoes.

Stuffed chicken breast with sun-blushed tomatoes and olive mash

INGREDIENTS	4 PORTIONS	10 PORTIONS
Chicken suprêmes	4 × 170g	10 × 170g
Sun-blushed tomato	100g	250g
Parmesan	50g	125g
Mashed potato	400g	1kg
Black olives	3tbsp	7tbsp
Assorted peppers	½ of each	1 of each
Button onions	12	40
Baby asparagus	8	20
Baby fennel	4	10
Olive oil and tomato reduction	6tbsp	15tbsp
Good-quality salt and pepper	To taste	To taste

Method of work

1 Chop the sun-blushed tomatoes and mix with a little grated Parmesan then place the mixture under the skin of the chicken suprêmes.

2 Season the chicken and wrap in cling film to form cylindrical shapes then chill.

3 Warm the mashed potato and add chopped black olives and the remaining Parmesan.

4 Cut the peppers into diamonds and blanch, blanch the asparagus and cut into lozenges, peel and roast the button onions, trim the fennel and blanch.

5 Make a reduction by boiling a few sun-blushed tomatoes per person in olive oil until very soft then liquidise.

6 Cook the chicken in a saucepan of water for approximately 10 minutes. Remove from the cling film and fry in butter until golden.

7 Pipe the mashed potato onto the plate. Slice the stuffed chicken and arrange overlapping. Finish with the vegetables tossed in hot butter and the reduction.

Suprême of duck en croute with spinach

INGREDIENTS	4 PORTIONS	10 PORTIONS
Duck breasts	4 × 170g	10 × 170g
Puff pastry (10cm × 10cm)	5 sheets	13 sheets
Butter	100g	250g
Baby spinach	200g	500g
Fresh cranberries	50g	125g
Duck jus	200ml	500ml
Caster sugar	10g	25g
Red wine	50ml	125ml
Oranges	1	3
Eggs	1	3
Good-quality salt and pepper	To taste	To taste

Method of work

1 Trim the duck breasts and remove the fat, then seal in a hot pan all over. Chill and season.

2 Take three-quarters of the rolled out puff pastry and wrap thinly around the duck. Brush with beaten egg.

3 With the remainder of the puff pastry, form a trellis and wrap around the outside, brush again with beaten egg.

4 Chill for 30 minutes.

5 Bake the duck at 170°C for 25 minutes. Remove from the oven and rest for 5 minutes.

6 Heat the cranberries and add the zest of the oranges then add the sugar. Deglaze with red wine and orange juice, reduce then add the jus.

7 Wilt the spinach in butter and season.

8 Place the spinach on the plate, duck on top and cranberry jus around.

Roast Barbary duck breast glazed with honey and five spice, confit chestnuts, glazed button onions and baby carrots, red wine sauce

BILL HULL

INGREDIENTS	4 PORTIONS	10 PORTIONS
Barbary duck breasts	4	10

Method of work

1 Trim sinew and feather stubs from breasts.

2 Place back in the fridge to harden fat, score fat with sharp knife.

3 Season well with salt and pepper, place skin side down in warm frying pan, no extra oil.

4 Render fat slowly then increase temperature, cook skin side down until golden brown for about 6 minutes.

5 Seal flesh side gently then place back on skin side and finish in 180°C oven for 3–4 minutes.

6 Place on cooling rack and rest for 10 minutes.

Glaze

INGREDIENTS	4 PORTIONS	10 PORTIONS
Manuka honey	100ml	250ml
Five spice	5g	12g
Red wine vinegar	15ml	35ml

Method of work

1 Dry roast the five spice, add vinegar and reduce until dry.

2 Add honey, bring to boil and simmer for 2 minutes.

3 Keep warm.

Confit chestnuts

INGREDIENTS	4 PORTIONS	10 PORTIONS
Peeled chestnuts	12	30
Duck fat	150ml	400ml
Sprig of thyme	1	2
Small bay leaf	1	2
Salt	5g	12g
White peppercorns	6	15

Method of work

1 Melt duck fat in a small heavy bottomed pan and add all ingredients.

2 Cover with parchment and tight fitting lid.

3 Bring to simmering point, place in 160°C oven for 45 minutes or until soft.

Glazed button mushrooms

INGREDIENTS	4 PORTIONS	10 PORTIONS
Peeled button onions	12	30
Castor sugar	5g	12g
Unsalted butter	5g	12g
Salt	2g	5g
Water		

Method of work
1 Place onions in a pan that is just big enough for the onions to fit in one layer.
2 Add butter, salt and sugar.
3 ¾ cover with water and a cartouche, cut a small hole in the middle.
4 Place over high heat and boil rapidly, shake the pan occasionally.
5 When water has evaporated remove cartouche and let the sugar and butter caramelise lightly.
6 Roll the onions to brown evenly, tip onto grease proof paper.

Baby carrots

INGREDIENTS	4 PORTIONS	10 PORTIONS
Baby carrots turned to 1½ inch in length keeping part of the stalk	12	30
Castor sugar	5g	12g
Unsalted butter	5g	12g
Salt	2g	5g
Water		

Method of work

Repeat as for onions.

Pomme purée
See recipe page 270.

Red wine sauce

INGREDIENTS	4 PORTIONS	10 PORTIONS
Duck bones chopped into small pieces	250g	600g
Shallots finely sliced	50g	125g
Clove garlic crushed	1	2
Small bouquet garni	1	2
Duck fat	50ml	125ml
Red wine	350ml	700ml
Ruby port	150ml	400ml
Demi glace	350ml	700ml
Lemon juice	To taste	To taste
Unsalted butter	25g	60g
Seasoning		

Method of work

1 Heat duck fat in a heavy bottomed pan until smoking, add duck bones and caramelise until golden brown.
2 Tip out bones and degrease pan, add shallots and garlic, lightly colour.
3 Place bones back with aromats, add red wine, reduce by two thirds.
4 Add demi glace, reduce until coating consistency is reached skimming regularly.
5 Pass through muslin, place in clean sauce pan reheat and monter au beurre.
6 Season with salt, pepper and lemon juice.

To finish

1 Reheat chestnuts, onions and carrots.
2 Brush glaze onto skin of cooked duck breasts and place under a hot grill until caramelised and hot.
3 Cut duck breasts into 6 equal pieces.
4 Place hot pomme purée in a piping bag, pipe into centre of a bowl.
5 Arrange carrots onto purée.
6 Place duck around the purée and place the chestnuts and onions alternately between duck pieces.
7 Sauce around duck and garnish with picked chervil.

Guinea fowl breast with mustard cream, pancetta and oyster mushrooms

INGREDIENTS	4 PORTIONS	10 PORTIONS
Guinea fowl suprêmes	4 × 170g	10 × 170g
White chicken stock	200ml	500ml
Double cream	200ml	500ml
English mustard	40g	100g
Mashed potato	300g	750g
Onions	200g	500g
Oyster mushrooms	100g	250g
Pancetta	40g	100g
Creamed horseradish	1tbsp	2tbsp
Butter	50g	125g
Olive oil	20ml	50ml
Flat leaf parsley	4 leaves	10 leaves
Good-quality salt and pepper	To taste	To taste

CHEF'S TIP

Vary the type of mushrooms used, e.g. chanterelle, shitake, cep or morel. The delicacy of guinea fowl is enhanced by wild mushrooms.

Method of work

1 Cut the pancetta into lardons. Season the suprêmes and pan fry with the pancetta. Place in the oven 180°C for 10–12 minutes.
2 Add the chicken stock and reduce by half. Add the double cream and reduce again by half, add the horseradish and mustard. Correct the seasoning, consistency and pass.
3 Remove from the oven and set the guinea fowl and lardons to one side to rest.
4 Sauté the oyster mushrooms in butter.
5 Finely dice the onions and sweat in olive oil until transparent. Mix with the mashed potato and, using a little flour, form small cakes. Shallow fry until golden.
6 Arrange a potato cake on the plate. Slice the guinea fowl and lay on top. Spoon sauce around and finish with lardons, mushrooms and flat leaf parsley.

Breast of duck, duck faggot and confit with jasmine sauce

INGREDIENTS	4 PORTIONS	10 PORTIONS
Butter	50g	125g
Small ducklings (1kg)	2	5
Clear honey	2tbsp	5tbsp
Finely diced onion	100g	250g
Veal jus	125ml	300ml
Garlic, finely chopped	1 clove	2 cloves
Pearl barley	20g	50g
Fresh thyme	1 sprig	3 sprigs
Fresh parsley	1 small bunch	2 small bunches
Bay leaf	1	2
Duck livers	2	5
Duck hearts	2	5
Pig's caul	4 good pieces	10 good pieces
Veal stock	1000ml	2500ml
Finely diced carrots	50g	125g
Chopped shallots	50g	125g
Diced leeks	50g	125g
Red wine	100ml	250ml
Lime juice	¼ lime	½ lime
Blanched pistachio nuts	40g	100g
Sultanas marinated in jasmine tea	40g	100g
Sea salt and black pepper	To taste	To taste
Fondant potatoes	4	10
Red onion marmalade	40g	100g
Savoy cabbage parcels	4	10

CHEF'S TIP

Add a little chicken forcemeat to the farce to bind it and make carving easier.

Method of work

1 Cook the pearl barley by bringing to the boil in salted water and cooking for 1 hour. Refresh immediately. Sweat the onions and garlic in some vegetable oil. Add the veal jus to cover the onions and garlic. Allow to reduce. Remove from the heat and allow to cool.

2 Mince the livers, hearts and thigh meat from the duck legs. Add to the reduction and incorporate the chopped fresh herbs. Season well. Fold in the cooked pearl barley. Wrap in pig's caul, creating one faggot per portion. Allow the faggots to rest in a refrigerator for at least 30 minutes before cooking. Colour the faggots in fat taken from the duck and then braise in the veal stock until just cooked.

3 Prepare the remaining legs into small ballotines. Stuff the legs with the pistachio nuts and sultanas that have been marinated in jasmine tea for 12 hours. Tie with string to keep the stuffing inside. These can now be braised and reserved in a warm place for service.

4 Remove the duck breasts from the carcasses and score the skin.

5 Fry the vegetables and the broken down duck carcasses. Drain off any excess fat. Place in a pan and cover with cold water. Add thyme, bay leaf and parsley stalks. Allow to simmer for 2 hours, strain, and bring back to the boil. Incorporate the braised faggot cooking liquor. Add the red wine.

6 Add the lime juice and bring back to boil. Adjust the consistency and the seasoning.

7 Season the duck breasts and fry with the skin side down until rendered and coloured. Brush warmed honey on the skin side and turn over to finish, cooking until golden brown and the breasts are still pink. Leave to rest in a warm place.

8 Carve each rested duck breast into thin slices and allow any juices to drain. Arrange on a plate with the red onion marmalade. Place the faggot on top of a cabbage parcel.

9 Take the ballotines and arrange on top of the fondant potato, check the seasoning and consistency of the sauce before serving.

Breast of duck with redcurrants and armagnac

INGREDIENTS	4 PORTIONS	10 PORTIONS
Butter	50g	120g
Duck breasts	4 × 200g	10 × 200g
Port wine	200ml	425ml
Redcurrant jelly	1tbsp	3tbsp
Fresh redcurrants	50g	125g
Jus lie	200ml	425ml
Lemon juice	A few drops	A few drops
Armagnac	2tbsp	5tbsp
Cocotte potatoes	12	30
Savoy cabbage parcel	4	10
Good-quality salt and pepper	To taste	To taste

Method of work

1 Heat the butter in a sauté pan. Season the duck breast well. Seal and colour the duck breasts on both sides in the hot butter and place into a hot oven, occasionally **basting** each breast with the fat. Cook for 8–9 minutes so that the breasts are cooked 'pink'. Remove from the oven, keep covered and warm and allow to rest.

2 Drain the fat from the pan. Add the port wine and reduce by three-quarters.

3 Add the redcurrant jelly and allow to melt. Add the Jus lie and bring slowly to the boil.

4 Adjust the consistency and seasoning and finish with lemon juice.

5 At the last moment add the redcurrants. Cover the sauce and keep warm for service.

6 Carve each duck breast into thin slices and allow any residual juices to drain. Arrange on a plate, overlapping slightly.

7 Add the Armagnac to the sauce, check the seasoning and consistency and spoon some over the duck. Serve with the cocotte potatoes and cabbage parcels.

Duckling with sherry vinegar sauce

INGREDIENTS	4 PORTIONS	10 PORTIONS
Ducklings	2	5
Vegetable oil	20ml	50ml
Chopped carrots	50g	100g
Chopped onions	50g	100g
Tomato concassé	40g	80g
Chopped celery	25g	50g
Garlic	2 cloves	4 cloves
Coriander seeds	½tsp	1tsp
Peppercorns (coarsely crushed)	½tsp	1tsp
Bouquet garni	1	1
Sherry vinegar	25 ml	50ml
Dry white wine	15ml	25ml
Chicken stock	1.25 litres	2.5 litres
Tomato purée	¼tsp	½tsp
Sea salt	1tsp	2tsp
Dijon mustard	½tsp	1tsp
Butter	40g	80g
Good-quality salt and pepper	To taste	To taste

Method of work

 CHEF'S TIP

Remove any white sinew from the duckling suprêmes. This will minimise any distortion during roasting.

1 Check the ducklings for quality. Remove the suprêmes and legs and keep refrigerated before use. Reserve the legs for later use. Chop the carcasses.

2 Heat the vegetable oil in a large casserole. Add the duck carcasses, wings and necks and brown over a moderate heat, stirring frequently. Cook for approximately 15 minutes. Lift the pieces of duck out of the casserole and remove all excess fat.

3 Place the pieces of duck back into the casserole with the carrot, onion, celery, tomato, garlic, coriander seeds, peppercorns and bouquet garni. Cook over a moderate heat for 3–4 minutes to soften the vegetables. Add the vinegar and wine and reduce.

4 Add the stock, tomato purée and salt. Bring to the boil and simmer for 35 minutes or until the stock has reduced by half.

5 Strain the stock into a bowl and reserve to one side. Skim off any fat that has risen to the top after 10 minutes. Whisk in the mustard and reserve for finishing.

6 Preheat an oven to 220°C. Season the suprêmes with salt and pepper. Place in a small roasting tin without any fat or oil and roast for 10 minutes.

7 Turn the suprêmes over and return to the oven and cook for 10 minutes further. Rest in a warm place for approximately 5 minutes.

8 Heat the reserved stock until warm and then whisk in the softened butter little by little to finish the sauce. Cover the sauce and keep warm for service.

9 Cut the suprêmes into thin slices. Dress each plate with the cooked duck and lightly dress with the prepared sauce. Serve the rest of the sauce separately.

Roast goose with semolina dumplings

INGREDIENTS	4 PORTIONS	10 PORTIONS
Young oven-ready goose	1 × 2.5kg	3 × 2.5kg
Medium-sized dessert apple	1	3
Onion	1	3
Fresh tarragon	1 sprig	3 sprigs
Water	250ml	750ml
Brown chicken stock	400ml	1200ml
Butter	150g	450g
Eggs	4	12
Semolina	250g	750g
White bread	200g	600g
Soured cream	125ml	375ml
King Edward potatoes	450g	1350g
Sea salt	To taste	To taste
Freshly ground nutmeg	To taste	To taste
Dessert apples	4	12
Butter	40g	120g
Cranberries	2tbsp	6tbsp
Caster sugar	3tbsp	9tbsp
Lemon juice	½ lemon	1 lemon
White wine	2tbsp	6tbsp
Good-quality salt and pepper	To taste	To taste

Method of work

1   Rinse the goose, pat dry, cut off the fat by the vent and season inside with salt. Peel, halve and core the apple, stuff into the goose together with the whole onion and tarragon sprigs. Pour the water into a large roasting pan. Bring to the boil on top of the stove, then lower in the goose.

2   Roast for approximately 1½–2 hours in a preheated oven at 220°C. Baste frequently with the cooking juices. After an hour, remove the stuffing from the goose and place in the roasting pan. Return to the oven.

3   Beat the butter until light and creamy in texture. Add the eggs a little at a time, beating well between each addition. Then add the semolina. Leave the egg and semolina mixture to stand for 1 hour in a refrigerator.

4   **Steep** the diced bread in the soured cream to soften. Steam the potatoes until quite soft then peel, chop coarsely and lay out on a baking sheet. Place into the oven and lower the temperature to 200°C and dry out the potatoes for approximately 5 minutes. Push through a coarse sieve and season with salt and nutmeg, mixing thoroughly. Work this potato into the semolina dough.

5   Remove the goose from the roasting pan and keep warm. Add the stock to the pan, bring to the boil and pass through a fine sieve lined with muslin cloth. Skim off any excess fat and adjust the seasoning and consistency of the jus.

6   Form the dough into small dumplings and drop gently into boiling salted water. Cook for approximately 15 minutes.

7   Core the remaining apples and place in a buttered, ovenproof dish. Fill the cavities with the cranberries and sprinkle with sugar, dotting the remaining butter on top. Bake in an oven at the highest heat for 15–20 minutes. Add the lemon juice and wine and cook for a further 5 minutes until the juice has reduced.

8   Carve the goose into thin slices and allow any residual juices to drain. Arrange on a plate. Check the seasoning and consistency of the sauce and spoon some over the goose. Serve with two semolina dumplings per portion and one baked apple. Serve the rest of the sauce separately.

Seared chicken livers with a Madeira jus, saffron risotto and Parmesan crisp

INGREDIENTS	4 PORTIONS	10 PORTIONS
Chicken livers	12	30
Madeira	35ml	70ml
Brown chicken jus	50ml	145ml
Finely diced onion	40g	100g
Chopped flat leaf parsley	4tbsp	10tbsp
Butter	100g	250g
Arborio rice	100g	250g
Saffron white chicken stock	400ml	1 litre
Grated Parmesan cheese	100g	250g
Fresh chervil	¼ bunch	1 bunch
Good-quality salt and pepper	To taste	To taste

Method of work

1 Take half the Parmesan cheese and place onto a non-stick mat or silicone paper in a long rectangular shape, approximately 5cm wide by 20cm long.

2 Bake in the oven at 180°C until bubbling and very slightly golden.

3 Remove from the oven and trim back into shape with a knife (keep on the hot tray).

4 Wrap the cheese around a circular mould and press the two ends together to form a circle.

5 Allow to cool and set hard.

6 Sweat the onions in a little butter and oil, then add the rice and cook for a further 2 minutes. Add the hot stock and continue to cook the risotto until al dente. Finish with butter, Parmesan and flat leaf parsley.

7 Quickly fry the chicken livers in a hot pan until pink, then deglaze with Madeira and add the brown chicken jus.

8 Place the crisp in a bowl and fill with risotto, top with the livers and drizzle the sauce around, garnish with chervil.

Suprême of turkey wrapped in bacon with turkey ballotine

INGREDIENTS	4 PORTIONS	10 PORTIONS
Turkey suprême	1 × 600g	1 × 1.5kg
Streaky bacon	10 rashers	20 rashers
Turkey leg	1 small	1 large
Cumberland sausage meat	200g	500g
Dried cranberries	50g	125g
Fresh cranberries	80g	200g
Sugar	As required	As required
Turkey jus	120ml	300ml
Good-quality salt and pepper	To taste	To taste

Method of work

1 Lay the bacon **rashers** onto cling film. Season the turkey suprême with pepper and roll tightly.

2 Remove all bone, skin and sinew from the turkey leg. Mix the dried cranberries with the sausage meat and spread on top.

3 Roll the leg and tie at 2cm intervals. Wrap in cling film and then in foil.

4 Steam or poach the suprême for 40 minutes, remove to a roasting pan and remove the cling film. Roast for a further 40 minutes or until a core temperature of 70°C has been reached for 5 minutes.

5 Place the ballotine in an oven and bake for 1 hour.

6 Place the fresh cranberries in a pan with the sugar and heat for 2–3 minutes until the cranberries start to release their juices.

7 Add the jus and bring to the boil, simmer for 2–3 minutes.

8 Carve the suprême and ballotine and serve with seasonal potatoes and vegetables.

Medallions of turkey en papillote with lemon, sage and onion

INGREDIENTS	4 PORTIONS	10 PORTIONS
Turkey medallions	8 × 75g	20 × 75g
Lemon	1	3
Sage	¼ bunch	½ bunch
Onion (finely chopped)	1 medium	2½ medium
Butter	100g	250g
White wine	8tbsp	20tbsp
Fondant potatoes	4	10
Green beans tied with chive	4 bundles	10 bundles
Sea salt and white pepper	To taste	To taste

Method of work

1 Sauté the onion in a little oil until light golden brown.

2 Lay out a square of tin foil 15cm × 15cm, then place a piece of silicone paper on top.

3 Brush a little melted butter onto the paper and arrange the lightly browned onion, chopped sage (reserve a few sprigs) and thinly sliced lemon on top.

4 Bar mark the turkey medallions on one side to form a quadrillage effect.

5 Arrange the turkey on top of the mixture and drizzle with white wine, sea salt and ground white pepper.

6 Fold the paper and foil over the turkey, crimping the edges to form an airtight pouch. Leave to marinate for 30 minutes.

7 Place the pouch in a hot oven, 180°C for 10 minutes.

8 Arrange a fondant potato, a green bean bundle and a pouch on the plate.

9 Just before serving, cut the pouch open to expose the turkey.

10 Garnish with deep fried sage leaves.

Pot-roasted snipe in stout with onion and rosemary dumplings

INGREDIENTS	4 PORTIONS	10 PORTIONS
Snipe (whole)	4	10
Stout	250ml	750ml
Game stock	250ml	750ml
Plain flour	50g	125g
Butter	50g	125g
Mirepoix of root vegetables	400g	900g
Carrot, celery, turnip, swede into macédoine	100g of each	220g of each
Soft flour	95g	230g
Baking powder	5g	20g
Water	100ml	250ml
Beef suet	50g	125g
Olive oil	1tbsp	2tbsp
Onion (finely chopped)	1	2
Fresh rosemary (finely chopped)	1tbsp	2tbsp
Peas	50g	125g
Curly kale	75g	180g
Good-quality salt and pepper	To taste	To taste

Method of work

1 Preheat an oven to 180°C.

2 Season and flour each whole snipe. Melt the butter in a large ovenproof casserole dish. Place the snipe into the dish and lightly colour on all sides.

3 Remove the snipe and leave to one side. In the same dish, brown the mirepoix of vegetables, season well and add the stout and game stock and bring to the boil. Return the snipe to the casserole dish, cover with a lid and cook in the preheated oven for 45 minutes.

4 In a small saucepan season and sweat down the onions with the olive oil and rosemary until tender. Remove from the heat and cool.

5 Once cooled, stir in the suet and sieve in the soft flour and baking powder. Slowly add the water until a dough is formed. Shape into medium size round balls, allowing one per portion.

6 In a pan of boiling salted water blanch and refresh the macédoine of vegetables and cook the dumplings until they float. Remove from the water and leave to cool slightly.

7 Once the snipe is cooked, remove from the sauce and leave to one side to rest. Pass the sauce through a strainer or chinois into a clean pan. Add the blanched macédoine of vegetables to the sauce and correct the seasoning and consistency.

8 Now return the snipe and dumplings to the sauce, adding the peas and curly kale. Place back in the oven at 180°C and cook for a further 15 minutes.

9 For service, allow one snipe and dumpling per portion with a serving of vegetables and sauce.

 CHEF'S TIP

Always remove excess flour from products before frying to stop the starch from burning and leaving a bitter taste in the final dish. This will also prevent lumps of raw flour appearing in a sauce.

Tandoori pigeon with sag aloo and a caramelised lemon and coriander dressing

INGREDIENTS	4 PORTIONS	10 PORTIONS
Squab pigeon breasts	4	10
Tandoori paste or spice mix	3tsp	8tsp
Olive oil	30ml	80ml
Maris piper potatoes (cut into macédoine)	500g	1.25kg
Baby spinach leaves	200g	500g
Ground cumin	1tsp	3tsp
Ground coriander	1tsp	3tsp
Ground turmeric	1tsp	3tsp
Garam masala	2tsp	5tsp
Vegetable stock	300ml	750ml
Lemons	2	5
Cardamom pods	6	15
Natural yoghurt	100g	250g
Fresh coriander	¼ bunch	½ bunch
Clear honey	1tsp	2½ tsp
Good-quality salt and pepper	To taste	To taste

CHEF'S TIP

Experiment using other marinades, such as tikka or garlic and chilli. Pigeon is a strongly flavoured bird and this will come through even when other strong flavours are used.

Method of work

1 Place the tandoori paste and the pigeon breasts in a large bowl. Mix the breasts into the paste so that they are completely coated. Remove and place on a tray. Cover with plastic film and leave to marinate in a refrigerator for a minimum of one hour.

2 In a small sauté pan heat the olive oil then add the diced potatoes and sweat down without colour for a few minutes.

3 Season and add the ground cumin, turmeric and coriander. Continue to cook for a few minutes so that the spices have cooked out. Add the vegetable stock so that the potatoes are just covered. Season with salt and pepper and simmer until the potatoes are tender. Add the garam masala and the baby spinach.

4 Remove from the heat and allow the spinach to wilt into the potato mix. Stir well so that all the spices and the spinach are incorporated. Check the seasoning.

5 To prepare the dressing, peel and segment the lemons, chop the coriander roughly and open the cardamom pods, removing the seeds. In a shallow pan heat the honey, lemon segments and cardamom seeds until the honey starts to boil and caramelise. Remove from the heat and cool.

6 Once the honey and lemons has cooled, stir in the yoghurt and chopped fresh coriander.

7 Preheat the oven to 200°C. Place the marinated pigeon breasts onto a roasting tray and roast for approximately 10 minutes until the pigeon is cooked through. Remove from the oven and rest for a minimum of 5 minutes.

8 To serve, place the sag aloo into a ring in the centre of a plate, draining any excess liquid in the process. Arrange the breasts on top and pour the yoghurt sauce around the serving plate.

Steamed roulade of woodcock with Jerusalem artichoke purée and braised baby gem lettuce

INGREDIENTS	4 PORTIONS	10 PORTIONS
Woodcock (whole)	4	10
Leaf spinach, washed and de-stalked	100g	250g
Sun-dried tomatoes	120g	300g
Jerusalem artichokes (peeled)	400g	1kg
Double cream	100ml	250ml
Baby gem lettuce	2	5
Butter	50g	125g
Orange zest and juice	1 orange	3 oranges
Vegetable stock	500ml	1.25 litres
Good-quality salt and pepper	To taste	To taste

Method of work

1   For each woodcock, using a sharp boning knife cut along the back of the bird, cutting the flesh away from the carcass. The bird should be left intact but with the main bone structure removed.

2   Once the bird is open, cut the wing and drumstick joints off so that the other wing bone and the thigh bone can be easily removed. Now the whole bird has been boned it can be stuffed.

3   Season with salt and pepper and lay the spinach leaves across the opened-out bird. Next, lay across the sun-dried tomatoes. Tightly roll up the bird – roll from side to side, not from tail to tip.

4   Tightly roll up in plastic film and tie at both ends, so that the roulade is sausage shaped.

5   In a medium sized saucepan place half the vegetable stock and the peeled artichokes with salt and pepper. Bring to the boil and simmer until the artichokes are tender.

6   Remove the artichokes from the stock and place into a blender with the cream. Blend to a smooth purée. Empty the purée into a small pan and dry the mixture slightly over the heat.

7   Remove the outer leaves of the baby gems, trim the bases and cut in half lengthways. Melt the butter in a sauté pan. Place the baby gems into the pan, flat side down, so that they start to fry.

8   Add the orange juice, zest and the remaining stock, bringing to the boil. Place a cartouche over the tops of the baby gems and simmer on the stove until soft and tender.

9   Place the roulades into a steamer and cook for 10–15 minutes until firm to the touch. Remove from the steamer and allow to rest for 5 minutes. Remove the plastic film.

10   To serve, carve the woodcock roulades into even slices. Pipe or quenelle the artichoke purée onto a plate and then lay the slices of woodcock over the purée. Cut the baby gems in half again lengthways and arrange around the outside.

 CHEF'S TIP

When peeling Jerusalem artichokes, leave them in water with lemon juice or a touch of vinegar to prevent them oxidising.

Pheasant legs stuffed with a mousseline of duck liver and juniper, cep cream sauce and fondant potato

INGREDIENTS	4 PORTIONS	10 PORTIONS
Pheasant legs	4	10
Pheasant breast	2	5
Duck livers	250g	625g
Juniper berries (soaked in the gin below)	100g	250g
Gin	30ml	75ml
Double cream	300ml	750ml
Onion	1	2
Garlic	1 clove	2–3 cloves
Thyme	A few sprigs	A few sprigs
Butter	50g	125g
Brown chicken stock	150ml	400ml
Dried cep mushrooms	20g	50g
Pig's caul	80–100g	200–250g
Fondant potatoes	4	10
Fresh chopped chives and chervil	30g	80g
Good-quality salt and pepper	To taste	To taste

CHEF'S TIP

Dried wild mushrooms can be an economic commodity. As they are dried their flavour is much stronger. They are as good as fresh mushrooms for flavouring stocks, but only half the amount is required.

Method of work

1 Tunnel bone each pheasant leg to remove the thighbone. Neatly trim the drumstick flesh.

2 Season the duck livers. Over a high heat, quickly pan fry the livers and the soaked juniper berries in a shallow pan. Flambé with the gin. Remove from the heat and allow to cool.

3 In a food processor blend the pheasant breast and duck liver. Pass the mix through the back of a sieve to remove any sinew or large pieces.

4 Semi whip half the cream, ensuring the bowl used is freezing cold before use, then fold in the passed pheasant breast. Season, cover, place in a fridge and chill.

5 Once chilled, place the mixture into a piping bag with a plain tube and pipe into the legs. Carefully wrap the filled legs in the pig's caul before wrapping in plastic film and chilling further in the refrigerator.

6 Preheat an oven to 180°C.

7 Soak the cep mushrooms in a small pan of boiling water for 10 minutes. Remove the ceps and drain any excess water.

8 In a sauté pan gently sweat the garlic, onion and thyme in a little butter. Add the ceps, stock and a small amount of the water the ceps were soaked in and reduce by half. Add the remaining cream. Continue to cook for a further 5–10 minutes to infuse flavour into the sauce.

9 Using a hand blender or a food processor, blend the sauce ingredients together to maximise the cep flavour. Pass through a chinois. Adjust the consistency and seasoning before serving.

10 Season the stuffed legs. In a medium-hot pan with a small amount of oil seal the legs to give colour. Then place into a hot oven to cook for about 25 minutes. Remove from the oven and allow to rest.

11 To serve, lay the fondant potato on the plate and lean the ballotine against it. Warm the sauce, add the chopped chives and chervil at the last minute and spoon around the meat.

Roasted crown of partridge with butternut squash fondant and braised red cabbage and creamed Brussels sprouts

INGREDIENTS	4 PORTIONS	10 PORTIONS
Crown of partridge	2	5
Mirepoix	150g	400g
Unsalted butter	125g	250g
Butternut squash	1	3
Brown chicken stock	400ml	1 litre
Red cabbage	1	2
Sultanas	100g	250g
Grated dessert apples	100g	250g
Brown sugar	100g	250g
Raspberry vinegar	100ml	250ml
Game stock	200ml	500ml
Redcurrant jelly	50g	125g
Brussels sprouts	160g	400g
Double cream	100ml	250ml
Good-quality salt and pepper	To taste	To taste

Method of work

1 Preheat the oven to 180°C.

2 Soften 100/200g of the butter. Season the crown of partridge and coat the breasts with the butter. Place the crown on a tray with the mirepoix on the base. Roast in the oven for 15–20 minutes until golden brown and cooked all the way through. Use a digital thermometer to measure the temperature of the partridge inside. Remove from the oven, place on a cooling rack and rest.

3 Drain off any excess fat from the tray and then place on a stove and heat through. Add the game stock and deglaze the pan. Simmer for a few minutes then pass through a fine chinois into a clean pan. Warm the sauce. Add the redcurrant jelly and melt into the sauce. Correct the seasoning and consistency.

4 Warm the chicken stock in a small saucepan. Peel the butternut squash and cut into 4cm slices. Using a cutter cut out cylinder-shaped pieces, one per portion. Place the peeled and shaped butternut squash pieces in a small tray, brush with melted butter. Add stock so the squash pieces are two-thirds immersed, then place in the oven for 30–35 minutes until the squash is soft and lightly coloured on top. Remove from the stock and keep warm.

5 Put the raspberry vinegar, brown sugar, sultanas and grated apple into a heavy-based saucepan and bring to the boil. **Shred** the cabbage and add to the boiling vinegar mixture. Place a lid over the top and cook until the cabbage has become soft. Remove the lid and continue cooking until the liquid has reduced.

6 Prepare the Brussels sprouts by trimming the stalks and quartering. Heat a frying pan with a small amount of butter, fry the sprouts until softened and add the double cream.

7 Cook the cream until it has thickened slightly, season well and then remove from the pan and liquidise to a purée.

8 To serve, remove the breasts from the crown and arrange on the plate. Place a butternut fondant next to the breast and a spoonful of the cabbage. Spoon the creamed Brussels sprout next to the breast.

Quail and black pudding sausages with parsnip purée, étuvée of leeks and cider sauce

INGREDIENTS	4 PORTIONS	10 PORTIONS
Quail meat (leg and breast removed from the bone)	600g	1.5kg
Black pudding	200g	500g
Breadcrumbs	150g	375g
Double cream	100ml	250ml
Onions diced	50g	125g
Egg	1	3
Sausage skins (soaked in water and drained)	100g	250g
Parsnips	480g	1.2kg
Vegetable oil	40ml	90ml
Leeks	400g	1kg
Partridge or chicken stock (brown)	200ml	500ml
Cider	100ml	250ml
Unsalted butter	100g	250g
Double cream	250ml	600ml
Good-quality salt and pepper	To taste	To taste

CHEF'S TIP

Making sausages can be a good and cost-effective way of utilising leftover meats.

Method of work

1 Finely chop the black pudding and the quail meat and pass through a mincing machine. Soak the breadcrumbs in the smaller quantity of cream.

2 Preheat an oven to 180°C.

3 Fry the onions in a small amount of the butter in a frying pan until transparent but no colour. Allow to cool.

4 Mix the minced meat, egg and onions together to form a paste. Fold in the breadcrumbs and beat to a paste. Season well.

5 Fill a piping bag fitted with a plain tube with the sausage mix. Place the sausage skin over the end of the tube and fill the skin with the quail mixture. Pipe and twist the skin until enough length has been made to make one sausage per person. Place on a tray in a refrigerator to set.

6 Wash and peel the parsnips and remove the cores. Heat a roasting tray with a small amount of the butter, add the parsnips and season. Place in a preheated oven. Roast until soft and slightly caramelised. Remove from the oven and pass through a ricer. Beat in a little butter, seasoning and cream until a smooth purée consistency has been obtained.

7 Slice the leeks and wash them well. In a sauteuse, melt some butter and add the leeks to sweat down until softened. Season to taste.

8 In a saucepan reduce the cider and stock by half and add the 250/600ml of cream. Reduce the liquid until it coats the back of a spoon. Check the seasoning.

9 In a frying pan seal the sausages with the vegetable oil. Then place in a preheated oven at 200°C for 15–20 minutes until cooked all the way through and golden brown.

10 To serve, quenelle the mash. Slice the sausage at an angle and sit on top of the parsnips. Lay a little leek over the sausage and spoon the sauce around.

Sautéed saddle of rabbit with prune and Armagnac sauce

INGREDIENTS	4 PORTIONS	10 PORTIONS
Saddle of rabbit	4	10
Prunes	350g	875g
Armagnac	250ml	625ml
Chicken stock	250ml	625ml
Butter	125g	325g
Bouquet garni	1	1
Finely chopped parsley	30g	75g
Celeriac	75g	3
Desiree potatoes	150g	400g
Olive oil	30ml	75ml
Baby spinach	250g	700g
Salted butter	25g	60g
Nutmeg	10g	25g
Good-quality salt and pepper	To taste	To taste

Method of work

1 Preheat an oven to 180°C. Soak the prunes in the Armagnac for a minimum of 30 minutes. Remove half of the prunes from the Armagnac, chop and set aside.

2 Put the chicken stock and bouquet garni and the remaining liquor and prunes into a pan and reduce by half. Once reduced remove the bouquet garni, and using a hand blender blend the butter into the reduced liquor. Pass through a chinois.

3 Once amalgamated, stir in the chopped reserved prunes and chopped parsley. Season and keep warm to one side.

4 Season and pan fry the saddle of rabbit quickly for about 5 minutes. Place on trays in the preheated oven for approximately 15 minutes. Allow to rest for approximately 5 minutes. Carve the loins off the saddle and slice into thin strips across each loin.

5 Peel and grate the celeriac and potatoes into a bowl. Season and leave for 5 minutes. Remove from the bowl and squeeze so that any excess liquid is removed. Place a 6cm ring for each portion in a frying pan and heat on a stove. Add a touch of oil into each ring then place some of the potato and celeriac mixture into each ring. Fry on both sides until golden brown and cooked through. Remove from the rings and place on a cooling rack. Keep warm.

6 Put the salted butter in a shallow pan and heat on a stove. Wash and dry the spinach, then add to the butter and wilt. Sprinkle in the nutmeg and season. Remove from the pan and drain any excess water.

7 To serve, place the rosti of potato on the base then a layer of spinach. Arrange the rabbit around in a circle shape. Spoon the sauce over the rabbit.

 CHEF'S TIP

Try using different dried fruit with game dishes as the sweetness helps bring out the rich game flavour of the meat. Cranberries can give a nice sweet and sour effect.

Roasted loin of venison with baba ganoush and balsamic syrup

INGREDIENTS	4 PORTIONS	10 PORTIONS
Loin of venison	500g	1.2kg
Sumac spice	100g	250g
Aubergine	4	10
Tahini paste	1tsp	2.5tsp
Garlic	1 clove	3 cloves
Lemon juice and zest	1 lemon	3 lemon
Olive oil	100ml	250ml
Balsamic vinegar	200ml	500ml
Red peppers	3	8
Fresh coriander	¼ bunch	½ bunch
Reduced game stock	100ml	250ml
Demerara sugar	2tbsp	5tbsp
Good-quality salt and pepper	To taste	To taste

Method of work

1   Preheat an oven to 180°C.

2   Split the aubergine and roast in the preheated oven in a little olive oil. Cool until the outside is golden and crisp and the centre is soft and cooked through.

3   Cool the aubergine and remove the flesh. Pass through a course sieve. Purée the garlic and add to the aubergine along with the tahini, lemon juice and zest and the olive oil, season to taste.

4   Cut the peppers into quarters and remove the seeds, place onto a roasting tray and blister the skin under the salamander.

5   Remove from the heat and place the peppers into a plastic bag so that the peppers steam and the skin can easily be removed. Remove the skin and dice the flesh into a brunoise. Fold the peppers through the aubergine mixture.

6   Combine the balsamic vinegar, reduced game stock and sugar together in a saucepan and reduce to a coating consistency. Chop the coriander and stir into the sauce.

7   Season the loin of venison well with salt and pepper and the sumac spice. Seal in a very hot pan with a small amount of oil until golden all over. Place into the hot oven and roast for about 6–8 minutes until cooked to a medium pink stage. Remove from the pan and allow to rest for 5–10 minutes before carving.

8   To serve, slice the loin into thin slices, place a spoonful of the aubergine mix along the centre of the plate. Arrange the loin over the top of the aubergine mix so that the degree of cooking of the venison can be seen, run the sauce around the outside of the plate.

CHEF'S TIP

For venison, the longer the resting period, the more tender the meat becomes.

Assessment of knowledge and understanding

You have now learned about the use of different types of poultry and how to prepare and cook a variety of poultry dishes using different commodities and preparation techniques.

To test your level of knowledge and understanding, answer the following short questions. These will help to prepare you for your summative (final) assessment.

Quality identifications

1 List three types of chicken.

i) _____   ii) _____

iii) _____

2 List three quality points you should look for when receiving poultry.

i) _____   ii) _____

iii) _____

3 Explain why free range and organic methods of rearing are so important when considering the quality of poultry.

_____

_____

Materials and storage

1 Explain why a heavy-bottomed sauté pan should be used when making sauté chicken dishes that have the sauce finished in the same pan.

_____

_____

Preparation

1 Explain the term 'sauté' in relation to cooking chicken.

_____

2 Explain the difference between white and dark meat in poultry.

_____

3 Describe the method of preparation for spatchcock.

_____

Cooking

1 Explain the reason for resting poultry prior to carving.

_____

Health and safety

1 State two healthy options when finishing poultry dishes.

i) _____

ii) _____

Quality points and types of game

1 Name four types of feathered game and a suitable dish for each.

i) _____ ii) _____

iii) _____ iv) _____

2 Name two types of small furred game and a suitable dish for each.

i) _____ ii) _____

Preparation techniques

1 List and detail the procedure to fully joint a wild rabbit.

_____

_____

2 Describe the process of trussing a whole game bird and give examples of two dishes suitable for a trussed bird.

_____

_____

Storage of game

1 Explain why it is best to drain raw or defrosting game regularly of excess blood and juices.

_____

_____

2 Discuss why it is best to store game in a separate refrigerator to other food items.

_____

_____

CHEF'S PROFILE

Name: ANDRE GARRETT MCA

Position: Head Chef

Establishment: Galvin at Windows

Current job role and main responsibilities: Ensuring high standards and pushing for culinary excellence. Also linking between Chris Galvin and the Hilton Hotel on Park Lane.

When did you realise that you wanted to pursue a career in the catering and hospitality industry? I was 14 years old and washing up in a local hotel in my home town of Bath. I caught the bug of the kitchen and decided to go to college, so they took me on as an apprentice chef.

Training:
I went to Bath College and did my City and Guilds 706/1 and 2 Food Preparation and Cookery. I had very good teachers – Mr Maslin was especially helpful to me. After college I started at Hunstrete House Hotel.

Experience:
After 2 years at Hunstrete House Hotel and my apprenticeship, I knew it was time to come to London. I came and knocked on the door of Nico Ladenis at Chez Nico and was lucky to get a job as Commis. I stayed with Nico for 5 years at a number of his establishments, but I finished as Chef de Partie at Nico at 90 Park Lane, where he gained three Michelin stars. Afterwards I spent time with Bruno Loubet and progressed to Sous chef at the Landmark Hotel fine dining restaurant. After this I met up with Chris Galvin at the Orrery and became his Sous chef. Later I was promoted to Head Chef and continued to run the Orrery for 3 more years.

What do you find rewarding about your job?
I like the fact people find pleasure in what I do and it is nice at the end of the day to know you've done a good job. I am now finding it interesting to train the next generation of chefs.

What do you find the most challenging about the job?
Getting up every day and striving to do better than before.

What advice would you give to students just beginning their career?
It is going to be hard for a long time but it is very rewarding. Be patient and learn. Ask lots of questions and make sure you work for someone who can teach you well.

Who is your mentor or main inspiration?
My mentor would be Chris Galvin; he has given me great opportunities and advice. I am inspired by every great chef and restaurateur.

What traits do you consider essential for anyone entering a career as a chef?
Patience, flexibility, motivation, determination and speed.

A brief personal profile:
- Travel and sport is what I like to do out of the kitchen.
- My job has been very good to me and I have also done very well in competitions. This is something that has motivated me and helped me to focus.
- Prix Pierre Tattinger, international finalist, 2000.
- Roux Scholor 2002.
- Bocuse dor 2007, 10th place.

Can you give one essential kitchen tip or technique that you use as a chef?
Be very organised and precise. Always cook with a timer.

CHEF'S PROFILE

Name: MARK ASKEW

Position: Executive Chef

Establishment: Gordon Ramsay Holdings

Current job role and main responsibilities:
I liaise with all chefs and department heads to oversee current operations in all the kitchens within the group. I am also involved in ongoing and future restaurant openings and consultancy projects.

When did you realise that you wanted to pursue a career in the catering and hospitality industry?
I decided to pursue this career whilst working part-time when at school.

Training:
Craven College, Skipton, Yorkshire. I trained for two years to gain the 1961/2 City and Guilds.

Experience:
1   Savoy Grill
2   Pierre Koffman at Tante Claire
3   Michel Bourdin at the Connaught
4   Nico Ladenis at Nico's
5   Aubergine
6   Maison de Bricount
7   Gordon Ramsay Restaurant

What do you find rewarding about your job?
The sense of achievement, as well as helping to maintain the pride and passion of the group.

What do you find the most challenging about the job?
Providing consistency in the delivery of our product and standard of service.

What advice would you give to students just beginning their career?
To be 100 per cent committed; ambitious, enthusiastic and passionate.

Who is your mentor or main inspiration?
Gordon – we share the same ideals.

What traits do you consider essential for anyone entering a career as a chef?
Dedication, enthusiasm and passion.

Can you give one essential kitchen tip that you use as a chef?
To learn from others' mistakes, along with their achievements. Also, keep your eyes open!

Ballotine of English free-range chicken with foie gras and truffle

INGREDIENTS	4 PORTIONS
Chicken breast suprêmes (with skin on)	4 × 150g
Foie gras	100g
Sea salt and freshly ground black pepper	To taste
Double cream	50g
Black truffle (preferably from Perigold, finely diced)	20g
Knobs of butter	A few
Chicken jus	
Chicken bones	1kg
Oil	2tbsp
Carrot (chopped)	1
Leek (chopped)	1
Celery sticks (chopped)	2
Thyme	A few sprigs
Bay leaf	1
Garlic cloves (peeled)	3
Tomato purée	2 tbsp
Sea salt and freshly ground black pepper	To taste

Method of work

1 First, prepare the chicken jus. Preheat an oven to 200°C. Place the chicken bones on a roasting tray and roast for 20 minutes until browned. Heat the oil in a large stockpot and add the chopped vegetables. Stir over high heat for a few minutes until nicely browned. Add the herbs, garlic and tomato purée. Stir for another couple of minutes before adding the browned chicken bones. Cover with cold water, bring to the boil and skim off the froth and scum. Reduce the heat and simmer for 3 hours then pass through a chinois.

2 Boil the chicken stock in a clean, wide pan until reduced to the desired flavour and consistency. Season with salt and pepper.

3 Trim the chicken breast and leave the skin on. Remove the false fillets and purée them to a fine paste. Push the purée through a fine mesh (or drum) sieve to remove any sinew or large pieces. Chill the paste for an hour, then slowly incorporate the cream and return to the refrigerator.

4 Chop the foie gras into 1cm cubes. Heat a pan until hot, season the foie gras and lightly sauté until it is golden brown. Drain off the excess fat and transfer the foie gras to a plate and allow to cool completely. Chill the foie gras for at least 20 minutes then mix with the chicken purée along with the diced truffle. Season well. Spoon the mixture into a piping bag fitted with a large plain nozzle and chill again until ready to use.

5 Cut a 4cm-deep slit along the thicker side of the chicken breasts. Pipe the chicken purée into the slit, fold in the flaps and carefully stretch the skin of the chicken breasts to cover the purée. Wrap each stuffed breast tightly with cling film and secure both ends to achieve a neat cylindrical shape, about 12cm long. Chill for at least 1 hour.

6 When ready to serve, poach the chicken ballotine in boiling water for 6–7 minutes. The chicken should only be partially cooked but hold its shape. Remove from the pan, discard the cling film and pan fry with a few knobs of butter for 3–4 minutes each side until the skin is golden brown and the chicken is cooked through. Rest for a few minutes while you reheat the chicken jus for serving.

Serving suggestion

One of the most popular ways we have served this dish in the past is to arrange the diagonally cut chicken ballotine on buttered cabbage then surround it with braised baby carrots, onions, sautéed morels and light chicken jus.

9

Advanced skills and techniques in producing fish and shellfish (Unit 307)

LEARNING OUTCOMES

The aim of this chapter is to enable the candidate to develop the necessary advanced skills, knowledge and understanding of the principles in preparing and cooking fish and shellfish to dish specifications. The emphasis in this chapter is on developing precision, speed and control in existing skills and perfecting more refined and advanced techniques.

There are **two** outcomes to this unit. At the end of this chapter the candidate will be able to:

■ Prepare fish and shellfish dishes and associated products
■ Produce fish and shellfish dishes, associated products and garnishes

Chefs inspecting the day's catch at Newlyn, with a local fisherman and the project director from Seafood Cornwall

FISH

For the professional chef, fish has possibly become the most important ingredient on the menu. It is one of the most fulfilling foods to prepare and cook and there is a wide variety of fish and shellfish available to choose from, but the chef must reflect on the health aspects of fish, select carefully from the wide variety available and ensure that the menu choice helps to contribute positively to the issues of fish sustainability. When selecting fish for a menu, the chef should consider the quality, freshness, availability – due to weather conditions or seasonality – and suitability for different cooking techniques.

FISH TYPES

Fish can be divided into two distinctive types:

1 *Pelagic* – fish that swim relatively close to the surface of the sea.

2 *Demersal* – fish that are found on or near the seabed.

Demersal fish can be further divided into subcategories:

- Flat
- Round
- Oily
- Non-bony.

CATEGORIES OF FISH

Pelagic fish	Flat fish	Round fish	Oily fish	Non-bony fish
Herring	Brill	Cod	Salmon	Monkfish
Mackerel	Dover sole	Conger eel	Trout	Ray (skate)
Sardine	Lemon sole	Grey mullet	Tuna	Shark
Sprat	Megrim sole	Hake		
	Turbot	Pollack		

The sea contains a wide variety of flat fish and round fish. The colour and pattern of their skin is used as camouflage to protect them from potential predators. Most fish have darker shades of skin on the top of the body, which makes them blend into the sea floor when viewed from above. When viewed from below, the pale undersides blend in with the light from above.

The percentage of weight loss should be taken into account when considering fish dishes for a menu. It is unusual to have more than 60 per cent of usable flesh when preparing filleted fish. If preparing round fish for grilling whole, there will be an approximate 5 per cent weight loss from the discarding of the trimmed fins and the gutting, with a further 10 per cent loss if the head is removed.

To estimate the weight loss of fish, the calculation below should be applied:

$$\frac{\text{Total waste weight}}{\text{Total original fish weight}} \times 100 = \% \text{ wastage}$$

CHEF'S TIP

If there has been several days of bad weather, the choice of fresh seafood will be limited. Be guided by your fish supplier, and remember that there are fish that can be substituted, such as megrim instead of lemon sole and pollack or gurnard instead of cod.

CHEF'S TIP

Stocks of skate have been depleted in certain regions, and in Cornwall almost all the fish landed and sold as skate are in fact ray. The two names are interchangeable, which is quite confusing for chefs and customers. The species of ray landed include: blonde rays, owl rays, star rays and thornback rays.

John Dory fish at market

FISH SEASONALITY

	Variety	Jan.	Feb.	March	April	May	June	July	Aug.	Sep.	Oct.	Nov.	Dec.
Round white	Bass	✓	✓	✓					✓	✓	✓	✓	✓
	Bream						✓	✓	✓	✓	✓	✓	✓
	Cod	✓	✓	✓	✓	✓	✓	✓	✓	✓	✓	✓	✓
	Gurnard	✓	✓						✓	✓	✓	✓	✓
	Haddock	✓	✓	✓	✓	✓	✓	✓	✓	✓	✓	✓	✓
	Hake	✓	✓						✓	✓	✓	✓	✓
	Huss	✓	✓	✓	✓	✓	✓	✓	✓	✓	✓	✓	✓
	John Dory	✓	✓	✓	✓	✓				✓	✓	✓	✓
	Ling	✓	✓	✓	✓	✓	✓	✓		✓	✓	✓	✓
	Monkfish	✓	✓	✓	✓	✓	✓	✓	✓	✓	✓	✓	✓
	Pollack					✓	✓	✓	✓	✓	✓	✓	✓
	Red mullet		✓	✓	✓	✓	✓	✓	✓	✓	✓	✓	
	Red snapper	✓	✓	✓	✓	✓	✓	✓	✓	✓	✓	✓	✓
	Redfish	✓	✓	✓	✓	✓	✓	✓	✓	✓	✓	✓	✓
	Sea bream	✓	✓	✓	✓				✓	✓	✓	✓	✓
	Whiting	✓	✓	✓	✓	✓	✓	✓	✓	✓	✓	✓	✓
Flat fish	Brill	✓	✓				✓	✓	✓	✓	✓	✓	✓
	Dab	✓	✓	✓			✓	✓	✓	✓	✓	✓	✓
	Dover sole	✓	✓	✓			✓	✓	✓	✓	✓	✓	✓
	Halibut	✓	✓	✓			✓	✓	✓	✓	✓	✓	✓
	Lemon sole	✓	✓	✓	✓			✓	✓	✓	✓	✓	✓
	Megrim	✓	✓	✓	✓			✓	✓	✓	✓	✓	✓
	Plaice	✓	✓				✓	✓	✓	✓	✓	✓	✓
	Skate	✓	✓			✓	✓	✓	✓	✓	✓	✓	✓
	Turbot	✓	✓	✓	✓	✓	✓	✓	✓	✓	✓	✓	✓
Oily fish	Eel	✓	✓	✓	✓	✓	✓	✓	✓	✓	✓	✓	✓
	Herring	✓	✓	✓	✓			✓	✓	✓	✓	✓	✓
	Mackeral	✓	✓	✓	✓	✓	✓	✓			✓	✓	✓
	Salmon	✓	✓	✓	✓	✓	✓	✓	✓	✓	✓	✓	✓
	Sardines	✓	✓	✓	✓	✓	✓	✓	✓	✓	✓	✓	✓
	Trout	✓	✓	✓	✓	✓	✓	✓	✓	✓	✓	✓	✓
	Tuna	✓	✓	✓	✓	✓	✓	✓	✓	✓	✓	✓	✓
	Wild salmon		✓	✓	✓	✓	✓	✓	✓				

Key: ▨ in season ☐ out of season

COMMERCIAL FISHING

The figures below illustrate the quantities of fish landed by UK vessels into the UK each year. In 2005, the five most popular species of fish landed were:

SPECIES	TONNES LANDED
Mackerel	120,600
Herring	76,400
Haddock	47,600
Blue whiting	28,800
Cod	13,800

Source: UK Sea Fisheries Statistics, DEFRA

The decline of the North Sea cod stocks is a serious problem for the UK. The pressures on fish stocks have made the UK seafood industry adapt, so that fish stocks are better managed in order to meet present needs without compromising the needs of the future. Consumers can, however, still eat fish, a fact that is recognised by leading environmental fisheries campaigners at the WWF (the global conservation organisation) and the Marine Conservation Society.

Chefs and consumers must be more inquisitive and taste a wider range of seafood in order to reduce the pressure on more traditional species – such as cod and skate. There are 21,000 species of fish and shellfish in the world, and at least 100 different varieties available in the UK.

Cod landed in the UK is caught within strict management regimes. The control measures already in place at a European level to help preserve stocks include, for example, the closure of certain fisheries during the spawning seasons, catch quotas and restrictions on the type of fishing gear that can be used. The quota system sets safe limits for catches agreed by fishermen, scientists and government. Cod is caught within these agreed limits so consumers can eat it without concern.

Fish is also traded on an international market. The UK's buyers, processors and retailers source imported supplies from sustainable sources to compensate for reduced landings from their own fleets while work is undertaken to recover stocks in the North Sea. Obviously, purchasing fish from further distances increases the carbon footprint of the ingredient, and it may also lead to concerns over quality and freshness. Currently almost 90 per cent of the cod eaten in the UK comes from waters outside the UK, such as Icelandic and Norwegian waters.

 CHEF'S TIP

When selecting fish for menus try to use alternative under-utilised local varieties, such as pollack, coley or dab. All have great flavours and are not in short supply.

Over-fishing

Many once-common fish, such as cod and skate, are now quite rare, with cod close to commercial collapse. Due to over-fishing, the productivity of our seas

A small fishing boat, Cornwall

VIDEO CLIP
Sea fishing

and rivers is becoming exhausted. The UN Food and Agriculture Organization reports that nearly 70 per cent of the world's fish stocks are now fully fished, over-fished or depleted. If a responsible attitude to fishing is not adopted and the public does not embrace changes to eating habits, the consequences on the world's fisheries will become disastrous. Consumers can contribute to the responsible management of fish stocks by demanding that the fish they eat is from sustainable, managed stocks and that the way in which it is caught or farmed causes minimum damage to the marine environment.

Fishing methods

Fishermen use a variety of methods to catch fish, but each is based on one of four basic techniques:

1 Pulling an open net through a shoal of fish, either above the seabed or on the seabed itself; this captures the fish in the path of the net and is known as trawling or dredging.

2 Enclosing an area with a net and then advancing inward, trapping the fish within the encircled area; this is sometimes known as purse-seining or seining.

3 Snaring passing fish in set nets.

4 Attracting fish to either bait or bright lures, such as in lining or potting.

Trawling

There are three types of trawler:

1 Beam

2 Mid-water

3 Bottom.

A beam trawler has two nets (one on either side of the boat), each suspended from a metal beam. The nets have chains in the front edge, which will generally dig 3–8cm into the seabed to help gather the demersal fish – such as cod, monkfish and sole – into the net.

This type of fishing has attracted many critics because of the potential for damage to the seabed and because the nets pick up everything that gets in their way (including urchins and starfish, which are not used). Most skippers of these trawlers use technology such as sonar, echo sounders and computerised 3D maps to find the softer, sandy ground that is suited to this type of trawling. It would be counterproductive to trawl on rocky ground or over wrecks as this would damage the nets. Recent research has shown that 95 per cent of beam trawlers now use wheels on their beams to help increase fuel efficiency and reduce contact with the seabed.

Fisherman repairing a trawler net

Netting

Static nets are fixed on the seabed (known as tangle nets), around wrecks or at sea (known as gill nets), and are left for several hours before being hauled in. This method tends to capture a broad range of species, such as monkfish, pollack, turbot, hake and spider crabs, although this will always depend on locality and location. Mesh sizes are controlled to avoid catching small and immature fish.

Smaller inshore boats use the netting method

Handlining

This method is used by inshore and day boats, where baited hooks on lines are dropped into the sea. The number of hooks used per line depends on the species being caught. Handlining is used mostly for mackerel, sea bass, pollack and cod.

This is a preferred method because each fish can be marked and traced and is generally in very good condition. Small fish are rarely caught, but if caught they are returned alive immediately. Line fishing also has no unwanted by-catch. Chefs and customers will pay a higher price for fish caught by handlining.

Handlining for mackerel on a small inshore boat

Caring for the catch and inspection at the market

Catching fewer fish but ensuring that they are effectively cared for can result in increased freshness, quality and value in the fish caught. Seafish Quality Advisors, working mainly in Scotland, Northern Ireland, Cornwall and the Humber, provide free independent and unbiased assessment on catch quality for fishermen and their crews.

Fish are inspected at the market for standards of grading, size, gutting, washing, icing and presentation, and the quality advisors can advise on how to improve quality of preservation and presentation, thus increasing the value of the catch. A scored analysis report shows the quality of the fish compared with the average for a particular port.

Skippers on pelagic vessels are encouraged to track times of hauls and record the temperature of tanks and details of the frequency and type of cleaning carried out aboard. This information is forwarded to processors and customers.

Quality advisors have also been working with skippers to show that if they weigh fish boxes at sea, and not over-fill them, the quality of the catch is improved. By restricting boxes to a stated weight, and labelling when and where caught, fish can achieve an increased value at market.

Handline caught mackerel stored in a seawater slush

Small handline boats use large plastic tubs filled with a slush of ice and seawater (usually held at a temperature of 0°C). The fresh catch is put into the slush straight from the line to maintain its freshness and quality.

CHEF'S TIP

The first hour after the fish has been caught is the most crucial for maintaining its quality and freshness. Therefore, the correct storage and rapid chilling of fish as soon as it is caught significantly improves shelf life, appearance and keeping qualities.

Tagged line-caught sea bass

Newlyn fish market, Cornwall

VIDEO CLIP
Billingsgate fish market

Seafood Cornwall and Seafood Scotland have employed former skippers as Seafood Quality Advisors. This is another significant quality control step to help ensure that fish suppliers and chefs receive the best possible standard of fish.

Tagging: the mark of quality

In 2001 the South West Handline Fishermen's Association (SWHFA) was among the first UK fisheries to gain accreditation from the Marine Stewardship Council (MSC), for its handline mackerel scheme. Mackerel carrying the MSC mark is guaranteed to have been caught in south-west waters using the traditional method of handline fishing. Recently, the SWHFA has introduced tagging schemes for handline caught sea bass and pollack, clearly identifying these fish as being caught in Cornish waters. Customers who purchase these species with tags can match the tag numbers with the fisherman and boat on a website (www.linecaught.org.uk).

This method has developed a new market, where small numbers of dedicated boats can sell directly to suppliers using this tag as a sign of quality and sustainability. The volume of fish caught is very small compared with what a trawler will catch in one day, but the fish is arguably better quality and there is no 'unwanted catch'. The fish will also have a smaller carbon footprint because the boats used are smaller and do not travel so far out to sea. Because sustainability of fish supplies is the major factor, the emphasis is on the quality rather than the quantity.

THE FISH MARKET

After fish has been landed, some is sold at the fish market in the port of landing and some is sent to other markets around the UK, such as Billingsgate in London. The quality of product and food safety issues are of utmost importance throughout this process. UK seafood markets are constantly taking steps to ensure that only the best quality product reaches the customer. There is constant investment in innovative procedures, such as temperature controlled fish halls and electronic auctions and/or remote bidding. Also, major new investments have been made in building new markets at some ports, such as Hull and Peterhead.

What to look out for when purchasing fish

■ Fresh whole fish will have eyes that are bright and not sunken and the skin will have a shiny, moist and firm appearance. There will be a pleasant sea-fresh aroma if the fish is really fresh.

■ When buying fillets, look out for neat, trim fillets and a white translucent appearance.

■ Smoked fish should always appear glossy and have a fresh smoked aroma.

■ When purchasing frozen seafood, check that the fish is frozen solid with no signs of partial thawing. Ensure that the packaging is undamaged and there is no sign of freezer burn to the fish.

FISH FARMING

Aquaculture is an important industry in the UK, made up of an established shellfish sector and a rapidly developing fish sector. Many of the sheltered bays, estuaries and lochs around the UK coastline are suitable for farming a wide range of species. With the development of new equipment that can withstand more extreme weather conditions, opportunities to move to sites further offshore are likely to arise. The shellfish species that are currently produced in UK waters include:

■ Mussels

■ Oysters

■ Clams

■ Scallops.

The main fish species being farmed at the moment are:

■ Salmon

■ Halibut

■ Turbot.

The farming of haddock and Dover sole is still at the research or semi-commercial level. Farmed sea bass is also now starting to appear in UK supermarkets.

How fish are farmed

Young fish are produced in land-based hatcheries and then transferred to sea cages for growing on to market size. This is taking place in Scotland, where the infrastructure for producing salmon is well established, and some of the producers are diversifying into other species. Norway is another country where this is happening. Recirculation systems are gaining interest, especially in areas where there are no sheltered sites for the mooring of cages.

The selection of a suitable site is crucial to the success of any aquaculture business. Growth and survival of the stock, whether fish or shellfish, are influenced by a range of physical and biological factors, including seawater temperature, exposure of the site to the elements, dissolved oxygen and pollutants. Sites near large urban and industrial developments are generally unsuitable for cultivation because of potential pollutants in the water. More specifically for shellfish, growth and survival are also affected by water flow rates, food (phytoplankton) in the water, predators and fouling organisms. Starfish and crabs, abundant in estuaries and coastal waters, are probably the most damaging of all the shellfish predators.

Sustainability of fish and shellfish

Around the world, some types of fish, especially in certain areas, are threatened by being over-fished. At the same time, we're eating more fish and shellfish in this country and across Europe. Fish and shellfish farming (and other types of what are known as 'sustainable aquaculture') have a significant role to play in meeting our demand for fish and shellfish, along with fishing at sea.

Here are some examples of how we can help maintain the fish and shellfish levels for the future:

■ Try to choose fish and shellfish that comes from responsibly managed sources; this means it will have been caught in a way that conserves fish stock for the future. Or choose fish and shellfish that have been produced sustainably; this means it will have been farmed in a way that allows the fish population to continue in the future. (See below for where to find advice on choosing sustainable seafood.)

■ Read the labels on fish. This often tells you where the fish comes from as well as what species it is. This can be important because stocks of certain types of fish might be declining in some areas but not in others.

■ Look for assurance scheme logos ('eco-labels'), for example, the Marine Stewardship Council's use a 'blue tick' as their logo.

■ Be adventurous – try something new. If you eat fish regularly, try eating a wider variety of fish to help reduce the environmental impact.

For help choosing sustainable seafood see the following websites:

The Marine Conservation Society (MCS) is a UK charity that offers a viewpoint on the sustainable supply of both farmed and wild seafood. They provide an online website containing information on choosing sustainably caught fish: www.fishonline.org.

The Marine Stewardship Council (MSC) is a global organisation with standards for assessing the sustainability of fishing. The MSC runs a certification and labelling programme for sustainable wild seafood. The assessments are made by independent third-party accredited certifiers. For more information about the MSC see: www.msc.org.

Seafish is an organisation that seeks to promote good quality sustainable seafood, and is funded by government fisheries departments in England, Scotland, Wales and Northern Ireland. See: www.seafish.org.

The great majority of the fish caught in the UK is landed in Scotland and **The Scottish Government** recently launched its 'Eat more fish' initiative, which aims to promote the consumption of Scottish seafood. Its website also provides some useful links to fish sustainability information.
See: www.scotland.gov.uk/topics/fisheries/fish.

Seafood Scotland is a regional body set up to market, promote and develop responsibly caught Scottish seafood. See: www.seafoodscotland.org.

ADVANCED PREPARATION TECHNIQUES

Preparation of a whole salmon

Clean the cavity of the salmon

Remove the scales

Remove the head with a heavy knife

Fillet by cutting along the backbone

Trim the side of salmon

Remove the belly, trimming the side of salmon

Remove pin bones from the side of salmon

Cut traditional suprêmes from the side of salmon

Cut modern style suprêmes from a side of salmon

Examples of the two styles of suprême

Preparation of a whole trout

Cut the trout along belly so the guts can be removed

Remove the guts from the cavity

Remove the blood line and wash thoroughly

Remove the fins

Fillet by cutting along the backbone

Continue to fillet as a double fillet

Remove double fillet from the bone

A double fillet of trout

Bone removal

Remove the head of the trout

Press down the backbone to loosen it from the flesh

Remove all the pin bones and backbone

Trout with head and bones removed

Removing a double fillet (cross cutting) from a plaice

Make an incision for the removal of the double fillet from the plaice

Continue the process of removing the double fillet

Continue along the bones as closely as possible, ensuring no flesh left on the bones

Continue across the fish to remove the double fillet

Remove the roe from the double fillet

VIDEO CLIP
Preparing a délice and paupiette

FISH RECIPES

Pan fried fillet of red mullet with lemon thyme noodles, fine ratatouille sauce and crispy spring onion

INGREDIENTS	4 PORTIONS	10 PORTIONS
Red mullet fillets	4 × red mullet fillets	10 × red mullet fillets
Linguini noodles (cooked with cream and chopped thyme and lemon juice)	400g	1 kg
Courgette	40g	100g
Aubergine	40g	100g
White onion	40g	100g
Mixed peppers	40g	100g
Tomato coulis	8tbsp	20tbsp
Spring onions	1 bunch	2½ bunches
Butter	50g	125g
Olive oil	50ml	125ml
Black olives	2tbsp	5tbsp
Good-quality salt and white pepper	To taste	To taste

 CHEF'S TIP

The mullet should only be gently cooked to retain as much of its flavour and nutrients as possible. However, the dish requires a crispy skin so ensure the fish is skin-side down for at least 80 per cent of the cooking time.

Method of work

1 Prepare the fillets by cutting into a **butterfly**. In a frying pan heat a little oil until it just begins to smoke.

2 Season and lay the fish into the pan, skin-side down, and **shallow fry** until the skin just begins to crisp without burning.

3 Turn the fish over and allow to cook for a further 30 seconds.

4 Neatly dice the courgettes, aubergines, peppers and onions. Sweat in a little butter in a heavy-based saucepan until just cooked and season well. Reserve to one side.

5 Using a pestle and mortar, grind the black olives and remaining olive oil into a paste.

6 Slice the spring onions finely into julienne and dry them of any excess water. Place into hot oil (180°C) and deep fry until they are crisp. Reserve under hot lamps for service.

7 Ensure the linguini noodles are cooked and well seasoned then arrange in the centre of the plate. Lay the cooked fish on top.

8 Arrange the fine ratatouille vegetables around the edge and spoon the warmed tomato coulis around the plate, finish with drops of black olive purée and the crispy spring onion.

Poached Cornish pollack with Caerphilly mash, baby leek étuvé, langoustine and saffron beurre blanc

INGREDIENTS	4 PORTIONS	10 PORTIONS
Pollack fillets	4 × 160g	10 × 160g
Mashed potato	400g	1 kg
Caerphilly cheese	40g	100g
Baby leeks	12	30
Butter	50g	125g
Langoustines	12	30
Beurre blanc sauce	200ml	500ml
Saffron	pinch	2 pinches
Fish stock	300ml	750ml
Fresh dill	4tsp	10tsp
Good-quality salt and white pepper	Pinch	Pinch

Method of work

1 Prepare and wash the langoustines. Poach in the fish stock, remove and allow to cool. Save the claws for decoration and carefully remove the flesh from each tail.

2 Put the langoustine tail shells into a little of the fish stock and slowly reduce to a glaze, extracting as much flavour from the shells as possible.

3 Pass the langoustine glaze and carefully whisk into the beurre blanc, add the saffron to infuse the flavour and colour.

4 Poach the pollack in the fish stock until the flesh is creamy and just set. A lightly buttered cartouche may be required to help with the cooking process.

5 Slice the baby leeks into lozenges and cook in a little stock and butter until tender, season well and reserve for service.

6 Heat the mashed potato in a heavy-based saucepan with a little butter and add the grated Caerphilly cheese. Check the seasoning, and while still hot pipe onto a warmed service plate. Top with the poached fish.

7 Finish with the baby leeks, langoustine tails and one set of claws for decoration. Serve with the beurre blanc and the fresh dill.

Confit sea trout, citrus and poppy seed gnocchi, pickled fennel and Noilly Prat veloute

Infused oil

INGREDIENTS	4 PORTIONS	10 PORTIONS
Sunflower oil	50ml	100ml
Olive oil	50ml	100ml
Lemon	¼ zest	½ zest
Orange	¼ zest	½ zest
Lime	¼ zest	½ zest
Thyme	2 sprigs	5 sprigs
Bay leaf	1	3
White peppercorns	6	13

Method of work

1 Heat all ingredients to 60°C, remove from heat, cover tightly and leave at room temperature for 24 hours, strain and reserve.

Sea trout

INGREDIENTS	4 PORTIONS	10 PORTIONS
Pavé of sea trout	4 × 80g	10 × 80g

Method of work

1 Place pavés in individual vacuum pack bags with 50 ml of the strained oil.
2 Cook in a water bath at 60°C for 6 minutes.
3 Remove from bag and season well.
4 Place skin side up under a hot grill to crisp skin.

Gnocchi

INGREDIENTS	4 PORTIONS	10 PORTIONS
Gnocchi dough	200g	500g
Orange, lime and lemon zest	Pinch	Pinch
Blue poppy seeds	Pinch	Pinch
Salted butter	50g	125g

Method of work

1 Mix zest into dough and cut into 25g pieces.
2 Roll dough under the palm of the hand to create a torpedo shape.
3 Cook in boiling salted water and refresh in iced water.
4 Fry in butter until lightly coloured and finish with poppy seeds.
5 Drain on absorbent paper.

Pickled fennel

INGREDIENTS	4 PORTIONS	10 PORTIONS
Head of fennel	½	1
Salt	5g	12g
Fennel seeds	2g	5g
Castor sugar	25g	60g
White wine vinegar	50ml	120ml
Water	200ml	500ml

Method of work

1 Slice fennel very thinly.
2 Place the rest of the ingredients in a pan and bring to boil until sugar and salt are dissolved.
3 Pour over fennel and cover with cling film, leave to marinate for 30 minutes.

Noilly Prat veloute

INGREDIENTS	4 PORTIONS	10 PORTIONS
Sliced shallots	50g	120g
Unsalted butter	10g	25g
Noilly Prat	100ml	250ml
Double fish stock (reduced by half)	150ml	400ml
Double cream	50ml	120ml

Method of work

1 Sweat shallots in butter until soft, no colour.
2 Add Noilly Prat and reduce by half.
3 Add fish stock and reduce rapidly until syrupy.
4 Add cream, bring to boil and pass through fine chinois.

To finish

1 Place fennel in centre of plate.
2 Sit sea trout on top, place two gnocchi on trout.
3 Spoon veloute around, garnish with grilled orange segments and picked chervil and dill.

Pan fried sea bream, crushed ratte potatoes and stuffed baby artichokes, roast langoustines and sauce vierge

INGREDIENTS	4 PORTIONS	10 PORTIONS
Fillets of sea bream	4	10

Method of work

1 Season the fillets and fry in a hot pan with oil and butter, skin side down until crisp, then turn over and leave to cook for 30 seconds.
2 Place on absorbent towel.

Crushed ratte potatoes

INGREDIENTS	4 PORTIONS	10 PORTIONS
Ratte potatoes, boiled and skinned	400g	1kg
Olive oil	To taste	To taste
Lemon juice	To taste	To taste
Chopped chives		

Method of work

1 Crush the potatoes with a fork and gently heat on the stove adding olive oil until creamy.
2 Finish with salt and pepper, lemon juice and chives.

Stuffed baby artichokes

INGREDIENTS	4 PORTIONS	10 PORTIONS
Baby artichokes	4	10
Fennel brunoise	25g	60g
Carrot brunoise	25g	60g
Celery brunoise	25g	60g
Shallot brunoise	25g	60g
Piece of pancetta	25g	60g
Lemon	½	1
Olive oil	100ml	220ml
Saffron	Pinch	Pinch
Bouquet garni	1	2
Fish/ vegetable stock	200ml	450ml
Chopped parsley	Pinch	Pinch

Method of work

1 Turn artichokes and toss in lemon juice.
2 Sweat vegetables and bacon in oil for 2 minutes, add artichokes and lemon juice.
3 Cover with stock, add saffron and bouquet garni, simmer until artichokes are tender.

4 Remove artichokes and scoop out choke.
5 Strain vegetables and cut bacon into brunoise, mix together with the parsley.
6 Season and stuff artichokes with mixture.
7 Keep warm.

Roast langoustines

INGREDIENTS	4 PORTIONS	10 PORTIONS
Large langoustines, shelled and deveined	4	10
Unsalted butter	25g	60g
Lemon juice	To taste	To taste
Salt and pepper		

Method of work
1 Heat butter until foaming, add langoustines and toss quickly.
2 Place into a 200°C oven for 2 minutes, add lemon juice and season, remove from pan, pour butter over and serve immediately.

Sauce vierge

INGREDIENTS	4 PORTIONS	10 PORTIONS
Brunoise shallots	50g	120g
Tomato concassé	100g	250g
Extra virgin olive oil	150ml	400ml
Lemon juice	1/2	2
Basil chiffonade	1 tbsp	3 tbsp
Parsley chiffonade	1 tbsp	3 tbsp
Roasted fennel seeds	1 tsp	3 tsp

Method of work
1 Mix ingredients just before serving.

Grilled marine conservation tuna with borlotti beans, red peppers and parsley potatoes, rocket pesto

INGREDIENTS	4 PORTIONS	10 PORTIONS
Marine conservation tuna steaks cooked on a griddle to rare	4 × 150g	10 × 150g

Borlotti beans and red peppers

INGREDIENTS	4 PORTIONS	10 PORTIONS
Cooked borlotti beans	400g	1kg
Red peppers	2	5
Olive oil	100ml	220ml
Red wine vinegar	To taste	To taste

Method of work

1 Blister peppers with a blow torch until blackened.
2 Place in a plastic bag and tie, leave to cool down.
3 Remove peppers and peel of the skin, take 1 pepper and cut into fine strips.
4 Cut the other pepper into dice and blend with the olive oil in a blender until smooth.
5 Adjust seasoning and add vinegar to taste.
6 Mix the beans and pepper strips into the pepper and oil purée.

Parsley potatoes

INGREDIENTS	4 PORTIONS	10 PORTIONS
20 cocotte size potatoes	20	50
Olive oil		
Chopped parsley		

Method of work

1 Carefully simmer potatoes in salted water. When cooked drain and dry, toss in oil and parsley, season well.

Rocket pesto

INGREDIENTS	4 PORTIONS	10 PORTIONS
Fresh rocket leaves	200g	500g
Pine nuts	50g	110g
Clove garlic	1	2
Extra virgin olive oil	150ml	400ml
Freshly grated parmesan	100ml	220ml

Method of work

1 Place oil, pine nuts and garlic into a blender, blend until nuts and garlic are chopped finely.
2 With the motor still running add the rocket leaves and blend until they form a paste.
3 Add parmesan and blend for 20 seconds, season.

To finish

1 Place hot bean mixture in the centre of a bowl, top with the tuna.
2 Sit potatoes on top of tuna and spoon the pesto around.
3 Garnish with a poached egg and anchovy fillets.

Seared sea bass with curry oil, yoghurt, onion bhaji and spiced plum chutney

INGREDIENTS	4 PORTIONS	10 PORTIONS
Sea bass	4 × 150g	10 × 150g
Diced potatoes	400g	1kg
Turmeric	2tsp	5tsp
Fresh baby spinach	200g	500g
Mustard seeds	1tsp	3tsp
Curry powder	2tbsp	5tbsp
Olive oil	200ml	450ml
Greek yoghurt	50ml	125ml
White onions sliced	2	5
Flour	100g	250g
Garam masala	2 tbspn	5 tbspn
Plums (stoned and chopped)	500g	1250g
Red chillies chopped	2	5
Brown sugar	6tbsp	15tbsp
Cinnamon stick	1	3
Red wine vinegar	50ml	125ml
Red onion chopped	2	5
Good-quality salt and white pepper	To taste	To taste

 CHEF'S TIP

There is very little connective tissue in fish, making it very fragile during cooking. All fish should be cooked as little as possible to maintain its shape and moisture content.

Method of work

1 Mix the plums, red chillies, sugar, cinnamon, red wine vinegar and chopped red onion together. Simmer for 4 hours until totally broken down and thickened, chill and store in an airtight container.

2 Mix the curry powder with a little olive oil to form a paste, then gradually add the remaining oil. Simmer for 1 hour until the spices are cooked through and the oil is brightly coloured and flavoured.

3 Thin the yoghurt with a little water or fresh milk until it resembles a sauce consistency.

4 Bring the washed potatoes to the boil with the turmeric, a little water to cover and the mustard seeds. When cooked, pour off any excess water and add the spinach over the heat, allow the mix to break down a little.

5 Mix the sliced onions with the garam masala, a little water and the flour and leave the paste aside for 1 hour.

6 Form small flat bhajis and deep fry until golden in colour.

7 Sear the seasoned sea bass in a shallow pan of oil, skin-side first, and finish cooking in a hot oven until just cooked.

8 Spoon the yoghurt on the plate and drizzle on the curry oil.

9 Position the potato mixture, with the sea bass on top, the plum chutney and then the onion bhaji to serve.

Monkfish and tiger prawn skewers with sweet potato sagaloo, Shishu cress and spiced pineapple compôte

INGREDIENTS	4 PORTIONS	10 PORTIONS
Monkfish	320g	800g
Peeled tiger prawns	320g	800g
Sweet potato	400g	1kg
Fresh spinach	100g	250g
Coconut milk	1 × 400g tin	2½ × 400g tins
Turmeric	2tbsp	5tbsp
Mustard seeds	2tsp	5tsp
Shishu cress	1 punnet	2½ punnets
Pineapple	¼	1 whole
Cinnamon stick	1	3
Stock syrup	100ml	250ml
Chilli flakes	pinch	2 pinches
Good-quality salt and white pepper	To taste	To taste

Method of work

1 Soak the bamboo skewers in water for 1 hour. Put the prawns and diced monkfish alternately onto the skewers (one portion should equal a total weight of 160g).
2 Dice the sweet potato and cook with turmeric, mustard seeds and coconut milk until tender. Add the torn spinach leaves and allow to wilt with the residual heat from the potato mixture.
3 Dice the fresh pineapple and simmer in the stock syrup with the cinnamon and chilli flakes until just tender. Cool down and refrigerate in an airtight container.
4 Shallow fry the fish skewers and finish in the oven if required. Use the excess syrup glaze to brush over as they cook in the oven.
5 Place the sweet potatoes on the centre of the serving plate with the skewers and pineapple **compôte** and garnish with Shishu cress.

CHEF'S TIP

To test if fish is correctly cooked, the flesh should feel tender to the touch and offer little resistance.

Roasted pavé of salmon, wilted pak choy, shitake mushrooms and a tomato butter sauce

 CHEF'S TIP

When roasting fish, always constantly baste with olive oil or butter to help maintain the moisture and prevent it from burning in a dry heat.

INGREDIENTS	4 PORTIONS	10 PORTIONS
Salmon pavé	4 × 160g	10 × 160g
Pak choy	4	10
Shitake mushrooms (quartered)	200g	500g
Unsalted butter	100g	250g
Tomato fondue (passed and reduced)	50ml	125ml
Beurre blanc	100ml	250ml
Olive oil	50ml	125ml
Good-quality salt and white pepper	To taste	To taste
Lemon juice	To taste	To taste

Method of work

1 Preheat an oven to 200°C. Brush the salmon **pavé** with olive oil and season well. Place onto a roasting tray and roast until just slightly undercooked in the centre.

2 Cut the pak choy down the centre and wash well. Sweat in butter in a shallow pan and season.

3 Sauté the shitake mushrooms until tender and season with salt, pepper and a few drops of lemon juice.

4 Mix the tomato fondue with the beurre blanc and correct the seasoning and the consistency.

5 Carefully arrange the pak choy and the shitake mushrooms on the service plate and position the roasted salmon on top.

6 Spoon the sauce neatly around the plate and serve.

Poached paupiette of lemon sole with salmon and lemongrass mousseline, champagne and chervil fish cream sauce

INGREDIENTS	4 PORTIONS	10 PORTIONS
Lemon sole fillet	8 × 60g	20 × 60g
Salmon mousseline	240g	600g
Lemongrass	2 sticks	5 sticks
Carrot	100g	250g
Leek	100g	250g
Courgette	100g	250g
Mouli	100g	250g
Unsalted butter	100g	250g
Fish cream sauce	175ml	400ml
Champagne	50ml	125ml
Fresh chervil	¼ bunch	½ bunch
Fish stock	200ml	500ml
Good-quality salt and white pepper	To taste	To taste

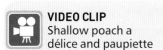

VIDEO CLIP
Shallow poach a délice and paupiette

Method of work

1 Lightly bat out the skinned fillets of lemon sole between plastic film.

2 Finely chop the lemongrass, quickly blanch in boiling water and refresh in iced water. Add to the salmon mousseline.

3 Pipe the mousseline onto one half of the sole fillet and fold the other half on the top. Retain in a refrigerator ready for cooking.

4 Cut the vegetables into long julienne strips and sweat in butter in a shallow pan. Season well and retain warm until needed for service.

5 Lightly poach the paupiette of sole in the fish stock with a cartouche until just cooked. Retain warm for service.

6 Chop half of the fresh chervil and add to the fish cream sauce with a little of the champagne. Bring to the boil and check the seasoning and consistency.

7 Place buttered vegetables on the bottom of the plate and rest the sole on the top. Nape with the fish cream sauce and garnish with a sprig of chervil.

Grilled gravadlax with crisp potatoes, oyster mushrooms, rocket and puy lentil cream

INGREDIENTS	4 PORTIONS	10 PORTIONS
Thin supreme of gravadlax	4 × 100g	10 × 100g
Diced Maris Piper potatoes	400g	1kg
Oyster mushrooms	100g	250g
Fresh rocket	200g	500g
Puy lentils (braised with brunoise of vegetables)	50g	125g
Fish cream sauce	100ml	250ml
Fresh dill	6tsp	15tsp
Good-quality salt and white pepper	To taste	To taste

Method of work

1 Thoroughly wash the gravadlax and dry well. Char grill, creating a quadrillage effect. Retain warm for service.

2 Wash the diced potatoes under running cold water for approximately 2 minutes to rinse off the starch. Drain well. Deep fry the potatoes in groundnut oil at 150°C, until blanched. Drain well and place onto a tray lined with absorbent paper. Chill in a refrigerator.

3 Sauté the mushrooms then mix with the fresh rocket.

4 Deep fry the potatoes at 190°C until golden brown. Drain the potatoes, season well and mix with the rocket and sautéed mushrooms.

5 Arrange the potato mix on the service plate with the gravadlax on top.

6 Chop half the fresh dill and mix with the lentils and fish cream sauce then spoon around the plate.

7 Finish with the remaining sprigs of fresh dill.

CHEF'S TIP

When deep frying fish or potatoes, try to use groundnut oil as this has a superior quality when cooking.

Seared hot-smoked halibut with treacle-cured bacon, chestnut mushrooms, wilted baby gem and pesto vinaigrette

INGREDIENTS	4 PORTIONS	10 PORTIONS
Hot-smoked halibut	4 × 160g	10 × 160g
Treacle-cured bacon	200g	500g
Chestnut mushrooms	200g	500g
Baby gem lettuce	2	5
Pesto dressing	50ml	150ml
White wine vinegar	50ml	50ml
Olive oil	150ml	150ml
Good-quality salt and white pepper	To taste	To taste

Method of work

1 Cut the treacle-cured bacon into lardons and the chestnut mushrooms into quarters. Ensure there is no dirt or grit in the mushrooms.

2 Wash the baby gem lettuce and cut lengthwise into eight pieces.

3 Sauté the treacle-cured bacon lardons and add the quartered chestnut mushrooms. Once cooked, add the baby gems and wilt in the residual heat.

4 Heat a shallow pan with a little olive oil. Sear the halibut for approximately 2 minutes on each side to colour and warm through.

5 Reduce the pesto to a slightly runnier consistency with the white wine vinegar and olive oil.

6 Set the bacon mixture in a stainless steel ring in the centre of a service plate, lay the halibut on top and spoon the dressing around.

Peppered mackerel with Thai vegetable salad and ginger crème fraîche

INGREDIENTS	4 PORTIONS	10 PORTIONS
Mackerel fillets	4 fillets	10 fillets
Chinese leaf lettuce	¼	1 whole
Fresh carrot	100g	250g
Fresh mouli	100g	250g
Red onion	100g	250g
Spring onions	4	10
Cucumber	½	1½
Red chillies (cut into fine brunoise)	2tbsp	5tbsp
Garlic (cut into brunoise)	2tbsp	5tbsp
Ginger (cut into brunoise)	2tbsp	5tbsp
Lemongrass (cut into brunoise)	2tbsp	5tbsp
Champagne vinegar	50ml	125ml
Olive oil	150ml	375ml
Crème fraîche	50ml	125ml
Finely grated fresh ginger	20g	50g
Crushed black peppercorns	2tbsp	5tbsp
Good-quality salt	To taste	To taste

Method of work

1 To make the Thai dressing, combine the chillies, ginger, garlic and lemongrass with the vinegar and olive oil. Leave to stand at room temperature for a minimum of 24 hours to infuse all the flavours.

2 Sprinkle the mackerel fillets with the crushed peppercorns and lightly oil before placing onto a tray and under a **salamander** until cooked through.

3 Dress the washed and shredded Chinese leaf, finely sliced red onion, julienne of carrot and mouli, shredded spring onion and julienne of cucumber with the Thai dressing and warm together in a saucepan.

4 Mix the grated fresh ginger with the crème fraîche and season.

5 Arrange the salad on the service plate and set the grilled mackerel on top with a quenelle of crème fraîche on the fish.

Deep fried ray in turmeric flour with chive pomme purée and a mussel, tomato and tarragon liquor sauce

INGREDIENTS	4 PORTIONS	10 PORTIONS
Ray wing (boned and cut into 4cm × 4cm pieces)	20 pieces	50 pieces
Flour	50g	125g
Turmeric	2tbsp	5tbsp
Pomme purée (with double cream and butter)	400g	1kg
Chopped fresh chives	¼ bunch	1 bunch
Fresh live mussels	20	50
Chopped shallots	2	5
Dry white wine	100ml	250ml
Tomato concassé	50g	125g
Chopped fresh tarragon	4tsp	10tsp
Chilled unsalted butter (diced)	100g	250g
Good-quality salt and white pepper	To taste	To taste

Method of work

1 Prepare and wash the mussels, discarding any that are open. In a heavy-based saucepan, cook the cleaned mussels with the shallots and wine for 2 minutes with the lid firmly on.

2 Drain the mussels and pass the cooking liquor into a pan. The mussels should have all opened (discard any that remain closed). Pick the mussels and discard the shells.

3 Mix together the flour and the powdered turmeric and sieve together twice. Lightly flour the fresh ray wing pieces with the turmeric flour and deep fry at 190°C in groundnut oil until golden in colour.

4 Bring to the boil the retained mussel cooking liquor and reduce by one-third. Gradually add the chilled butter and blend in using a whisk over a heat. Add the mussels, tomato concassé and tarragon and correct the seasoning and consistency.

5 Heat the pomme purée with the chopped fresh chives and spoon into the base of the service dish.

6 Position the pieces of deep fried ray wing on top.

7 Spoon the sauce around the plate.

Monkfish and red mullet bourride

INGREDIENTS	4 PORTIONS	10 PORTIONS
Pieces of monkfish	4 × 60g	10 × 60g
Red mullet fillets (80g each)	4	10

Bourride

INGREDIENTS	4 PORTIONS	10 PORTIONS
Lobster shells chopped into small pieces	500g	1.25kg
Unsalted butter	50g	120g
Cognac	20ml	50ml
White wine	50ml	110ml
Noilly Prat	50ml	110ml
Fennel seeds	5g	12g
Small bay leaf	1	2
Sprig of thyme	1	2
Tomato purée	5g	12g
Crushed clove of garlic	1	2
Sliced shallots	50g	110g
Chopped parsley and chervil		
Fish stock	500ml	1.2 litres
Egg yolk	1	2
Olive oil	80ml	140ml
Pinch of saffron		
Salt and pepper		

Method of work

1 Sweat the lobster shells in butter until lightly coloured, then add shallots and garlic.
2 Add tomato purée and cook out for 5 minutes.
3 Add cognac and flame, add wine, Noilly Prat and cook out for 2 minutes.
4 Add fish stock, fennel seeds and saffron, simmer for 20 minutes.
5 Pass through a fine chinois and press bones.
6 Place in clean pan and keep warm.
7 Place egg yolk in a bowl and whisk with 5 ml of warm water, emulsify olive oil as with mayonnaise.
8 Gently heat liquid and whisk in egg and oil mix until thickened. Do not boil!
9 Finish with chopped herbs.
10 Grill the mullet and fry the monkfish, arrange on bowls and pour bourride over the fish.
11 Garnish with steamed turned potatoes and glazed baby leeks, carrots and broad beans.

Whiting fillets steamed with coriander, seared oriental salmon with sesame and breaded sole with sauce vierge

INGREDIENTS	4 PORTIONS	10 PORTIONS
Whiting fillets	4 × 50g	10 × 50g
Coriander seeds crushed	1tsp	2½tsp
Salmon fillets skinned	4 × 50g	10 × 50g
Hoi sin sauce	4tbsp	10tbsp
Sesame seeds	2tsp	5tsp
Lemon sole fillets	4 × 50g	10 × 50g
Flour	4tbsp	10tbsp
Whole eggs	2	5
Breadcrumbs	8tbsp	20tbsp
Sauce vierge	4tbsp	10tbsp
Tomato coulis	4tbsp	10tbsp
Good-quality salt and white pepper	To taste	To taste

Method of work

1 Prepare the whiting and fold into a delice. Season with salt and the crushed coriander, wrap in plastic film and steam in a steamer until just cooked.

2 Marinate the salmon in the hoi sin sauce and toasted sesame seeds. Shallow fry on both sides until the salmon is slightly underdone.

3 Roll the lemon sole into a spiral and pané à la Anglaise using seasoned flour, beaten egg and fine breadcrumbs. Deep fry in hot groundnut oil at 190°C.

4 Spoon a little warmed tomato coulis onto the service plate and rest the whiting on top.

5 Place a little of the warmed hoi sin sauce on the service plate and lay the salmon on top.

6 Spoon a little sauce vierge on the plate and set the deep fried lemon sole on top.

 CHEF'S TIP

To increase the flavour of fish when steaming, place it on a bed of fresh herbs or aromatic vegetables or spices.

SHELLFISH

Shellfish is a collective term for crustacean, mollusc and cephalopod seafood. Using shellfish can be a rewarding experience, both in preparation and cooking. Each group of shellfish includes a range of species, each with its own method of preparation.

■ *Molluscs*   Can have a single shell: univalves
Can have a pair of shells: bivalves
Can have no shell: cephalopods

■ *Crustaceans* Have an external skeleton

CLASSIFICATION OF SHELLFISH

UNIVALVE	BIVALVE	CEPHALOPOD	CRUSTACEAN
Limpets	Cockles	Octopus	Lobsters
Whelks	Mussels	Cuttlefish	Crabs
Winkles	Razor shell clams	Squid	Crayfish
Tower shells	Scallops		Prawns
Tusk shells	Oysters		Shrimps
	Carpet shells		Langoustine
	Paddocks		
	Clams		

Shellfish generally live in, on or near the seabed, on the continental shelf, shelf slope and in very deep water. They can be obtained in two ways; by farming or by harvesting from the wild. There are good and bad points for each method.

Larger crustaceans, such as lobsters, crabs and crayfish, are often caught by small inshore fisheries, and prawns, shrimps and langoustine may be targeted by trawlers. Langoustine is fished extensively in the North Sea.

Univalve and bivalve molluscs, including scallops, oysters, mussels, clams, cockles, whelks and snails, can all be gathered by hand, trapped or dredged. Cephalopods (squid, cuttlefish and octopus) can be harvested using nets or hook and line.

The most common way to gather scallops is to dredge the seabed with a net This method can result in by-catch of undersized individuals or other species and can damage the shells. An alternative method is diving, where divers collect the scallops by hand from the seabed. This method is more selective, and dived scallops will sell at a higher price.

SUSTAINABILITY

The Sea Fish Industry Authority (Seafish) works across all sectors of the UK seafood industry to promote good-quality, sustainable seafood. Its research and projects are aimed at raising standards, improving efficiency and ensuring that the fishing industry develops in a practical and sustainable way. Established in 1981, it is the UK's only cross-industry seafood body working with fishermen, processors, wholesalers, seafood farmers, chefs, caterers, retailers and the import/export trade.

Seafish is helping the industry to become more sustainable through a variety of activities:

- The Seafish Sustainable Fisheries Advisory Committee brings together fishermen and environmentalists from across all sectors of the seafood industry to consider the need for conservation and stability and to advise Seafish.

- Seafish marine technologists work with fishermen to develop and test trawling gear designs that are more selective and less damaging to the seabed.

- Guidelines have been produced for the use of square-mesh panels in prawn trawls, which reduce the by-catch of juvenile fish such as haddock and cod.

- An international research project on scallop dredge design to reduce environmental damage is co-ordinated by Seafish.

- A new trawl design with an escape hatch for dolphins is being developed.

Forthcoming projects include:

- Developing a UK training course in responsible fishing

- Co-ordinating a pilot project to develop a high-quality, low-volume sustainable pelagic fishery in Cornwall, and eventually a model which can be developed throughout the UK

- Investigating new ways to use the waste products left over from the UK's processing industry

- Leading an international project called Tracefish, developing a Europe-wide scheme which traces seafood from net to plate. This will help the seafood industry to deliver consistent, clear labelling for seafood so that consumers can make informed choices about what to purchase.

SHELLFISH PREPARATION

Bivalve molluscs

Scallops

Scallops are highly regarded and are expensive to purchase. The rounded, fan-shaped shells vary in size, from the smaller queen scallops about 7cm across to the larger ones up to 18cm across. The edible parts are the round white muscle and the orange and white roe (coral). The frilly gills and mantle can be used for soup and stocks.

Scallops can be opened by separating the shells with a knife. This can be done relatively easily once the basic techniques have been mastered.

■ Hold the scallop shell firmly, with the flat shell uppermost.

■ Place a thick knife between the shells by the hinge and push up to break the connection.

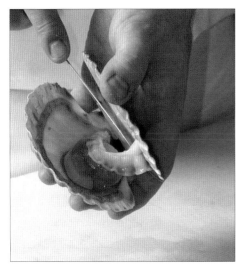

■ Slide the knife along the inside of the flat shell, remove the flat shell and discard.

■ Work the knife under the skirt (frilly gills) then under the white and coral to separate from the shell.

■ Discard the skirt or save for making a stock.

■ Separate the white from the coral and gently wash both and store until required.

If the scallops are fresh, well prepared and in excellent condition, they can be used raw, simply marinated with an acidic dressing to gently denaturise the flesh.

Clams

Clams are well known for the classic dish clam chowder, which is mainly associated with the east coast of the United States.

Razor shell clams

Razor shells clams are shaped like cut-throat razors. They are caught by tipping salt onto the sand: the shells pop out of the ground and are carefully harvested.

Oysters

Many species and varieties of oyster are found around the world and so oysters come in a many shapes and sizes. The best British oysters are the 'native' or 'flat' oysters. Other British oysters include 'rock' oysters. Natives are available from September to April, though they are at their best from late October to late February when the sea is colder. Pacific oysters are available all year.

Oyster shells must be scrubbed well before opening and an oyster knife should always be used to open the shells.

■ Place the blade of the oyster knife between the shells by the hinge, and using gentle force carefully lift.

■ Lift the top shell, sever the muscle and discard the shell.

■ Slide the knife under the oyster to free it, check for any loose shell and discard, remove any foam residue.

It is important to use an oyster knife because a normal kitchen knife could break. An oyster knife also has a small guard near the handle to help prevent the hand from slipping and cutting against the sharp shell.

Any oysters that have an unusual smell should be discarded. Native oysters are best eaten raw, and as soon as possible after capture. Raw oysters are traditionally eaten with lemon and a little cayenne pepper. Cooked rock oysters are used to produce chowders and fish stews.

Mussels

These molluscs, which have a distinctive oval blue-black shell, are often seen attached to rocks and wooden structures around coastlines worldwide. The vibrant orange-coloured meat inside is sweet and salty. Mussels should only be harvested from unpolluted waters between September and March; they should be left alone during the summer months. Cultivated mussels are also available.

Mussels

Purchase smaller or medium-sized mussels, and always buy more than you need because there will always be some dead ones that will need to be discarded.

Univalve molluscs

Whelks

Whelks resemble pointed snails when fresh, and are usually sold ready-cooked. Only retain the good whelks and discard any that are damaged or smell strongly.

Winkles

Winkles, known as 'black sea snails', are served as appetisers. They are usually sold pre-cooked, and can be seasoned with fresh tarragon or parsley and a little white wine. They are quickly and easily removed from their shells using a pin when cooked.

Cephalopod molluscs

Squid

Squid varies in size, from small ones of about 7cm to larger ones of about 25cm. Squid is available most of the year, either fresh or frozen. It freezes very well, and preparing squid is relatively straightforward. If the ink sac can be recovered intact from inside the squid, it can be used to colour and flavour risottos, pastas and sauces. There is a transparent flexible cartilage within the squid, which must be removed. Cooking must be either very quick or very slow, otherwise the flesh will be tough to eat.

Squid

Crustaceans

Lobster

Lobsters are more expensive than their close relatives the crabs because of the superior flavour and texture of their meat. When alive, lobsters' shells are mottled with dark green, blue and brick red colours, but they turn to their distinctive bright red on cooking.

Lobsters can grow to 4.5kg, but are best eaten at about 500g to 1.4kg. The smaller lobsters are more tender. Cold-water lobsters from the northern seas are considered the finest: the males have denser, meatier flesh, and the females have a more subtle flavour and an orange roe, the 'coral', which can be used to colour sauces.

Most of the lobster is edible, except the transparent bag-like stomach and the dark intestines. These should be removed with a sharp knife point. Do not remove the creamy green-grey liver, known as the 'tomalley', which has an excellent flavour. It can also be used to flavour sauces and soups.

Purchase lobsters that feel heavy for their size, with both claws intact, and preferably buy them while they are still alive and cook them yourself. A 1.4kg lobster should be enough for two portions.

VIDEO CLIP
Deep poaching lobsters in court bouillon

Lobster is best cooked simply – boiled, steamed or grilled – and can be served either hot or cold. Serve with melted butter, lemon juice or mayonnaise. Crack the claws with a hammer or back of a large knife to extract the meat. The shells can be used for fish soup, the base for bisque or a lobster sauce.

The reason for cooking lobsters alive is that once killed their flesh starts to deteriorate very quickly. Fishmongers and wholesalers will only buy live lobsters to sell, and in turn chefs and cooks, when cooking fresh lobster, will always choose live specimens for freshness. Lobsters sold in supermarkets in this country are generally sold already cooked as the demand for live lobsters is not as great as it is abroad.

Methods of cooking lobster

- The standard way of cooking is to place the live lobster head first into a pan of boiling water – the lobster dies very quickly.
- Another method is to freeze the live lobster for approximately 30 minutes to desensitise it and then cook it in boiling water.
- A third method it to kill the lobster before cooking: in one sharp blow, pierce the live lobster between the eyes, which kills it instantly, then cook it in the usual way.

Method of preparing lobster

Plunge the lobster into court bouillon *to cook*

Remove the claws

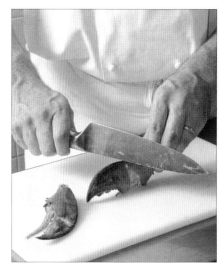

Crack the claws with the back of a knife

Remove the claw flesh in one piece

Split the lobster in half lengthwise

Turn the lobster and continue to cut

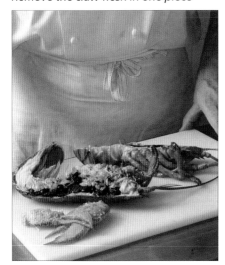

Remove the white flesh and discard the dark flesh

VIDEO CLIP
Lobster Thermidor

Crab

There are many varieties of crab and many regions throughout the world where crabs are abundant:

- *Europe* – the brown crab and the spider crab
- *Eastern USA* – the blue crab
- *Pacific coast of the USA* – the Dungeness crab

The soft brown flesh under the hard upper shell is strong and full-flavoured, this contrasts well with the sweet, delicate white flesh found in the claws and body. Male crabs often have larger claws and so more white flesh than females.

VIDEO CLIP
Dressed crab

Purchase crabs that feel heavy for their size and smell fresh and sweet, whether alive or cooked. If there is a smell of ammonia, do not buy. Crabs are best bought alive and cooked fresh. You will need approximately 115g of meat per portion – for this you will need about 450g of whole crab (with shell intact).

The brown crab from Europe is available all year. It reaches 20–25cm across and has heavy front claws with almost-black pincers. Its shell is rusty-red or brown, and its legs are hairy and red but mottled with white.

- Lay the crab on its back and remove the legs and claws by twisting.

- Hold the belly of the crab near the eyes and pull, this will come off in one piece.

- Inside you will see the grey fingers and a sack – discard these.

- Scrape the meat from the shell and claws (keep the brown meat and white meat separate).

- The inside of the claws can be accessed by cracking the shell with the back of a knife and then carefully peeling.

The velvet crab, sometimes known as the swimming crab, grows to 10–15cm. Its body is coated with short hairs, giving it a velvet-like appearance. It is one of the major crab species in UK waters, and is found in rocky areas near the shoreline and down to a depth of approximately 65 metres. Velvet crab fetches the highest price, especially abroad, such as in Spain, Portugal and France, where it is seen as a luxury food item.

The popularity of spider crab is increasing, and as the waters around the south-west coast of the UK begin warm up the population of these crabs is increasing. Tangle nets are the main fishing method used to capture spider crabs. Netting is less sustainable than potting; with potting there is no by-catch and undersized crabs can be returned to the sea alive. Avoid using immature crabs (the legal minimum landing size is 120mm maximum body width), egg-bearing crabs and fresh (not previously frozen) crabs caught during the spawning season (April to July).

Velvet crabs

Langoustine

Also known as Dublin Bay prawns, Norway lobster and scampi, these orange-pink shellfish from the north-east Atlantic and Mediterranean resemble small, slim lobsters. They are an expensive choice with little meat, but are delicious if freshly caught and cooked.

Spider crabs

The best specimens can be bought from late spring to late autumn and are cooked in the same way as lobster. Because of their smaller size, they need less cooking. Usually only the tail is sold. In their shells, 200g should be enough per portion, however removed from their shells, half this quantity will be enough. They are available frozen all year round.

Prawns

There are many prawn species and they vary in size from 5cm to 18cm long. King prawns grow even larger at up to 23cm. They also come in many colours, from the familiar common pink prawns to the brown-blue tiger prawns.

Prawns are available all year round, though usually frozen in the UK. Fresh raw prawns are the tastiest. They should be firm and springy with bright shells. If they are limp, soft or have an ammonia smell then discard them. Ensure frozen prawns are properly defrosted before heating.

Prawns can be prepared in the same way as langoustine but do not require scissors to cut and peel as the shells are much softer.

TRANSPORTATION AND STORAGE

The best transportation and storage for live crustaceans is to use a seawater or freshwater tank. For shellfish to be transported in these conditions the following points should be observed:

■ Controlled water temperature within the tanks

■ Good aeration of the water

■ Suitable water quality depending on the type of crustacean or mollusc

■ Species should be separated into independent tanks.

However, this method is costly and only catering establishments that specialise in serving shellfish will have this facility. Fish and shellfish suppliers will also have this facility on their own premises, but generally when being delivered crustaceans such as lobster, crabs and crayfish will be packed in cases (usually polystyrene), covered with wet cloths and kept in a refrigerated environment.

Follow these guidelines when storing fresh shellfish:

1 Keep the shellfish at a temperature of between 2°C and 8°C.
2 Keep shellfish in its packaging until preparation, this is to prevent moisture loss.
3 Ensure that all shellfish remain moist.
4 Molluscs should be kept in a container embedded in ice. The round side of the shell should face downwards to help collect and retain the natural juices.
5 Check regularly to make sure that they are still alive. Reject any dead or dying specimens.

SHELLFISH ALLERGY

Allergy to shellfish is quite common and people who are sensitive can react to a number of different types of shellfish, such as shrimps, prawns, lobsters and oysters. People who are allergic to one type of shellfish often react to others. Shellfish allergy can often cause severe reactions, and even the vapours from shellfish being cooked may be enough to trigger a reaction in some people.

Since November 2005, prepacked food sold in Europe must show clearly on the label if it contains crustaceans, including lobster, crab, prawns and langoustines. However, other groups of shellfish, such as molluscs (including mussels, scallops, oysters, and whelks), cephalopods (squid and octopus) or gastropods (snails) do not need to be labelled individually.

Shellfish is, however, recognised as being a healthy food which is low in cholesterol. It is important to support the UK's territorial fisherman and to utilise their skills in catching only what is required. This will help to increase the stock levels and generate a healthier UK economy.

SHELLFISH RECIPES

Deep fried oysters with a Thai salad

INGREDIENTS	4 PORTIONS	10 PORTIONS
Fresh oysters	12	30
White breadcrumbs	200g	500g
Lime juice and zest	1 lime	2 limes
Flour	100g	250g
Whole egg pasteurised	100ml	250ml
Chinese leaf lettuce (cut into chiffonade)	¼ lettuce	¾ lettuce
Assorted peppers (cut into julienne)	½ of each colour	1 of each colour
Red onion finely sliced	50g	125g
Baby gem lettuce (cut into chiffonade)	1	2
Julienne of carrot	80g	200g
Thai dressing	200ml	500ml
Good-quality salt and white pepper	To taste	To taste

Method of work

1 Carefully remove the fresh oysters from their shells and wash to remove any grit.
2 Marinate the oysters in the lime juice for 5 minutes.
3 Pané the oysters through the flour, then the beaten egg and finally the breadcrumbs with the finely grated lime zest mixed through.
4 Prepare the vegetables as required and dress with the Thai dressing.
5 Season well and arrange on a serving plate.
6 Quickly deep fry the oysters at 180°C until golden and serve on top of the salad.

Seared scallops with a sweet caper dressing and cauliflower purée

INGREDIENTS	4 PORTIONS	10 PORTIONS
Fresh scallops	12	30
Curry powder	5g	10g
Capers	80g	200g
Caster sugar	2tbsp	5tbsp
White wine vinegar	40ml	100ml
Vegetable stock	100ml	250ml
Cauliflower	¼	¾
Béchamel sauce	50ml	125ml
Olive oil	2tbsp	5tbsp
Fresh dill	4 sprigs	10 sprigs
Good-quality salt and white pepper	To taste	To taste

Method of work

1 Carefully remove the scallops from the shells and remove the corals.

2 Trim the scallops, wash, dry and dust lightly with the curry powder.

3 Drain and wash the **capers**, then blend with the vinegar, oil and sugar to form the dressing.

4 Cut the cauliflower into small florets and cook in the vegetable stock until tender. Drain and blend the cauliflower with the béchamel until smooth, pass through a sieve. Season to taste.

5 Quickly sear the scallops in a hot pan with a little oil for 1 minute on each side.

6 Spoon the purée and dressing onto a serving plate, arrange the scallops on top and finish with a sprig of fresh dill.

Tiger prawn and lemongrass cakes with chilli jam

INGREDIENTS	4 PORTIONS	10 PORTIONS
Minced tiger prawns (reserving one whole tail per portion)	16	40
Lemongrass brunoise	1tbsp	2½tbsp
Red chilli brunoise	2tbsp	5tbsp
Shallot brunoise	1tbsp	2½tbsp
Red wine vinegar	50ml	125ml
Caster sugar	100g	250g
Cornflour	50g	125g
Soy sauce	2tbsp	5tbsp
Fresh garlic (finely puréed)	1tsp	2½tsp
Ginger purée	1tsp	2½tsp
Mizuna	50g	125g
Good-quality salt and white pepper	To taste	To taste

Method of work

1 Preheat an oven to 180°C.

2 Mix the minced prawn meat with the lemongrass, garlic, ginger, cornflour, soy sauce and seasoning. Leave for 20 minutes.

3 Boil the vinegar and sugar until it becomes syrupy.

4 Add the chilli and shallots and simmer for a further 5 minutes. Cool down for service.

5 Divide the prawn paste into equal pieces, one per portion. Dust with a little cornflour and form into round shapes.

6 Fry until golden in a little heated oil, remove from the pan and bake in the preheated oven for 2 minutes.

7 Add the whole tails at the last minute to the pan and flash fry until just cooked.

8 Arrange a cake and tail with some jam and mizuna on the plate and serve.

Mussels cooked with a garlic cream sauce, sun-dried tomato bread and baby rocket salad

INGREDIENTS	4 PORTIONS	10 PORTIONS
Fresh mussels	400g	1kg
Garlic	1 clove	3 cloves
Dry white wine	50ml	125ml
Shallot brunoise	2tbsp	5tbsp
Double cream	150ml	375ml
Sun-dried tomato bread	4 slices	10 slices
Baby rocket	75g	180g
Lemon oil	2tbsp	5tbsp
Fish stock	100ml	250ml
Fresh coriander	4 sprigs	10 sprigs
Good-quality salt and white pepper	To taste	To taste

Method of work

1 Place the mussels, shallots, chopped garlic and white wine in a hot saucepan. Cover with a tight-fitting lid and cook for 2 minutes. The mussels should have all opened (discard any that remain closed).

2 Remove the mussels and keep warm, add the fish stock to the saucepan and reduce by half over a medium heat.

3 Add the double cream and reduce until the sauce thickens to the correct consistency.

4 Return the mussels to the sauce and warm through gently, check the seasoning.

5 Quickly toast the slices of bread and set into a serving bowl.

6 Add the mussels and the sauce.

7 Dress the rocket with lemon oil and arrange neatly to the side of the bowl and serve with the coriander.

CHEF'S TIP

Before cooking mussels always ensure that they are washed well under plenty of cold running water. Remove all beards and barnacles. Any mussels that are still open at this point should be discarded.

Fried medallions of lobster with coral pasta and a bisque foam

INGREDIENTS	4 PORTIONS	10 PORTIONS
Fresh lobster (hen)	1	3
Fresh egg pasta dough	200g	500g
Shellfish bisque	100ml	250ml
Fresh full fat milk	50ml	125ml
Double cream	50ml	125ml
Lemon thyme	Sprig	Sprig
Butter	100g	250g
Good-quality salt and white pepper	To taste	To taste

Method of work

1   Remove the coral from the hen lobster and add to the pasta dough during the initial process of mixing the ingredients.

2   Kill the lobster by plunging a knife through the cavity in the centre of its head.

3   Steam the lobster for 6 minutes and cool quickly.

4   Remove the tail meat and claws then reserve to one side.

5   Heat the bisque and separate into two, add double cream to one half and allow to reduce to form a sauce and season well.

6   Blanch the pasta in boiling salted water, drain and add to the sauce.

7   Slice the tail meat (2 slices per portion) and quickly fry in butter with the claws until golden and season.

8   Add the milk to the remaining bisque and blend using a handheld blender until a foam appears.

9   Lay the pasta neatly into a bowl, top with the lobster, spoon over the foam and finish with the lemon thyme.

Crab and grain mustard beignets with an iced gazpacho

INGREDIENTS	4 PORTIONS	10 PORTIONS
White crab meat	200g	500g
Grain mustard	2tbsp	5tbsp
Choux paste	100g	250g
Pink peppercorns	1tsp	2½tsp
Fresh chopped parsley	2tbsp	5tbsp
Tomato juice	100ml	250ml
Cucumber brunoise	1tbsp	2½tbsp
Red wine vinegar	50ml	125ml
Olive oil	2tbsp	5tbsp
Finely chopped garlic	1tsp	2½tsp
Fresh basil	4 leaves	10 leaves
Shallot brunoise	1tbsp	2½tbsp
Good-quality salt and white pepper	To taste	To taste

Method of work

1   Combine the prepared tomato, cucumber, shallot, garlic, vinegar and oil together. Season well and place in the freezer until required for service (it is essential that it is not allowed to freeze completely).

2   Mix the choux pastry with the crab, ground peppercorns, fresh chopped parsley and grain mustard and season well.

3   Quenelle the choux mixture neatly, one quenelle per portion, and deep fry in groundnut oil at 190°C until golden in colour and completely cooked through.

4   Spoon the chilled gazpacho into a cold serving bowl and drizzle a little olive oil around.

5   Set the crab beignet on top and dress with the chiffonade of fresh basil.

Langoustines cooked in a sweet curry sauce with coconut rice

INGREDIENTS	4 PORTIONS	10 PORTIONS
Langoustines	20	50
Unsalted butter	100g	250g
Finely chopped onion	4tbsp	10tbsp
Long grain rice	200g	500g
Fish stock	400ml	1 litre
Fresh coconut	¼	1 whole
Flat leaf parsley	4 sprigs	10 sprigs
Sweet curry sauce	200ml	500ml
Lemon juice and zest	½ lemon	1 lemon
Finely chopped garlic	2tsp	5tsp
Finely chopped red chilli	1tsp	2tsp
Good-quality salt and white pepper	To taste	To taste

Method of work

1 Preheat an oven to 180°C.
2 Take half of the unsalted butter and melt in a heavy-based saucepan, add the chopped onion and sweat until translucent.
3 Add the rice and cook for a further 2 minutes allowing the grains to become coated in butter and completely mixed with the onion.
4 Add the hot fish stock and bring to the boil, cover with a buttered cartouche and braise in the preheated oven for 10 minutes or until the rice has just cooked.
5 Remove from the oven, fluff the rice over with a fork and fold in the coconut, seasoning and chopped parsley.
6 Marinate the peeled langoustine tails in garlic and lemon for 5 minutes before quickly frying in the remaining butter.
7 Carefully place the langoustines into the sauce and cook for 1 minute.
8 Arrange the rice neatly in a bowl, add the langoustines and garnish with red chilli.

Scampi fritters with a baby herb salad and vine tomato coulis

INGREDIENTS	4 PORTIONS	10 PORTIONS
Shelled cooked scampi	20	50
Olive oil	100ml	250ml
Lemon zest and juice	1 lemon	3 lemons
Cayenne pepper	Pinch	Pinch
Self raising flour	100g	250g
Finely chopped parsley	1tbsp	3tbsp
Baby herbs (tarragon and dill)	100g	250g
White wine vinegar	50ml	125ml
Dijon mustard	1tbsp	3tbsp
Vine tomato coulis	4tbsp	10tbsp
Good-quality salt and white pepper	To taste	To taste

Method of work

1 Marinate the scampi in lemon, cayenne and a little olive oil.

2 Mix the flour and parsley and enough water to form a light batter, season well (reserve a little flour to coat the scampi).

3 Dust the scampi with flour, dip into the batter and deep fry at 180°C until golden brown.

4 Produce a vinaigrette with the mustard, vinegar and olive oil then dress the baby herbs.

5 Arrange the herbs on a plate, add the scampi and spoon over the tomato coulis.

Individual crayfish mousse with a saffron foam

INGREDIENTS	4 PORTIONS	10 PORTIONS
Crayfish (peeled)	15	40
Egg yolks	2	5
White wine	50ml	125ml
Onion macédoine	1tbsp	3tbsp
Leek macédoine	1tbsp	3tbsp
Celery macédoine	1tbsp	3tbsp
Butter	100g	250g
Fresh lemon sole (minced)	200g	500g
Egg whites	2	5
Double cream	200ml	500ml
Fish velouté	100ml	250ml
Fresh full fat milk	50ml	125ml
Saffron	Pinch	Pinch
Fresh chervil	Sprigs	Sprigs
Good-quality salt and white pepper	To taste	To taste

Method of work

1 Sweat the vegetables in butter for 3 minutes without colour. Add the crayfish and wine, cover with a lid and cook for 3 minutes.

2 Mince the crayfish with the lemon sole and chill over ice for 10 minutes.

3 Add the egg yolks and cream very slowly while continuously beating over the ice, season well.

4 Whisk the egg whites to firm peaks then fold into the crayfish mixture.

5 Spoon the mixture into buttered dariole moulds and cook in a bain marie in the oven at 165°C for 20 minutes.

6 Heat the velouté with the saffron threads until a yellow colour is achieved, add the milk and reboil. Blend until a foam is achieved.

7 Turn out the crayfish mousse onto a service plate and spoon over the foam, finish with sprigs of fresh chervil.

Assessment of knowledge and understanding

You have now learned about the use of the different types of fish and shellfish and how to produce a variety of fish and shellfish dishes utilising an array of commodities and cooking techniques.

To test your level of knowledge and understanding, answer the following short questions. These will help to prepare you for your summative (final) assessment.

Fish preparation

1 Explain why the removal of fins is important during preparation of exotic fish.

2 Describe how the skinning of Dover sole is different from the skinning of other flat fish and explain the process.

Shellfish quality identifications

1 Explain when oysters should be bought and in what condition.

2 Explain the difference between crustaceans, molluscs and cephalopods.

Shellfish preparation

1 Describe the method for opening oysters.

2 Explain how langoustines should be prepared before cooking.

3 Identify which parts of lobsters and crabs should be discarded and why.

Materials and storage

1 Describe how shellfish should be transported.

Cooking

1 Describe the cooking of crab.

Health and safety

1 List the months during which raw oysters should not be eaten.

CHEF'S PROFILE

Name: DAVID CAVALIER

Position: Food Innovation Director

Establishment: Charlton House Catering Services Ltd

Current job role and main responsibilities: Food innovations, menu development and training. A large part of my role is to oversee 500 chefs within 140 different units on a day-to-day basis.

When did you realise that you wanted to pursue a career in the catering and hospitality industry? When I was 12 years old a French chef, who later became a great friend, was staying at our house. I was intrigued by the food he made for our family – it was very different to the meals my mother prepared.

Training:

I started working as a pot wash in the school holidays. I then got myself enrolled on a full-time catering course where I completed the City and Guilds qualification. From there I gained employment at top London hotels, such as the Dorchester, Grosvenor House and the Berkeley, while continuing with a one day a week course to achieve my City and Guilds 706/3.

Experience:

After working in the London hotels I went to America to work at the Stamford Court Hotel in San Francisco and the Belair Hotel in Los Angeles. I also spent two years in France, immersing myself in French culture and food while working at two Michelin-starred establishments. Upon my return to the UK, I opened my first small restaurant, Pebbles, in Aylesbury. From there I opened restaurant number two, Cavalier's, in London and then L'Escargot in Soho. I have consulted on many projects, from Chapter One to Regal Hotels to Pyrex cookware, spent some time as Executive Chef at Mosimann's, and in 2000 I gained another Michelin star for myself in just nine months. I am now concentrating on contract catering at Charlton House.

What do you find rewarding about your job?

Seeing customers' happy faces after they have experienced a wonderful meal. To me, this is the end result of hard work, being creative and mentoring chefs along the way.

What do you find most challenging about the job?

Always maintaining a consistently high level of food and service.

What advice would you give to students just beginning their career?

Catering is a long road, and it's not a job but a way of life. Once you have decided to follow this route, be passionate and fully committed. You will then find the area in which you excel.

Who is your mentor or main inspiration?

The young French chef who ignited my interest in food, François le Coz.

What traits do you consider essential for anyone entering a career as a chef?

Focus, natural flair, ability, talent, drive, enthusiasm and commitment.

Can you give one essential kitchen tip or technique that you use as a chef?

Never send out food that you are not 100 per cent happy with – keep your mistakes in the kitchen!

Roast scallops with wild mushroom ravioli

INGREDIENTS	4 PORTIONS
Scallops (cleaned with roe removed)	12
Sea salt and freshly milled black pepper	To taste
Asparagus	To garnish
Chervil	To garnish
Scallop mousse	
Scallop meat	300g
Egg yolks	2
Whipping cream	400ml
Sea salt and cayenne pepper	To taste
Ravioli	
Chopped shallots	20g
Crushed garlic	5g
Olive oil	
Mixed wild mushrooms	100g
Sea salt and freshly milled black pepper	To taste
Fresh thyme (blanched)	5g
Pasta dough	200g
Celeriac purée	
Celeriac (peeled and chopped into 3cm cubes)	1
Olive oil	
Double cream	150ml
Butter	15g
Sea salt and freshly milled black pepper	
Cappuccino sauce	
Diced raw celeriac	100g
Shallots	50g
Unsalted butter	120g
Cleaned beards and outer muscle of scallops	12
Fish stock	200ml
White wine	75ml
Dry vermouth	75ml
Garlic	5g
Whipped cream	100ml
Butter (for frothing the sauce)	40g
Cold full fat milk	50ml

Method of work

1. For the scallop mousse, blend the scallop meat to a paste, add the egg yolks and then blend again while slowly adding half the cream.

2. Pass through a chinois, then blend and add the remaining cream. Season with salt and cayenne pepper.

3. To make the ravioli, sweat the shallots and garlic in oil. Increase the heat and sauté the mushrooms. Season with salt, milled pepper and thyme. Leave to cool, then fold through 100g of the scallop mousse.

4. Roll out the pasta dough and cut to the required size. Fill the ravioli with the mushroom mixture and seal by pinching the edges. Blanch for two minutes in boiling salted water, then refresh in ice-cold water.

5. For the celeriac puree, put the celeriac on a foiled-lined ovenproof baking tray and drizzle with olive oil. Place another sheet of foil over the top and seal. Bake at 180°C until it starts to soften (about 10 minutes).

6. Purée the celeriac in a blender and pass through a sieve. Put into a saucepan, add cream and butter, season with salt and pepper, and stir over a medium heat until smooth.

7. For the cappuccino sauce, sweat the celeriac and shallots in 20g butter, add scallop beards and outer muscle, fish stock, wine, vermouth, garlic and 80ml cream. Simmer until the celeriac is almost a purée. Blend well and pass through a strainer.

8. To assemble the dish, pan roast the scallops and season with salt and pepper. Reheat the ravioli for two minutes in salted boiling water. Reheat the celeriac purée.

9. To finish to cappuccino sauce, heat a small quantity of the strained liquid in a saucepan and add a spoonful of whipped cream and a small amount of butter and milk and combine to a light frothy foam by using a hand blender.

10. To serve, pipe the celeriac purée to one side of the plate. Place three roast scallops on top of the purée and the ravioli to the other side of the plate. Spoon over the cappuccino sauce and garnish with asparagus and chervil. Serve immediately.

10

Advanced skills and techniques in producing pâtisserie and fermented products (Unit 308)

LEARNING OUTCOMES

The aim of this chapter is to enable the candidate to develop the necessary advanced techniques knowledge and understanding of the principles in preparing and cooking pâtisserie, cakes and fermented goods. The emphasis in this chapter is on developing precision and control in existing skills and perfecting refined and advanced techniques. Included in this chapter is information on materials, ingredients and equipment.

There are **three** principal outcomes to this chapter. At the end of this chapter the candidate will be able to:

- Produce paste products
- Produce cakes and sponges
- Produce dough and batter products

INTRODUCTION

The art of pastry making can be attributed to the Egyptians, who were the first to make basic yeast cakes. The ancient Greeks and Romans produced a variety of confections, made primarily from seeds, honey, almonds and flour. The introduction of sugar to Europe via Asia gave impetus to the first French pastry cooks, who were then called *oubloyers* after a type of waffle (oublies).

Great innovations in pastry making were later introduced in other countries, notably Italy, Switzerland and Spain. However, the greatest innovator worked at the beginning of the nineteenth century was Marie-Antoine **Carême** (1784–1833), who took **pâtisserie** to new heights through his introduction of ornate designs and by perfecting the recipe for puff pastry.

New techniques are being developed all the time as the modern pastry kitchen is well equipped with innovative machinery and small equipment. These also help the chef to produce high-quality, standardised products that are well presented and economical.

Identifying the correct tools and equipment for each job is as important as reading recipes carefully. As mundane as this might sound, the careful identification of the correct ingredients, tools, equipment and production method is the first stage to creating success as a pastry chef.

VIDEO CLIP
French pâtisserie

Electric pastry break for rolling out puff pastry and dough

INGREDIENTS USED IN PASTRY WORK

Fats

Fats are used in pastry making to add flavour and texture. Certain fats are referred to as 'shortenings' because they give a tender, crumbly texture to pastes by shortening the strands of gluten, preventing them from coming together and producing a tough finish to the pastry. Flakiness in a pastry is produced by creating layers of fat between layers of paste. When placed into an oven to bake, the fat melts and pockets of air expand from where the fat was present. This expansion separates the layers of paste which, after baking process is complete, will produce a flaky pastry. This is the basis of puff pastry.

Different types of fat – butter, suet, margarine, lard and shortening

There are two basic types of fats: unsaturated and saturated. The chart below shows the main differences:

UNSATURATED FATS	SATURATED FATS
Usually of vegetable origin Are soft or liquid at room temperature Monounsaturated fatty acids have double-bonded carbon atoms with one hydrogen atom attached. These can be found in both animal and vegetable fats and especially in olive oil Polyunsaturated fatty acids have more than one double bond. Good sources are walnut and sunflower oils	Usually of animal origin Are solid at room temperature Highly evident in butter, lard, coconut oil and cocoa butter Filled to capacity with hydrogen atoms; each carbon atom is bonded to two hydrogen atoms

Hydrogenated fats

Since the turn of the twentieth century, manufacturers have been making hydrogenated fats – solid pastry shortenings and margarines – from liquid seed-based oils. Hydrogenated fats are essentially unsaturated fatty acids that have been saturated with hydrogen. This gives the fat the desired texture for baking and also extends its shelf life. Most of these compound fats have no flavour and are free of salt.

Hydrogenated fats have excellent shortening capabilities and can be used in the production of convenience pastes, especially puff paste. When used with high-ratio flour for making cakes, high-ratio fat has the ability to absorb higher amounts of liquid than usual.

These fats are usually stored in coloured plastic wrapping otherwise light may destabilise the colour. They must be kept covered in a refrigerator. Do not store next to produce with strong odours, such as cheese.

Margarine

This product was developed in France in the nineteenth century as an inexpensive fat to supplement inadequate supplies of butter. Modern margarine is made from hydrogenated liquid vegetable oils and has a minimum of 80 per cent fat and a maximum of 16 per cent water. The water content is usually derived from a skimmed milk product, which helps to deliver flavour and colour. Salt may also be added; this type of margarine is sometimes known as 'stick' or 'table' margarine. Pastry margarine is formulated to produce a higher melting point and has a good plasticity to aid the production of certain pastes. Margarine is best stored covered in a refrigerator at 1–4°C.

Butter

This is the most widely used fat in the production of pastes. It is composed of milk fat, lactose, water and casein and can have salt added to improve flavour and shelf life. Unsalted butter is sometimes specified in recipes due to its intense creaminess. Because it is a saturated fat, butter is stable and is slower to become rancid than unsaturated fats. However, the storage criteria for butter are the same as for margarine.

Lard

This is a rendered fat derived from pork fat. It has no colour but it does have a distinct flavour. In paste recipes, such as pâte brisée, lard is usually combined with butter or margarine to create a shorter textured finish. Storage is the same as for margarine.

Suet

Commercial suet can be either beef fat obtained from around the kidneys or a vegetable fat that has been hydrogenated and mixed with a little flour to prevent the pieces sticking together. Suet is a hard fat and does not have creaming properties. Traditionally it is used for the production of suet paste and puddings. It should be stored in a refrigerator in an airtight container.

Eggs

Fresh eggs will keep for up to four weeks in a refrigerator. To determine the freshness of an egg, crack it onto a plate and check that the white is holding the yolk firmly in the centre and that the yolk is standing high rather than flat. Eggs keep best when stored away from foods with strong odours, such as cheese, onions or garlic, because the eggshell is porous and will allow air and moisture to enter the egg.

Eggs can be purchased frozen and pasteurised and also dried. Chefs will often use pasteurised eggs in the professional pastry kitchen because of their ease of use and also to help reduce the risk of salmonella. Always read the label on the packaging because other ingredients may also be present, products such as salt to aid shelf life and beta-carotene to simulate the colour of egg yolk.

THE USE OF CONVENIENCE PASTES

Puff paste and filo paste

Being able to purchase ready-made and ready-to-use pastes has been both a revelation and a concern for many chefs in the industry. The issues of ease of production, use of human resources, cost and standardisation of the product suggest that the purchase of convenience commodities is inevitable in many high-turnover restaurants. In contrast, the issues of quality, freshness and flavour can discourage the purchase of such products, especially in the case of 'artisan' pâtisseries and restaurants.

The popularity of filo paste is largely attributed to its success as an easy to use, convenient paste – it is no longer necessary to spend the time needed to make it from fresh. Other pastes that require skilled labour and are potentially time inefficient can also now be presented on a menu with relative ease, such as puff paste and strüdel paste.

Most pastes can be purchased as a convenience product in either a frozen or fresh variety. If using frozen paste it is important that the paste is correctly defrosted in a refrigerator and in the packaging in which it was first purchased (provided that it is hygienic and intact). The paste should then be stored as for fresh paste: wrapped in plastic film, refrigerated and accurately labelled.

The word 'convenience' simply refers to something that is easy to use. Another convenient way of using pastes is to prepare large batches of different pastes using your own recipes and techniques, thus ensuring quality, and then to freeze them individually for use at a later date.

LES PÂTES FRIABLE – SHORT PASTE VARIETIES

This family of tart and pie pastes comprises several different varieties, each one having its own method of preparation and use. All of the pastes are easy to prepare, but they do require careful handling and an understanding of their individual characteristics.

There are five different short pastes which come under the collective heading of *les pâtes friable*, all of them being short, crisp and friable (crumbly):

■ Shortcrust pastry – *la pâte brisée*

■ Lining paste – *la pâte à foncer*

■ Sweet paste – *la pâte sucrée*

■ Shortbread/sable paste – *la pate sablée*

■ Linzer paste – *la pâte à linzer*

Two main methods are used to obtain the crispness characteristic of these pastes:

1 *Sablage* (rubbing in) – the aim of this method is to coat the particles of flour with a layer of fat to protect them from the liquid ingredients. This prevents the gluten from becoming activated, which would result in a tough paste with a hard crust.

2 *Creaming* – in this method the liquid ingredients are first combined with the butter and worked to a smooth cream. This mixture contains a high proportion of fat. The flour is added at the last stage and is not manipulated for as long as in the 'rubbing in' method and therefore the fat tends not to penetrate the flour particles.

BASIC RECIPES FOR SHORT PASTES
Shortcrust paste *Pâte brisée*

INGREDIENTS	MAKES APPROXIMATELY 400G
Soft flour	250g
Butter	160g
Whole egg	1
Good-quality salt	5g
Cold fresh milk or water	1tbsp

Method of work

1 Sift the flour onto a clean work surface or into a stainless steel bowl.
2 Cut the butter (at room temperature) into small pieces and rub into the flour with the salt.

3 When the butter has been rubbed into the flour, incorporate the cold liquid and the whole egg.

4 Gently amalgamate the ingredients, forming a light dough. Do not overwork this paste.

5 Wrap well in polythene or silicone paper and place in a refrigerator for 30 minutes before using.

Lining paste *Pâte à foncer*

INGREDIENTS	MAKES APPROXIMATELY 500G
Soft flour	250g
Softened butter	125g
Caster sugar	20g
Whole egg	60g
Cold water	40ml
Good-quality salt	5g

Method of work

1 Sift the flour onto a clean work surface or into a stainless steel bowl.

2 Cut the butter (at room temperature) into small pieces and rub into the flour with the sugar and the salt.

3 When the butter has been successfully rubbed into the flour, incorporate the cold water and the whole egg.

4 Gently amalgamate the ingredients, forming a light dough. Do not overwork this paste.

5 Wrap well in polythene or silicone paper and place in a refrigerator for 45 minutes before using.

Sweet paste *Pâte sucrée*

INGREDIENTS	MAKES APPROXIMATELY 530G
Soft flour	250g
Butter	100g
Caster sugar	80g
Whole egg	100g
Good-quality salt	5g
Vanilla pod or extract	Optional

Method of work

1 Place the flour onto a clean work surface or into a stainless steel bowl. Make a well in the centre.

2 Cut the butter (at room temperature) into small pieces and place in the centre of the well with the salt and sugar.

3 Work the butter and sugar with your finger tips until completely creamed together and pale in colour.

4 Slowly incorporate the whole egg, mixing well until the mixture is completely smooth and creamy. At this stage you can add a few drops of vanilla extract to help flavour the paste.

5 Gradually draw the flour into the creamed butter and when all ingredients are thoroughly mixed, lightly work the paste to a smooth texture. Do not overwork the paste at this point.

6 Wrap well in polythene or silicone paper and place in a refrigerator for 60 minutes before using.

Shortbread paste *Pâte sablée*

INGREDIENTS	MAKES APPROXIMATELY 500G
Soft flour	250g
Ground almonds	30g
Unsalted butter	140g
Icing sugar	100g
Whole egg	60g
Good-quality salt	5g
Vanilla extract or zest of 1 lemon	optional

Method of work

1 Sift together the flour and ground almonds onto a clean work surface or into a stainless steel bowl.

2 Cut the softened butter into small pieces and place into the centre of the flour well with the sieved icing sugar.

3 Cream together the butter and sugar with the salt and then slowly incorporate the whole egg. Mix well and add any additional flavours (such as the vanilla or lemon) at this point.

4 Gently incorporate the flour with the other ingredients, forming a light dough. Do not overwork this paste.

5 Wrap well in polythene or silicone paper and place in a refrigerator for a minimum of 2 hours before using.

Preparation points for short pastes

It is important to be aware of the roles of the different ingredients. For instance, any increase in the fat content will shorten the paste by reacting with the gluten in the flour. It will also enhance the flavour the paste if the correct type of fat is used (butter).

■ *La pâte à foncer* – This paste is always prepared using the sablage technique. The use of water as the binding agent produces a very elastic

paste that must be rested for 30 minutes before use. The paste must be rested again after the food items have been prepared.
Baking temperature: 230°C

■ *La pâte sucrée* – This paste may be prepared using either the sablage or the creaming technique. The paste is soft and fragile, therefore it must be handled carefully. Flour should be used when rolling out the paste, but too much will produce a heavier texture to the finished item.
Baking temperature: 200°C

■ *La pâte sablée* – It is extremely short and difficult to use. This is due to the high fat and egg content. This should be used in small quantities and kept refrigerated at all times. Finished products should be kept in an airtight container otherwise they will quickly become soft; this is due to the hygroscopic properties of the product.

LE PÂTE FEUILLETAGE – PUFF PASTE

Uses of puff pastry

■ Vol-au-vents

■ **Fleurons** and various savoury decorations

■ Tart shells for assorted large and individual tarts

■ Chaussons aux pommes

■ Pithiviers

■ Mille feuilles.

Characteristics of puff paste

Puff paste has a specific structure, consisting of numerous alternating layers of *détrempe* (the basic paste) and *beurrage* (the butter or fat used). This structure is obtained by repeatedly folding and rolling the paste; this is known as giving the paste a 'turn'.

The puff paste itself should always have a somewhat firm consistency and should be completely chilled to at least 5°C while laminating. The détrempe must not become too elastic during processing. It is therefore important not to overwork the ingredients while preparing the paste.

Five different methods for making puff paste

1 *French method* – It is essential to work on marble, using the 'envelope' method to position the fat inside the paste. Fold and give three 'book' turns.

2 *English method* – Roll the détrempe out to an oblong and place the beurrage on one-third of it. Give six single turns.

 CHEF'S TIP

A variety of puff pastry made with oil can be traced back to the ancient Greeks. In France, records show a type of puff pastry being made in the thirteenth century, and a charter written by Bishop Robert of Amiens in 1311 mentions desserts using puff pastry. The creation of *talmouses* (puff pastry wrapped around a savoury farce) popularised this pastry in the early fifteenth century. Carême, in his book *Le Pâtissier Royal*, honoured Feuillet by describing his pastries as beautiful and inspiring.

3 *Scottish method* – Beurrage is incorporated to the détrempe in pieces. This is a fast method.

4 *Reversed method* – This method reverses the positions of the two principal elements. The détrempe is assembled in the same manner as in a basic puff paste. The butter is softened, then mixed with flour. A simple blending of the two ingredients is sufficient.

5 *Viennois* – This method is basically the same as the French method but with a subtle difference. Enriching ingredients are added to the détrempe to give better flavour and colour to the finished article, for example the addition of egg yolks.

Tenderness versus flakiness in pastry pastes

⊙ Fat   ▬▬ Paste

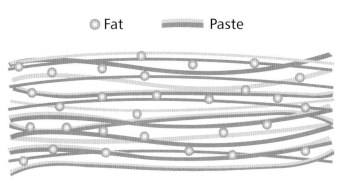

Tender paste with the fat more evenly distributed in smaller, finer pieces. The fat melts into the pastry paste creating tenderness by coating gluten strands but producing little flakiness.

Flaky paste with fat in pea-sized pieces unevenly distributed in the pastry paste. The fat melts into the pastry paste creating spaces during baking which separates the layers producing flakiness.

Tender paste versus flaky pastes

BASIC RECIPES FOR PUFF PASTES

Three-quarter puff pastry recipe with pastry margarine
Pâte feuilletée

INGREDIENTS	MAKES APPROXIMATELY 530G
Strong flour	1kg
Butter	150g
Pastry margarine	600g
Lemon juice	1tbsp
Salt	30g
Cold water	500ml (approx)

Method of work

1 Sift the flour into a bowl. Combine the salt, lemon juice and water.
2 Rub the butter into the flour.
3 Mix in the liquid to form a firm but elastic paste, depending on the flour used and the product to be made.
4 On a lightly floured marble top roll out the paste to form a rectangle twice as long as broad and about 20mm thick.
5 Take a square of pastry margarine (also 20mm thick) which will fit neatly on to one end of the rolled out paste.
6 Fold the paste over the fat to enclose it. Seal the edges well.
7 Roll out the paste to 15–20mm thick; it must be four times as long as it is broad and a precise rectangle.
8 Give one book turn (double turn). Cover with plastic film and rest in a refrigerator for 20 minutes.
9 Repeat this three more times. It is then ready to use.

Puff pastry with butter *Pâte feuilletée*

INGREDIENTS	MAKES APPROXIMATELY 530G
Strong flour	1kg
Butter	250g
Pastry (dry) butter	750g
Lemon juice	1tbsp
Salt	30g
Cold water	500ml (approx)

Method of work

1 Sift the flour into a bowl.

2 Combine the salt, lemon juice and water.

3 Rub the butter into the flour.

4 Mix in the liquid to form a firm but elastic paste, depending on the flour used and the product to be made.

5 On a lightly floured marble top, roll out the paste to form a rectangle twice as long as broad and about 20mm thick. (Alternatively, a large envelope can be produced; the French method.)

6 Take a square of pastry margarine (also 20mm thick) which will fit neatly on to one end of the rolled out paste.

7 Fold the paste over the fat to enclose it. Seal the edges well.

8 Roll out the paste to 15–20mm thick. It must be four times as long as it is broad and a precise rectangle.

9 Give one book turn (double turn). Cover the paste with plastic film and rest in a refrigerator for 20 minutes.

10 Repeat this three more times. It is then ready to use.

Notes on puff pastry

■ *Flour* – use strong flour. Most white flour milled in the UK is no longer bleached and contains grey particles which look like ash. This will give a dull look to raw paste but will not affect the paste itself. Ensure the gluten content of the flour is high; it is this and not the overall protein content that is important.

■ *Salt* – any type of salt that is easily soluble can be used.

■ *Water* – cold tap water is adequate. The quantity required will vary according to the flour.

■ *Fat* – unsalted butter has a higher moisture content than pastry margarine. It is helpful to prepare it in a flat, plastic square about 20mm thick. Butter makes puff pastry more appetising and colourful, but pastry margarine is easier to work with. A little malt extract added to the paste can compensate for lack of colour.

- *Temperature* – it is possible to make puff paste in a warm kitchen, up to 22–25°C, but working with butter will become progressively more difficult.
- *Rolling* – always put the puff paste in the refrigerator, covered in plastic film, to rest before turns (although it may be unnecessary to refrigerate paste that contains pastry margarine).
- *Work surface* – marble is the best surface to use because it remains cool longer than stainless steel. It is also slightly porous, which makes rolling easier. Keep it cleaned at all times.
- *Single turn* – involves folding the sheet of puff paste into three.
- *Double turn* – also called a 'book turn', involves folding the paste sheet into four. The two sides are folded into the middle and then closed up like a book.
- *Rotating* - after each turn it is important to rotate the folded paste through 90 degrees before rolling it out again. Always roll out evenly, treating the paste with care.
- *Baking temperatures* – bake at 210°C to ensure the pastry cooks thoroughly before it colours too much.

PÂTE À CHOUX – CHOUX PASTE

Explanation of the method

During the first part of the production the chef is looking to dry out the mix of water, fat, flour, sugar and salt. This will denature and change the structure of the starch found in flour, resulting in a thick paste.

The second phase is the 're-moisturisation' of the paste through the addition of eggs in order to obtain a paste of piping consistency. This paste therefore contains a lot of moisture (that remaining from the first part of the process and that from the addition of the egg). During the baking the moisture will create steam, which acts as the raising agent for the paste.

- *Water* – the water can be half or totally replaced with milk. The resulting paste will be finer, more enriched and slightly softer in texture, but it may be a little heavier.
- *Fat* – the choice (butter or margarine) and quantity of fat will depend on the role required of the finished paste. The proportion can vary between 400g and 500g per litre of liquid. Salted butter is the preferred fat due to its colour and flavour-enhancing properties.
- *Salt* – this helps to improve the flavour. Use a fine salt, and ensure it is correctly weighed so as not to produce an over-salted taste.
- *Sugar* – the role of sugar is to produce a good colour during baking. Use a fine-grained sugar (caster). The quantity of sugar may be varied according to the temperature of the oven: for a higher oven temperature, a smaller quantity of sugar should be used.

 CHEF'S TIP

The origin of choux paste dates back to the sixteenth century. Its invention is attributed to an Italian pastry chef named Popelini, who created a gâteau called *Le Popolin*. The gâteau was made from a paste dried out on the stove and which resembled a type of raw pasta dough. This paste was also know as *la pâte à chaud*.

■ *Eggs* – the eggs should never be added to the **panada** when it has first been made as the temperature of the initial paste (approximately 82–88°C) will cook the egg protein. This will make the paste less elastic and less able to retain steam and so will limit its ability to rise. The eggs should always be added when the paste is warm to the touch as this will aid the general incorporation and mixing process. The protein value of eggs helps to give colour to the paste. Eggs also help to produce the blown texture of choux paste.

■ *Flour* – strong flour should be used. The quantity of flour may vary between 500g and 800g per litre of liquid according to the recipe.

During baking, the heat from the oven will turn the moisture in the paste to steam. At the same time, the eggs and the starch from the flour begin to coagulate, forming a layer on the outside of the paste which retains the steam. The steam inflates the paste, which continues to coagulate and becomes solid as it has cooked. The result is the choux pastry's distinctive blown appearance.

BASIC RECIPE FOR CHOUX PASTE

Choux paste *Pâte à choux*

INGREDIENTS	20 ÉCLAIRS OR 40 PROFITEROLES
Water	150ml
Butter	60g
Strong white flour	90g
Sugar	5g
Salt	5g
Whole eggs	3

Method of work

1 Place the water and butter into a saucepan and bring to the boil.
2 Take off the heat and stir in the sieved flour, salt and sugar.
3 Return to the heat and cook out, continuously stirring until it leaves the sides of the pan clean.
4 Allow to partly cool.
5 Beat in the eggs a little at a time, making sure that they are well incorporated.

 CHEF'S TIP

When drying out the panada, do so only until it leaves the side of the pan clean. Do not overcook the panada otherwise the fat content will separate.

 CHEF'S TIP

The eggs should be beaten first and added gradually when the panada has cooled. This will aid the mixing process and ensure the eggs are totally integrated into the panada.

STRÜDEL

Strüdel paste

The strüdel paste consists of flour, water, salt, sugar, eggs and oil. It is important to give as much elasticity to the paste as possible. To help create this elasticity, use a fine graded strong flour that is high in gluten. Once the paste has been made it is brushed with oil and allowed to rest for about 60 minutes.

The paste is then worked by hand, using fingertips which have been dipped in oil. It is gradually stretched from underneath until it is paper thin. This process should be carried out on a large, flour-dusted linen cloth.

Strüdel filling

The ingredients for strüdel filling vary from recipe to recipe. This may be due to regional preferences and traditions, or to individual chefs changing the components of a recipe at their own discretion. However, certain rules should always be followed in the make-up of a strüdel filling. The main one is that the recipe should have an equal balance of wet and dry ingredients: if the filling is too wet the strüdel may collapse, and if it is too dry it will not be pleasing to the palette.

 CHEF'S TIP

The word 'strüdel' is a derivative of the old German word *streden*, which means to boil or bubble. This is an apt description of the finished pastry as it often appears very wrinkly and bubbly on the surface. The actual pastry is thought to have originated from Bavaria in southern Germany or in Austria, and was the creation of a Hungarian pâtissier. It has also been suggested that strüdel is a relative of baklava, the Turkish sweet which comprises very thin layers of paste sandwiched together with a filling of chopped nuts and a honey-based syrup.

 VIDEO CLIP
Strüdel paste

Strüdel paste being pinned out on a floured cloth

Strüdel paste being stretched gently by hand

RECIPE FOR STRÜDEL
Apple strüdel *Apfel strüdel*

CHEF'S TIP

You can replace the apples and add your own fruit of choice to create an alternative variety of strüdel, but you must always balance the water content of the fruit against the dry ingredients in the filling to prevent the strüdel from collapsing.

CHEF'S TIP

Make the strüdel paste the day before you need to use it. This will allow the paste to rest even longer, improving its flexibility.

VIDEO CLIP
Making apple strüdel

INGREDIENTS	
Strüdel paste	**2 LARGE STRUDELS**
Strong graded flour	700g
Olive or vegetable oil	110g
Warm water (37°C)	180g
Whole eggs	3
Vinegar	3tsp
Salt	5g
Sugar	5g
Apple filling	**1 LARGE STRUDEL**
Bramley apples (sweet apples taste bland after cooking)	1.5kg
Lightly roasted ground almonds	150g
Brioche crumbs	150g
Cinnamon sugar	125g
Finely grated zest of lemon	1 lemon
Sultanas macerated in dark rum	200g
Melted butter	200g

Method of work

To prepare the paste
1 Place the flour, salt and sugar in a bowl and make a well in the centre.
2 Add the oil, eggs, water and vinegar. Using an electric mixer, mix until the paste is soft and comes away from the sides of the bowl. The paste should be elastic to the touch.
3 Transfer the paste to a lightly floured surface and knead well for approximately 15 minutes or until it is soft and pliable.
4 Depending on the number of strudels to make, divide the paste into two or three pieces. Using a pastry brush, lightly brush the pieces of paste with oil, cover with plastic film and leave to rest for a minimum of 60 minutes on the side of a table (not in a refrigerator).

To prepare the filling
1 Peel and slice the apples thinly and mix with a little cinnamon if desired.
2 Fry the brioche crumbs in a little melted butter until they turn a very light golden colour.

To prepare the strüdel
1 Spread a linen cloth, dusted with flour, over a table and initially pin out the paste.
2 Very carefully begin to stretch the paste using fingertips dipped in a little oil. The paste should eventually be stretched paper thin.

3   After stretching, trim the edges and brush the paste with the melted butter. Carefully build up layers of filling with each ingredient, apples first and then the remaining ingredients.

4   Fold in the ends of the paste and, using the cloth, roll it carefully to resemble a Swiss roll. Transfer onto a baking sheet and brush with melted butter.

5   Place in the oven at 225°C and bake for approximately 35–45 minutes. Two-thirds of the way through baking, remove the strüdel from the oven and dredge with icing sugar. Replace to continue baking.

HOT WATER PASTE FOR SAVOURY PIES

Hot water paste may be sweet or savoury. Savoury hot water paste is used for pork pies, veal and ham pies, game pies and a variety of terrines. The paste must be used while it is warm; if it is too hot it will be difficult to handle and if it is too cold it is liable to crack during handling.

VIDEO CLIP
Hot water paste

Pork pies

To shape a pork pie case successfully, a block of approximately 10cm in diameter is required. Special wooden blocks are available for this purpose, but if one is not available a suitable alternative – such as a tin can or individual mousse ring mould – can be used.

The heel of the hand is used to form a cup shape, with the paste around the mould. The block is then rotated while pressing firmly to raise the paste up the side. The paste is then allowed to set and is removed from the block.

The meat filling is made into a ball and dropped into the case and then carefully pressed to remove any air spaces. The lid is made from the same pastry, which is rolled to a thickness of 3mm and cut with a plain cutter a little larger than the diameter of the pie. A hole is cut in the top of the lid to act as a steam vent. The top inside edge of the lid is washed with egg or water and the lid is then placed on the case. It is pressed firmly into the sides and pinched with fingers or crimpers to seal. The sides and top are washed with egg and decoration applied to the top, such as diamonds of paste or leaf shapes. It is essential that the meat is thoroughly cooked to help prevent the build up of food-poisoning bacteria.

RECIPE FOR HOT WATER PASTE
English pork pie using hot water paste

INGREDIENTS

Hot water paste	MAKES APPROXIMATELY 900g
Lard	150g
Good-quality salt	10g
Soft white flour	500g
Water	250ml
Filling	MAKES APPROXIMATELY 400g
Shoulder of pork (boned)	300g
Fresh chopped thyme	10g
Fresh chopped sage	10g
Fresh chopped parsley	10g
Good-quality salt	10g
Chopped, sweated onion	75g
White veal or chicken stock	25ml
Powdered white pepper	5g
Stock	
Gelatine	

Method of work

To prepare the paste

1 Sift the flour and the salt together into a stainless steel bowl.
2 Boil the water and the lard together, ensuring that the lard has completely melted.
3 Pour the liquid into the flour and begin to mix carefully with a spoon.
4 Gently amalgamate the ingredients. When you are able to touch the paste by hand, begin to knead.
5 Use immediately. Keep the paste warm by placing an upturned stainless steel bowl over it on the work surface to keep in the heat and moisture.

To prepare the pie

1 Mince the pork shoulder coarsely and then combine with the rest of the filling ingredients.
2 Keeping a quarter of the paste warm, roll out the rest and carefully line a well-greased raised pie mould.
3 Add the filling and press down firmly. Roll the remaining paste out to create a lid.
4 Egg wash the edges of the pie and seal the edges, trimming off any surplus paste. Cut a 1cm-diameter hole in the centre of the pie lid. Decorate the lid as appropriate.

 CHEF'S TIP

If the pie colours too quickly during baking, cover with either silicone paper or foil and continue baking. An oiled silicone paper funnel can be inserted into the hole in the lid to keep the hole open, allowing steam to escape during cooking.

5 Egg wash and place into a preheated oven at 230°C for 20 minutes, then reduce the oven temperature to approximately 160°C and bake for a further hour.

6 Remove from the oven and leave to cool for 30 minutes. Fill with a hot stock containing dissolved gelatine to create an **aspic** inside the pie (approximately 400ml stock to 5 leaves of gelatine).

7 Cool and serve as desired.

RECIPES
Suet paste

CHEF'S TIP

Vegetable suet can be used to replace the beef suet if vegetarian products are required.

INGREDIENTS	MAKES APPROXIMATELY 500G
Soft flour	250g
Baking powder	5g
Beef suet	150g
Good-quality salt	3g
Cold water	125ml
Caster sugar (optional)	25g

Method of work

1 Sift together the flour, **baking powder** and salt into a stainless steel bowl. Add the suet and lightly mix in.

2 If using sugar as part of the recipe, add to the water to dissolve. Make a well in the centre of the flour mixture and add the water or sugar solution.

3 Mix lightly together to form a firm paste. Rest for 5 minutes in the bowl covered with plastic film before using.

 CHEF'S TIP

Suet is a hard fat that surrounds beef kidneys (to protect them) and is grated and lightly floured for commercial use. It is creamy white in colour, should be dry to the touch and can be stored in a refrigerator for 2–4 weeks in a sealed container. Ensure suet does not come into close proximity to strongly flavoured ingredients as it easily absorbs aromas.

Leek and goat's cheese tartlette *Tartelette de fromage de chèvre et poireau*

INGREDIENTS	4 PORTIONS	10 PORTIONS
Shortcrust paste (pâte brisée, see recipe on p. 296)	200g	500g
Full-fat goat's cheese	100g	250g
Chopped fresh mixed herbs (basil, chives, parsley)	2tbsp	5tbsp
Leeks	1	2
Eggs	1	3
Single cream	150ml	400ml
Ground black pepper and good-quality salt	To taste	To taste

Method of work

1 Roll out the paste thinly. Line the tartlet tins and chill for 15 minutes in a refrigerator.

2 Preheat an oven to 200°C. Bake the cases blind for approximately 10 minutes. Reduce the oven temperature to 190°C.

3 Wash, slice and dry the leeks. Quickly sweat them off in a little butter to begin the cooking process. Put aside to cool.

4 Place the cheese, herbs and leeks in a bowl and mix until well blended. Add the egg, cream, salt and pepper and mix again.

5 Divide the mixture evenly into the pastry cases and return to the oven for 10–15 minutes, until the filling has just set.

6 Serve warm or cold.

Lemon tart *Tarte au citron*

INGREDIENTS	8 PORTIONS (1 × 30CM TART RING)	16 PORTIONS (2 × 30CM TART RING)
Sweet paste (pâte sucrée, see recipe on p. 297)	250g	500g
Lemons	4	8
Eggs	9	18
Castor sugar	380g	700g
Double cream	300ml	600ml
Icing sugar	50g	100g

Method of work

1 Preheat an oven to 200°C.

2 Butter a flan ring and carefully line with the paste. Leave to rest for 15 minutes in a refrigerator.

3 Blind bake in the preheated oven for approximately 20 minutes.

4 Lower the oven temperature 150°C.

5 Wash the lemons and finely grate the zests. Extract the juice and mix together.

6 Break the eggs into a bowl and lightly beat in the castor sugar. Add the cream and lemon and mix. Remove any froth from the top. Place in a refrigerator before use.

7 Pour the filling into the pastry case and bake for approximately 30 minutes or until the lemon filling has just set.

8 When cooked, carefully remove the flan ring.

9 Leave to cool at room temperature for at least 1 hour.

10 Portion the tart and dust the top of each slice with icing sugar before serving. The tart can be caramelised using a blowtorch or under a salamander.

Chocolate and banana tart with a coconut ice cream and a mango compôte

INGREDIENTS	4 INDIVIDUAL TARTLETTES	10 INDIVIDUAL TARTLETTES OR 1 × 20CM TART RING
Dark couverture chocolate (70 per cent)	80g	220g
Unsalted butter	50g	110g
Whole egg	55g	150g
Egg yolk	1	3
Caster sugar	30g	75g
Icing sugar	50g	100g
Banana (to slice and caramelise)	1	2
Sweet paste (pâte sucrée, see recipe on p. 297)	250g	550g
Ripe mango	1	2
Water	250ml	400ml
Caster sugar	75g	180g
Lemon juice and zest	½ lemon	1 lemon
Under-ripe banana	1	2
Light stock syrup	75ml	150ml

Method of work

1 Melt the dark chocolate **couverture** and butter together.

2 Whisk the eggs and sugar until thick in a food processor, fold together with the melted dark couverture and cool.

3 Line individual tartlette cases with the sweet paste and bake blind.

4 Cut the banana into small slices and sprinkle over with a little icing sugar. Quickly caramelise using a blowtorch or a hot salamander. Add three or four slices to the bottom of the blind-baked tartlette cases.

5 Pour the dark couverture mixture equally into each tartlette and bake at 150°C for 6–10 minutes. Leave to one side to keep warm.

6 For the mango compôte, cut and stone the mango, removing the skin, and cut into small dice.

7 Bring all the other compôte ingredients to the boil in a saucepan. Add the mango and cook over a low heat for 3–4 minutes until tender. Leave to one side to cool.

8 For the banana crisps, preheat an oven to 110°C. On a slicing machine, slice the bananas lengthwise as thinly as possible. Submerge each slice in a light stock syrup for two minutes. Place the slices on a silicon mat and dry in the oven for about 30 minutes. Form into desired shapes and cool.

9 Serve the tartlette either warm or at room temperature with ice cream and the compôte.

CHEF'S TIP

Use a good-quality high cocoa content dark chocolate for this recipe to obtain depth of flavour and consistency in the tartlettes. As an alternative to the basic sweet paste, substitute 25g of flour from the recipe with 25g of cocoa.

Red berry streusel tart *Tarte streusel aux fruits rouges*

INGREDIENTS	1 × 20CM TART	3 × 20CM TARTS
Lining paste (pâte à foncer, see recipe on p. 297)	175g	550g
Pistachio crème		
Melted butter	50g	125g
Icing sugar	50g	125g
Ground almonds	50g	125g
Whole eggs	40g	100g
Cornflour	5g	20g
Crème pâtissière	50g	100g
Pistachio paste	10g	40g
Kirsch	5g	20g
Cinnamon streusel		
Ground almonds	40g	100g
Butter	40g	100g
Soft flour	40g	100g
Caster sugar	40g	100g
Powdered cinnamon	1g	2g
Red berry garnish		
Cherries steeped in kirsch	30g	100g
Raspberries	30g	100g
Strawberries	30g	100g
Redcurrants	30g	100g

Method of work

1 Line a tart ring with lining paste. Cover in plastic film and leave to rest in a refrigerator until required.

2 To make the pistachio crème, mix together the melted butter, ground almonds, icing sugar, eggs and cornflour to a smooth paste.

3 Fold in the crème pâtissière and the pistachio paste. Mix well and finally add the kirsch.

4 Pipe this preparation into the base of the lined tart to about two-thirds of the way up.

5 Ensure all the fresh berries are well washed and prepared. If the strawberries are too large, cut them up so that all the berries are similar in size.

6 Mix the berries together with some of the juice/kirsch from the cherries. Place a layer of this fruit gently on top of the pistachio crème.

7 Bake in a preheated oven at 170°C for approximately 20 minutes.

8 To make the streusel, rub the ground almonds, butter, sugar and cinnamon into the flour, until a large crumb has been produced. Place this in a ring on top of the tart and place back into the oven for a further 10 minutes.

9 Decorate the centre with some fresh berries and dust with icing sugar for service.

CHEF'S TIP

Use fresh fruit that is in season. This will produce a finer aroma and personality to this tart. Source fruits from a supplier as local as possible to help ensure it is fresh and in good condition.

Gâteau Basque

INGREDIENTS	8 INDIVIDUAL PORTIONS	16 INDIVIDUAL PORTIONS
Butter	125g	250g
Hazelnut tant pour tant (equal quantities of ground hazelnuts and icing sugar)	50g	100g
Caster sugar	125g	250g
Good-quality salt	3g	5g
Finely grated lemon zest	½ lemon	1 lemon
Egg yolks	2	4
Whole egg	½ egg	1 egg
Soft flour	250g	500g
Baking powder	5g	10g
Almond filling	MAKES APPROXIMATELY 500g OF FILLING	MAKES APPROXIMATELY 1kg OF FILLING
Full fat milk	175ml	350ml
Vanilla pod	½ pod split	1 pod split
Egg yolks	3	6
Caster sugar	40g	70g
Custard powder	10g	20g
Cornflour	5g	10g
Ground almonds	100g	200g
Dark rum	5ml	10ml
Fresh apricots poached in syrup or tinned	250g	500g

CHEF'S TIP

With the tant pour tant, ensure that you pass both the icing sugar and the ground nut content through a sieve twice. This will help to aerate the composition of ingredients and aid creaming with the butter.

CHEF'S TIP

Larger tarts can be presented rather than individual ones. You may have to bake this for about 10 minutes longer.

Method of work

1 To make pâte à Basque, cream the butter with the tant pour tant, caster sugar, salt and lemon zest.
2 Incorporate the egg yolks and whole egg gradually.
3 Sift the flour and baking powder together. Add the sifted flour and begin to knead the ingredients into a paste. Take care not to overwork the paste. Place in a refrigerator wrapped in plastic to rest for at least 1 hour.
4 Preheat an oven to 177°C.
5 To make the almond cream, bring to the boil the milk and vanilla pod.
6 Whisk together the egg yolks, caster sugar and custard powder and cornflour.
7 Combine the ingredients together and cook out, stirring constantly, to make a basic crème pâtissière.
8 Reserve to one side, adding a little melted butter to the surface of the crème to prevent a skin forming.
9 Incorporate the dark rum and ground almonds and reserve to one side.
10 To assemble the gateau, line individual flan rings with the pâte à Basque and pipe the base with the pastry cream mixed with the ground almonds.
11 Place the quartered apricots on top of the pastry cream and place a disc of the pâte à Basque on top of the flan. Glaze with egg wash.
12 Place in a fridge to rest for 30 minutes. Mark the top with a sharp knife.
13 Bake in an oven at 177°C for approximately 30 minutes. Halfway through baking sprinkle a few flaked almonds and icing sugar on top.
14 De-mould and serve warm with a hot apricot sauce and an appropriate accompaniment such as vanilla ice cream.

Lemon meringue pie

INGREDIENTS	1 × 20CM PIE	2 × 20CM PIES
Lining paste (pâte à foncer, see recipe on p. 297)	200g	400g
Lemon filling		
Butter	125g	250g
Caster sugar	125g	250g
Eggs	4	8
Lemon zest and juice	2 lemons	4 lemons
Swiss meringue		
Egg white	250g	375g
Caster sugar	125g	180g
Icing sugar	125g	180g

 CHEF'S TIP

To help to stabilise the Swiss meringue further, a pinch of cream of tartar can be added during the cooking stage. With constant whisking and the protective effects of sugar and the cream of tartar, you can heat this meringue mixture up to 78°C and still maintain a successful, although dense, foam.

Method of work

1 Line a 20 cm tart ring with the paste and bake blind with minimal colour.
2 To prepare the filling, combine the finely grated lemon zest and juice in a saucepan with the caster sugar and butter.
3 Bring the ingredients to the boil, ensuring that the butter has completely melted.
4 Gradually add the beaten eggs, constantly stirring vigorously with a whisk until all of the egg content is successfully incorporated and the mixture has cooked out to a thick and creamy consistency.
5 Pour this lemon cream into the blind-baked tart case and leave to cool and set.
6 To prepare the Swiss meringue, mix all the ingredients together in a stainless steel bowl and place into a bain marie over simmering water.
7 Whisking continuously to aerate the egg whites, heat the mixture to 60°C. Use a thermometer or digital probe to accurately gauge the temperature.
8 Immediately transfer the egg white mixture into a mixing machine with a whisk attachment and beat until cold. The meringue will now begin to completely aerate as it cools down.
9 Transfer the Swiss meringue to a piping bag with a plain tube and pipe onto the set lemon cream in a decorative manner.
10 Lightly dust the meringue with icing sugar and place into a hot oven at 180°C to colour the meringue. Serve either at room temperature or warm as desired.

Linzer torte

INGREDIENTS	1 × 20CM TORTE	2 × 20CM TORTE
Soft white flour	175g	350g
Ground hazelnuts	75g	150g
Icing sugar	60g	120g
Finely grated lemon zest	1 lemon	2 lemons
Grated nutmeg	Pinch	Pinch
Powdered cinnamon	5g	10g
Butter	120g	240g
Egg yolks	2	4
Raspberry jam	175g	350g
Lemon juice	¼ lemon	½ lemon

Method of work

1 Preheat an oven to 175°C.

2 Sift together the flour, ground hazelnuts, icing sugar, cinnamon and nutmeg. Repeat this process to consolidate the aeration and mixing of the ingredients.

3 Dice the butter and rub in with the lemon zest until the mixture reaches a crumbly texture. Add the egg yolk and carefully form into a paste.

4 Wrap the paste in plastic film and rest in a refrigerator for 30 minutes.

5 Cut the rested Linzer paste in half. Roll out one half and use it to line the flan ring. Using the **thumbing up** technique to ensure an evenly lined pastry case.

6 Mix the jam with the lemon juice and spoon it into the lined case.

7 Roll out the paste that was set aside and cut into a lattice pattern.

8 Drape over the top of the torte base and seal the edges well.

9 Place in the oven to bake for approximately 30 minutes.

10 To finish, dust with icing sugar and fill the centres of the squares with more jam if required. Serve warm or chilled with crème chantilly.

 CHEF'S TIP

This is a traditional torte that takes its name from the Austrian town of Linz, where it is served in coffee houses as an afternoon pastry. It can be stored in a refrigerator for up to a day after production. Do not store next to strongly flavoured products such as cheese.

Tranche Saint Honoré

INGREDIENTS	10 PORTIONS	20 PORTIONS
Tranche		
Basic choux paste (see recipe on p. 304)	150g	300g
Basic puff paste trimmings	250g	500g
Egg wash (whole egg beaten with a pinch of salt)	1 egg	1 egg
Crème chiboust	APPROXIMATELY 800g OF CRÈME	APPROXIMATELY 1.5kg OF CRÈME
Fresh full fat milk	350ml	700ml
Vanilla pod	½ pod split	1 pod split
Egg yolks	6	12
Caster sugar	70g	120g
Custard powder	20g	40g
Cornflour	10g	20g
Granulated sugar	300g	500g
Water	80ml	150ml
Glucose	25g	45g
Egg whites	6	12

CHEF'S TIP

The use of glucose in the Italian meringue is essential as it helps sugar crystals to form in the meringue. To create a firm meringue, more sugar per egg white (70g per egg white) is required; this should help the crème chiboust retain its stability.

CHEF'S TIP

For the crème chiboust you can add 1½ sheets of gelatine to the crème pâtissière base to help set the cream. This will make it easier to serve. You can also enhance the flavour of this crème by adding finely grated orange zest to the boiling milk and some Grand Marnier at the final stage.

Method of work

1 On a floured surface, roll out the puff paste into a 35cm × 11cm rectangle. (Use puff paste trimmings rather than virgin paste to reduce the rise in this pastry.) Prick with a fork or pastry dock.

2 Using a piping bag with a 1.2cm plain nozzle, pipe the choux paste lengthways down each edge of the puff paste, leaving a gap of approximately 1cm from the edge.

3 Egg wash the puff paste and the choux paste. Leave to rest in a refrigerator for 30 minutes before baking.

4 Pipe small choux buns, about 1.5cm in diameter, onto a separate baking sheet. Brush with egg wash and press lightly with the back of a fork.

5 Bake at 220°C for about 10 minutes with the vents of the oven open (if you have this facility). Lower the temperature to 200°C and bake the small choux buns for a further ten minutes and the base for a further 20 minutes. Remove and cool on a wire rack when cooked.

6 To make the crème chiboust, bring to the boil the milk and vanilla pod.

7 Whisk together the egg yolks, caster sugar, custard powder and cornflour.

8 Combine the ingredients and cook out, stirring constantly, to make a basic crème pâtissière.

9 Reserve to one side, adding a little melted butter to the surface of the crème to prevent a skin forming.

10 To create an Italian meringue, carefully boil the granulated sugar, water and glucose to 121°C. Meanwhile, whisk the egg whites to soft peaks. Gently pour in the hot sugar solution in a thin stream while still whisking. Continue to beat at a low speed until the mixture is completely cold.

11 While the crème pâtissière is still slightly warm, using a whisk stir in one-third of the meringue. Next, using a spatula, fold in the remaining meringue until completed incorporated. Do not over mix or the crème will collapse.

12 To assemble the tranche, cut a small hole in the base of each profiterole with the point of a knife or a cream horn mould. Dip the tops into some caramelised sugar and place onto a baking sheet to cool.

13 When cool, fill the profiteroles with some of the crème chiboust.

14 Pipe the crème chiboust decoratively down the centre of the baked choux/puff pastry base.

15 Place the profiteroles down the sides of the tranche, using a little of the caramelised sugar to help adhere if you wish.

16 Leave the Saint Honoré in a refrigerator for approximately 2 hours before serving.

17 Garnish the dessert traditionally with a sugar veil, or for a more modern effect add some piped sugar.

Pear Bourdaloue tart *Poire flan Bourdaloue*

INGREDIENTS	1 × 20CM TART (8 PORTIONS)	2 × 20CM TARTS (16 PORTIONS)
Sweet paste (la pâte sucrée, see recipe on p. 297)	175g	350g
Crème pâtissière	75g	150g
Unsalted butter	100g	225g
Tant pour tant	225g	450g
Eggs	2	4
Soft white flour	30g	60g
Almond flavour or dark rum	30g	60g
Poached pear halves	8 halves	16 halves
Sieved apricot jam	50g	100g
Stock syrup	25g	50g
Chopped pistachio nuts or flaked almonds	25g	50g

Method of work

1 Preheat an oven to 180°C.

2 Cream together the tant pour tant and the unsalted butter.

3 Slowly beat in the eggs, flour and almond flavour or dark rum.

4 Mix the crème pâtissière into the almond preparation and set aside in a refrigerator. For a traditional Bourdaloue filling, create a mix using two parts crème d'amande to one part crème pâtissière.

5 Line a tart mould with the sweet paste and trim the edges.

6 Pipe the Bourdaloue preparation into the bottom of the lined tart case to just two-thirds full.

7 Slice each pear half thinly and arrange on top of the filling.

8 Place in the oven and bake for approximately 35 minutes.

9 Carefully remove from the oven and cool on a wire rack. In a small saucepan, bring the apricot jam and stock syrup to the boil, stirring constantly to produce an apricot glaze. Apply the hot apricot glaze carefully with a pastry brush and decorate with the chopped pistachio nuts or flaked almonds.

10 Serve warm or chilled.

 CHEF'S TIP

You can vary the type of fruit used, but it is best to use fruits such as apples, quinces and plums due to the baking time of the tart.

Strawberry club sandwich *Club sandwich aux fraises*

INGREDIENTS	4 PORTIONS	10 PORTIONS
Shortbread paste (pâte sablée, see recipe on p. 299)	200g	500g
Passion fruit purée	140ml	350g
Passion fruit (whole with seeds)	2	5
Fresh full fat milk	160ml	400g
Caster sugar	75g	180g
Cornflour	10g	25g
Soft white flour	15g	40g
Egg yolk	1	3
Whipping cream	200ml	500ml
Fresh strawberries	280g	700g
Earl grey tea (with sugar to taste)	150ml	375ml
Passion fruit purée	140ml	350g
Icing sugar for dusting	50g	100g

Method of work

1 Preheat an oven to 200°C.

2 Roll the pâte sablée to about 2mm thick and cut out sandwich triangles about 15cm along the longest edge. Each triangle should be of identical size. Three triangles per portion.

3 Pile them on top of each other and make a hole through the middle using a skewer. Transfer separately onto baking sheets lined with a silicone baking mat and rest in a refrigerator for 15 minutes.

4 Place in the oven to bake until set but without too much colour. Remove and cool on a wire rack.

5 To make the crème, aerate the whipping cream to soft peaks.

6 Combine half of the passion fruit (reserve the other half for the sauce), purée and milk and heat to simmering point.

7 Blend the sugar, egg yolk, cornflour and flour whisked with 2 tablespoons of cold milk.

8 Add to the simmering liquid and cook out, stirring continuously.

9 Cool the mixture quickly then carefully fold in the whipped cream.

10 To make the sauce and serve, mix the tea (which has been previously made with water and sweetened with a little sugar), the remaining passion fruit and purée together. Refrigerate in a covered bowl.

11 Place a teaspoon of the crème in the centre of a plate. Position a triangle of pastry on it.

12 Put a dessertspoon of the crème on top and arrange some strawberries on it.

13 Repeat the procedure, layering the club sandwich and finishing with a third pastry triangle on top.

14 Place a small strawberry on the end of a sugar or bamboo skewer and push the skewer through the holes in the pastry to hold the sandwich together.

15 Splash the jus around the sides of the plate and dust the top of the sandwich with icing sugar. Serve immediately.

CHEF'S TIP

Dip a whole small strawberry into caramelised sugar and let the sugar slowly drip and set to create a sugar spike; use this instead of the bamboo skewer.

Gâteau Paris Brest

INGREDIENTS	10 PORTIONS	20 PORTIONS
Basic choux paste (see recipe on p. 304)	300g	500g
Egg yolks	6	12
Caster sugar	125g	250g
Cornflour	20g	40g
Custard powder	20g	40g
Fresh full fat milk	500ml	500ml
Vanilla	Optional	Optional
Crushed praline	100g	200g
Selection of fresh fruits for decoration (e.g. raspberries, kiwi, apple and orange)	200g	400g
Caramel sauce		
Granulated sugar	50g	100g
Cold water	40ml	80ml
Double cream	250ml	500ml

Method of work

1 Fill a piping bag fitted with a large star nozzle with basic choux paste. Pipe individual choux rings onto a lightly greased baking sheet.

2 Sprinkle the top with some flaked almonds and egg wash the tops. Bake at 220°C for about 15 minutes. Cool on a wire rack.

3 To make the praline cream, whisk the egg yolks with the sugar and then mix in the cornflour and custard powder.

4 Bring the milk to the boil in a saucepan with the vanilla.

5 Add the boiled milk to the egg mixture and stir until smooth. Add the vanilla if required. Return to the saucepan and bring to the boil, stirring constantly. Make sure the cream is the correct consistency, then cool it by pouring onto a clean work surface, such as a marble slab. Keep turning it back on itself for 2–3 minutes using a palette knife.

6 When cooled, stir in the praline. Reserve to one side.

7 For the caramel sauce, using a heavy-based saucepan dissolve the sugar in the water and bring to boiling point over a medium heat.

8 Wash down the inside of the pan with a clean pastry brush and clean water to prevent any sugar crystals forming. Continue to cook the sugar solution to a deep amber colour.

9 Remove from the heat and carefully add the double cream.

10 Set back onto the heat and slowly bring back to the boil, stirring constantly with a wooden spoon. Simmer while stirring for 2 minutes.

11 Pass through a chinois and store until required for use. (This sauce can be used either hot or cold.)

12 To serve, cut each individual gâteau in half lengthways and pipe some of the praline cream inside.

13 Decoratively arrange the fresh fruit on top of the cream. Place the top of the choux ring back on top of the filling and arranged fruit.

14 Dust with a little icing sugar and place in the centre of the dessert plate.

15 Pour some caramel sauce around the gateau, decorate as desired and serve.

CHEF'S TIP

The traditional presentation of this gâteau is as a multi-portioned confection with just the praline cream. To create a lighter praline cream you can substitute the pastry cream base for a preparation of crème chantilly and fold the crushed praline into this. The finish for the gâteau is a light dusting of icing sugar.

Profiteroles with pistachio ice cream *Profiteroles aux glace de pistache*

INGREDIENTS	20 PORTIONS	40 PORTIONS
Profiteroles		
Basic choux paste (see recipe on p. 304)	150g	300g
Chopped pistachios	45g	70g
Nibbed sugar	25g	50g
Pistachio ice cream		
Fresh full fat milk	225ml	550ml
Skimmed milk powder	20g	40g
Double cream	35ml	70ml
Egg yolks	25g	50g
Caster sugar	50g	100g
Glucose syrup	15g	25g
Pistachio paste	35g	70g
Ice cream stabiliser	3 g	5g
Kirsch	5g	10g

Method of work

1 Fold two-thirds of the chopped pistachio nuts into the paste.

2 Using a piping bag with a large star nozzle pipe individual profiteroles onto a baking sheet.

3 Sprinkle the top with the remaining chopped pistachio nuts and the nibbed sugar crystals. Lightly dust with icing sugar. Bake at 190°C for about 20 minutes with the vents of the oven open (if the oven has this facility). Remove when cooked and cool on a wire rack.

4 To make the pistachio ice cream, bring to the boil the milk, cream, stabiliser, pistachio paste and **glucose** syrup.

5 Whisk together the egg yolks, caster sugar and milk powder.

6 Combine the ingredients and reheat to 85°C stirring constantly.

7 Reserve to one side. Add the kirsch and cool down to a minimum of 4°C within one hour.

8 Freeze in an ice cream machine and reserve in a freezer in piping bags with star tubes for use.

9 To serve, cut the profiteroles in half lengthways.

10 Pipe the pistachio ice cream into the bottom half of the profiteroles.

11 Place the tops back on and dust with icing sugar.

12 Serve approximately three profiteroles per portion and present with an appropriate garnish and a raspberry coulis.

 CHEF'S TIP

Alternative ice cream or sorbet preparations can be used in this recipe. However, in order to help accentuate the flavour of the ice cream and also to settle the fat content in the mixture it is advisable to leave the cooked mixture to mature for 24 hours in a refrigerator at 0–3°C.

Warm cherry samosas with Amaretto bavarois

 CHEF'S TIP

The samosas can be deep fried instead of baked. This will help to achieve an all round golden colour, but it will also increase the fat levels to the palette when eating.

INGREDIENTS	4 PORTIONS	8 PORTIONS
Cherry samosas		
Melted butter	60g	120g
Filo paste sheets	4	8
Griottines soaked in kirsch	125g	200g
Cornflour	5g	10g
Icing sugar	60g	120g
Amaretto bavarois		
Fresh full fat milk	175ml	375ml
Amaretto	25ml	50ml
Egg yolks	2	3
Caster sugar	40g	60g
Whipping cream	175ml	375ml
Gelatine	2 leaves	4 leaves
Pre-crystallised white chocolate (see chapter 11)	200g	400g
Acetate strips (to line the mould)	4	8

Method of work

1 Gently heat the griottines in a saucepan. Mix the cornflour with a little cold water. Add the diluted cornflour and cook until the griottines and kirsch mixture has thickened. Retain some of this for the **bavarois**.

2 Take two sheets of the filo paste, brush one with the melted butter and place the other on top. Cut into strips and place the cooled griottine mixture in the centre. Fold into a samosa shape. Repeat this process for the required number of samosas.

3 Brush the samosas with the melted butter and dust well with the icing sugar. Bake on a lined baking sheet at 200°C until golden brown in colour.

4 Purée the remaining filling in a blender with a little Amaretto to create a coulis to use for decoration.

5 To prepare the bavarois, beat together the egg yolks and the caster sugar and soak the gelatine leaves in cold water to soften.

6 Bring the milk to the boil. Add the milk to the egg yolks, mix together and return to the pan. Stirring constantly, cook out the egg custard to approximately 82°C.

7 Add the softened gelatine, stir in well until melted, pass through a sieve and cool down the custard as quickly as possible.

8 Temper the white chocolate and spread over each acetate strip (see chapter 11). Carefully place each strip inside each mould to form a collar for the bavarois. Use any leftover chocolate for decoration to finish the dessert.

9 When the custard with the Amaretto is half set, whip the cream to the ribbon stage and gently fold into the custard.

10 Pipe bavarois mixture into each mould until half full. Spoon a teaspoon of the griottine mixture into the centre of each bavarois. Pipe in the rest of the bavarois mixture to retain the griottines in the centre. Level off the top and place in a refrigerator to set.

11 To serve, place the cherry samosas into the centre of the plate, with the amaretto bavarois to one side. Decorate as required and finish with the griottine coulis. Serve immediately.

CAKES, BISCUITS AND SPONGES

Over the past few years, the production and presentation of cakes, gâteaux and torten within Europe and North America have changed significantly. For these types of pâtisserie the emphasis is now on producing individual portions, individually decorated with glazes and fruits or chocolate decorations. There is a trend towards lightness in texture and design of the dessert or cake – the use of biscuit jaconde, dacquoise and mousses seems to highlight this very well.

Unusual flavours and combinations are now being used in conjunction with sophisticated presentations, and influences from the Eastern and Indian regions and the Caribbean are now mixed with more traditional and classical European styles.

This chapter explains the various base components used in the production of modern-style and classical cakes, biscuits, sponges and scones.

USE OF FATS IN BAKERY AND CAKE MAKING

Fats that are solid at room temperature (e.g. butter) tend to be derived from animal sources. There are, however, a few exceptions, such as hydrogenated vegetable shortenings, cocoa butter and some tropical fats, which are derived from plants. Fats that are liquid at room temperature are referred to collectively as 'oils'. These tend to originate from plants, such as olives, maize, nuts and seeds. Oils can be chemically processed into solid form (hydrogenated), which will increase their shelf life.

Fats perform many different functions in baking, for example they provide flavour. They also create tenderness in the baked product by coating the strands of gluten present in batters and doughs. Fats add moisture and a rich quality that will help to increase the shelf life of many products. When creamed together with sugar, fats can also hold a great amount of air, and when used jointly with other leaveners (such as baking powder) this will help baked goods to rise.

Solid fats with a high melting point will help to provide flakiness to pastes and laminated dough products, such as croissants and puff pastry, by creating distinct fine layers of fat between sheets of dough. Fats can also impart flavour when used for frying, such as deep frying of doughnuts and beignets.

Choosing an appropriate fat to use for a particular recipe will make a big difference to the result. One of the main points of consideration is the fat's plasticity. The greater the plasticity of a fat (e.g. vegetable shortening), the less pleasant it may be to eat because it will tend to leave a coating on the tongue. This is because highly plastic fats have a higher melting temperature. Butter is plastic at a cool room temperature, but once refrigerated it becomes harder and less plastic. Vegetable shortening will still have a good degree of plasticity even when refrigerated, which makes it easier to use in some laminated recipes.

Butter and vegetable shortening are both capable of holding air and are therefore good to use as creaming agents. When creaming, butter should always be soft enough to be beaten and therefore trap air. This happens best at temperatures between 19°C and 21°C. The flavour and colour of butter make it the most desirable fat for use in the production of cakes, biscuits and sponges. Vegetable shortening will hold more air than butter because it contains less water, but it has the drawbacks of a lack of colour and flavour and a slightly greasy feel on the tongue during eating.

Storage of fats

Solid fats absorb odours and strong flavours and therefore need to be stored correctly in the refrigerator, away from strongly flavoured ingredients. They can also be frozen for several weeks. Liquid fats will turn rancid more quickly and should be stored in airtight containers in a dark, cool and dry area. The longer a fat is stored, the greater the chance of it turning rancid. Liquid fats can be stored in a refrigerator; however, they can turn semi-solid at these cooler temperatures and must be brought back to room temperature before use.

USE OF EGGS IN BAKERY AND CAKE MAKING

Fresh shell eggs are undoubtedly best for most cuisine and bakery purposes. However, the time required for cracking the eggs, the inevitable waste, the mess caused by egg shells and the ever-present possibility of the inclusion of a stale egg in a mixing all highlight the benefits of using good brands of frozen pasteurised eggs.

Fresh eggs are made up of three main components:

1 *Shell* – calcium carbonate   12%
2 *White* – protein: albumen   58%
3 *Yolk* – protein: lecithin   30%

The average weight of an egg is 50 grams.

Eggs have various uses in cookery, especially in the pastry section:

■ Eggs are used as moistening agents
■ They absorb a large quantity of air when manipulated (whisked)

CHEF'S TIP

The ability of a fat to hold its own shape at room temperature but still have the capacity to be moulded is known as 'plasticity'.

CHEF'S TIP

Hydrogenated vegetable shortenings are liquid oils that have undergone the chemical process of hydrogenation, which changes the oil to a solid. This gives the added benefit of a longer shelf life.

■ They act as enriching agents in food products, giving better structure, flavour and appearance

■ Egg yolk coagulates at 65–71°C

■ Egg white denatures at 60–65°C.

Basic composition of eggs

Both egg white and egg yolk contain a large proportion of water, some protein, fats and minerals, but in slightly different quantities.

COMPOSITION OF EGGS: PER CENT

	EGG YOLK	EGG WHITE	WHOLE EGG
WATER	50–50.5	86–87	73–75
PROTEIN	16–16.5	12–12.5	12–14
FAT	31–32	0.25	10–12
MINERALS	0.8–1.5	0.5–0.6	0.8–1.5

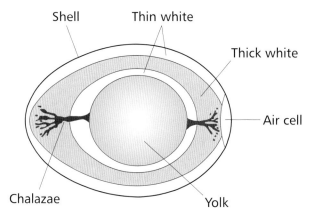

The structure of an egg

Storage of eggs

Fresh eggs should be stored in a cool but not too dry place, refrigeration at 2–3°C is ideal. Egg shells are porous and so eggs will absorb strong odours.

When an egg is stored, the thick white gradually absorbs moisture and therefore thins down. The yolk, in turn, absorbs moisture and begins to spread. Eventually the water will evaporate from the egg through its porous shell and is replaced by air. Since water is heavier than air, fresh eggs will be heavier than stale ones.

Frozen eggs

The use of frozen eggs is becoming more widespread due to fears of contamination of fresh eggs and the issue of wastage. There were initially problems with some imported frozen eggs, which were contaminated with *Salmonella* and other food poisoning bacteria. To overcome this, legislation was introduced in January 1964 stating that all eggs to be frozen must first be pasteurised.

Pasteurised frozen eggs must be defrosted gently before use. Immerse the can in cold running water until defrosted. When defrosted, remove the eggs from the can, thoroughly mix and then bring to room temperature. On no account should eggs be defrosted by the application of heat or the eggs will be denatured and lose their efficiency. Once defrosted, pasteurised eggs should be used without delay as, like all forms of egg, they are an extremely good medium for the growth of bacteria.

USE OF DRIED FRUIT IN BAKERY AND CAKE MAKING

Many types of fruit are available dried. Whereas fruit in its natural state is bursting with fresh, sweet juices, when dried it changes character completely. It becomes dense, concentrated in flavour and often not particularly attractive to look at, being wrinkled and leathery.

Dried fruit is an excellent source of dietary fibre, and although much of the moisture has been removed, most of the nutrients found in the fresh fruit are retained (apart from vitamin C). Dried fruit is higher in calories, volume for volume, than fresh fruit. When rehydrated, the nutritional value of the dried fruit approximates that of fresh fruit. Some fruits absorb larger volumes of liquid than others: tree fruits such as apples and pears increase by between three and five times their volume after soaking, vine fruits such as currants and raisins by about twice their volume.

Dried fruits also have the capacity to take on additional flavours when rehydrated, such as from fruit juices, alcohol, spices and tea. This is especially valuable when producing fruit cakes.

Not all dried fruit is soaked before use. Fruits such as dates, figs and raisins can be eaten as they are.

Before using dried fruits in cake recipes it is best to wash them then soak them in the required flavoured liquid. The fruit can be soaked for long periods of time, especially for rich fruit cakes for weddings and Christmas festivals, where the richness and moisture of the fruit will help to prolong the shelf life of the actual cake.

Dried fruits are often purchased in packs and can make very good winter fruit salads or compôtes.

AERATION PROCESSES IN CAKES AND SPONGES

There are four methods of aeration used in the preparation of cakes, biscuits and sponges. These are:

1 *Panary* – yeast
2 *Chemical* – baking powder
3 *Physical* – whisking and beating
4 Combination

Panary aeration

In 1859, the French scientist Louis Pasteur discovered that dough is aerated by living micro-organisms, which convert sugar into carbon dioxide (CO_2) . This is the principle behind panary fermentation, which is brought about by the action of enzymes in yeast and flour. Fermentation in breads and doughs is dealt with later in this chapter, but it is also a prime concept in baked products such as pâte à savarin.

The initial gas production during panary fermentation comes from the breakdown of simple sugars present in the flour or in other added ingredients. Further glucose is made available by the conversion of other carbohydrates in the flour by specific enzymes. The gas is held within the structure of the gluten network, which gradually becomes more elastic during the fermentation process, and so the dough rises. Two by-products of this fermentation process are acids and alcohol, which make a contribution to the overall dough flavour.

When in the oven, gas production is accelerated until the yeast is killed by the heat, at which point activity ceases. The expansion of air and gas and the pressure of water vapour cause an increase in volume, which is maintained by the coagulation of all the proteins present as baking continues.

Chemical aeration

Historically, cakes originated from the practice of using up surplus ingredients – sugar (probably in the form of honey), fats or oils – by adding them to fermented dough. This produced a rich and pleasant range of finished goods.

This basic method continued to be used until the introduction of chemical aeration, when it was discovered that certain chemicals would give off gas when mixed with moist ingredients and then heated.

An examination of old recipe books shows that chemical aeration was known and in use many centuries ago. Certainly, **bicarbonate of soda** has been in use for over 200 years, and before that pearl ash, a pure form of potash obtained from deteriorating wood and vegetable matter, was used. It was discovered that if potash was added to **gingerbread** dough it would become aerated during storage before baking. Potassium carbonate obtained from residues of beet sugar refining was another known aerating chemical.

Old recipe books also refer to muriatic acid, now known as hydrochloric acid. When mixed with bicarbonate of soda, the resulting reaction releases carbon dioxide and leaves a residue of sodium chloride (common salt).

A mixture of tartaric acid and bicarbonate of soda then came into favour, tartaric acid in turn being superseded by cream of tartar. Cream of tartar, however, was much more expensive than tartaric acid and more of it is necessary for a given amount of bicarbonate of soda. This mixture is known as baking powder.

Baking powder may be produced by combining one part bicarbonate of soda with two parts cream of tartar. Efficient baking powder should liberate the maximum amount of gas during baking. It must also be harmless and should not be unpleasant in taste or aroma.

Carbon dioxide generated by the chemical reaction becomes entangled in the gluten and albumin framework of a cake. This holds the gas and expands until the proteins coagulate, at which point the aerated structure becomes comparatively rigid.

The baking powder has a delayed action – only a small amount of carbon dioxide is given off when the liquid ingredients are added. The majority of the gas is released when the mixture is heated, therefore cake and pudding mixtures will not lose their ability to rise if they are not cooked immediately.

 CHEF'S TIP

If too much baking powder is used in a recipe the flavour of the cake will become quite salty as the sodium residue builds up.

 CHEF'S TIP

Over time the shelf life of baking powder is shortened because it absorbs moisture from the air, which weakens it. A quick test to determine whether baking powder is still active is to mix a little of it with some malt vinegar. If the powder is active it will quickly foam.

Hints on using baking powder:

- Mix the baking powder thoroughly with the flour
- Replace the lid tightly on the tin after use
- Measure accurately
- Do not slam the oven door in the early stages of cooking
- Excess baking powder causes a cake to collapse in the middle and dumplings to break up
- Insufficient baking powder results in a close, heavy texture

---

Physical aeration

Beating particular mixtures of ingredients will cause air to become incorporated into the mixture, resulting in a baked product with a light texture. This is known as physical aeration. Two principal bakery ingredients are capable of holding air when beaten: fats and eggs. It is probable that eggs were the first ingredient aerated in this way, but animal fats can also be made much lighter by beating, particularly when blended with other ingredients, such as sugar.

Beating eggs denatures the protein content by breaking it down into smaller fragments and allows air to be trapped. As the aeration of the egg continues, the denatured protein surrounds the air bubbles and locks in the air, preventing it from escaping. This process helps in the production of cakes and sponges by creating a lightness and leavens the cake (makes it rise) as it bakes.

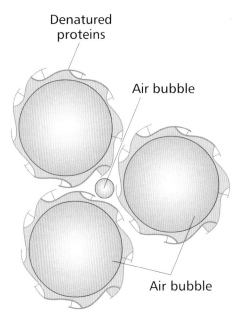

Aeration of albumin

When beaten, egg white can hold more air than either whole egg or egg yolk, and for this reason it is the ideal medium for meringues, soufflés and royal icing.

Short pastry is also lightened by physical aeration, but to a lesser extent. Air is introduced either when the fat is rubbed in to the flour or when the fat and sugar are beaten prior to mixing into the flour.

Combination method

A simple example of a combination method is that used for Danish pastry, when butter is laminated into fermented dough. This combines panary aeration with aeration by lamination.

The combination of physical and chemical aeration is quite common. A mixture of fat, sugar and eggs is beaten during the first stages of production. The aeration is then supplemented by the addition of baking powder during the later stages.

An example where panary and chemical aeration are combined is the fermented scone. This is made using a preliminary yeast fermentation which is then incorporated with other ingredients to which baking powder has been added.

RECIPES
Rich fruit cake

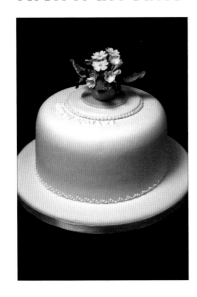

INGREDIENTS	1 × 20CM ROUND CAKE	1 × 30CM ROUND CAKE
Soft flour	180g	360g
Dark brown muscovado sugar	180g	360g
Unsalted butter	180g	360g
Washed currants	225g	450g
Washed sultanas	225g	450g
Seedless raisins	90g	200g
Glacé cherries	50g	100g
Mixed peel	150g	300g
Ground almonds	75g	150g
Eggs	3	6
Mixed spice	5g	10g
Nutmeg	2g	5g
Ground mace	2g	5g
Good-quality salt	2g	5g
Zest and juice of lemon	1 lemon	2 lemons
Brandy	75ml	150ml
Sherry	50ml	100ml

Method of work

1 First line your tin with a double layer of greaseproof parchment. Then clean and prepare the fruit, halve the cherries.

2 Mix all the fruit together with the lemon juice, zest and alcohol. This mixture can be left for about one week in advance of making the cake.

3 Sift the flour and spices together.

4 Beat the butter until soft and light. Add the sugar to create a good aeration. Gradually incorporate the egg.

5 Stir in the ground almonds and fold in the flour and spices.

6 Add the fruit with the liquid and mix well together. Transfer to the baking tin.

7 It is extremely important to follow the correct recipe balance. Preheat an oven to 140°C. Put a tray containing 1 pint of water into the oven; this will create steam within the oven and help the cake rise evenly. Remove the tray of water half way through the baking process. The cake should be cooked after 3½–4 hours.

8 Leave the cake in the tin for one day. Add a soaking mixture of rum and sherry every two days for one week. Wrap the cake in wax paper and place in an airtight container. The cake should be mature after three weeks.

 CHEF'S TIP

To calculate the size of cake required, eight portions are generally cut from each 450g of finished cake.

Decorating the cake

3. Carefully roll up the marzipan and lay it over the cake.

1. Select the correct sized board to present the cake. Trim the top of the cake to create a level surface.

2. Knead the marzipan (if required) and pin out so that it is at least 8cm larger than the actual cake. Brush some boiled apricot jam over the cake to completely seal it.

4. Manipulate the marzipan so it completely covers the cake and creates a protective skin.

5. Leave the marzipan to dry for at least 24 hours before attempting to cover with the cover paste (icing). Using the same method, cover the cake with the cover paste, but brush a little alcohol onto the marzipan to help the cover paste to adhere. Smooth out any creases using a special smoothing paddle or the palm of your hand.

6. Using a piping bag with a small (number one) plain tube, pipe small decorative sequences over the cake using royal icing.

7. Write the name of the person that the cake is for (or the message for the cake) onto some silicone paper. Carefully place this onto the top of the cake and using a small pin, prick the outline of the words directly onto the cake to form a guide to pipe over.

8. Pipe over the guide marks using royal icing.

9. Finish off with a pre-made decorative motif or flowers as desired.

Separated egg sponge

INGREDIENTS	1 SMALL BAKING SHEET	2 SMALL BAKING SHEETS
Fresh eggs	4	8
Soft flour	110g	220g
Caster sugar	110g	220g
Vanilla flavour	A few drops	A few drops

 CHEF'S TIP

Replace one-third of the flour with potato flour to make the finished sponge soft and flexible for use as a Swiss roll.

Method of work

1 Line a baking sheet (35cm × 25cm × 2cm deep) with silicone paper or a silicone baking mat. Preheat an oven to 200°C.

2 Separate the eggs. Aerate the egg yolks with two-thirds of the caster sugar and the vanilla essence in a bowl until stiff and almost white in colour.

3 Meanwhile, aerate the egg whites with the remaining caster sugar to a stiff peak.

4 Mix in a little of the aerated egg whites to the yolk mixture.

5 Carefully fold in the sieved flour and then the remainder of the egg whites. At this stage you must fold in very carefully using a plastic spatula so as not to knock the air out of the preparation. Pipe the mixture onto the prepared baking sheet in fingers (biscuit à la cuillère) or spread onto the sheet and use as a base for gâteaux.

Flourless chocolate sponge

INGREDIENTS	2 × 20CM ROUND CAKE TINS	4 × 20CM ROUND CAKE TINS
Egg yolks	5	10
Cocoa powder	40g	80g
Caster sugar	55g	110g
Egg whites	5	10
Caster sugar	75g	150g
Vanilla flavour	A few drops	A few drops

 CHEF'S TIP

This sponge recipe can be used for desserts, gâteaux and cakes.

Method of work

1 Prepare the cake tins with silicone paper or line a baking sheet with silicone paper or a silicone baking mat. Preheat an oven to 200°C.

2 Whisk the egg yolks and the smaller quantity of caster sugar to a sabayon stage over a bain marie of warm water (softly aerated).

3 Create a meringue with the egg whites and the larger quantity of caster sugar.

4 Sieve the cocoa powder and carefully fold in to the egg yolk sabayon with some vanilla flavour.

5 Gently fold in the meringue mixture and then deposit onto the prepared baking sheet or cake tins.

6 Bake in the oven until the sponge contracts from the sides and it feels springy to the touch.

Biscuit jaconde

CHEF'S TIP

Biscuit jaconde is a flexible, highly moisturised biscuit designed to be used decoratively in association with cakes, torten, mousses, bavarois and other entremets.

VIDEO CLIP
Using a silk screen to make a biscuit jaconde

CHEF'S TIP

Other colours can be achieved in the stencil paste. Just replace the cocoa powder with 20g soft flour and add the appropriate coloured/flavoured paste.

CHEF'S TIP

A textured effect can be produced by liberally sprinkling chopped pistachio nuts, hazelnuts, poppy seeds or desiccated coconut over the silicone baking mat before carefully spreading on the biscuit mixture.

INGREDIENTS	2 LARGE BAKING SHEETS	4 LARGE BAKING SHEETS
Stencil paste		
Icing sugar	50g	100g
Unsalted butter	50g	100g
Egg whites	55g	105g
Soft flour	40g	80g
Cocoa powder	10g	20g
Biscuit		
Icing sugar	190g	375g
Ground almonds	190g	375g
Whole eggs	250g	500g
Soft flour	50g	100g
Melted butter	40g	75g
Egg whites	130g	260g
Caster sugar	25g	50g

Method of work

1 Line a baking sheet (45cm × 35cm × 2cm deep) with a silicone baking mat. Preheat an oven to 240°C.

2 To make the stencil paste, beat the icing sugar and the softened butter. Add the egg whites and fold in the sieved flour and cocoa powder together. Mix to a smooth paste.

3 To make the biscuit, pass the icing sugar and ground almonds through a sieve twice.

4 Whisk the sieved mixture with the whole eggs to a ribbon stage on an electric mixing machine.

5 Sieve the flour.

6 Create a meringue with the egg whites and caster sugar.

7 Fold the sieved flour into the sabayon of eggs and almonds and then fold in the melted butter. Carefully fold in the meringue.

8 To create the frieze effect, spread the stencil paste using a decorative template or rake onto a baking sheet lined with a silicone baking mat. Freeze the baking sheet until the mixture is hard.

9 Thinly spread the biscuit mixture over the frozen stencil paste (about 5mm).

10 Bake at 240°C for about 5 minutes. The biscuit should be moist, springy to the touch and on no account dry.

11 Remove from the oven, cool, carefully remove from the silicone baking mat. Store wrapped in cling film in a refrigerator and use as required.

Dacquoise

INGREDIENTS	4 × 20CM DISCS	8 × 20CM DISCS
Egg whites	220g	440g
Caster sugar	80g	160g
Hazelnut tant pour tant	190g	380g
Almond tant pour tant	170g	340g

Method of work

1. Line a baking sheet with a silicone baking mat. Preheat an oven to 180°C.
2. Create a meringue with the egg whites and the caster sugar.
3. Carefully combine both tant pour tant preparations into the meringue using a plastic spatula to maintain as much aeration as possible.
4. Place into a disposable piping bag with a plain tube and pipe discs on to the baking sheet.
5. Bake in the oven for approximately 20 minutes.

Heavy Genoese sponge

INGREDIENTS	2 TRAYS	4 TRAYS
Butter or cake margarine	225g	450g
Caster sugar	225g	450g
Whole eggs	5	10
Soft flour	250g	500g
Cornflour	30g	60g
Baking powder	10g	20g
Vanilla	To taste	To taste
Good-quality salt	3g	5g

Method of work

1. First line the baking trays (15cm × 8cm × 5cm deep) with silicone paper. Preheat an oven to 180°C.
2. Beat the fat with the sugar to a light aerated consistency. Add the salt and vanilla.
3. Slowly add the eggs, clearing the mixture each time before adding another quantity.
4. Fold in the sieved flour, baking powder and cornflour.
5. Deposit into the moulds and place in the oven to bake for approximately 40 minutes.

Japonaise

INGREDIENTS	2 × 20CM DISCS	5 × 20CM DISCS
Egg whites	5	10
Caster sugar	150g	300g
Ground hazelnuts	150g	300g
Cornflour	25g	50g
Caster sugar	60g	120g

CHEF'S TIP

Keep any excess Japonaise and reduce to crumbs. Keep in an airtight container and use for decorating various gâteaux (e.g. Gâteau Succés).

Method of work

1 Line a baking sheet with a silicone baking mat. Preheat an oven to 160°C.
2 Mix together the hazelnuts, cornflour and the smaller quantity of caster sugar.
3 Create a meringue with the larger quantity of caster sugar and the egg whites.
4 Carefully fold in the dry mix to the meringue and quickly pipe onto the prepared baking sheet.
5 Place in the oven to bake for approximately 15–20 minutes. Remove from the oven to cool. When nearly cooled cut out the required shapes or discs. When it is totally cooled down it will dry out like a meringue.

Schweizwein torten

INGREDIENTS	1 × 20CM TORTEN RING	2 × 20CM TORTEN RINGS
Sweet wine mousse		
Sweet white wine	250ml	500ml
Caster sugar	70g	140g
Egg yolks	4	8
Whipping cream	250ml	500ml
Orange zest	1 orange	2 oranges
Gelatine	5 leaves	10 leaves
Vanilla	½ pod	1 pod
Neutral glaze		
Light stock syrup	200ml	400ml
Gelatine	2 leaves	4 leaves
Additional ingredients		
Sweet paste (pâte sucrée; see recipe on p. 297)	100g	200g
Almond flavoured separated egg sponge (see recipe on p. 331)	1 × 16cm disc	2 × 16cm disc
Sieved raspberry jam	100g	200g
Mixed prepared fresh fruits (e.g. strawberry, kiwi, fig, orange segments)	250g	500g

Method of work

1 Cut out a 16cm diameter circle of the rolled out sweet paste. **Dock** the paste and lay onto a baking tray lined with silicone paper. Bake blind. Remove from the oven and leave to cool.

2 Soften the gelatine in cold water.

3 Spread the disc of sweet paste with the sieved jam and place in the base of the torten ring.

4 Place a circle of the almond flavoured sponge on top, then add the mixed fruit. At this stage you can place a collar of biscuit jaconde around the side of the torten if required.

5 Whisk the orange zest, caster sugar and egg yolks over a bain marie to create a light aeration. Meanwhile, warm the wine in a saucepan to 80°C. Slowly add to the egg yolk while whisking continuously to form a sabayon.

6 Add the softened gelatine and make sure it is dissolved completely into the sabayon.

7 Remove from the bain marie and slowly whisk until the mixture has cooled down. Place into the refrigerator to half set.

8 Whip the cream to a ribbon stage and carefully fold into the sabayon. Pour into the torten ring and set in a refrigerator for at least 2 hours.

9 Make the neutral glaze by warming the stock syrup and adding the softened leaves of gelatine. Ensure that the gelatine has completely melted, then cool down over a bain marie of cold water.

10 When the torten has completely set and the glaze has cooled sufficiently, glaze the top of the torten and refrigerate for another 15 minutes. Remove the torten from the ring and serve with a raspberry coulis.

Sacher torte

INGREDIENTS	1 × 20CM ROUND CAKE TIN	2 × 20CM ROUND CAKE TINS
Sponge		
Butter	105g	210g
Caster sugar	75g	150g
Egg yolks	3	6
Melted dark chocolate	40g	80g
Soft flour	100g	200g
Baking powder	5g	10g
Ground almonds	25g	50g
Cocoa powder	30g	30g
Egg whites	3	6
Caster sugar	30g	60g
Chocolate glaze		
Fresh milk	100g	210g
Double cream	75g	150g
Icing sugar	50g	100g
Water	50g	100g
Liquid glucose	50g	100g
Dark chocolate	375g	750g
Additional ingredients		
Apricot jam	100g	200g
Dark rum or kirsch	25ml	50ml

Method of work

1 Line the baking tins with silicone paper. Preheat an oven to 180°C.

2 To make the Sacher sponge, cream the butter and the larger quantity of caster sugar together to aerate. Slowly add the egg yolks and the melted dark chocolate.

3 Sift together the baking powder, flour, ground almonds and cocoa powder twice. Incorporate into the creamed chocolate butter preparation.

4 Create a meringue with the smaller quantity of caster sugar and the egg whites. Carefully fold this into the chocolate preparation. Deposit the mixture into the prepared tins and place into the oven to bake.

5 Remove from the oven when fully cooked and turn out onto a wire cooling rack.

6 To make the Sacher glaze, place the milk, water, icing sugar, cream and glucose into a saucepan and slowly bring to the boil.

7 Meanwhile, melt the chocolate in a bain marie.

8 Remove the boiled cream liquid from the stove and add the melted chocolate. Mix together to a silky smooth consistency. Pass through a fine sieve and leave to cool to 20°C.

9 To prepare the base, cut the chocolate sponge into three equal layers. Macerate each layer with the alcohol and brush the surface with some boiled apricot jam thinned with a little of the alcohol. Reassemble the layers and place onto a cake board. Brush the remaining apricot glaze over the Sacher sponge.

10 With the glaze at the correct temperature (nearly at setting point), ladle the glaze over to completely cover the sponge. Leave to set. Using a little of the chocolate glaze pipe the name 'Sacher' on top of the torte and decorate with a little chocolate.

Pear and chocolate mousse cake

INGREDIENTS	1 × 20CM ROUND CAKE TIN	2 × 20CM ROUND CAKE TINS
Pear compôte		
Poached pears	550g	1150g
Unsalted butter	50g	100g
Caster sugar	100g	200g
Vanilla	½ pod	1 pod
Pear liqueur	25g	50g
Nougatine		
Caster sugar	75g	150g
Pectin (optional)	1g	2g
Glucose	25g	50g
Butter	75g	125g
Flaked almonds	50g	100g
Dark chocolate mousse		
Melted dark chocolate	350g	550g
Whipping cream (half whipped)	480g	680g
Additional ingredients		
Flourless chocolate sponge (see recipe on p. 331)	2 discs	4 discs
Biscuit jaconde (3cm wide strip to fit the circumference of the torten ring; see recipe on p. 332)	1 strip	2 strips
Cocoa powder	50g	100g

The different preparations required to assemble the mousse cake

Method of work

1 For the compôte, take the pears that have been poached in syrup and cut into 5mm dice. Melt the butter in a heavy-based pan then add the sugar and the split vanilla pod. Cook until a light caramel starts to appear and then add the pears and a little of the syrup. Cook for a further 3–4 minutes to evaporate most of the liquid. Add the alcohol and flambé then set aside to cool for later use.

2 For the nougatine, warm all the ingredients together in a saucepan and then roll the contents between two sheets of silicone paper. Remove the top sheet and bake in the oven until golden brown. Cut discs out of the nougatine when it has cooled a little.

3 For the dark chocolate mousse, melt the chocolate at 50°C. Combine with a little of the semi-whipped cream then mix together with the rest of the cream.

4 In a stainless steel torten ring, place the first disc of chocolate sponge in the base and moisten with a little extra liqueur. Place a disc of the nougatine on top. Wrap a strip of the biscuit jaconde around the inside of the ring. Half fill the torten with the chocolate mousse. Place the second chocolate sponge disc on top and spoon the compôte of pears over the disc. Finally fill the torten ring to the top with the chocolate mousse.

5 Leave to set in a refrigerator for at least 2 hours. Dust the top with the cocoa powder for decoration before removing the torten ring.

6 Serve with a crème chantilly.

Strawberry and lemon mousse cake

CHEF'S TIP

A classical pâte à bombe recipe is to beat cooked sugar (118°C) and egg yolks over a bain marie to a sabayon stage. This modern version for the lemon mousse recipe has the addition of water, glucose and milk powder to stabilise the egg yolk content. Cooking to 85°C will ensure that the eggs cook out completely without splitting the mixture.

INGREDIENTS	1 × 20CM TORTEN RING	3 × 20CM TORTEN RINGS
Lemon mousse		
Egg yolks	90g	180g
Water	90g	180g
Milk powder	30g	60g
Glucose	20g	40g
Lemon zest	3 lemons	6 lemons
Gelatine	10 leaves	20 leaves
Water	60g	120g
Lemon juice	180g	360g
Whipping cream (half whipped)	300g	600g
Italian meringue		
Egg whites	90g	180g
Caster sugar	90g	180g
Glucose	40g	80g
Water	40g	80g
Strawberry gel		
Strawberry purée	350ml	700ml
Gelatine	4 leaves	8 leaves
Water	25ml	50ml
Chopped fresh strawberries	100g	200g
Neutral glaze		
Stock syrup	320g	600g
Gelatine	4 leaves	8 leaves
Additional ingredients		
Dacquoise discs	1 × 18cm	3 × 18cm

Method of work

1 To prepare the lemon pâte à bombe base for the mousse, place the egg yolks, water, glucose, lemon zest and milk powder into a stainless steel saucepan and whisk while cooking out on the stove to 85°C.

2 Meanwhile, make the meringue to the Italian method by boiling the sugar, water and glucose to 121°C. Aerate the egg whites using an electric mixing machine until firm. Slowly stream the cooked sugar into the egg whites while beating on the machine. Continue to beat at a low speed until all the sugar has been incorporated and the meringue has cooled.

3 Fold the lemon pâte à bombe into the meringue. Melt the gelatine in a bain marie of hot water and add to the lemon mixture.

4 Carefully fold the lemon juice into the half whipped cream. Fold in all the ingredients together to create the lemon mousse.

5 Bring the strawberry purée to the boil. Soften the gelatine in the water and add to the hot purée. Strain onto the chopped strawberries and set in 150mm diameter rings.

6 Bring the stock syrup to the boil. Add the softened gelatine off the heat. Pass through a sieve and cool until required for glazing.

7 Lay the disc of dacquoise in the base of the torten ring. Add some of the lemon mousse to cover the base. Turn out the strawberry gel and place into the centre. Cover with the lemon mousse, filling to the top of the ring. Refrigerate for 2 hours.

8 Remove the torten ring and glaze. Set up in the refrigerator once again and decorate as desired.

Lemon tuilles

INGREDIENTS	25 TUILLES	50 TUILLES
Lemon zest	2 lemons	4 lemons
Icing sugar	85g	170g
Melted butter	60g	120g
Egg whites	70g	140g
Soft flour	85g	170g

VIDEO CLIP
Orange tuilles

CHEF'S TIP

Alternative flavours can be used, such as vanilla, cinnamon, orange, hazelnut and almond. Simply add the flavour to this basic recipe.

Method of work

1 Preheat an oven to 220°C.
2 Beat together the icing sugar, egg whites, melted butter and the finely grated lemon zest.
3 Mix in the flour and place the tuille mixture into a refrigerator to chill and set up. This can take approximately 1 hour.
4 Using a template, spread the mixture onto a baking sheet lined with a silicone baking mat.
5 Place in the oven and bake until the tuille begins to colour to a golden brown.
6 Remove from the oven and manipulate over a rolling pin into the classical tuille shape.

Classic tuilles

INGREDIENTS	25 TUILLES	50 TUILLES
Caster sugar	500g	1kg
Glucose	50g	100g
Melted butter	250g	500g
Flaked almonds	250g	500g
Water	200ml	400ml
Soft flour	150g	300g
Pistachio nuts	100g	200g

Method of work

1 Preheat an oven to 200°C.
2 Place the sugar, glucose, water, butter and almonds in a saucepan and bring to the boil, stirring constantly.
3 Remove from the heat and stir in the sieved flour. Ensure that the flour is incorporated thoroughly.
4 Put into a bowl and cool, then place in a refrigerator to chill down.
5 Place well-spaced piles of the mixture (approximately one teaspoon) on baking sheets lined with silicone paper. Flatten thoroughly.
6 Sprinkle with the pistachio nuts and place in the oven. Bake until golden brown.
7 Remove from the oven and cool for approximately 1 minute, then shape over a rolling pin and allow to cool.

Griddle scones

INGREDIENTS	12 SCONES	24 SCONES
Soft flour	225g	450g
Bicarbonate of soda	1tsp	2tsp
Cream of tartar	2tsp	4tsp
Butter	25g	50g
Caster sugar	25g	50g
Fresh milk	150ml	300ml

Method of work

1 Preheat a griddle or heavy-based frying pan and lightly oil the surface.
2 Sift the flour, bicarbonate of soda and cream of tartar into a bowl and rub in the butter.
3 Gradually stir in the sugar and the milk to form a soft paste.
4 Divide the paste in half and lightly knead on a lightly floured surface.
5 Roll each piece out to 1cm thick and cut out individual scone rounds. Place them onto the prepared griddle and cook for about 5 minutes per side, until the scones are evenly brown. Place onto a wire rack to cool.
6 Serve as quickly as possible with jam and cream accompaniments.

CHEF'S TIP

Wholemeal flour can replace the white flour in this recipe, although a little extra milk will be required to balance the overall consistency of the finished paste.

Almond biscotti

INGREDIENTS	2 × 500G LOGS	4 × 500G LOGS
Unsalted butter	125g	250g
Caster sugar	225g	450g
Whole eggs	1	3
Aniseed	4g	8g
Lemon zest	½ lemon	1 lemon
Almond flour	To taste	To taste
Soft flour	850g	1.7kg
Good-quality salt	5g	10g
Baking powder	7 g	15g
Flaked almonds	85g	170g
Vanilla flavour	To taste	To taste

Method of work

1 Preheat an oven to 180°C.
2 Cream the butter and the caster sugar together. Add the egg to the creamed mixture and beat together. Add all the flavourings and mix well.
3 Sift the flour, salt and baking powder. Gradually combine with the creamed butter.
4 Fold in the almonds.
5 Scale off at 500g each and roll into thin baguette shapes.
6 Bake in the oven on a baking tray lined with silicone paper for 20 minutes. Remove from the oven and slice thinly while still slightly warm.
7 Place the slices back into the oven (or until they have reached a golden colour). Turn over and bake for a further 8 minutes.
8 Cool on a wire cooling rack and store in an airtight container.

FERMENTED PRODUCTS

To make good bread and fermented dough products it is important to understand the functions of the basic components (flour, salt, water and yeast) and how they can be controlled and the appropriate methods of making dough for different types of bread products.

VIDEO CLIP
A professional bakery at work

FERMENTED DOUGH METHODS

There are four basic methods of producing fermented dough, each method has its own characteristics and applications:

1 Bulk fermented dough

2 'No-time' dough

3 Ferment and dough

4 Sponge and dough.

Bulk fermented dough (straight dough)

This is the process bakers and chefs use to make bread. It is a simple and effective method that is used in many recipes.

Flour and salt are blended together with water and yeast. These are mixed to a smooth, clear dough. The dough is then covered with a plastic sheet or damp kitchen cloth to prevent it drying out and forming a skin ('skinning'). It is given a 'bulk fermentation time' (BFT), allowing fermentation to occur over a set period of time. The next stage is carefully **knocking back** (de-gassing) the dough after the BFT and lightly **kneading** to encourage continued yeast activity, develop the gluten in the flour and ensure an even dough temperature.

The dough is rested for a few minutes, covered as before, then scaled off for shaping into the various products required by the baker or chef. The shaped dough products are then allowed to **prove** for a second time before baking. The total BFT can vary from 1 to 12 hours, depending on the recipe and the quantities of the ingredients, so it is important to always follow the recipe given.

 CHEF'S TIP

The fermentation process starts the development of flavour in the dough. Enzymes in the flour and yeast release simple sugars from the starch molecules in the flour.

'No-time' dough (activated dough development)

This method speeds up the fermentation through the addition of an improver. The improver contains chemicals and minerals that would normally be produced naturally during fermentation if allowed to continue over a longer time. This process is used by large-scale producers of packaged breads, such as supermarkets and large bakeries.

CHEF'S TIP

Retarding fermented dough means to slow down the fermentation process by placing the dough into refrigerated storage (1–4°C). This suppresses the activity of the yeast. Dough can therefore be produced the day before it is required and 'retarded' overnight before finishing and baking the next day.

CHEF'S TIP

Generally, the longer the fermentation time, the better the flavour developed within the dough. This is because the enzymes have more time to break down the starch molecules into sugars.

Flour, salt, yeast, water and the improver are blended and mixed to a soft dough. An electric mixing machine is required as the mixing time is approximately double the normal time. The mixing speed is also higher to help develop the gluten quickly and to warm the dough to a specific temperature. Fermentation progresses quickly due to the effects of the improver on the other ingredients, so cutting down the time required to produce large quantities of fermented dough products. When this stage is complete the dough is ready for scaling off, moulding into the required shape and proving before baking.

Extra yeast is required in some recipes that use improvers as the normal growth rate of the yeast can not keep up with the speed of the fermentation. As this process does not allow time for the gluten to mellow, about 4 per cent extra water is usually added to the dough.

No-time dough is ideal for production systems with limited time, facilities and space. Improvers also assist prolonged quality maintenance, making these doughs suitable for retarding in a refrigeratered area. Improvers also help to make reasonable breads from weaker flours.

Ferment and dough

This process is intended for heavily enriched dough to allow yeast to become accustomed to high levels of fat and sugar, which slow yeast activity considerably.

The first stage is to produce a ferment; the yeast is blended to a thin batter and fermented with about 20 per cent of the recipe's flour and all of the water. Fermentation time depends on the yeast content, but it is ready when it begins to drop back (the ferment rises so much that it cannot support its own bulk and starts to drop back). It is best fermented in a proving cabinet as it needs to be sufficiently warm after dropping back to maintain the correct dough temperature.

The ferment is then blended with the remaining flour, salt, fat and other enrichening ingredients to form a dough. The dough is then bulk fermented for approximately the same time as the ferment and then scaled off. This method is sometimes known as a 'flying ferment'.

Sponge and dough

This method is used by many artisan bakeries and chefs who wish to create natural, full-flavoured and textured breads.

The 'sponge' is a thick batter which ferments slowly, helping to maximise the amount of flavour in the finished bread. It is made by combining equal amounts of liquid, flour and yeast and may contain some salt. It is then left to ferment for between 6 and 24 hours, depending on the recipe and the amount of yeast used. This is sometimes referred to as a 'poolish'. It is then made into a soft dough with the addition of more liquid and flour. The dough can be used almost immediately as the yeast is fully activated.

This method will sometimes create a sour dough that is packed full of the natural flavours of the acids developed during the slow fermentation process.

Determining the water temperature for a dough

Certain dough recipes specify a particular working temperature for the dough to ferment correctly. This represents the temperature the dough should be before fermentation begins. If the dough is too cold, fermentation will be slow. The following method is recommended for determining the temperature of the water for the dough:

1 Measure the temperature of the flour to be used

2 Subtract that value from twice the required dough temperature

3 The result will be the required water temperature

The equation to find the correct water temperature for dough.

$$\text{WATER TEMPERATURE} = \frac{(\text{REQUIRED DOUGH} \times 2)}{\text{TEMPERATURE}} - \frac{\text{FLOUR}}{\text{TEMPERATURE}}$$

CHEF'S TIP

The act of mixing dough in an electric mixing machine produces energy. This is transferred to the dough as heat and so will increase its temperature. If using this method of mixing, it is best to reduce the water temperature slightly.

EQUIPMENT

Small quantities of fermented dough can be kneaded by hand.

However, this takes time and most chefs will prefer to use an electric mixer with a dough hook attachment.

A proving cabinet (prover) is a standard piece of equipment in patisseries and bakeries. The first prove should be between 25°C and 28°C. The second prove must be warmer, but never hotter than 40°C. If you do not have a proving cabinet, wrap the bowl containing the dough in a plastic bag and leave it in an appropriately warm place.

Provided that the dough has been properly handled, you will not need a steam-injected oven. Preheat the oven to a temperature ranging from 180°C to 200°C. The larger the bread loaf or brioche, the lower the heat setting should be.

Non-stick loaf tins are best for producing a rich brioche Nanterre loaf

IMAGES COURTESY OF RUSSUMS.CO.UK

Non-stick baking mats reduce the expense of purchasing silicone paper and can be washed and re-used

A heavy-duty mixer with a dough hook can be invaluable when producing large quantities of fermented dough

Digital thermometers give a quick and clear reading of the core temperature of the dough

CHEF'S TIP

Many ferments can be fermented in a refrigerator. The longer, cooler fermentation process allows more flavour to develop. This is also known as 'retarding'; the yeast activity slows down but continues slowly.

MAKING A FERMENT

Using a ferment will help to produce breads and yeast-based products with more flavour, improved crust colour and better texture. It will also allow the chef to reduce the yeast content and can increase the shelf life of the products.

Many top bakeries and kitchens maintain ferments from day to day for many months, ranging from basic recipes to natural starter-based recipes that contain little or no yeast at all. There are various methods of producing a ferment.

■ *Method 1* – retain a 200g piece of dough from the first batch of bread you make. This can be kept in the refrigerator or a cool room. Add this to the next batch of dough to enhance it. Retain another 200g from the new batch of dough to use the following day.

■ *Method 2* – an extension of the above method is to retain 200g of dough and leave it for 2 days at a temperature of 12–18°C in an airtight plastic container. Add the same amount of water (200g) and double its weight in flour (400g). Mix well until a dough is formed. This process is known as 'refreshing'. The dough will need to be refreshed every 5 days, or when some of the ferment is used to create a bread dough.

■ *Method 3* – the third method is to produce a natural starter using a good-quality stoneground organic flour with a high gluten content. A typical recipe for this method is:

– raisins, apples or sultanas	250g
– sugar	25g
– water (at 20°C)	250g
– fresh yeast	4g

Place the fruit in a clean plastic container. Cover the fruit with the water (a natural mineral water if possible) and add the sugar and the yeast. Leave for approximately 4–5 days, until the fruit can be seen to be fermenting. Press the fruit mixture through a sieve and measure the following ingredients:

– fermented fruit juice	250g
– strong organic stoneground flour	350g

Knead for 5 minutes at a low speed to create a firm dough and leave to rest in a warm place for a minimum of 4 hours. Refresh with ferment with the following ingredients:

– water	250g
– strong organic stoneground flour	375g

Knead for 5 minutes at a low speed. Leave to rest in a cool place or in a refrigerator and use after 24 hours. A starter dough can now be produced from this ferment by using the base recipe below. Alternatively, keep refreshing the ferment every day; for every 200g used, refresh with 100g flour and 100g water.

CHEF'S TIP

Two varieties of bacteria are present in sour dough: *Acetobacter* and *Lactobacillus*. These give off acetic and lactic acids during fermentation, which help to impart the strong flavour required.

MAKING A STARTER (POOLISH)

To make a starter you will require the following ingredients:

–	water	300g
–	ferment	100g
–	strong organic stoneground flour	540g

Carefully place the ferment into the water and slowly add the flour. Combine the ingredients together to create a soft textured dough. Sprinkle some flour into the bottom of a bowl and place the starter into it. Set in a prover and leave for up to 5 hours (or until it has doubled in size). The fermentation time can vary. This starter can now be used for the country bread recipe on page 343.

ENRICHING INGREDIENTS

Bread and fermented goods are sometimes enriched with a variety of additional ingredients. These are included to help increase the food value, add to the flavour, produce a softer crumb and retard staling. Fermentation is slower in enriched dough.

■ *Sugar* – this is an ingredient that requires careful usage in the presence of yeast. It should be used sparingly and should never come into direct contact with yeast because the yeast will be chemically broken down and become inactive. Sugar will help to increase the water retention of the dough, which will in turn enhance the softness of the crumb. However, sugar is used in fermented products to produce a sweet flavour, to give colour to the crust or to create a decorative effect on certain finished products (such as fondant and nibbed sugar).

■ *Milk* – as with water, milk will contribute to the moisture content of the product. Its fat content will also help to ensure that the dough will have a softer crumb. It also plays a role in helping to colour the crust and crumb during baking. Because of its natural sugar content, milk will have an important influence on the flavour of the fermented product. Generally, milk powder is usually used in the production of bread.

Butter, eggs, spices, honey and milk

- *Egg* – an average fresh egg will weigh approximately 50g, of which nearly 60 per cent is egg white. The white has a high water concentration and contains minute traces of fat. The protein found within the white, **albumin**, has the ability to create a foam. Egg yolk has a high fat content and contains little water. It also contains the protein lecithin, which has the ability to emulsify fat-based and water-based ingredients. Egg yolk can be used in fermented goods to provide colour, additional liquid and fat content. It can also help to increase the shelf life of the product.

- *Butter* – the high fat content of butter means it is used primarily to create a softer texture to the baked dough. It will also add some colour and flavour to the overall finish. Butter contains approximately 16 per cent water, and in the case of fermented goods such as brioche it will considerably change the texture, colour and flavour of the finished product. Salt may have to be reduced when using salted butter or margarine (which contains approximately 2 per cent salt).

- *Spices, herbs, fruits, vegetables and flavourings* – these are all added to enhance the flavour and texture of the finished product. Because of their varying fat or sugar contents they will have an effect on the fermentation process and may slow it down considerably. During fermentation the chef or baker should always observe the physical reactions taking place in the dough to gauge the consequence of the added enriching agents.

BRIOCHE

Brioche is a very rich bread. There are four basic classes of brioche, describing the levels of richness:

- Surfine
- Fine
- Ordinaire
- Commune.

The classes roughly correspond to the amounts of butter and egg used in the brioche and therefore how rich it is in taste, colour and texture. Commune contains the least amounts of egg and butter and so is the least rich.

Brioche is at its best within the first couple of hours of baking, once it has cooled, and should be eaten within a day. Brioche can be frozen, but it will lose its texture and will generally not be as pleasant.

There are two basic processes of making pâte à brioche. The first is a straight dough method (see recipe on p. 329), where all the ingredients are mixed together. The second uses a **levain** (a yeast sponge), which is added to the dough (see recipe on p. 338).

Types of brioche

Brioche comes in many shapes and sizes:

◼ *Mousseline* – a round brioche. Can be baked in a cylindrical tin, buttered and lined with greaseproof paper. The dough is moulded into a ball, placed into the tin and proved until above the sides.

◼ *À tête* – the brioche with the well-known head on top. Small brioches can weigh from 50g, large ones up to 1kg. Always baked in fluted moulds.

◼ *Nanterre* or *Nantaise* – made in a straight-sided loaf tin, either in one piece or by laying balls of dough next to each other.

◼ *Couronne* or *Pompe* (in Marseilles) – a large ring, snipped at intervals with scissors to produce a decorative effect. The ring is made by moulding a ball, making a hole in the centre and forming into a ring by gradually increasing the size of the hole.

◼ *La tresse*– a plaited loaf that resembles the Jewish cholla breads.

CHEF'S TIP

Brioche can be stored in a refrigerator, but it must be wrapped in plastic film and stored away from strong smelling foods such as cheese.

Goods made from brioche

Croûtes:

◼ *Aux fruits* – slices of brioche sprinkled with icing sugar, glazed, covered with a fruit compote mask with a kirsch-flavoured apricot sauce.

◼ *Lyonnaise* – slices of brioche spread with a chestnut purée, coated with apricot glaze and sprinkled with roasted flaked almonds. Served dressed as a crown with the centre filled with marrons glacés.

◼ *Madère* – slices of brioche formed into a crown with the centre filled with a macédoine of fruits, sultanas, currants and raisins and coated with Madeira-flavoured apricot sauce.

◼ *Bostock* – stale Nantaise is cut into slices, imbibed with stock syrup, spread with crème d'amande, dusted with icing sugar and glazed in a hot oven.

◼ *Goubaud* – produced by lining a flan ring with brioche paste. Another piece of paste is rolled into a rectangle, sprinkled all over with pieces of **glacé** fruit macerated in kirsch, rolled up and cut into 2cm slices. The slices are placed into the prepared ring, egg glazed, proved and baked. After cooling on a wire cooling rack it is finished with apricot glaze and a kirsch water icing.

Kitchen uses:

◼ Coulibiac

◼ Foie gras en croûte

◼ Loaves for sandwiches, rolls and fingers

◼ Crumbs (Chapelure) for coating suprême of chicken and similar dishes.

RECIPES
Blinis

CHEF'S TIP

Blinis can be used for canapés and hors d'oeuvre and are traditionally served with ice-cold caviar and soured cream. They are sometimes used as an accompaniment to smoked and cured fish.

Blinis pan

INGREDIENTS	15 INDIVIDUAL	30 INDIVIDUAL
Strong flour	110g	220g
Buckwheat flour	110g	220g
Fresh yeast	10g	20g
Warm milk (30°C)	280g	560g
Separated eggs	2	4
Good-quality salt	To taste	To taste
Finish		
Clarified butter	200g	400g

Method of work

1 Sieve the flours together. Mix the fresh yeast in with the warm milk.

2 Add the flour to the milk to create a light dough.

3 Cover the bowl with plastic film and leave to ferment for up to 1 hour.

4 Add the egg yolks and beat in well. Rest the mixture for a further 30 minutes.

5 Aerate the egg whites to soft peaks with a little salt added. Carefully fold into the fermented batter with a spatula.

6 Place small non-stick blinis pans onto a stove to heat and pour a small amount of the clarified butter into each one.

7 Ladle some of the blinis mixture into each pan and fry on both sides until just cooked; the **blinis** should be springy to the touch. Serve as soon as possible.

Brioche, using the straight method

Brioche à tête

INGREDIENTS	25 BRIOCHE À TÊTE OR 2 LOAVES	45 BRIOCHE À TÊTE OR 4 LOAVES
Strong flour	500g	1kg
Fresh yeast	25g	50g
Fresh milk	75ml	150ml
Good-quality salt	15g	30g
Caster sugar	50g	100g
Type of brioche		
Commune		
Eggs	4	8
Butter	125g	250g
Ordinaire		
Eggs	6	12
Butter	200g	400g
Fine		
Eggs	6	12
Butter	350g	700g
Surfine		
Eggs	8	16
Butter	500g	1kg

Method of work

1. Preheat an oven to 220°C.
2. Warm the milk to 30°C. Dissolve the yeast and sugar in the milk.
3. Sieve the flour and salt together. Add to the milk/yeast mixture with the eggs to form a smooth and elastic dough. It is easiest to use an electric mixer.
4. Carefully **cut in** the soft butter and mix in well. Place in a refrigerator to rest for at least 1 hour.
5. For brioche à tête, scale off 50g each and mould into 'boules'.
6. Create the 'heads' (têtes) by rolling the side of the hand one-third of the way up each boule to separate off a piece of dough for the head.
7. Place each boule into a prepared individual fluted tin and press the head firmly in the centre of the body. Glaze with an egg wash.
8. Bake in the preheated oven. The baking time will vary according to the size of the brioche so take care and inspect the brioches every five minutes during baking.

Creating the head for a brioche à tête

Placing boules into individual fluted moulds

Ensuring the heads are positioned correctly

Brioche, using the levain method

INGREDIENTS	1 LOAF OR 18 ROLLS	2 LOAVES OR 40 ROLLS
Levain ingredients		
Fresh milk	130ml	260ml
Slower acting fresh yeast (French hirondelle; if using British yeast then use only 20g and 40g)	25g	50g
Strong flour	250g	500g
Dough ingredients		
Strong flour	750g	1.5kg
Good-quality salt	20g	40g
Caster sugar	25g	50g
Size 4 fresh eggs	10	20
Unsalted butter (keep at a temperature which leaves it plastic and manageable; not cold and hard or too warm and soft)	700g	1.4kg
Egg wash glaze		
Whole egg	125g	200g
Caster sugar	25g	50g
Good-quality salt	Pinch	Pinch

Method of work

1 Preheat an oven to 220°C.

2 To make the levain, warm the milk to approximately 30°C. Dissolve the yeast in the milk. Combine the flour with the yeast/milk to obtain a stretchy and elastic dough. This will take 10 minutes by hand, less in a machine at medium speed.

3 Shape into a ball and stand in a bowl of tepid water (20–25°C). Leave to ferment and develop. When it is ready it will look like a large swollen sponge floating on the surface of the water.

4 When the levain is nearly ready make the dough. Combine the flour, salt and sugar. Make a well in the centre of the flour and pour in 10 lightly beaten eggs.

5 Work the eggs into the flour. Knead by hand for about 15 minutes.

6 Temper the butter by flattening it with your hand or a rolling pin. Take about a quarter of the dough and work it into the butter. Combine the butter with the rest of the dough and mix until smooth, either by hand or using a machine.

7 Incorporating the levain is a very delicate process. It is easiest to use an electric mixer and a dough hook. However, if you are working by hand lay the soft levain onto the slightly flattened dough and knead the two ingredients together.

8 Prove the dough until it is well risen.

9 Knock it back on the work surface. Fold it back into three, as though you were preparing puff pastry. Flatten it and again fold into three. Wrap the dough in plastic and chill for 2 hours.

10 To finish the brioche, lightly **grease** a bread tin. Unwrap the brioche dough and place in the tin. If making buns, scale into the required 50g weight and mould.

11 Prove the brioche at below 40°C. It should double in size. To test whether it is ready, lightly press the surface with a finger; the depression should spring back.

12 Brush the top of the brioche with the egg glaze, made by mixing the egg, sugar and salt together.

13 Bake in a preheated oven. The baking time will vary according to the size of the brioche, from a few minutes to 45 minutes. Remove when golden brown and cooked through.

Stöllen

INGREDIENTS	3 LOAVES	6 LOAVES
Ferment ingredients		
Warm water	150ml	300ml
Milk powder	15g	30g
Whole egg	100g	200g
Caster sugar	30g	60g
Fresh yeast	60g	120g
Strong flour	80g	160g
Dough ingredients		
Strong flour	600g	1.3kg
Good-quality salt	5g	10g
Caster sugar	80g	160g
Mixed spice	3g	5g
Unsalted butter	125g	250g
Fruit		
Currants	60g	120g
Sultanas or raisins	60g	120g
Mixed peel	100g	200g
Glacé cherries	50g	100g
Juice and finely grated lemon zest	½ lemon	1 lemon
Dark rum	25ml	50ml
Flaked almonds	50g	100g
Rope of marzipan	3 × 75g	6 × 75g

Method of work

1   Preheat an oven to 200°C.

2   Wash the currants and sultanas/raisins and drain. Place them into a stainless steel bowl with the mixed peel, cherries, flaked almonds and juice and zest of lemon and then add the dark rum. Leave to **macerate** for at least 1 hour.

3   To make the ferment, blend the yeast with the milk powder, egg, sugar, water and flour. Set the ferment at 26°C for 30 minutes. When it is ready it will begin to drop back.

4   Mix the dough ingredients together and incorporate the butter by **rubbing in**.

5   Blend the ferment with the flour mixture to form a soft dough. Blend in the fruit ingredients carefully; avoid breaking or bruising the fruit.

6   Bulk ferment for 1 hour.

7   Carefully knock back to release only some of the fermentation gasses. Scale off each loaf at 450g.

8   For each loaf, knead the dough into a rectangle slightly longer than the marzipan rope. Fold in the sides to prevent the marzipan from leaking.

9   Place the marzipan in the centre and then roll up. Set the stöllen onto a baking sheet lined with a silicone mat and prove for a further 45 minutes.

10 Bake in the preheated oven for approximately 40 minutes. Remove from the oven and while still hot brush well with melted butter. Leave to cool for five minutes and brush once more with melted butter then completely coat with sieved icing sugar.

11 Leave to cool on a wire cooling rack.

12 When cold wrap well in plastic film and store in a cool, dry area. To serve, simply slice and warm under a salamander with a little unsalted butter to spread.

Kneading the dough into a rectangle slightly longer than the marzipan rope

Folding in the sides to prevent the marzipan from leaking

Placing the marzipan before rolling up the stöllen

Ciabatta

INGREDIENTS	2 LOAVES	4 LOAVES
Ferment ingredients		
Strong flour	175g	350g
Fresh yeast	3g	5g
Water (at 20°C)	90g	180g
Dough ingredients		
Strong Italian flour	225g	450g
Good-quality salt	8g	15g
Fresh yeast	5g	10g
Water (at 28°C)	170g	340g
Olive oil	25g	50g
Finish		
Flour for dusting	50g	100g

Method of work

1 Mix the ingredients for the ferment together to form a soft dough. Place in a clean bowl and cover with plastic film then leave in a closed cupboard for 12–24 hours to slowly ferment.

2 Preheat an oven to 220°C.

3 For the dough, mix the yeast with the water and pour into the flour and mix in. Add the ferment and the remaining ingredients. Knead the dough well for at least five minutes.

4 Transfer to a lightly oiled surface and mould into a ball. Place the dough into a bowl, cover with a clean kitchen cloth and leave to rest for 1½ hours until risen.

5 Gently knock back the dough and divide it into equal quantities, according to how many ciabattas you wish to make.

6 Form each piece of dough into a rectangle and fold it in three (as if for laminating). Fold in half lengthways and seal the edges so that you have produced a long rectangle shape.

7 Leave to prove on well-floured tea towels for approximately 45 minutes.

8 Flour a baking tray. Pick up each ciabatta, turn it over, stretch it lengthways slightly and place onto the baking tray.

9 Spray the inside of the oven with a little water and quickly slide the ciabattas into the oven. Bake for approximately 20 minutes.

10 Remove from the oven and leave to cool on a wire cooling rack before serving.

Focaccia

INGREDIENTS	1 FLAT LOAF	2 FLAT LOAVES
Ferment ingredients		
Strong flour	150g	300g
Fresh yeast	7g	15g
Water (at 20°C)	200g	400g
Dough ingredients		
Strong Italian flour	375g	725g
Good-quality salt	10g	20g
Water (at 20°C)	150g	300g
Olive oil	20g	40g
Finish		
Fine sea-salt crystals	20g	45g
Fresh rosemary leaves	20 leaves	50 leaves
Olive oil	40ml	90ml

Method of work

1 Mix the ingredients for the ferment together to form a soft dough. Place in a clean bowl and cover with plastic film and leave in a closed cupboard at room temperature for 2 hours to slowly ferment.

2 Preheat an oven to 220°C.

3 To make the dough, mix the water and oil together and add the ferment. Combine the flour and salt and knead until soft.

4 Place in a clean bowl and leave to rest for 15 minutes.

5 Turn the dough out onto an oiled surface and fold and gently knead the dough for a few minutes. Leave to rest for 10 minutes and then repeat the process.

6 Lightly flatten the dough onto a baking tray rubbed with olive oil. Stretch the dough out until it reaches the corners of the tray, but ensure that it is at least 2cm thick.

7 Cover with a clean kitchen cloth and leave to prove for 25 minutes.

8 Sprinkle a little water, olive oil, sea salt and rosemary leaves on top. Press down onto the dough with your finger tips to create a dimpled effect.

9 Bake in the oven for 15 minutes then reduce the temperature to 180°C for a further 15 minutes. Remove from the oven and leave to cool on a wire cooling rack.

 CHEF'S TIP

When working with a soft dough such as focaccia, it is important to keep the work surface and your hands clean and oiled with a little olive oil.

Croissants

INGREDIENTS	15 INDIVIDUAL	30 INDIVIDUAL
Strong flour	500g	1kg
Good-quality salt	10g	20g
Fresh yeast	25g	40g
Caster sugar	30g	60g
Fresh milk (at 20°C)	300ml	600ml
Butter	250g	500g
Finish		
Egg wash	100g	150g

Method of work

1 Sieve the flour, salt and sugar together. Mix the fresh yeast in with the milk.

2 Add the flour to the milk to create a soft dough.

3 Place in the prover to ferment at 28°C for 25 minutes.

4 Gently knock back the dough for 10 minutes. Roll out the dough into a rectangle to a thickness of 8mm.

5 Soften the butter and spread it over two-thirds of the surface of the dough. Fold the dough in three, turn a quarter of the way around and roll out again to 5mm thick.

6 Fold the dough into three again and wrap in plastic film and refrigerate for 1 hour. Repeat the rolling and folding process one more time and rest in the refrigerator for a further hour.

7 Roll out the dough to 5mm thick and cut into rectangular strips. Cut out triangles from the strips and roll up into a croissant shape.

8 Alternatively, cut into smaller rectangles, place a stick of chocolate in the centre of each and roll up.

9 Preheat an oven to 220°C.

10 Place all the croissants onto a baking tray set with silicone paper or a silicone baking mat. Lightly egg wash each croissant and prove at no warmer than 27°C for up to 2 hours or until they have doubled in size.

11 Place into the oven and bake for approximately 15 minutes. Cool on a wire cooling rack before serving slightly warm.

VIDEO CLIP Croissants

Knocking back the dough

Rolling out the dough into an 8mm-thick rectangle

Folding the dough over the softened butter

Rolling out the dough to 5mm thick after turning a quarter of a turn

Rolling up the triangles of dough into croissant shapes

Alternatively, roll up smaller rectangles with a stick of chocolate in the centre

Croissants placed onto a baking tray set with silicone paper

Country bread

INGREDIENTS	3 LOAVES	6 LOAVES
Water	500g	1kg
Good-quality salt	20g	40g
Wheatgerm	10g	20g
Starter	350g	700g
Strong flour	700g	1.4kg
Rye flour	80g	160g
Finish		
Flour for dusting	As required	As required

Method of work

1 Preheat an oven to 230°C.
2 Place the starter in the water with the salt, wheatgerm, flour and the rye flour. Knead in a mixing machine at a low speed for 10 minutes.
3 Place into the prover to prove for 1 hour.
4 Scale off the dough at 500g per loaf. Rest the dough for 10 minutes under a sheet of plastic or a clean kitchen cloth.
5 Shape the dough into fat batons and place onto dusted linen cloths. Prove again for a minimum of 4 hours at 20°C, with a high humidity if possible.
6 Dust with flour and cut a decorative marking on the top of each bread. Bake for 45 minutes.

Savarin

INGREDIENTS	12 INDIVIDUAL SAVARIN RINGS	24 INDIVIDUAL SAVARIN RINGS
Savarin		
Strong flour	200g	400g
Good-quality salt	5g	10g
Caster sugar	15g	30g
Fresh yeast	10g	20g
Eggs	2	4
Water (at 35°C)	100ml	200ml
Soft butter	50g	100g
Additional ingredients		
Crème chantilly	400ml	800ml
Mixed fruits	500g	1kg
Sugar decoration	12	24
Preserved vanilla stick	12	24

Baba and savarin doughs are prepared using the same method as for brioche. Always use a good-quality, high-gluten flour and simply cream or soften the butter. Baba and savarin doughs are softer than a brioche dough because the weight of the liquid ingredients is equal to that of the flour.

Method of work

1 Preheat an oven to 200°C.
2 Dissolve the yeast and sugar in the water.
3 Sift the flour and salt together. Add to the water/yeast with the eggs to form a smooth and elastic dough. It is easier to do this task using an electric mixing machine.
4 Carefully cut in the softened butter and mix in well. Place in a refrigerator to rest for at least 1 hour.
5 Take care when preparing the moulds. Wipe the moulds with a lightly oiled kitchen towel. Do not butter heavily unless you have previously experienced problems with baked savarins sticking to the moulds. Too much butter on the moulds can pit the surface of the savarin, giving an unattractive appearance and rendering them less able to absorb syrup.
6 Pipe the mixture into the prepared non-stick individual savarin moulds. Place in the prover until doubled in size.
7 Place into the oven to bake for approximately 20 minutes. Remove from the oven and leave to cool on a wire cooling rack.
8 To present, bring to the boil a large pan of stock syrup flavoured with dark rum, lemon zest, orange zest and cinnamon sticks. Set on a very low heat and add the savarins to soak up the syrup. The hotter the syrup, the quicker the savarins will absorb it.
9 Remove the savarins from the syrup and leave to drain and cool.
10 Decorate as required with fresh fruit and crème chantilly.

CHEF'S TIP

For babas, prepare the raisins, checking them for stones, then rinse and drain them. The raisins are added to the dough at the last minute, just before moulding. Normally, raisins make up about 20–25% of the overall weight of the dough.

CHEF'S TIP

The rising times for babas and savarins are minimal. The temperature does not need to be so precisely controlled as with bread. Even though baba and savarin doughs are much softer than brioche dough, it is still important that the gluten is activated and that the dough has enough elasticity.

Warm water is used in this recipe for two main reasons;

1 It will penetrate the flour and reach the gluten more quickly than cold water, giving the dough maximum body and elasticity. This method can be used because the dough requires practically no rising time; 10 minutes maximum. Letting the dough rise too long can negatively affect the gluten in the dough; the heat and acidity generated by rapid fermentation cause the gluten to break down.

2 Warm water helps activate yeast. This is important because the rising time for babas and savarins is so short.

Babas and savarins should be baked in a moderate oven, 180–200°C, for individual sized cakes and a slightly slower oven, 170–180°C, for larger cakes. The cakes should be placed in the oven without being glazed. If oven vents are available, they should be left open during baking to enhance the drying and colouring of the dough. To check that they have been baked, the cakes should slip out of the moulds quite easily. They should be pale brown on the bottom and very dry.

The pâte à savarin can be used to make a range of products:

■ *Pomponette* – piped into tartlette moulds

■ *Marignan* – piped into barquette moulds

■ *Baba* – piped into baba moulds or dariole moulds

■ *Savarin* – piped into savarin moulds

Danish pastries

INGREDIENTS	15 INDIVIDUAL	30 INDIVIDUAL
Strong flour	450g	900g
Good-quality salt	5g	10g
Butter	25g	50g
Fresh yeast	15g	30g
Caster sugar	30g	60g
Fresh milk (at 20°C)	250ml	500ml
Whole egg	1	2
Butter	200g	400g
Finish		
As required		

Method of work

1 Preheat an oven to 220°C.

2 Sieve the flour into a warm stainless steel basin and rub the smaller quantity of butter into the flour.

3 Make a well in the centre of the mixture.

4 Mix half the milk with the yeast and the remainder of the milk with the salt, sugar and eggs.

5 Pour the solutions into the well and mix thoroughly. Knead the dough until it is an elastic consistency and free of any lumps.

6 Cover with plastic film and leave to rest for at least 20 minutes at room temperature. Carefully knock back the dough.

7 Roll out the dough to an 8-mm thick rectangle, as for the croissant recipe.

8 Soften the butter and spread over two-thirds of the surface of the dough. Fold the dough into three, turn a quarter of the way around and roll out again to 5mm thick.

9 Fold the dough into three again, wrap in plastic film and refrigerate for 1 hour. Repeat the rolling and folding process one more time and rest the dough in the refrigerator for a further hour.

10 Roll out and cut and shape as required and add any fillings. Place onto silicone baking mats and prove at 27°C for up to 2 hours or until they have doubled in size.

11 Bake in the oven for approximately 15 minutes. Cool on a wire cooling rack before serving slightly warm.

VIDEO CLIP
Technique for
Danish pastries

CHEF'S TIP

It is preferable to make the paste a day before you need to use it.

Variations for finishing Danish pastries

Moulins à vent

Cut the rolled dough into equal squares (approximately 9cm × 9cm). Glaze the sides with egg wash. Pipe a small rosette of almond cream in the centre using a piping bag with a plain tube. Fold the four corners into the centre. Place a small disc of paste on top in the centre. Prove and bake. Glaze the pastries with a hot apricot glaze as soon as they are removed from the oven.

Tortillons

Roll out the dough sheet to 3mm thick. Cut out 6cm × 12cm rectangles and glaze with egg wash and sprinkle with granulated sugar. Then cut a slit in the centre and intertwine: pull one end through the cut slit and pull through to the other side. These can then be filled with almond cream if desired, and are baked and finished as above.

Apricot Danish pastry

Roll out the dough to 2mm thick. Cut out discs 10cm in diameter and place into the bottom of 8cm-diameter moulds. Fill with crème pâtissière and place an apricot half on top. Roll out a top sheet for the pastries, preferably using a marking device such as a perspex template to create a design. Garnish and leave to prove for 45 minutes at 28°C. Bake at 180°C for 15 minutes. Glaze with a hot apricot glaze and cool.

Pistachio and chocolate roulade

Roll out the dough to 2mm thick. Mix the crème pâtissière with the pistachio paste and spread onto the dough. Add a few chocolate drops and roll up to form a roulade. Cut into slices about 2cm thick (approximately 60g). Place the end of the roll underneath to prevent it from unfurling. Leave to prove for about 45 minutes and bake at 180°C for 15 minutes. Glaze with apricot glaze and sprinkle with chopped pistachio nuts.

Assessment of knowledge and understanding

You have now learned about the use of the different types of complex pastes and how to produce a variety of tarts, pies and confections utilising an array of commodities.

To test your level of knowledge and understanding, answer the following short questions. These will help to prepare you for your summative (final) assessment.

Quality identifications

1 Name four types of fat used in the production of pastes and state two uses of two of the fats mentioned.

i) _____ ii) _____

iii) _____ iv) _____

2 Explain the quality points to look for when producing puff paste.

_____

3 State the quality points to look for when producing a separated egg sponge.

_____

4 State two advantages to using a prover, and what you would need to use if there is not one available.

i) _____ ii) _____

Equipment and materials

1 Explain why you would use a refrigerator to help rest paste before rolling out.

_____

2 Explain why when producing strüdel paste is it necessary to use a linen cloth during the stretching of the paste and finishing of the strüdel.

_____

3 State which two fats are ideal for aeration and creaming.

i) _____ ii) _____

4 State two advantages of using a prover, and what you would need to use if there is not one available.

i) _____ ii) _____

Preparation methods

1 Describe the effect that gluten has on puff pastry.

_____

2 Describe how you would laminate croissant dough.

_____

3 State three roles that fat plays in baking cakes.

i) _____ ii) _____

iii) _____

4 If the temperature required for dough is 38°C, and the temperature of the flour is 17°C, what temperature does the water need to be.

Cooking methods

1 Describe how you would test a choux bun to see if it is correctly baked.

2 Explain the process of lamination and why it is crucial to the success of puff paste.

3 Explain the difference between a savarin and a brioche.

4 Identify the critical quality points for the following baked products:

- Brioche

- Focaccia

- Danish pastry

Healthy options

1 Suggest what changes the chef can make to the recipe for a pear Bourdaloue tart to create a healthier option.

CHEF'S PROFILE

Name: WILLIAM CURLEY

Position: Pâtissier Chocolatier

Establishment: William Curley (Richmond upon Thames, soon to be Mayfair and Belgravia)

Current job role and main responsibilities: Owner of William Curley. We produce fresh (on the day) pâtisserie, handmade chocolates, ice cream and baked goods. We encourage and train young chefs to be future pâtissiers and chocolatiers.

When did you realise that you wanted to pursue a career in the catering and hospitality industry?
I didn't grow-up dreaming of being a chef, although I did enjoy the odd cake. I left school with no qualifications and decided to enrol at a local college. It was on the spur of the moment that I went for a cooking class.

Training: I spent two years at Glenrothes College in Fife doing the 706/1 and 706/2 City and Guilds. I also went on to pass the 706/3 advanced pastry City and Guilds course. Although it was a job, I always regard working at Gleneagles under Ian Ironside (I arrived when I was 17 and stayed for three years) as very much part of my ground training.

Experience: I worked for Pierre Koffmann at La Tante Claire (three Michelin stars), Raymond Blanc at Le Manoir aux Quat' Saisons (two Michelin stars) and Marco Pierre White at The Restaurant/Oak Room (three Michelin stars). I spent six years working for what I felt were the best restaurants in the country at the time. These experiences very much shaped me as a chef – they gave me focus, developed my skills and gave me a non-compromising attitude. From there, at the age of 27, I become Chef Pâtissier at The Savoy under Anton Edelmann; he gave me a huge opportunity. At times I must have driven him mad, but his support in a job where I was responsible for 21 chefs and for running the River Restaurant, private rooms, bakery, banquetting and afternoon teas was enormous. I also trained in Belgium at Maison du Bouche, Pierre Romeyer (three Michelin stars) for a season and I worked for Marc Meneau at L'Esperance (three Michelin stars) after winning the William Heptinstill Scholarship.

What do you find rewarding about your job?
Seeing how our shop has grown is very satisfying and knowing that the public will travel for miles to buy our pâtisserie and chocolates. Having my own shop is what I dreamt of for many years – to fulfil this dream is very rewarding.

What do you find the most challenging about the job?
To keep the standard that you believe in and not compromising on ingredients. Make an extra effort to create beautiful (not only look but taste) pâtisserie and chocolates!

What advice would you give to students just beginning their career?
Work in as many high-quality places as you can to get a solid foundation for your work. Our industry can be a bit of a marathon; a good base where you understand the basics will stand you well in the long run.

Who is your mentor or main inspiration?
The six chefs I worked and trained under – Raymond Blanc, Anton Edelmann, Ian Ironside, Pierre Koffmann, Marco Pierre White and Pierre Romeyer. When I was at Glasgow College of Food and Technology, my lecturer Willie Pike was a great inspiration – he is also very funny.

What traits do you consider essential for anyone entering a career as a chef?
To be a great, I believe you must truly enjoy cooking. Being determined and focused also helps.

Can you give one essential kitchen tip or technique that you use as a chef?
Never take shortcuts!

Seasonal fresh fruit tartlets

INGREDIENTS

Sweet pastry

Soft flour	480g
Unsalted butter	280g
Caster sugar	140g
Whole eggs	100g

Frangipane

Unsalted butter	250g
Icing sugar	250g
Whole eggs	250g
Ground almonds	250g
Plain flour	50g

Pastry cream

Milk	500g
Vanilla	1 pod
Egg yolks	120g
Caster sugar	100g
Flour	50g

Grand Mariner syrup

Water	450g
Sugar	375g
Grand Marnier	200g

Other ingredients

Neutral nappage	As required
Chocolate decorations	As required
Seasonal fruits: strawberry, raspberry, blackberry, blueberry, mango, kiwi fruits, grapes, plums, nectarines (cut into chunks and slices)	As required

Method of work

1. To make the pastry, chop the unsalted butter into cubes and sieve the soft flour.
2. Crumb together the soft flour and butter, until no lumps are left.
3. Add the caster sugar and salt and mix in.
4. Gradually add the eggs, mix until the mixture is smooth and a homogeneous mass.
5. Place the paste onto a floured tray, wrap with cling film and rest in the refrigerator for at least 1 hour before use.
6. Roll out the sweet pastry to 3–4mm thick. Line tartlet moulds and allow to rest for 30 minutes in the fridge.
7. To make the frangipane, sieve the flour and soften the unsalted butter.
8. Place the softened butter and icing sugar in a mixing bowl and cream together.
9. Beat the eggs and gradually add slowly.
10. Add the ground almonds. Once incorporated add the flour.
11. Pipe the frangipane into the tartlet cases to half full.
12. To bake the tartlets, preheat an oven to 180°C.
13. Bake for 15–20 minutes, then allow to cool on a wire cooling rack.
14. To make the pastry cream, boil together the milk and vanilla pods.
15. Simultaneously whisk together the egg yolks and caster sugar, whisk until the mixture thickens slightly and turns light in colour.
16. Sieve the flour and add into the mixture, whisk until smooth.
17. Add half of the milk to the base, whisk until there are no lumps.
18. Pass through a fine strainer, return the mixture to the pan (ensuring the vanilla pod is retuned to the pan).
19. Using a whisk, stir the mixture continuously. When it comes to the boil, reduce the temperature to a simmer. Continue to stir and cook out for 8–10 minutes.
20. Remove the pastry cream onto a shallow tray, wrap with cling film and cool rapidly.
21. To make the Grand Mariner syrup, boil together the water and sugar.
22. Allow to cool completely then add the Grand Marnier. Keep in an airtight container.
23. To Assemble, punch the tartlets with the Grand Marnier syrup.
24. Pipe a ring of pastry cream onto each tartlet.
25. Place fruits on the tartlet as required (you can support the fruits by surrounding with plastic).
26. Glaze the tart with nappage and decorate as required.

CHEF'S PROFILE

Name: THIERRY DUMOUCHEL

Position: Director

Establishment: Boulangerie-Pâtisserie-Chocolatierie

Current job role and main responsibilities:
Boulanger, pâtissier, chocolatier.

When did you realise that you wanted to pursue a career in the catering and hospitality industry?
From a very young age. I was brought up on a farm around fresh produce and learned to love food.

Training:
Roven College de Boulangerie Pâtisserie

Experience:
1   Pelletier
2   Fauchon
3   Dallayau
4   Cordon Bleu
5   Alan Ducasse
6   Relais Chateau

After meeting and marrying my Leeds-born wife, I set up my own production unit in Garforth, Leeds, producing high-class breads, pastries, cakes and chocolate. I also have two successful shops in Garforth and Harrogate and now have a mobile outlet visiting local offices during the week and food fairs at weekends.

What do you find rewarding about your job?
Creativity!

What do you find the most challenging about the job?
Finding staff with the relevant skills.

What advice would you give to students just beginning their career?
Take every opportunity to learn. Get as much experience as possible. Go to demonstrations, read magazines, visit as many establishments as possible for work experience.

Who is your mentor or main inspiration?
My father. He taught me how to work hard. He is a farmer.

What traits do you consider essential for anyone entering a career as a chef?
To be fit, motivated and determined. To be able to observe and learn.

Can you give one essential kitchen tip that you use as a chef?
Reduce wastage as much as possible to keep costs down.

11

Advanced skills and techniques in producing desserts and petits fours (Unit 309)

LEARNING OUTCOMES

The aim of this chapter is to enable the candidate to develop the necessary advanced skills in and knowledge and understanding of the principles in producing hot, cold and frozen desserts and petits fours. This covers the development of more refined and advanced techniques and includes information on materials, ingredients and equipment.

There are **two** principal outcomes to this chapter. At the end of this chapter the candidate will be able to :

- Produce hot, cold and frozen desserts
- Produce petits fours

INTRODUCTION

The first desserts have consistently been attributed to the ancient Egyptians, who began harvesting honey from bees at around 5500 BC. A variety of fruits, nuts and cereals were also important ingredients, from which confections were created to show off great wealth during banquets and for use as gifts during religious festivals. Many of these ingredients (especially honey) were also used medicinally.

The European discovery of sugar in Asia in the twelfth century played a significant role in the development of more complex desserts. In the fifteenth century, the recently opened trade routes with Africa, Asia, East Asia and the Americas allowed spices and chocolate to be used as flavourings for desserts as well as for medicinal purposes, previously the main use of such extravagant commodities.

Eventually, these new ingredients became widely available and Europe was recognised as the focus of the development of more sophisticated recipes. The most famous chef of the early nineteenth century was Marie-Antoine Carême (1784–1833). His spectacular architectural constructions of sugar, meringue, pastries and desserts earned him great fame as the 'king of chefs and chef to kings'. Most of his career was spent in the service of nobility and royalty, such as the Prince Regent, Tsar Alexander I and Napoleon I. Throughout his career he dedicated his skills to the art of the pâtissier and generally changed the way menus were created and food was served. By the time of Carême, desserts were large, elaborate set pieces, often fashioned in great detail.

In the twentieth century, advances in technology such as refrigeration, sophisticated ovens and air transportation contributed immensely to the production of both simply designed and more complex desserts, and their popularity continues to grow. With the advent of a more diet-conscious public, desserts have had to adapt by using less sugar and fat commodities, but they retain their sense of decadence, art and flavour.

The skill of the pastry chef is to be able to create a dessert that is appealing to the eye, stimulates the palette through flavour, aroma, temperature and texture, and maintains a lightness that will not leave the customer feeling overindulged.

THE USE OF SPICES IN DESSERTS AND PÂTISSERIE

Spices offer the chef a wide range of rich flavours for use throughout the menu. Influences from China, India, Thailand and other countries can be used to create different fusions of cuisines and exciting new dishes.

Spices are the dried fruits, flowers, buds, seeds, roots or bark of plants. Sometimes more than one part of a plant is used, and the same plants (such as coriander) may also give us a herb. All spices are best used as fresh as possible because the oils which give the aroma and flavour will deteriorate with age. Both ground spices and whole spices must be stored in airtight, lightproof plastic containers.

Spices are used in dessert and pastry production to create added flavour and colour to a finished product. Some of the commonly used spices are detailed below.

Anise

The distinctive aniseed flavour comes from the oils found within the seed. These oils are also found in unrelated plants, such as fennel and liquorice. This spice is used to flavour drinks, breads and pastries, but is also used as flavouring in crèmes and mousses.

Cardamom

Cardamom is best purchased as green pods, which contain the brown seeds packed full of flavour. Ground cardamom will rapidly lose its flavour. Cardamom is used in baking for pastries and in crèmes, sweet sauces and bavarois.

Cinnamon

Cinnamon is the dried bark of a tree found in Sri Lanka. It can be broken down into small pieces or ground to a powder. Cinnamon is used to flavour creams, syrups, apple tarts and sauces. It is one of the most commonly used spices in the pastry kitchen.

Cloves

Cloves are the dried buds from a tropical tree found in Tanzania. Cloves are usually purchased whole, and are used as flavouring for steamed puddings, apple pies and mincemeat.

Ginger

Ginger is one of the most widely used spices across the world. It is the root of a plant usually found in East Asia. It has a strong flavour and can be used fresh, dried, powdered or candied. When preserved in sugar or powdered it is used in breads, biscuits, cakes, drinks and creams. Ginger can also be used with a combination of other spices to create alternative flavourings, such as 'mixed spice' and 'Chinese five-spice'.

Nutmeg

This is the nut of an evergreen Indonesian tree. It is used grated or powdered to flavour cakes and various desserts and sauces. Ground nutmeg will lose its flavour if kept for too long. Mace is closely related to nutmeg; it is the dried 'cage' that separates the nutmeg from the outer fruit. It is more expensive than nutmeg and has a more delicate flavour.

Saffron

Saffron is the most expensive spice in the world. It is the orange-red stigmas of a purple flowering crocus. To produce 500g of saffron, up to a quarter of a million flowers are harvested, by hand. It is produced in Spain, India, Asia

Star anise

Ground cardamom

Cinnamon

Cloves

Ginger

Nutmeg

Saffron

Vanilla

 CHEF'S TIP

Keep all spices, whole or ground, in containers that are airtight and lightproof. Keep in a cool and dry cupboard. Only purchase small quantities at a time to help establish regular stock rotation and so ensure freshness and maximum flavour.

and North Africa. It has also been cultivated in England, near the town of Saffron Walden in Essex. It is used to flavour crèmes, sauces, cakes and breads.

Vanilla

There are approximately 75 different varieties of vanilla growing in the world's tropical regions. Initially discovered by the Aztecs and used to flavour cocoa-based drinks, vanilla is now produced predominantly in Madagascar, Indonesia, Réunion, Martinique, Tahiti and Guadalupe. Vanilla pods offer the best flavour and aroma for all desserts, crèmes, cakes and sauces. They should be split and infused in a liquid to impart as much flavour as possible. The pods can be reused two or three times. Dried pods can be stored in an airtight container with caster sugar so that the flavour of the vanilla permeates the sugar, creating vanilla sugar.

Genuine vanilla extract is an alternative to using pods. However, the labelling is not always clear and care must be taken to ensure that vanilla flavour is not substituted; this is a chemical-based vanilla flavouring that bears no resemblance to the aroma and flavour of real vanilla.

THE USE OF SALT

Salt (sodium chloride) is one of the most important ingredients in any recipe. It is a necessary part of the human diet and is present in many different types of natural food. All of the recipes mentioned in this book state that 'good-quality salt' is used. This is because the salt composition of human tissue is similar to that of seawater, and sea salt (such as large flake salt) provides one of the simplest ways of meeting our nutritional requirements. Good-quality sea salt retains the valuable natural trace elements which are often removed during the processing of some table salts. The distinctive flavour of a good-quality salt means that less is required for flavouring and cooking. This is an advantage for those wishing to reduce salt intake in their diet.

The production of sea salt relies on favourable dry weather conditions. Seawater for processing is taken after a period of dry weather, when the salt content is at its maximum. The water is transferred to large holding tanks where it is allowed to pass through a filtration system and settle. After further filtering it is drawn off as required and used to fill saltpans, where the water is evaporated off.

The large stainless steel saltpans are mounted on a brick heating system designed to give the specific heating pattern required to evaporate the water. During the evaporation of the water, salt crystals begin to form on the surface. These crystals are known as *fleur de sel* and can be removed and used as a special high-quality salt. However, as the crystals become heavier they sink to the bottom of the saltpan. The pans are allowed to cool slowly and the salt is then harvested. The salt is put into shallow drainage bins before finally being transferred to the salt store for drying and packaging.

Salt is available in many different forms, such as table salt, iodised salt, flake salt, kosher salt, unrefined sea salt, fleur de sel and flavoured salts, such as celery or garlic salt.

Salt can be used as a preservative because it discourages the growth of bacteria in food. It also allows a harmless flavour-producing bacteria to grow and thus improves the flavour of the food while preserving it at the same time.

The addition of salt will enhance flavour in many recipes, whether sweet or savoury. Salt is now combined with alternative flavouring commodities to provide contrast in flavour and texture, such as caramel and sea salt combined to create an interesting filling for chocolate.

Sea salt crystals

STABILISERS AND GELATINISATION

Various stabilisers, starches and emulsifiers are used throughout the kitchen to thicken or bind ingredients to create durable textures, different appearances and thickened liquids.

Starch

Starches are generally used to thicken sauces and creams and some fillings for gâteaux and tarts. Starch granules are made up of two types of molecule: *amylose*, which has a long, straight chemical chain of glucose sugars, and *amylopectin,* which has a branched chemical structure. These structures determine the different thickening properties. The amylose molecules require more liquid, higher temperature and longer cooking before the starch molecules are broken down; they then re-form on cooling.

Cornflour, arrowroot and rice

Gelatinisation is the process that starch molecules undergo to thicken a liquid. There are three stages of gelatinisation using starch:

THE THREE STAGES OF GELATINISATION

1   Heating the starch – the starch is heated with the liquid to be thickened

2   Absorbing the liquid – as the temperature rises, the bonds within the molecules of starch begin to break down, which allows them to take on board and trap liquid, causing the molecules to expand

3   Thickening the liquid – once the starch molecules have absorbed the liquid they become soft and have a gel-like texture, and as more heat is applied the liquid becomes thicker

Factors that affect gelatinisation

There are several factors that can affect the gelatinisation of liquids:

- *The amount of liquid used* – here must be an adequate balance of liquid to starch molecules to activate thickening.

- *Temperature* – different starches require different temperatures to thicken. Some starches, such as tapioca and potato starches, can be overheated, which can reverse the effects of gelatinisation and result in a thinner product.

- *Stirring* – overstirring can cause thinning of a mixture. The starch molecules are broken down and release any liquid that was absorbed.

- *Acids* – acids can break down starches, preventing them from swelling and thickening. If possible, acids should be added after gelatinisation has taken place. Alternatively, modified starches which are resistant to acid conditions can be used.

- *Egg yolks* – raw egg yolk contains an enzyme called alpha-amylase, which causes starches to break down. Pastry creams containing egg yolks should be brought to boiling point to destroy the alpha-amylase and so prevent it from breaking down the starch. Pastry creams that contain starch mixed with the egg yolk will not curdle when boiled due to the starch molecules protecting the yolks.

- *Sugar* – an excess of sugar can prevent gelatinisation by blocking the absorption of the liquid. When baking pastry, gelatinisation of starch is required to set the pastry. Pastry recipes with a high sugar content (such as pâte sablée) will therefore have a softer texture when cooked than recipes with lower sugar content. This is the basic principle for how sugars tenderise baked goods.

- *Time* – starches that have been stored for a long period of time may lose their ability to gelatinise and therefore a greater quantity of starch will be required to thicken a liquid.

Gelatine

Gelatine is a protein that is produced from the skin, connective tissue and bones of animals (primarily pork, veal and beef). These are soaked in an acid to break down the collagen and the gelatine molecules are then carefully extracted at low temperatures. Because the gelatine molecules are long and flexible, when they are warmed they disperse in liquids and will set the liquid into a gel. Gelatine will thicken and stabilise the consistency and texture of foods that cannot be further heated, such as ice cream.

Gelatine can be purchased in 2g sheets or in a granulated form. Gelatine sheets, which are also known as 'leaves', should be washed and bloomed in cold clean water to help remove any impurities and to soften the gelatine ready for the next stage of use. The liquid that is to be thickened must be

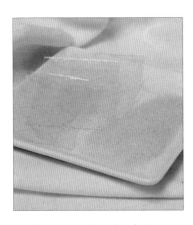

Leaf and granulated gelatine

heated, and the carefully drained gelatine sheets are then melted in the hot liquid.

When using granulated gelatine, the liquid to be thickened should be added cold to the required quantity of granules. The granules are then dissolved before the liquid is warmed over a bain marie. The granules will sometimes stick together, but constant warming and stirring will disperse them. The standard proportion advised by gelatine manufacturers is 7g granulated gelatine to 250ml liquid.

To set a dessert or ingredient after gelatine has been added it must be chilled in a refrigerator. The mixture can sometimes be set over an iced water bath while constantly stirring – this is a quicker method of setting.

Factors that affect gelatine

There are several factors that can affect gelatine:

- *The amount of gelatine used* – if too little gelatine is added to the liquid ingredients, insufficient gelling will occur. The amount required will vary between recipes, depending on the final texture desired, but a general rule is that six leaves of gelatine will set 480ml of liquid.

- *The amount of sugar added* – mixtures that contain a lot of sugar will take longer to gel, or may not even gel at all. More gelatine is added to compensate for this effect.

- *The amount of acid present* – acid can weaken the structure of gelatine and therefore more gelatine may be required to produce a set liquid.

- *Enzymes in fresh fruits* – the protease enzyme found in some fresh fruits, such as pineapple, kiwi fruit, melon, papaya and ginger, completely prevents gelatine from setting. This enzyme is inactivated or destroyed at 85°C, so canned or cooked fruit will not be affected.

- *The addition of salt* – salt reduces the strength of gelatine and so additional quantities may have to be added.

Other stabilisers

There are several other substances that work in a similar way to gelatine but which are derived from plants. Collectively referred to as 'gums', they are long chains of glucose sugars that are capable of absorbing large quantities of water:

- *Agar-agar* – derived from a seaweed, this has greater gelatinisation properties than gelatine so less is required for a recipe. It can be purchased in whole or powdered form and is suitable for vegetarian diets.

- *Carrageenan* – a similar substance to agar-agar and also a type of seaweed. Food manufacturers use this to thicken foods containing diary products, such as cottage cheese and ice cream.

■ *Gum Arabic* – derived from the sap of an African tree, this has been used to stabilise **icing**, frostings, glazes and some fillings and creams.

■ *Carob gum* – also derived from a tree (the carob tree), the seeds are used to make a gum that is used to stabilise ice creams and **sorbets**. An added benefit is that this substance will also improve a mixture's resistance to heat.

■ *Pectin* – many fruits contain **pectin**, but fruits that are particularly high in pectin are apples, plums, cranberries and citrus fruits. Pectin is used to thicken glazes, jams, jellies and preserves.

Considerations for balancing and scaling ingredients in recipes

All recipes and bakery formulas produce a specific number of servings of a given product. This meets the needs of the business in several ways; for example in portion control and cost control. But, if the chef requires more or less food to be produced and the recipe does not fit the amount of food required how do you alter the recipe to fit your needs?

Scaling a recipe means increasing or decreasing the amount of food a recipe produces. Though no strict guidelines govern how to scale a recipe, there are some practical considerations to help you adjust your recipes with greater success.

Changing a recipe's yield: points to consider

A recipe's yield could be, for example, ten portions of chocolate mousse. A recipe specifies the ingredients and the measurements required for a set amount. If the yield is either more or less than what you want to produce, you may need to scale the recipe.

Though some recipes, such as casseroles, stews and other main dishes, usually lend themselves to a simple increasing or decreasing of the amount of ingredients, others do not. For example, baked goods requiring leavening agents such as baking powder, baking soda or yeast, which may not work very well doubled or quadrupled.

Here are several factors to consider before increasing or decreasing the number of servings of a given recipe:

■ *Equipment* – when you scale a recipe, match your equipment to the volume of the food. Larger batches need bigger bowls and larger or extra baking pans. Likewise, smaller batches require smaller bowls and baking pans.

■ *Cooking times* – cooking times may stay the same. For instance, when preparing soufflés, it does not matter whether you bake six or twenty-six soufflés, the cooking time remains the same. Some recipes may, however, require a longer cooking time. Conversely, heavy sponge cake that serves eight portions will need a much shorter baking time than one that serves twenty portions.

- *Cooking temperature* – in most cases, you do not have to change the cooking temperature when you scale a recipe. The exception is when you have multiple items in the oven and may therefore require a slightly higher baking temperature.
- *Seasonings* – spices and other seasonings, including salt, do not always need to be increased or decreased in the same proportion as the other ingredients. Instead, add seasoning and flavourings to taste until you obtain the result you want.
- *Alcohol* – in recipes, alcohol such as white wine or rum can quickly overpower the flavour of the food if too much is used. Do not therefore increase the alcohol content as you would other ingredients. Consider also the effect that alcohol as an ingredient may have in certain recipes such as ice cream where additional alcohol will lower the freezing point of the ice cream mixture.

Best practice for scaling a recipe

In order to obtain the best results you should be familiar with your original recipe, experiment with your adjustments and make separate batches, if necessary.

- *Make the original recipe first*. Identify how the recipe should look and taste before you make any adjustments. The original is then a benchmark for comparing the success of the adjusted recipe. Plus, the original may yield fewer or more servings than expected and the recipe may not need to be adjusted after all!
- *Test first, and then serve*. You may not find success when scaling a recipe for the first time. So test your scaled dishes first, before serving them. Experiment with what works and what does not work. Ingredients interact with each other differently, and cooking methods, temperatures or times may need to be adjusted accordingly. Also, it is important to recognise the importance of using good quality ingredients and the detrimental effect that poor quality ingredients can have on the final result.
- *Make food in batches*. If you increase a recipe and lack the time to experiment, produce several individual batches. This way you end up with the amount you need based on the original recipe.

No specific rules dictate how to scale a recipe due to the diverse nature of the ingredients that we use. However, certain scientific formulas can explain how to produce the best soufflé, mousse or ice cream, based on the amount and type of fat, liquid and solids used.

BASIC DESSERT RECIPES

Crème diplomat

INGREDIENTS	MAKES 600G	MAKES 1.2KG
Fresh milk	250g	500g
Egg yolks	40g	80g
Caster sugar	70g	140g
Custard powder	20g	40g
Gelatine leaves	10 leaves	20 leaves
Kirsch	To taste	To taste
Whipped cream	310g	620g

Method of work

1 Bring the milk to the boil.

2 Mix together the egg yolks, caster sugar and custard powder. Add the boiled milk and return to the pan to cook out the mixture.

3 Strain through a fine chinois. Soften the leaves of gelatine in cold water.

4 Strain the gelatine sheets from any excess water and add to the hot, cooked custard. Stir until the gelatine has melted and been incorporated into the custard.

5 Cool the custard to 20°C then add the kirsch. Carefully fold in the whipped cream.

6 Use as required.

 CHEF'S TIP

Crème diplomat is a derivative of crème pâtissière and can be flavoured according to the requirements of the recipe by using a particular alcohol or a flavouring such as vanilla. Crème diplomat can be used as a filling in pastries, tarts, cakes and various desserts.

Chocolate sauce

INGREDIENTS	MAKES 1KG	MAKES 2KG
Water	710ml	1425ml
Caster sugar	400g	800g
Cocoa powder	60g	110g
Cornflour	20g	40g
Dark chocolate	125g	250g
Single cream	135ml	275ml

Method of work

1 Bring the water to the boil with the caster sugar.

2 Mix together the cocoa powder and the cornflour. Add the boiled sugar solution and return to the pan to cook out the mixture.

3 Chop the dark chocolate into small pieces and add to the mixture.

4 Stir continuously to melt the chocolate into the liquid. Ensure that the chocolate does not burn on the base of the saucepan.

5 Add the single cream and adjust the consistency.

6 Strain through a fine chinois.

7 Use as required.

CHEF'S TIP

This sauce can be stored in bulk in a refrigerator in a covered container. A little at a time can be taken to use either hot or cold.

Crème mousseline

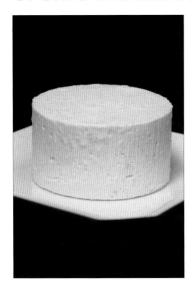

INGREDIENTS	MAKES 900G	MAKES 1.8KG
Fresh milk	500ml	1 litre
Egg yolks	6	12
Caster sugar	100g	200g
Flour	70g	140g
Vanilla	1 pod	2 pods
Unsalted butter	250g	500g

Method of work

1 Split the vanilla pod in half and remove the seeds. Add the pod to the milk and bring to the boil.

2 Mix together the egg yolks, caster sugar and the flour. Add the boiled milk and return to the pan to cook out the mixture.

3 Strain through a fine chinois.

4 Cut the butter into small pieces. Add one-third to the mixture while beating well and continue beating until it clears.

5 Cool the pastry cream to 20°C. Place the remaining butter in a mixing bowl and using a mixing machine beat until softened. On a medium speed add the pastry cream a little at a time. Ensure all the pastry cream is incorporated.

6 Beat a few minutes to produce a light and creamy finish.

7 Use as required.

 CHEF'S TIP

Crème mousseline will keep in a covered plastic container in refrigerated conditions for up to 4 days. The crème can be flavoured with fruit purées, alcohol, chocolate or praline.

Lemon cream

INGREDIENTS	MAKES 1KG	MAKES 2KG
Whole eggs	10	20
Caster sugar	360g	720g
Finely grated zest of lemon	5 lemons	10 lemons
Lemon juice	480g	960g
Caster sugar	300g	600g
Gelatine	5 leaves	10 leaves

Method of work

1 Bring to the boil the lemon juice, zest and the smaller quantity of caster sugar, stirring continuously. Meanwhile, soak the leaves of gelatine in cold water to soften.

2 Mix together the whole eggs and the larger quantity of caster sugar. Add this mixture to the boiled lemon mixture and place back onto the stove.

3 Cook out the lemon cream to 85°C, stirring constantly.

4 The lemon cream will thicken as it cooks out. Remove from the stove and add the softened gelatine (which has been squeezed to remove the excess water).

5 Strain through a fine chinois and chill in a refrigerator.

6 Use as required.

 CHEF'S TIP

This recipe can be used as an alternative to lemon curd and as a preserve, a flavouring for creams or an accompaniment to a dessert.

Coconut foam

INGREDIENTS	6 PORTIONS	15 PORTIONS
Coconut milk (tinned)	250ml	500ml
Yoghurt	80ml	175ml
Whipping cream	30ml	60ml
Icing sugar	40g	75g
Desiccated coconut	30g	60g
Gelatine	1½ leaves	3 leaves

Method of work

1. Soften the gelatine leaves in cold water.
2. Add the desiccated coconut to the coconut milk and bring to the boil in a saucepan. Reduce the liquid by half. Add the gelatine and melt into the hot coconut milk.
3. Mix together the reduced coconut with the yoghurt, cream and icing sugar.
4. Pass the mixture into an aeration canister. Chill in a refrigerator.
5. Charge the canister with two gas cartridges and use as required.

CHEF'S TIP

The coconut elements can be replaced with a fruit purée and an alternative liquid, such as mint-flavoured syrup.

Pâte à bombe

INGREDIENTS	MAKES 180ML	MAKES 360ML
Granulated sugar	40g	80g
Water	75g	150g
Egg yolks	3	5

Method of work

1. Place the water into a heavy-based saucepan and add the sugar. Heat slowly until the sugar dissolves.
2. Increase the heat, and using a sugar thermometer boil the sugar solution to 121°C (hard ball stage).
3. Meanwhile, whisk the eggs in an electric mixing machine until they have reached a pale yellow colour.
4. With the machine still whisking the egg yolks very carefully pour the hot sugar solution in a thin but steady stream onto the yolks. Continue until all of the hot sugar has been added.
5. Continue whisking to increase the volume of the mixture and to cool it down. The mixture should stand to a peak when cold.
6. The pâte à bombe mixture should be kept covered in a refrigerator for up to 2 days.

CHEF'S TIP

This classical preparation is an important base for other recipes, such as mousses, parfaits and iced soufflés. It provides a stabilised foam of egg yolks and sugar to be flavoured accordingly and sustain the addition of whipped cream or aerated egg whites.

Chocolate glaze

INGREDIENTS	TO COVER 1 CAKE	TO COVER 3 CAKES
Water	275g	550g
Whipping cream	250g	500g
Cocoa powder	125g	250g
Caster sugar	275g	550g
Liquid glucose	125g	250g
Gelatine	7 leaves	14 leaves

Method of work

1 Place the water into a heavy-based saucepan and add the glucose, whipping cream, cocoa powder and caster sugar. Heat slowly until the dry ingredients dissolve.

2 Increase the heat, and using a sugar thermometer boil the cocoa solution to 104°C.

3 Meanwhile, soften the gelatine in cold water.

4 Add the softened gelatine to the cocoa solution and stir well to melt. Pass through a fine sieve and leave to cool covered with plastic film.

5 Use the glaze to coat tarts, cakes and gâteaux, but only use it at a temperature of 30–35°C, when it is fluid but ready to set.

6 This glaze can be kept in a refrigerator for up to 3 days and melted for use as required.

 CHEF'S TIP

To melt the glaze place it in a microwave oven or on a bain marie. Try not to heat it above 40°C and always use it at the temperature stated in the recipe.

Muscat sabayon

INGREDIENTS	4 PORTIONS	10 PORTIONS
Egg yolks	3	8
Caster sugar	70g	170g
Water	50g	125g
Muscat (sweet white wine)	75g	200g
Vanilla	½ pod	1 pod

Method of work

1 Pour some water into a heavy-based saucepan large enough to hold a round-based mixing bowl on top. Heat the water on a stove to 45°C.

2 Combine the egg yolks, sugar, water, scrapped seeds from the vanilla pod and Muscat wine in the mixing bowl. Place onto the saucepan of heated water on a low heat.

3 Whisk continuously using a balloon whisk for about 12 minutes. Ensure that the water temperature for the bain marie does not exceed 90°C.

4 The mixture will aerate and a ribbon consistency should be obtained. The internal temperature of the sabayon should be 50°C with a smooth, aerated and light texture.

5 Use the sabayon while it is still warm. Serve as an accompaniment to a dessert such as a tart or as the main part of a dessert, in a wine glass with freshly picked strawberries and a biscuit à la cuillère.

CHEF'S TIP

This sabayon can be served cold, but it would be best to stabilise the aeration by adding a leaf of softened gelatine. Alternative alcohols can be used to create different flavoured sabayons, such as Marsala and eaux de vie.

Fruit coulis

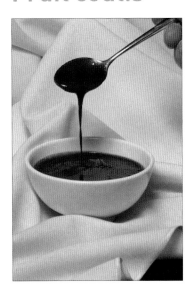

INGREDIENTS	4 PORTIONS	10 PORTIONS
Fresh fruit (such as raspberries, strawberries or redcurrants)	800g	1.7kg
Stock syrup	200ml	425ml
Lemon juice (optional)	1 lemon	2 lemons

Method of work

1 Carefully wash the fruit. Place into a food blender with the strained lemon juice and the stock syrup.

2 Purée the fruit mixture for approximately a minute until a smooth purée has been obtained.

3 Pass the purée through a fine chinois or muslin cloth and correct the consistency by adding more stock syrup or puréed raspberries.

4 The coulis is now ready for use, and will keep for 3–4 days in a refrigerator. Alternatively it can easily be frozen.

SOUFFLÉS

Soufflé is a French word derived from the verb *souffler*, which means to puff or to blow up. The soufflé was originally made in a croustade, which was a straight-sided pastry case into which the soufflé mixture was poured (but the croustade was never eaten). Modern practice it to use an ovenproof ramekin dish.

There are four main types of soufflé:

■ *Hot soufflé* – this is a very fragile and delicate blend of eggs, flour, butter and egg whites and can be sweet or savoury. Hot soufflés must be served the moment they are released from the oven.

■ *Pudding soufflé* – these are baked in a bain marie in a metal mould (dariole). They are turned out and always served with a sauce. Pudding soufflés are not as light in texture as a hot soufflé and are normally served for luncheon.

■ *Cold soufflé* – a soft mixture of meringue, cream, egg yolks and sugar together with gelatine. The soufflés are set in prepared soufflé dishes or ramekins and served cold.

■ *Iced soufflé* – this is prepared in a similar way to the cold soufflé but without the gelatine and is frozen like a parfait. A derivative of this type of soufflé is the omelette soufflé, which is produced directly onto a silver flat with a base of Génoise sponge, ice cream and fresh fruit, then decoratively covered with meringue and flash cooked under a grill or in a hot oven.

Ordinary hot sweet soufflés are served at the table in the dish that they were baked in. They are traditionally served without a sauce, but it is now commonplace to have a sorbet, ice cream or hot sauce as an accompaniment.

Soufflés are delicate and can be difficult to make. They are generally made using a base of crème pâtissière combined with a flavouring and aerated egg whites. The air trapped in the egg whites expands at cooking temperatures and the egg protein, along with the starch molecules found in the crème pâtissière base, will set the hot dessert. However, as the soufflé cools down the trapped air will escape and the soufflé will sink.

SOUFFLÉ RECIPES
Vanilla soufflé *Soufflé à la vanille*

INGREDIENTS	4 PORTIONS	8 PORTIONS
Fresh milk	250ml	500ml
Good-quality salt	3 g	5g
Caster sugar	40g	80g
Strong white flour	15g	30g
Cornflour	10g	20g
Egg yolks	3	6
Vanilla	1 pod	2 pods
Caster sugar	75g	150g
Egg whites	2	4
To coat the ramekin dishes		
Melted unsalted butter	50g	100g
Caster sugar	60g	120g

Method of work

1   Place the fresh milk, split vanilla pod (with the seeds removed) and salt in a saucepan and bring to the boil.

2   Sift together the flour and cornflour. Beat the egg yolks and the smaller quantity of caster sugar together and then mix in the sieved flour.

3   Slowly add the boiled milk to the egg mixture, whisking continuously to a smooth paste.

4   Return to the saucepan and back onto a medium heat. Stir until the mixture re-boils and the mixture is smooth and thickened.

5   Remove from the heat, transfer to a clean bowl, cover and cool.

6   Preheat an oven to 190°C. To prepare the soufflé dishes, brush the insides of the mould in vertical strokes with melted butter. Chill in a refrigerator until set. Brush a second layer of butter in the same way. Apply the sugar on the inside of the dish; rotate the dish to ensure that the inside is totally covered with the sugar.

7   Aerate the egg whites in a bowl until firm peaks are obtained and then gradually whisk in the remaining sugar.

8   Carefully fold in the meringue to the vanilla base and spoon equally into the prepared soufflé dishes. Level the tops with a palette knife.

9   Place on a baking tray and set in the preheated oven to bake for approximately 12–15 minutes. Remove from the oven and dust the tops immediately with icing sugar. Serve at once.

CHEF'S TIP

To create a chocolate version of this soufflé, replace some of the flour content with cocoa powder. Instead of coating the inside of the soufflé dish with caster sugar coat with grated chocolate.

ISTOCK / © JOHANNA DOORENBOSCH

Raspberry soufflé *Soufflé aux framboises*

INGREDIENTS	4 PORTIONS	8 PORTIONS
Fresh raspberries	110g	250g
Caster sugar	15g	40g
Lemon juice	A few drops to taste	A few drops to taste
Arrowroot	3g	8g
Water	25ml	60ml
Granulated sugar	60g	140g
Egg whites	3	6

Method of work

1 Preheat the oven to 200°C (400°F). Soufflés are baked at a high temperature to ensure a good rise.

2 Using a clean pastry brush, evenly coat the inside of the soufflé moulds with melted butter. Fill each mould with granulated sugar and shake out any excess sugar. If you have correctly buttered the moulds, the sugar will stick to the sides and base. The butter and sugar will prevent the soufflés from sticking to the sides of the mould and will allow the soufflé to rise evenly.

3 Prepare the soufflé base. Wash, dry and place the raspberries into a blender to purée into a paste. Put the raspberry paste and caster sugar into a stainless steel saucepan and stir over a medium heat until the mixture boils and thickens. Mix the arrowroot with a little cold water and add to the raspberry mixture. Allow it to boil for 1–2 minutes, and stir continuously. Remove from the heat and set aside.

4 Prepare the Italian meringue. Pour the water and granulated sugar into a heavy-based clean saucepan and place over medium to high heat. When bubbles start to form around the edge of the pan, insert a sugar thermometer in the mixture. When the sugar reaches 115°C, begin to aerate the egg whites in an electric mixer.

5 Place the egg whites in a large mixing bowl and whisk with an electric mixer on medium-high speed until foamy and slightly soft peaks have formed.

6 The sugar is ready when it reaches 118°C; this is called the 'soft ball' stage. Make an Italian meringue by pouring the cooked sugar between the side of the bowl and the whisk, as you continue whipping the egg whites. Be very careful not to pour the hot sugar onto the beaters, otherwise it will splash.

7 Continue whipping the meringue for approximately 5 minutes until the outside of the bowl is warm but not hot. Do not over whip the meringue or it will not incorporate evenly into the base and, when baked, the soufflés will have pieces of cooked egg white in their centre.

8 Fold the warm raspberry fruit base into the warm Italian meringue in two additions. Fold the two preparations together just enough until they are combined (you may still see small flecks of raspberry), being very careful not to deflate the mixture. It is important that both these mixtures be warm in order that they combine together smoothly. If one mixture is significantly cooler than the other, it will form a heavy mixture when the two are folded together. The warm meringue will also add stability to the unbaked soufflé by slightly cooking the egg whites, keeping the soufflé mixture from collapsing.

 CHEF'S TIP

The soufflé base with the Italian meringue folded into it can be kept in a refrigerator in soufflé moulds ready for service for up to two hours. Other fresh fruits or purées can be used as an alternative to raspberry (rhubarb, strawberry and blackberry, for example). Some small pieces of fruit can be added at the base of the soufflé mould before the mixture is piped in.

9   Place the soufflé mixture in a large piping bag with a 2 inch opening. Pipe the mixture into the prepared moulds. The best possible way to do this is to hold the pastry bag directly over each mould with the tip down. Place the tip inside the mould approximately 1 inch from the base. Applying an even pressure, pipe the mixture into the mould, lifting the pastry bag up as the mould fills. When you have piped level to the rim of the mould, stop squeezing and lift the tip straight up, leaving a small tail at the top of the soufflé. (The unbaked soufflés will hold at room temperature for 1 hour before baking.)

10   Place the moulds on a baking sheet and set the baking sheet in the centre of the oven. If the soufflés are too close to the base of the oven, the bottoms will burn before the insides are properly cooked. Bake for approximately 10 minutes until the soufflés have doubled in height and have begun to caramelise on top. Remove the baking sheet from the oven and dust the tops of the soufflés with icing sugar. Serve immediately.

Cold lemon soufflé with a lemongrass jelly and lemon tuille

INGREDIENTS	4 PORTIONS	10 PORTIONS
Cold lemon soufflé		
Gelatine	5 leaves	10 leaves
Egg yolks	3	6
Caster sugar	110g	260g
Lemon juice and finely grated zest	2 lemons	4 lemons
Egg whites	3	6
Whipping cream	200ml	500ml
Lemongrass jelly		
Sweet white wine	200g	400g
Caster sugar	15g	30g
Lemongrass	1 stick	2 sticks
Gelatine	3 leaves	6 leaves
Lemon tuille		
Finely grated lemon zest	1 lemon	2 lemons
Icing sugar	42 g	85g
Melted butter	34 g	67 g
Egg whites	38 g	78 g
Soft flour	42 g	85g
Additional ingredients		
Lemon cream (see recipe on p. 375)	75g	150g
Icing sugar	25g	50g
Caramel swirls	4	10
White chocolate acetate strips (1.5cm × 10cm; see recipe on p. 402)	4	10

Method of work

1 Prepare small ramekin dishes by attaching a strip of silicone paper to the outside of the dish so that it extends 2cm above the rim.
2 Soak the gelatine leaves in cold water.
3 Place the lemon zest and juice with the egg yolks and the sugar into a stainless steel mixing bowl.
4 Place the bowl over a bain marie of simmering water (not exceeding 90°C) and whisk continuously to thicken and aerate the mixture.
5 Add the gelatine and mix in until it has dissolved. Remove from the heat and continue to beat until cool.
6 Lightly whisk the whipping cream to the ribbon stage.
7 Stiffly aerate the egg whites.
8 Fold in the cream to the lemon mixture and then the egg whites.
9 Pour into prepared dishes and leave to set in a refrigerator for 1 hour.
10 To make the lemongrass jelly, select a small tray with 2cm sides. Warm a little of the wine with the sugar. Chop the lemongrass into small pieces and add. Infuse for 30 minutes.
11 Soften the gelatine in cold water and drain. Add to the warm lemongrass juice and melt. Strain this into the remaining wine and pour into the prepared container. Put in a refrigerator to set.
12 To make the lemon tuiles, mix the icing sugar and the egg whites. Add the lemon zest and soft flour. Finally, mix in the melted butter. Leave to rest in a cool place for 30 minutes.
13 Spread this mixture over a silicone baking sheet and place into a preheated oven at 200°C. Bake until the mixture turns light golden. Remove from the oven. Using a template cut rectangular strips of the tuille, one per portion (approximately 1.5cm × 10cm).
14 To serve, turn the lemongrass jelly out of the tray and cut into the same sized rectangles as the tuiles. Set the jelly on top of the tuile. Put the lemon cream in a piping bag with a small plain tube. Pipe small bulbs along the centre of the jelly and carefully position the white chocolate strip on top. Position this onto a rectangular plate and set the lemon soufflé next to it, with the paper removed, dusted with icing sugar and decorated with the caramel swirl.

Praline iced soufflé *Soufflé glacé au praline*

INGREDIENTS	4 PORTIONS	10 PORTIONS
Water	50ml	80ml
Granulated sugar	80g	170g
Egg yolks	4	8
Egg whites	3	5
Whipped cream	190ml	500ml
Praline (crushed)	55g	120g

Method of work

1 Prepare the moulds (usually ramekin dishes 8cm in diameter) with strips of acetate or silicone paper that have been measured to sit approximately 3cm higher than the rim of the mould that has been used. If using silicone paper, this may need to be folded twice to produce a structure strong enough to hold the mixture. Place the acetate or paper around the outside of the mould so that there are no gaps between it and the mould. To hold the collar firmly in place secure with a strip of adhesive tape.
2 To prepare the pâte à bombe base for this recipe mix and bring the granulated sugar and the water slowly to the boil. Using a sugar thermometer as a guide cook the sugar solution to 121°C.

When the iced soufflé is frozen, just before service scoop out some of the centre and fill the central well with fresh strawberries. These can be lightly sauced with a little strawberry coulis and decorated with whipped cream. This classical finished is called Soufflé Glacé Hericart

3 Carefully pour the hot sugar syrup onto the egg yolks while whisking continuously to aerate the mixture. Once all of the sugar has been added, keep whisking until it has cooled down and the mixture stands in soft peaks.

4 Aerate the egg whites in a separate bowl to create stiff peaks and ensure that the whipped cream is also correctly aerated ready for combining the preparations.

5 Fold in the whipped cream and the crushed praline to the pâte à bombe preparation.

6 Carefully fold in the aerated egg whites in two incorporation stages.

7 Fill the moulds to the top by piping the mixture into the moulds. Smooth the top with a small palate knife and place each filled mould onto a baking tray to place into a freezer.

8 The freezing process takes approximately 5 hours, depending on the inside temperature of the freezer being used.

9 Remove the acetate or paper band carefully from the iced soufflé. The soufflé is usually kept in the mould and decorated according to the style of the chef and a main ingredient used to flavour the dessert.

HOT DESSERT RECIPES
Coffee and date pudding with a rum and raisin ice cream

INGREDIENTS	6 PORTIONS	12 PORTIONS
Medjool dates (stoned and chopped)	175g	350g
Water	300ml	600ml
Bicarbonate of soda	1tsp	2tsp
Unsalted butter	50g	100g
Caster sugar	175g	350g
Whole eggs	2	4
Soft white flour	165g	330g
Baking powder	10g	25g
Strong espresso coffee	6tsp	12tsp
Toffee sauce		
Double cream	300ml	600ml
Light muscovado sugar	50g	100g
Black treacle	2tsp	4tsp
Unsalted butter	30g	60g
Rum and raisin ice cream		
Pâte à bombe (see recipe on p. 376)	180ml	360ml
Raisins	100g	200g
Dark rum	100g	200g
Water	30ml	60ml
Caster sugar	30g	60g
Fresh milk	120ml	250ml
Double cream	120ml	250ml

Method of work

1 Line a 22.5cm square baking tin with silicone paper and preheat an oven to 180°C.

2 Place the dates and the water into a heavy-based saucepan and bring to the boil. Continue to boil for 4 minutes then remove from the heat and add the bicarbonate of soda and coffee. Leave to stand.

3 Cream together the butter and sugar until light in colour and with a soft, fluffy texture. Gradually add the eggs, mixing continuously.

4 Combine the dates and water with the creamed butter mixture and fold in the flour and baking powder.

5 Pour the mixture into the prepared tin and bake for approximately 35 minutes or until the pudding is just firm to the touch.

6 To make the sauce, place the cream, sugar, treacle and butter into a saucepan and bring to the boil. Simmer for 3 minutes and pass through a chinois. Reserve warm.

7 To make the ice cream, wash the raisins in warm water and then place in a saucepan with the dark rum, sugar and water. Slowly bring to the boil and remove from the heat and cover with plastic film. Leave to cool and macerate for 24 hours before using.

8 Make the pâte à bombe and set aside. Place the milk and cream in a saucepan and bring to the boil, then leave to cool over a bain marie of iced water. Combine with the pâte à bombe and pour into an ice cream machine to churn. Halfway through the freezing process add the raisins and some of the dark rum liquor to taste. Continue to churn and freeze.

9 To serve, cut the pudding into portions and spoon the sauce over each pudding. Serve with a quenelle of the ice cream.

Chocolate fondant with spiced pears and vanilla ice cream

CHEF'S TIP

When making the vanilla ice cream, if possible cook the preparation 24 hours before churning and freezing. The vanilla pod should be kept in the preparation. The resultant flavour will be stronger with the texture of the finished ice cream much smoother.

INGREDIENTS	4 PORTIONS	15 PORTIONS
Whole eggs	2	8
Egg yolks	2	8
Caster sugar	60g	220g
Dark chocolate	100g	400g
Unsalted butter	75g	300g
Soft flour	30g	120g
Vanilla	To taste	To taste
Spiced pears		
Williams pears	4	10
Unsalted butter	25g	75g
Caster sugar	25g	75g
Cinnamon (powdered)	1tsp	3tsp
Star anise	1	3
Clove	1	3
Vanilla ice cream		
Fresh full fat milk	570ml	1140ml
Double cream	160g	320g
Milk powder	40g	75g
Vanilla	1	2
Caster sugar	110g	220g
Glucose	40g	80g
Egg yolks	2	4

Method of work

1 Preheat an oven to 175°C. Grease individual moulds well with melted butter.

2 Combine the eggs and sugar in a mixing bowl with the vanilla. Aerate until the volume has at least doubled.

3 Melt the chocolate and butter together in a microwave oven or in a bain marie and fold into the egg mixture.

4 Fold in the flour. Deposit the mixture into the prepared moulds to approximately half full.

5 Leave to rest in a refrigerator for 30 minutes.

6 Place into the oven to bake for 15 minutes. Remove from the oven and rest for 3 minutes then remove from the moulds.

7 For the spiced pears, wash, peel and cut the pears into brunoise. Place into a shallow pan with the butter, sugar and the spices and cook slowly. Half way through cooking place a cartouche of baking paper over the pan. Reserve warm for service.

8 For the vanilla ice cream, place the milk, cream, milk powder, half the quantity of sugar and split vanilla pod into a saucepan and slowly heat. At 45°C add the liquid glucose then bring to the boil.

9 Beat the remaining sugar and the egg yolks together and pour the boiled milk onto the yolks. Return to the pan and cook the mixture to 85°C, stirring continuously. Pass through a fine chinois into a bowl.

10 Chill quickly over a bain marie of iced water and then churn in an ice cream machine.

11 To serve, pack the spiced pears into a stainless steel ring in the centre of the service plate. Remove the ring. De-mould the chocolate fondant and place it carefully on top of the spiced pears. Spoon a quenelle of the vanilla ice cream on top of the fondant and decorate as required.

Apple and thyme crumble with mascarpone ice cream and salted caramel sauce

INGREDIENTS	4 PORTIONS	8 PORTIONS
Caster sugar	50g	100g
Butter	60g	120g
Ground almonds	55g	110g
Soft white flour	60g	125g
Bramley apples	3	6
Clear honey	25g	50g
Fresh thyme	1 sprig	2 sprigs
Unsalted butter	25g	50g
Sultanas	10g	20g
Salted caramel sauce		
Water	100g	200g
Granulated sugar	60g	120g
Double cream	50g	100g
Fleur de sel	2 g	4 g
Mascarpone ice cream		
Caster sugar	75g	150g
Egg yolks	3	6
Fresh full fat milk	250g	500g
Mascarpone	150g	300g

CHEF'S TIP

Always ensure that customers are aware of the nut content in the crumble topping for this recipe. Alternatively, the ground almond content can be replaced with flour and the butter content slightly increased.

Method of work

1. Preheat an oven to 180°C.
2. To make the crumble, mix the sugar with the butter. Incorporate the ground almonds and the flour and rub together to create a crumbly texture. Spread the mixture onto a baking sheet lined with a silicone baking mat and bake for 15 minutes. Remove from the oven and set aside.
3. Wash, peel and cut the apples into 1cm dice. In a shallow pan, cook the honey, butter and thyme to a light caramel. Add the sultanas and then add the apples. Place a cartouche of baking paper over the top and continue to cook until the apples are soft to the touch but still retain their shape.
4. Put the cooked apple mixture into the base of a 6cm stainless steel ring placed onto a silicone baking mat on a baking sheet. Place the crumble on top and return to the oven for 15 minutes to warm through and colour.
5. For the salted caramel sauce, place the water and sugar in a heavy-based saucepan and cook to a caramel. Deglaze carefully with the double cream and add the fleur de sel. Reboil and pass through a fine chinois. Reserve warm for service.
6. For the mascarpone ice cream, beat together the egg yolks and sugar. Meanwhile, place the milk and half of the mascarpone into a saucepan and bring to the boil. Add to the egg yolk mixture and mix well. Return to the saucepan and cook to 85°C, stirring continuously. Pass through a fine sieve and chill over a bain marie of iced water. Add the remaining mascarpone and freeze in an ice cream machine.
7. To serve, place the crumble onto the service plate and spoon the salted caramel sauce around it. Set a quenelle of the ice cream to the side and decorate accordingly.

Chocolate crêpe soufflé with orange and vanilla sauce

INGREDIENTS	4 PORTIONS	10 PORTIONS
Crêpes		
Soft white flour	100g	210g
Caster sugar	10g	30g
Cocoa powder	20g	40g
Good-quality salt	3 g	5g
Whole eggs	2	4
Fresh full fat milk	400ml	700ml
Orange and vanilla sauce		
Sweet white wine	300ml	650ml
Oranges	2	4
Vanilla	1 pod	2 pods
Caster sugar	50g	100g
Unsalted butter	70g	150g
Double cream	30ml	70ml
Chocolate soufflé centre		
Fresh milk	250ml	500ml
Dark chocolate (70% minimum cocoa content)	150g	320g
Caster sugar	40g	90g
Strong white flour	20g	40g
Cornflour	10g	20g
Egg yolks	3	6
Grand Marnier	4tbsp	10tbsp
Egg whites	3	6
Caster sugar	40g	80g

Method of work

1 Preheat an oven to 220°C.

2 To prepare the **crêpes**, combine the flour, cocoa powder, salt and sugar and slowly beat in the eggs. Stir in one-third of the milk and beat to a smooth paste. Add the rest of the milk and leave to rest in a refrigerator for 1 hour before using.

3 Stir the batter and pass through a chinois. Add a little sunflower oil to a crêpe pan and heat. Ladle a little of the batter and cook for approximately 1 minute on each side with very little colour. Place each cooked crêpe in between small sheets of silicone paper to retain the soft texture and refrigerate until needed.

4 To prepare the orange and vanilla sauce, add the wine, sugar and split vanilla pod to a saucepan and reduce by half. Segment the oranges and reserve to one side, retaining any juice with them. Add the double cream and cubed unsalted butter to the reduced liquor, whisk and cook until the fats emulsify into a sauce. Add the orange segments and reserve warm.

5 For the soufflé mixture, heat the milk in a saucepan until it just reaches boiling point. Meanwhile, sift the cornflour and flour together.

6 Beat the egg yolks and the first quantity of caster sugar together and then combine with the sieved flour. Melt the chocolate in a microwave or over a bowl of hot water.

7 Carefully pour the hot milk onto the egg yolk mixture, whisking continuously to prevent any lumps forming. Return to a clean saucepan.

8 Carefully heat up to simmering point, stirring constantly until the crème begins to thicken and the flour is cooked out. Transfer to a bowl and mix in the melted chocolate and Grand Marnier, cover with a buttered cartouche to prevent a skin from forming and leave to cool.

9 At the point of service, whisk the egg whites in a bowl while slowly adding the remaining caster sugar and aerate to a firm peak.

10 Carefully fold in the egg whites to the chocolate crème pâtissière and immediately pipe or spoon the mixture onto the middle of each crêpe. Fold each crêpe into quarters and pipe any remaining mixture into the cavities. Place onto a baking tray.

11 Bake in the preheated oven for approximately 5 minutes until well risen.

12 Serve immediately by dusting each crêpe soufflé with icing sugar and place into the centre of a plate. Spoon the orange and vanilla sauce with the segments around.

ICE CREAM

Ice cream is made by freezing a liquid mixture containing carefully balanced ingredients after it has been subjected to heat treatment. The conditions of the heat treatment are carefully governed by legal standards, and the process is subjected to regular scrutiny by local health officials.

Scrupulous cleanliness must be observed in every stage of ice cream making. The materials used can easily become contaminated and give rise to food poisoning bacteria. A special area should be reserved for the production of ice cream, appropriately equipped and kept solely for this purpose. Moreover, the equipment should be used solely for the making of ice cream. An abundant supply of hot and cold water for washing purposes is also essential.

The process of *pasteurisation* is essential to the production of ice cream. In 1864, while studying the fermentation of wines, vinegar, beers and milk, Louis Pasteur discovered that fermentation was caused by micro-organisms and realised that many infectious diseases derived from specific microbes. Pasteur ascertained that by boiling milk to over 100°C, all dangerous microbes could be destroyed. However, this heating also reduced the nutritional value of the milk itself. By carrying on his experimentation, Pasteur found out that heating milk to 65°C, keeping at this temperature it for 30 minutes, and then cooling it to 4°C destroyed all pathogenic microbes while leaving the main nutritional and structural characteristics of the milk unchanged.

It is important that all ingredients in the ice cream mix are subjected to heat treatment for the correct time periods and are then cooled down quickly. The treated ingredients must be kept covered to prevent any new contamination.

The Dairy Products (Hygiene) Regulations 1995 state that:

VIDEO CLIP
Ice cream

1 Pasteurised ice-cream shall be obtained by the mixture being heated—
   (a) to a temperature of not less than 65.6°C and retained at that temperature for not less than 30 minutes;
   (b) to a temperature of not less than 71.1°C and retained at that temperature for not less than 10 minutes; or
   (c) to a temperature of not less than 79.4°C and retained at that temperature for not less than 15 seconds, and then reduced to a temperature of not more than 7.2°C within 1½ hours and kept at such temperature until the freezing process is begun.

2 If the temperature of ice-cream has risen above minus 2.2°C at any time since it was frozen it shall not be sold or offered for sale unless—

(a) it has again been subjected to the heat-treatment to which as a mixture it was required to be subjected under paragraph 1 above; and

(b) after having again been frozen, it has been kept at a temperature not exceeding minus 2.2°C.

It is also essential that all hygiene regulations are followed, including those that relate to:

- Daily cleaning routines
- Preparation of the mixture and the close monitoring of temperature control
- The selling and dispensing of ice cream
- Customer hygiene measures
- Hygiene of specialist equipment, such as self-pasteurising machines
- Storage of ice cream.

Storage of ice cream

Ice cream should be stored at the lowest temperature possible, but in any event not higher than –20°C. However, at this temperature the ice cream is very hard and unsuitable for service. It should be brought out of storage prior to service and stored at a temperature of between –6°C and –12°C, according to the type of ice cream used and the consistency required for service.

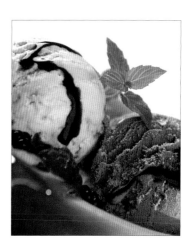

Ice cream should not be sold unless it has been kept at a temperature of –1°C or below since it was frozen. If the mixture has risen above –1°C since freezing, it must be heat treated again and then re-frozen.

TYPES OF ICES	
Sorbet	Made from fruit purée or pulp and stock syrup
Water ice	Made from fruit juice and stock syrup
Spoom	A sorbet mixture with Italian meringue
Granita	Crystallised flavoured syrup or fruit purée
Pâte à bombe	A special preparation of ice cream
Pâte à biscuit glacées	As a pâte à bombe mixture but in a biscuit mould, sometimes lightened with meringue
Soufflé glacé	Iced soufflé
Ice cream	Contains egg, cream and usually milk
Omelette soufflé	Ice cream encased in a meringue preparation on a base of Génoise and fruit
Marquise	Granita with crème chantilly folded in before service

ICE CREAM RECIPES
Madagascan chocolate parfait

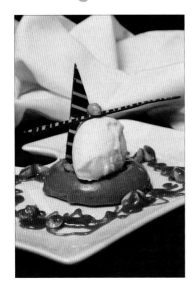

INGREDIENTS	4 PORTIONS	8 PORTIONS
Egg yolks	25g	50g
Caster sugar	30g	60g
Fresh full fat milk	45g	90g
Madagascan dark chocolate (66%)	65g	130g
Whipping cream	75g	150g
Caramelised hazelnuts		
Hazelnuts (toasted, skins removed and halved)	55g	110g
Demerara sugar	15g	30g
Good-quality salt	To taste	To taste
Warm water	A little	A little
Caramel salt and spice sauce		
Caster sugar	75g	150g
Liquid glucose	45g	90g
Double cream	350g	700g
Fleur de sel	2 g	4 g
Vanilla	1 pods	3 pods
Star anise	2	4
Cinnamon stick	½	1
Cardamom seeds	1g	3g
Decorative items		
Thin chocolate discs	4	8
Piped chocolate sticks	4	8
Vanilla ice cream	4 quenelles	8 quenelles
Decorative chocolate	4	8

Method of work

1 To prepare the chocolate parfait, place the milk into a heavy-based saucepan and bring to the boil. Meanwhile, beat together the egg yolks and sugar.

2 Pour the milk onto the egg yolks and mix well then return to the saucepan. Stirring constantly, cook the egg mixture to 85°C.

3 Melt the Madagascan chocolate and combine with the cooked out egg custard. Cool to 30°C in a refrigerator.

4 Carefully whisk the cream to aerate it to a ribbon stage. Gently fold in the cream to the chocolate mixture. Transfer the parfait mixture into individual savarin moulds (preferably flexible silicone moulds so it is easier to remove the frozen parfait) and freeze.

5 To make the caramelised hazelnuts, preheat an oven to 120°C. Toss the hazelnuts in a shallow pan with just enough warm water to make the nuts slightly sticky. Add the sugar and salt to taste and bring to the boil ensuring that the sugar coats the nuts. Turn the nuts out onto a baking sheet lined

 CHEF'S TIP

Madagascan chocolate is generally renowned for its fruity character and dark bitter flavour, so it is an ideal single-origin chocolate to use for this recipe. However, it can be replaced by alternative dark chocolates, but they will need to have a strong, bitter flavour.

with silicone paper then place in the oven and bake for 30 minutes. Remove from the oven and cool. The hazelnuts should be totally dry and crunchy after cooling. If not, return to the oven and bake longer. Store tightly covered in an airtight plastic container ready for service.

6   To make the caramel salt and spice sauce, infuse the fleur de sel, split vanilla pods, star anise, cinnamon and cardamom seeds in the cream for at least 2 hours, covered in a refrigerator.

7   Place the sugar in a heavy-based saucepan and heat. When the sugar begins to melt add the glucose. Continue cooking until a caramel has been reached. Deglaze the caramel with the infused cream and spices.

8   Bring back to the boil, pass through a fine chinois and cool.

9   To serve, turn out the frozen chocolate parfait onto the prepared chocolate disc and position it onto the serving plate. Deposit some of the caramelised hazelnuts in the centre of the chocolate parfait and around the plate. Spoon the caramel sauce onto the plate and finish with the quenelle of vanilla ice cream and chocolate decorations.

Iced parfait of strawberries, lavender ice cream and champagne strawberry salad

INGREDIENTS	4 PORTIONS	8 PORTIONS
Strawberry parfait		
Caster sugar	150g	300g
Glucose	15g	30g
Strawberry purée	3tbsp	5tbsp
Egg whites	3	6
Egg yolks	3	6
Caster sugar	75g	150g
Strawberry purée	125g	250g
Whipped cream	175ml	350ml
Dacquoise biscuit	4 small discs	8 small discs
Lavender ice cream		
Lavender flowers or seeds (edible)	1tsp	2tsp
Caster sugar	60g	120g
Fresh full fat milk	230ml	460ml
Egg yolks	3	6
Double cream	50ml	100ml
Strawberry champagne salad		
Washed and hulled strawberries	125g	250g
Champagne	75g	150g

Method of work

1 To prepare the strawberry parfait, create an Italian meringue with the larger quantity of caster sugar, glucose, smaller quantity of the strawberry purée and the egg whites, cooking to 118°C (soft ball stage).

2 Over a bain marie at approximately 90°C, whisk the egg yolks and smaller quantity of sugar. Slowly add the larger quantity of strawberry purée and cook out. Remove from the heat and carry on whisking to cool and aerate the mixture. When cool fold in the whipped cream and then the meringue.

3 Prepare individual ring moulds with a small disc of dacquoise in the base. Pour the parfait into the moulds and freeze.

4 To prepare the lavender ice cream, grind the lavender into the sugar and beat with the egg yolks.

5 Bring the milk and cream to the boil. Pour the boiled milk onto the egg yolk mixture, stir well and return to the saucepan. Cook out to 85°C, stirring constantly.

6 Pass through a fine chinois and cool over a bain marie of iced water. Churn in an ice cream machine.

7 For the champagne strawberry salad, cut the strawberries into brunoise and carefully combine them with the Champagne at the last moment. Leave to one side for service.

8 To serve, create some red coloured 'bubble' sugar for decoration. Present the de-moulded parfait in the centre of the plate with a quenelle of the lavender ice cream on top. Spoon the compôte around the plate and place the bubble sugar on top of the overall dessert.

Almond ice cream

INGREDIENTS	4 PORTIONS	8 PORTIONS
Fresh full fat milk	570ml	1140ml
Double cream	160g	320g
Milk powder	40g	75g
Softened marzipan	50g	100g
Caster sugar	80g	160g
Glucose	40g	80g
Egg yolks	3	6
Amaretto (optional)	25ml	50ml
Roasted flaked almonds	50g	100g

 CHEF'S TIP

Ice cream quickly absorbs the flavours of other ingredients stored alongside it. Ensure that a plastic container with a good seal is used for storage. Once ice cream has been made and frozen it is best to use it within a week.

Method of work

1 Place the milk, cream, milk powder and softened marzipan into a saucepan and slowly heat. At 45°C, add the liquid glucose and bring to the boil.

2 Beat the sugar and egg yolks together and pour the boiled milk onto the yolks. Return to the pan and cook the mixture, continuously stirring until 85°C has been reached. Pass through a fine chinois into a bowl.

3 Chill quickly over a bain marie of iced water. Add the Amaretto if required, then churn in an ice cream machine.

4 Serve in a chilled glass with some flaked almonds sprinkled over the top.

Fromage frais sorbet

INGREDIENTS	4 PORTIONS	8 PORTIONS
Fromage frais	200g	400g
Lemon juice	18g	36g
Sorbet syrup	175g	350g
Sorbet syrup		
Water	2.1 litres	
Granulated sugar	2.25kg	
Glucose	270g	

Method of work

1 To make the sorbet syrup, place the water, sugar and glucose in a saucepan and bring to the boil. Simmer for 2 minutes and strain into a sterilised plastic container. Leave to cool and refrigerate for use.

2 Place the fromage frais, sorbet syrup and lemon juice together in a bowl and mix well together.

3 Pass through a fine chinois and churn in an ice cream machine.

CHEF'S TIP

Use this sorbet syrup recipe as the base for all fruit sorbets. Use at a ratio of 1kg fruit purée to 550g sorbet syrup.

Apple and basil sorbet

INGREDIENTS	4 PORTIONS	8 PORTIONS
Green apple (such as Granny Smith)	140g	280g
Lemon juice	90g	190g
Caster sugar	110g	225g
Fresh basil leaves	5g	10g
Water	140g	280g
Milk powder	7g	14g

Method of work

1 Working quickly, cut the apples into pieces and place into a deep freezer (to prevent them turning brown).

2 Combine the water, sugar and milk powder together in a saucepan. Place on a medium heat and bring to the boil.

3 Pass the syrup through a fine chinois and chill to 4°C.

4 Chop the fresh basil and mix with the lemon juice.

5 Place the syrup and frozen apples into a blender and purée. Pass through a fine chinois then add the basil and lemon juice.

6 Place the mixture into an ice cream machine to freeze.

CHEF'S TIP

It is important that the apples are frozen as quickly as possible to prevent discolouration.
The citric acid found in lemon juice will also help to retain the natural colour of the apple. Always use the green skin of the apple to help with the flavour and colour of the sorbet.

Chocolate sorbet

INGREDIENTS	4 PORTIONS	8 PORTIONS
Whipping cream	250g	500g
Fresh milk	500ml	1 litre
Caster sugar	50g	100g
Cocoa powder	100g	200g
Dark chocolate (70%)	15g	30g

Method of work

1 Combine the cream and milk in a saucepan and place on a medium heat.

2 Add the sugar and cocoa powder. Stir in well and bring the liquid to the boil.

3 Remove from the heat and stir in the chopped chocolate. Pass through a fine chinois and leave to cool then freeze in an ice cream machine.

COLD DESSERT RECIPES

Vanilla brûlée with passion fruit cream and apple and basil sorbet

INGREDIENTS	4 PORTIONS	8 PORTIONS
Coconut crisp		
Egg whites	40g	80g
Caster sugar	60g	125g
Desiccated coconut	75g	130g
White rum	6g	12g
Zest of lime	1 lime	2 limes
Passion fruit cream		
Passion fruit pulp	30g	50g
Lime juice	3g	7g
Vanilla	½ pod	1 pod
Caster sugar	30g	60g
Whole egg	33g	65g
Unsalted butter	50g	100g
Vanilla brûlée		
Egg yolks	27g	55g
Full fat milk	35g	70g
Double cream	90g	180g
Caster sugar	23g	45g
Vanilla pod	½	1
Gelatine	2 leaves	4 leaves

INGREDIENTS	4 PORTIONS	8 PORTIONS
Basil and pineapple base		
Water	500ml	1 litre
Caster sugar	150g	300g
Fresh basil	11g	22g
Sliced pineapple with the core cut out (6cm × 3cm)	4 slices	8 slices
Assembling the dessert		
Dried pineapple crisp	4	8
Sugar stick	4	8
Apple and basil sorbet (see recipe on p. 393)	4 quenelles	8 quenelles
Sauce Anglaise	60ml	120ml

Method of work

1 Preheat an oven to 210°C.

2 To make the coconut crisps, mix the egg whites and sugar together and add the coconut, white rum and lime zest.

3 Place between two sheets of silicone paper and roll out as thinly as possible. Put into a freezer to set and then cut individual discs out of the sheet.

4 Place the discs onto a baking sheet lined with a silicone baking mat. Bake for 2 minutes then reduce the oven temperature to 170°C for a further 7 minutes.

5 To make the passion fruit cream, place the passion fruit pulp, lime juice and vanilla into a small saucepan and bring to the boil.

6 Mix together the eggs and sugar. Add the boiled passion fruit to the eggs and mix well. Return to the saucepan and cook out the mixture to 85°C as for a crème Anglaise. Immediately cool the passion fruit cream over a bain marie of iced water.

7 Slowly beat the softened butter into the passion fruit cream. An electric mixer will ensure that the butter emulsifies with the passion fruit cream. Reserve in a refrigerator for later use.

Add the boiled passion fruit to the eggs and mix into the butter

Slowly beat the softened butter into the passion fruit cream

Bake the brûlée for 60 minutes or until just set

CHEF'S TIP

The method of producing the vanilla brûlée departs from the classical method because of the need to ensure that the brûlée is set sufficiently to support the sorbet. This is an example of changing the method of preparation and recipe to suit the requirements of a particular dish.

8 To make the vanilla brûlée, preheat an oven to 90°C. Mix all the ingredients together except the gelatine. Pour this into an ovenproof dish and bake in the oven for 60 minutes or until the brûlée has just set.

9 Soften the gelatine in some cold water and drain. Remove the brûlée from the oven and place into a food blender immediately with the gelatine and process to a soft, cooked liquid. Pour the liquid into individual small savarin moulds (preferably flexible silicone moulds) and freeze.

10 When frozen, de-mould and leave to defrost on a tray in a refrigerator.

11 To make the basil and pineapple base, place the water, sugar and basil into a saucepan and bring the contents to the boil.

12 Place the slices of pineapple into a high-sided tray and pour over the basil syrup and cover with plastic film. After the syrup has cooled, put the pineapple into a refrigerator and leave to macerate for 24 hours.

13 To serve, set the coconut biscuit in the centre of the serving plate. Place the pineapple slice on top and pipe the passion fruit cream into the centre of the pineapple.

14 Position the savarin ring of vanilla brûlée on top of the pineapple with the quenelle of sorbet on top.

15 Finish with a dried pineapple crisp and sugar stick and spoon the sauce around the plate.

Pour the basil syrup over the pineapple slices

Position the savarin ring of vanilla brûlée on top of the pineapple

Almond cake with fig ice cream and a red fruit soup

INGREDIENTS	4 PORTIONS	8 PORTIONS
Almond cake		
Double cream	120g	240g
Raw almond paste	90g	180g
Egg yolks	60g	120g
Egg whites	90g	180g
Caster sugar	45g	90g
Fig ice cream		
Pâte à bombe (see recipe on p. 376)	180ml	360ml
Fresh figs	200g	400g
Dried figs	50g	100g
Raspberry purée	70ml	140ml
Double cream	120ml	250ml
Red fruit soup		
Red fruit berries (such as raspberries, blackberries, redcurrants and strawberries)	500g	1kg
Demerara sugar	25g	50g
Vanilla	1 pod	3 pods

Method of work

1 Prepare individual round stainless steel moulds by brushing with melted butter and lining with silicone paper. Ensure the silicone paper is 3cm higher than the ring. Brush butter onto the inside of the silicone paper. Place the moulds onto a baking sheet lined with a silicone baking mat. Preheat an oven to 180°C.

2 Place the double cream, raw **almond paste** and egg yolks into a food blender and mix the ingredients together for a few seconds. Remove from the blender and place the almond mixture in a mixing bowl.

3 Create a meringue with the egg whites and caster sugar.

4 Carefully fold in the meringue to the almond mixture a little at a time to maintain the aeration as much as possible.

5 Pour the almond batter into the moulds to two-thirds full and bake in the oven for 10 minutes.

6 To make the fig ice cream, place the fresh figs, dried figs and raspberry purée into a food blender and liquidise.

7 Combine the fig purée with the pâte à bombe and mix in the double cream.

8 Freeze in an ice cream machine.

9 To make the red fruit soup, place the fruit, sugar and split vanilla pods into a stainless steel bowl and cover tightly with plastic film.

10 Place the bowl onto a saucepan of simmering water and turn the heat down low. Maintain this for 2 hours; the heat generated will cause the fruit to shed its juices.

11 Put the fruit through a chinois without squeezing. Reserve the juice warm for service.

12 To serve, place the warm almond cake in the centre of a bowl and spoon the fruit soup around it. Finely chop a fresh fig and place into the soup. Set a quenelle of the fig ice cream on top of the almond cake and decorate as required.

Terrine of two chocolates

INGREDIENTS	1 TERRINE	2 TERRINES
White chocolate mousse		
White chocolate	200g	400g
Whipping cream	300ml	600ml
Gelatine	2 leaves	3 leaves
Grand Marnier	15ml	25ml
Dark chocolate mousse		
Dark chocolate	200g	400g
Whipping cream	300ml	600ml
Additional preparations		
Sheet of Japonaise (40cm × 20cm; see recipe on p. 334)	1 sheet	2 sheets
Crème Anglaise	400ml	750ml
Grand Marnier	To taste	To taste
Segmented oranges	3	6
Fresh mint	5g	10g
Caramel sticks for garnish	2 per portion	2 per portion

Method of work

1 Line a terrine mould with plastic film. Carefully cut four strips of Japonaise. Place one strip in the bottom of the terrine mould and one on each side so that the mould is lined.

2 Melt the white chocolate in a bain marie to no more than 45°C. Meanwhile, half whip the cream. Soften the gelatine in cold water and squeeze out. Melt the gelatine with the Grand Marnier.

3 Fold the white chocolate into the whipped cream to create a smooth mixture and add the melted gelatine.

4 Deposit the white chocolate mousse into the lined terrine mould half way up. Put in a refrigerator to set.

5 Melt the dark chocolate and whip the second quantity of whipping cream in the same way. Combine the two ingredients carefully to a smooth mousse and deposit on top of the set white chocolate mousse.

6 Set a final strip of the Japonaise on top of the terrine to totally encase the mousses. Place in a refrigerator to set for 2 hours.

7 Chop the fresh mint into julienne and mix with the segmented oranges. Any residual orange juice can be added to the crème Anglaise with the Grand Marnier.

8 To serve, remove the two chocolate terrine from the mould and using a large knife that has been warmed in hot water, slice a generous portion of the terrine and set on a serving plate. Garnish with the salad of mint and orange and serve with the Grand Marnier sauce.

 CHEF'S TIP

Milk chocolate can be used as an alternative to white chocolate, but gelatine will not be required to set the mousse because of the presence of cocoa solids. Jaconde sponge or hazelnut Génoise could be used instead of Japonaise.

Bavarois Rubané *Ribboned Bavarois*

The ribboned Bavarois can consist of any number of colours and flavours, however pink or red (strawberry or raspberry), white (vanilla) and chocolate are the usual flavour combinations. On this occasion, we have combined chocolate, vanilla and pistachio.

INGREDIENTS	4 PORTIONS	10 PORTIONS
Bavarois base		
Fresh milk	400ml	1 litre
Egg yolks	3	8
Caster sugar	75g	200g
Leaf gelatine	6	14 leaves
Whipped cream	300ml	800ml
Additional flavours		
Split vanilla pod	1 pod	3 pods
Dark chocolate (70% cocoa)	40g	90g
Pistachio paste	To taste	To taste

Method of work

1 Soak the gelatine leaves in cold water for approximately 10 minutes to soften, then drain and squeeze to remove excess water.

2 Bring the milk to the boil and mix together the egg yolks and caster sugar.

3 When the milk has boiled, removed from the heat and mix carefully with the egg yolks and sugar mixture. Pour into the saucepan and return to the stove, stirring constantly while heating the mixture to 83°C or until it has cooked and coats the back of a wooden spoon. The mixture should not be allowed to boil.

4 Add the softened gelatine and stir in until dissolved.

5 Strain through a sieve or chinois and divide the mixture into equal portions in three separate bowls. Allow to cool, stirring occasionally.

6 Flavour each bowl with the required flavouring. Add the vanilla to the first by scraping the seeds out into the mixture. For the second, ensure that the chocolate has melted fully and add to the slightly warm egg mixture before it has completely cooled. For the third bowl add the pistachio paste until you are satisfied that the flavour and colour are correct.

7 When the vanilla mixture is cold, fold in a third of the whipped cream and pour into the selected moulds that you are using for the dessert. Allow to almost set in a refrigerator and then repeat the process with the chocolate mixture. Allow this to almost set also and then repeat this process once more for the pistachio mixture.

8 Allow to completely set in a refrigerator and remove from the mould when ready for service. Decorate as required with some crème chantilly.

Passion fruit mousse cake

INGREDIENTS	1 MOUSSE CAKE	3 MOUSSE CAKES
Passion fruit purée	280ml	575ml
Caster sugar	15g	30g
Lemon juice	½ lemon	1 lemon
Gelatine	6 leaves	12 leaves
Egg whites	120g	240g
Caster sugar	150g	300g
Water	50g	100g
Whipping cream	280ml	575ml
Dacquoise disc (see recipe on p. 333)	1 × 16cm	3 × 16cm
Biscuit jaconde	1 strip	3 strips
Glaze		
Cocoa powder	20g	40g
Stock syrup	100ml	240ml
Gelatine	2 leaves	3 leaves

 CHEF'S TIP

This recipe can be adapted to use other forms of fruit purées, such as banana, raspberry, cassis, mango and strawberry.

Method of work

1 Soften the gelatine in cold water and squeeze out the excess water once softened. Melt the gelatine in a bain marie.

2 Prepare a 22cm torten ring by lining the sides with the biscuit jaconde and placing the disc of dacquoise in the base.

3 Mix together the passion fruit purée, smaller quantity of sugar, lemon juice and melted gelatine. Leave to half set in a refrigerator.

4 Create an Italian meringue with the egg whites, larger quantity of sugar and water.

5 Softly aerate the whipping cream to a ribbon stage. Fold in the cream to the passion fruit purée and then gradually incorporate the meringue.

6 Set into the prepared torten ring and place in the refrigerator to set for 2 hours.

7 To make the glaze, soften the gelatine in cold water and warm up the stock syrup. Add the gelatine and allow to melt, then cool the syrup to 30°C. Lightly dust the top of the mousse cake with the cocoa powder and then quickly apply the glaze using a large palette knife. Return to the refrigerator to set. De-mould the ring when required for service.

Cappuccino crème brûlée

VIDEO CLIP
Brûlée

INGREDIENTS	4 BRÛLÉE	8 BRÛLÉE
Double cream	350ml	700ml
UHT milk	125ml	250ml
Strong espresso coffee	50ml	100ml
Tia Maria	2tbsp	4tbsp
Large egg yolks	6	12
Caster sugar	75g	150g
Demerara sugar	50g	100g
Vanilla foam		
Fresh full fat milk	120ml	240ml
Icing sugar	10g	20g
Vanilla	½ pod	1 pod
Powdered albumin	2g	4g

Method of work

1 Preheat an oven to 140°C.

2 Place the cream and milk into a heavy-based saucepan and bring to the boil. Add the espresso coffee and Tia Maria.

3 Beat together the egg yolks and sugar until pale. Pour the boiled mixture onto the egg yolks and mix well.

4 Pass the liquid through a fine chinois and pour into prepared coffee cups. Place the cups in a bain marie and bake in the preheated oven for approximately 50 minutes or until the brûlée is set. To test, the brûlée should be slightly wobbly and springy to the touch and the core temperature should read at least 80°C.

5 Remove from the oven and cool in a refrigerator.

6 To serve, sprinkle the demerara sugar on top and caramelise with a blowtorch.

7 For the foam, place the milk, sugar, vanilla seeds scraped from the pod and the dried albumin into a bowl. Using a hand blender, froth the milk quickly and spoon onto the top of the brûlée and serve immediately.

Garnishes and decorations: chocolate acetate collars

INGREDIENTS	20 COLLARS
Pre-crystallised chocolate	300g

Method of work

1 Cut acetate into a strip of the size required. Place on a clean, smooth surface.
2 Spread the chocolate thinly and evenly onto the acetate strip.
3 Leave to set slightly.
4 Form the acetate strip into a loop, or use it to line the inside of a mould, giving the collar shape. Allow for a 2cm overlap.
5 Leave to set and harden before carefully peeling away the acetate.

CHEF'S TIP

The acetate can only be used once. These collars can be used to contain desserts such as mousses, crèmes and cakes.

Garnishes and decorations: piped chocolate in sugar

INGREDIENTS	20 PIECES
Pre-crystallised chocolate	300g
Caster or demerara sugar	300g

Method of work

1 Evenly spread the sugar onto a tray.
2 Using a small piping bag, pipe the chocolate into your required design onto the sugar.
3 Leave to harden before removing and using as a decoration.

Garnishes and decorations: deep fried spaghetti sticks

INGREDIENTS	10 STICKS
Spaghetti sticks (dried)	10
Cocoa powder	50g

Method of work

1 Preheat a deep fat fryer to 170°C.
2 Dust the spaghetti sticks lightly in cocoa powder.
3 Place the spaghetti into the deep fat fryer and cook until browned and brittle (this may take 2 minutes).
4 Drain and dry. Use as a garnish for a dessert.
5 An alternative is to blanch the spaghetti in water and then refresh in cold water. Pat dry and pane in cocoa powder before deep frying. The effect produced will be more of a nest of coca pasta.

COCOA

Cocoa tree

Cocoa flower

Cocoa pod

The cocoa tree grows in warm and humid climates around the equator. Plantations can be found in the tropical rainforests of Africa, Asia and Latin America. Africa produces the largest proportion of the world harvest today, providing up to 65 per cent of the world's cocoa. The tree itself is quite fragile and needs other tall-growing plants, such as palm trees or banana plants, to give it protection from strong winds and the burning sun.

There are three principal varieties of cocoa, although many hybrids have been produced by chocolate companies over the years.

- *Criollo* – known as 'the king of cocoa' due to its exceptional flavour qualities, but is the most fragile variety.

- *Forastero* – this is a stronger type that is easier to cultivate and produces larger yields of cocoa. It has a stronger and more bitter flavour than the criollo and is usually blended with other varieties.

- *Trinitario* – this is a cross-breed of the criollo and forastero types and gives a strong but refined flavour.

VIDEO CLIP
Barry Callebaut Factory and Academy: types of chocolate

Harvesting takes place twice a year and is always undertaken by hand because of the delicate nature of the process. After the pods have been gathered, the outer shell is opened and the pulp is removed. The cocoa beans are then extracted from the pulp and then left to ferment for up to seven days. Fermentation is important for developing colour and flavour in the beans. After the fermentation, the beans are spread out to dry naturally in the sun for up to seven days. They are turned regularly to stop the fermentation process.

Before the cocoa beans can be processed into chocolate, beans from various origins are blended according to the requirements of the recipe. The cocoa bean shells are removed and the beans are broken down into 'nibs', which are then roasted to increase the flavour of the cocoa.

Cocoa pulp

Cocoa beans fermenting

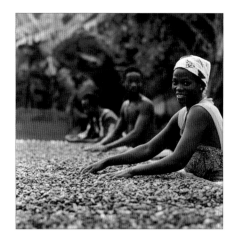

Fermented cocoa drying

The roasted cocoa nibs are then ground. The heat produced during this procedure melts the cocoa butter, which is removed by being pressed out. The cocoa solids will now be formed into a dry cake and used as the base ingredient in the production of chocolate or processed into a fine cocoa powder.

The next stage in chocolate making is conching, whereby the cocoa solids and cocoa butter are slowly mixed in tanks over a period of time. This develops the flavour of the chocolate and breaks down the particles into a smooth texture. Further ingredients are then added: cocoa butter, sugar, vanilla and soya lecithin. The chocolate is then tempered and set into blocks or drops, which are then packaged for storage and distribution.

Couverture is the term used for chocolate in which the fat content is pure cocoa butter. In family or bakers' chocolate the cocoa fat content is replaced by a vegetable-based fat. This has a detrimental effect on the texture and hardness of the chocolate but makes the product cheaper to purchase and easier to use. When used for making chocolates, decorations or moulded chocolates, couverture first has to go though a process of tempering called 'pre-crystallisation'.

MELTING CHOCOLATE

Melted dark couverture

Dark, milk and white couverture all contain cocoa butter. When the chocolate is warmed, the fat crystals in the cocoa butter melt and the chocolate becomes liquid. This starts to occur at 25°C, but cocoa butter contains a variety of fat crystals, some of which will not melt until a temperature of 37°C has been reached. To make sure that the mass of chocolate is totally melted it is common practice to heat the chocolate to 45°C. The following practices must be applied when melting chocolate:

- Ensure that the chocolate does not come into direct contact with the heat source otherwise it may burn.
- Use a dry bain marie or chocolate melting pot to prevent the chocolate coming into contact with moisture.
- If storing melted chocolate for a long period of time, it is important to stir the chocolate regularly to prevent the cocoa butter rising to the surface.

PRE-CRYSTALLISING CHOCOLATE

If chocolate has been melted at 45°C then poured into a mould and left to set without further processing, the following will occur:

VIDEO CLIP
Pre-crystallisation

- The chocolate will take a long time to harden
- When the chocolate has eventually hardened it will have a grainy structure and a greyish colour
- The chocolate will stick to the mould.

The reason for this is that as the chocolate cools, crystals form in the cocoa butter, but these crystals are unstable. Cocoa butter actually contains six different forms of crystal, but only one is stable. It is this form of crystal that makes chocolate hard and shiny with a deep and even colouring. The chocolate will also turn out of the mould easily.

There are several different techniques used to pre-crystallise chocolate; crystals can be created in melted chocolate through manipulation and temperature control or by adding chocolate that already contains the stable crystal.

Tabletop pre-crystallising

It is preferable to use a marble or a granite worktop, which will retain heat better than stainless steel.

1 Melt the chocolate to 45°C.
2 Stir well.
3 Pour two-thirds of the chocolate onto the work surface. Leave the remaining chocolate in the bain marie.
4 Spread the chocolate over the work surface, moving it around with a palette knife and a scraper. This movement cools down the chocolate mass evenly. The chocolate will begin to thicken as it cools. This is an indication the stable crystals are forming.
5 At 27°C the chocolate will be too thick to process and use. Return it to the bain marie and mix together well with the remaining warm chocolate.
6 This will create the right amount of stable crystals throughout the chocolate, which is now ready to use as required.

 CHEF'S TIP

Time, temperature and movement are the three essential factors in this method. If the chocolate is too thick after pre-crystallising, simply raise the temperature by 1°C to re-melt some of the stable crystals.

It is easy to focus on just the temperature when preparing chocolate. This will not guarantee that there are sufficient stable crystals present in the chocolate. Pre-crystallising is a form of 'tempering', in other words bringing the chocolate to a certain temperature. However, if the chocolate is just left to cool down to 32°C after melting, it will have been tempered but not pre-crystallised. Without the stirring and moving around of the chocolate required to form the crystals, the result will be a chocolate that hardens slowly, is dull and sticks in the mould.

The seeding method

This method uses ready-to-use pre-crystallised chocolate callets or small pieces of chopped chocolate block, which are added to the chocolate being processed.

1 Melt the chocolate to 45°C.

2 Stir well.

3 Add 15–20 per cent of callets or chopped chocolate block and stir well into the melted chocolate; these pieces contain the stable cocoa crystals. They will slowly melt and cool down the mass. When the chocolate reaches its correct processing temperature, stir well again; it will be completely pre-crystallised.

4 If all the crystals melt quickly before the correct temperature has been reached, just add a small extra quantity and stir in well until the correct temperature has been obtained.

CHEF'S TIP

To test if the chocolate if ready, dip the tip of a palette knife into the melted chocolate. It should harden within five minutes and have a nice sheen. If you have too few crystals the chocolate will not harden. If you have too many crystals the chocolate will not have a sheen.

Couverture callets

Stirring the callets into the chocolate mass

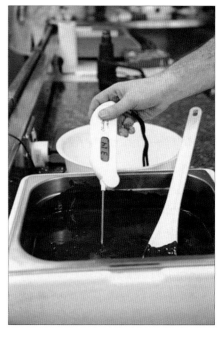

The correctly pre-crystallised chocolate

TEMPERATURE CONTROL FOR CHOCOLATE

The ideal processing temperatures after melting and pre-crystallisation are different for the three different types of chocolate (dark, milk and white). This is attributed to their different compositions; for instance, the higher the quantity of milk fats (milk and white chocolate), the lower the processing temperature.

Irregular cooling can create a dull appearance and a soft structure in the finished chocolate. The ideal temperature to cool and harden chocolate is 10–15°C. A refrigerator with air circulation set to this temperature range is ideal for setting chocolate.

Dark chocolate: processing temperature is 31–32°C

Milk chocolate: processing temperature is 30–31°C

White chocolate: processing temperature is 28–29°C

SHELF LIFE AND STORAGE OF CHOCOLATE

The ideal temperature for storing chocolate is 12–20°C, and the temperature should not fluctuate. At higher temperatures the chocolate becomes soft and will lose its sheen, and at lower temperatures it may be affected by condensation. Chocolate that has been stored at a lower temperature should, when required for use, be left to acclimatise in its original packaging for a few hours until it reaches ambient temperature.

Chocolate is sensitive to humidity and easily absorbs smells and flavours. It is also liable to oxidisation if it is exposed to light, direct sunlight and air for too long. Therefore, chocolate should be stored in a cool, dry place, completely sealed from light and air. Always ensure that the packaging is resealed after using.

Finished products are also very sensitive to temperature, foreign smells, flavours, light, air and humidity and to the effects of time and transportation. Typical changes that can occur during storage of chocolate products include:

■ *Fat bloom* – a thin layer of fat crystals on the surface of the chocolate. The chocolate loses its sheen and a soft, milky white bloom appears on the surface, giving the finished chocolate an unattractive appearance. Fat bloom is caused when fats in the chocolate crystallise or when the fats in the ganache/filling migrate to the chocolate layer. The appearance of fat bloom can be delayed by storing the chocolate at a constant temperature of 10–15°C.

 CHEF'S TIP

The ideal room temperature when working with chocolate is 20°C.

 CHEF'S TIP

Cocoa solids contain naturally occurring antioxidants. Since white chocolate contains no cocoa solids, it lacks these antioxidants and so will be more susceptible to oxidation than other chocolates.

 CHEF'S TIP

Chocolate should be stored in a well-ventilated area with no strong odours. Always ensure that the packaging is secure.

■ *Sugar bloom* – in contrast to fat bloom, sugar bloom creates a rough, coarse layer on top of the chocolate. Sugar bloom is mainly caused by condensation, which can form on the surface of chocolate if storage temperatures are too low or if the chocolate is left in a refrigerator for too long. This moisture will dissolve the sugar within the chocolate and when the moisture evaporates, the sugar re-crystallises on the surface. Avoid rapid changes of temperature to help prevent this occurrence.

If the storage time for chocolate can be kept short, the quality of the product will be much better. Each type of chocolate will have a different shelf life, which is measured from the initial production date and is shown on the packaging. Because of the milk fat solids present in white and milk chocolate, these have shorter shelf lives than dark chocolate. Chocolates that contain a filling need special consideration. Chocolates made with cream or butter fillings have a very short storage life (the recipes shown in this chapter have a shelf life of one week), provided they are stored in ideal conditions. The substitution of cream or butter with alternative ingredients (such as light sugar solutions) will help to increase shelf life.

RECIPES

Honey and cinnamon moulded chocolates

INGREDIENTS	40–50 CHOCOLATES
Dark chocolate (minimum 60% cocoa)	250g
Milk chocolate (minimum 32% cocoa)	250g
Double cream	250g
Clear honey	80g
Cinnamon	2 sticks or 20g powder
Pre-crystallised dark chocolate	50g
Pre-crystallised white chocolate for moulding	1kg

VIDEO CLIP
Moulding

Method of work

1 Place the double cream in a saucepan with the cinnamon and bring to the boil. Remove from the heat and leave to infuse for 15 minutes.

2 Melt the dark and milk chocolates together and add the cinnamon-infused cream. Blend well with a whisk.

3 Add the honey and allow the **ganache** to cool.

4 Prepare the chocolate moulds by polishing well with cotton wool to ensure there are no marks, dust or remaining chocolate.

5 Take a little pre-crystallised dark chocolate and using a plastic disposable glove, dip a finger into it. Rub some chocolate into each mould and leave to set.

6 If desired, at this stage a fine spray of coloured cocoa butter can be applied to build up a pronounced presentation of the finished chocolate. Leave to set.

7 Using the pre-crystallised white chocolate, fill the moulds. Shake out any air bubbles in the chocolate.

8   Pour out the excess chocolate and make sure all the edges and corners in the mould have been covered.

9   To leave a clean finish, remove any remaining chocolate from the top and the edges using a palette knife.

10 Invert the mould onto a wire rack or silicone paper for 4 minutes. Scrape off any remaining chocolate that has dripped down the mould and leave to harden for a few minutes.

11 Place the ganache into a disposable piping bag and pipe into the centre of each chocolate shell. Take care not to pipe too much ganache into the chocolate shell; it is best to leave a 2mm gap from the top. Make sure the ganache is not too warm otherwise it will melt the chocolate shell. Leave the filling to solidify.

12 To close the chocolates, put a small amount of the pre-crystallised white chocolate onto the mould and spread over each moulded ganache chocolate. Scrape off any excess chocolate and leave to set at 10°C for 30 minutes.

13 Tap the moulds gently onto a sheet of paper and carefully turn out the chocolates.

 CHEF'S TIP

Wear gloves when removing chocolates from the mould to avoid fingerprints.

The ingredients required for the ganache

Rubbing pre-crystallised dark chocolate into each mould

The moulds sprayed with coloured cocoa butter

Filling the moulds with pre-crystallised white chocolate

Pouring out the excess white chocolate

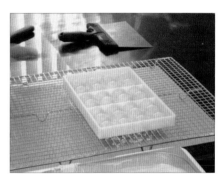
Inverting the moulds onto a wire rack

Scraping off the excess chocolate

The chocolate shells filled with ganache

Scraping off excess chocolate after closing the moulds

Raspberry moulded chocolates

CHEF'S TIP

Invert sugar is created by mixing basic sugar syrup with a small amount of acid, such as lemon juice or cream of tartar. This will break down the sugar (sucrose) into two simple sugars (fructose and glucose) and so reduce the size of the sugar crystals. Adding this to the chocolate filling recipe will help to create a smoother texture in the product.

INGREDIENTS	40–50 CHOCOLATES
Dark chocolate (minimum 64% cocoa)	300g
Raspberry purée	150g
UHT cream	125g
Caster sugar	10g
Invert sugar	25g
Unsalted butter	60g
Alcohol (framboise or kirsch)	15g
Pre-crystallised dark chocolate (minimum 64% cocoa) for moulding	1kg

Method of work

1 Melt the dark chocolate.
2 Place the raspberry purée, caster sugar and invert sugar into a saucepan and bring to the boil. Using a sugar thermometer, continue cooking the purée to 104°C.
3 Add the UHT cream carefully and stir in. Incorporate into the dark chocolate and add the alcohol. Leave to cool.
4 When cool, beat in the softened unsalted butter.
5 Follow the method for moulding the chocolates in the previous recipe, but using the dark chocolate.

Boiling the raspberry purée

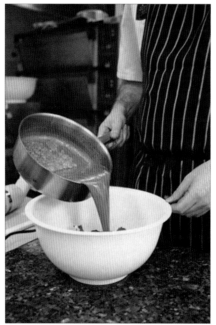

Pouring the cooked raspberry cream onto the dark chocolate

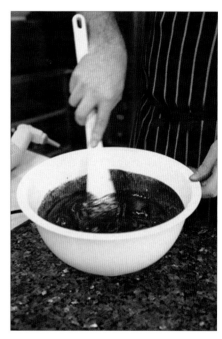

Mixing the ingredients together well to form a stable emulsion

Filling the moulds with the pre-crystallised dark chocolate

Pouring out the excess chocolate, tapping the base of the moulds with the handle of the palette knife

Starting to remove the excess chocolate

Sliding the edge of the palette knife down to the bain marie to collect the excess chocolate

Carefully removing any remaining chocolate

Letting the chocolate crystallise and harden before adding the filling

Vanilla chocolate truffles

INGREDIENTS	40–50 CHOCOLATES
Dark chocolate (minimum 70% cocoa)	400g
Whipping cream	325g
Milk chocolate (minimum 36% cocoa)	200g
Invert sugar	40g
Unsalted butter	50g
Vanilla	1 pod
Pre-crystallised dark chocolate (minimum 64% cocoa) for dipping	1kg
Cocoa powder	500g

Method of work

1 Melt the dark and milk chocolate together.
2 Bring the cream to the boil with the split vanilla pod. Remove from the heat and leave to infuse for 5 minutes.
3 Pour the infused cream onto the chocolate and add the invert sugar. Combine the ingredients well.
4 Beat in the softened unsalted butter when cold.
5 Fill a disposable piping bag with the truffle filling and pipe out small truffle shapes onto silicone paper. Leave to harden for at least 3 hours in a refrigerator.
6 Dip the individual truffles into the pre-crystallised dark chocolate. Shake off any excess chocolate.
7 Immediately place the truffles into a container filled with cocoa powder and roll until completely covered with a fine layer of the powder.

CHEF'S TIP

Alternatively, the truffles can be rolled in sieved icing sugar or small chocolate shavings for different effects.

Pralines

INGREDIENTS	40–50 CHOCOLATES
Milk chocolate (minimum 38% cocoa)	100g
Praline paste	220g
Pure hazelnut paste	50g
Unsalted butter	50g
Pre-crystallised milk chocolate (minimum 38% cocoa) for moulding	1kg

Method of work

1 Melt the milk chocolate to 40°C.
2 Add the praline paste and the hazelnut paste.
3 Blend together to form a smooth paste and beat in the softened butter.
4 Prepare the moulds using the pre-crystallised milk chocolate, as described previously (see page 409). An alternative is to marble with a little pre-crystallised white or dark chocolate to create an interesting design.
5 Pipe the praline filling into the prepared moulds and finish by topping off and leaving to set.

Acetate curls

1. Lay a sheet of acetate on a sheet of plastic film on a work surface. Pour some pre-crystallised chocolate onto the acetate and spread it over the surface evenly.

2. Leave the chocolate to begin to set. While the chocolate is still pliable and not fully hardened, quickly make curved cuts from the inside of the acetate to the edge, without cutting through the acetate.

3. Place a sheet of silicone paper over the acetate and quickly roll up the acetate before the chocolate sets. Leave to harden for approximately 15 minutes.

4. When the chocolate is set, carefully unravel the acetate sheet. The chocolate curls will break off where the cuts were made.

5. The finished curls ready for use.

VIDEO CLIP
Decorative acetate work

SUGAR CONFECTIONERY

Sugar confectionery has a long and widespread history. Honey was the first source of sugar and was used to conserve fruits, herbs and grains. The ancient Chinese and Egyptians coated fruits, flowers, grains and plants with honey and served them as sweet treats. The Greeks and Romans also used honey to conserve raisins and other fruits. The Roman Empire, which influenced cookery techniques across in Europe, introduced the first confiture (or preserved fruit) recipes.

Sugar cane was first discovered in the south Pacific, where the sweet juice was extracted by pressing the juice from the cane. Sugar manufacturing began in the eastern Mediterranean as the trade routes between Asia and the Western regions slowly developed. The Arabs appear to have been the first to use sugar to create confections such as almond paste.

Sugar confections developed rapidly after they were first introduced to the Europeans. During the crusades, Europeans came in contact with many new ingredients, including various spices and sugar cane. The chefs to the noble courts and royalty began to experiment with sugar and candy making, and recipes for sugar bonbons had appeared by the sixteenth century. Candies were developed and given as precious gifts for weddings, birthdays and religious festivals. They were mainly reserved for the upper classes because sugar was so rare and expensive at this time.

The further development of sugar confections expanded when sugar became more available and the price began to fall due to the new large sugar plantations in Europe's colonies and to the later discovery of beet sugar. By the eighteenth century, bonbons were being made by many artisans in Europe. In France, the confiseurs were known as *marchands de plaisirs* (pleasures sellers) and their bonbons were made with flowers, essences, oils and spices.

Today, most sugar confections are made in factories, although modern candies have developed from the long tradition of artisan candy making. Confiseurs can still be found in well-structured pastry kitchens, where they provide a selection of bonbons and produce basic pastry ingredients such as marzipan, raw almond paste, pralines, fondants and nougatines.

SUGAR CONFECTIONERY BASES

Most of the bases made by confectioners are also available as finished products under a range of different brand names. Today, most hotels, restaurants, caterers and even pastry shops will purchase them to help save time and improve consistency of the final product. However, it is crucial for a professional chef to have the knowledge and the skills to produce them. Creating these bases will produce finished products that are fresher and more individual than products made with industrially produced bases.

VIDEO CLIP
A sugar artist at work

■ *Marzipan* (almond paste) – A paste made of ground almonds (or almonds mixed with other nuts) and cooked sugar. Trimoline and sorbitol (used as stabilisers) and flavourings can also be added. This is a primary ingredient that is widely used in any pastry kitchen. Marzipan is also used in a number of sugar confections.

■ *Raw almond paste* – A paste made of ground almonds and sugar. This is a primary ingredient in the production of various cakes, such as pound cakes, sponges and pain de gênes.

■ *Praline* – a paste made of caramelised sugar and roasted hazelnuts. Praline is a primary ingredient in various pastry products, used to flavour candies or as a filling in chocolates and cakes.

■ *Fondant* – A cooked sugar syrup that is re-crystallised by mechanical agitation. It can be flavoured and coloured as required. In the past fondant was used extensively in sugar confections. Today it is mainly used for glazing or covering pastries, sweets, cakes and choux pastries.

■ *Nougatine* – A mixture of caramelised sugar with glucose and nuts. Unsalted butter and fresh vanilla can be added to improve the flavour. To protect it against humidity, a drying agent, such as powdered pectin, can be added. In the pastry kitchen it is used in mousses, ice creams, croquembouche and many chocolate fillings.

■ *Caramelised nuts* – caramelised, sugar-coated roasted nuts are used for a few sugar confections, but mainly in industrially produced candies or candy bars. They are also used in mousses, cakes and ice creams and in chocolate making.

■ *Sugar syrups* – These have many different purposes in candy making, and may be used either as part of the recipe or in a finishing process (dipped, crystallised, powdered or glazed). The most important characteristic of sugar syrups is their sugar density. This can be determined using a saccharometer or a refractometer and is measured in degrees **Baumé** or degrees **Brix.** Measuring sugar density is very important in the production of sorbets and sauces to help control the freezing process and consistency of a sauce.

SUGAR CONFECTION FAMILIES

Candies have been classified into groups based on a specific ingredient or a specific technique. Collectively they are called sugar confections or sugar candies (*bonbons de sucre*).

Lollipops

■ *Cooked sugars* – A sugar solution (often with the addition of glucose) is cooked until enough water evaporates to ensure the hard setting of the bonbon. These candies can be moulded, cut or pressed. Sugar and glucose syrups are both unflavoured and colourless, so the chef can be very creative in the choice of flavours and colours to be added. Examples of cooked sugars are lollipops and bonbons.

Caramels

■ *Caramels* – These are composed of sugar, water, milk, glucose and butter. The sugar is usually caramelised with the liquid content and then re-cooked to the desired temperature and colour. They are produced from light brown to darker shades, depending on the strength of flavour being sought. After cooking and cooling, they are cut and wrapped. Nuts or other flavours can be added. Among the most famous found in Europe are caramels with salted butter from Brittany and toffees from the United Kingdom. Chewy caramels, hard caramels and toffees all belong in this family.

Nougats

■ *Nougats* – The term 'nougat' is derived from the Latin word *nugatum* (of nuts), and there is a Roman recipe from **Apicius** made using nuts, honey and eggs. Nougat was first seen in Marseille and has became popular and famous throughout the south-eastern areas of France. There are four types of nougats in France:

– Nougat de Montélimar: 28–30 per cent almond content

– Honey nougat: minimum 20 per cent honey content

– Nougat provençale: 25 per cent honey with almond, coriander, hazelnuts and aniseed

– Black nougat: the same as provençale but not aerated or caramelised

The addition of egg whites or gelatine allows air to be incorporated to increase the volume and makes a difference in the texture between the nougats. Sugar and honey are cooked and then mixed with egg whites or gelatine. Roasted nuts, dried or candied fruits, and spices can be added and the nougats are cut when cold and set.

■ *Dragées* – These take their name from the popular almonds covered with honey favoured by the Greeks called *tragemata*. The first mention of dragées is found in the archives of the French town of Verdun (1220 AD). The technique used is to cover a whole nut or other filling in regular layers of sugar that are made hard and smooth. The centre can be made of whole nut, chocolate, nougat, marzipan or fondant. Dragées used to be made by hand, but today they are produced industrially in factories. The dragées are slowly covered with sugar syrup (maintained at a constant temperature) in a revolving pan until crystallisation takes place. They are traditionally used in Europe at celebrations of baptism and marriage.

■ *Gums* – Gums are centuries old, and in the past were used as medicines. They are made using gum Arabic, a natural vegetable substance. Purified, powdered and diluted in warm water, the gum is added to sugar syrup and glucose and then flavoured and coloured as required. Bonbons are then cast in starch moulds and when set are crystallised in sugar syrup before serving.

■ *Fruit jellies* – These delicacies are among the oldest candies and were introduced from the Far East along with candied fruits and the art of confiture. Fruit purées, sugar (a minimum of half the purée weight), glucose and pectin are cooked to the desired temperature. Pectin is added to help set the jellies and citric acid is mixed in prior to casting to ensure the setting of the pectin. Fruit jellies can be moulded and cut after cooling. They are usually covered with granulated sugar or crystallised in saturated sugar syrup.

■ *Liquorice* – Liquorice candies are made using a substance extracted from the root of the liquorice plant. This plant was valued in the Middle Ages as an aid in digestion, and at the end of the seventeenth century an Englishman was the first to use it to create a confection. The roots are cleaned and crushed before being heated in water. The solution is purified, filtered and concentrated to obtain the final flavouring. There are two kinds of liquorice: a hard type, made of liquorice, sugar syrup, glucose and gum Arabic, and a soft type, in which wheat flour and powdered sugar are added to liquorice flavouring and the candy is pushed through a machine to form strings or ribbons.

Liquorice

■ *Jams, marmalades and jellies* – Jams are made from whole or pieces of fresh fruits and are set with the aid of pectin. Marmalades are made from strained fruit purées such as Seville oranges. Jellies are made from strained fruit juice.

Jellies

■ *Candied fruit* – Fruit is dipped into a sulphur bath before being blanched in hot water and candied in a sugar solution. The sulphur lightens the original colour of the fruit and kills any bacteria that could later cause fermentation. Blanching is a crucial step. If the fruit is not blanched enough it may dry out and impart an unpleasant colour. If it is blanched too much, the fruit may become too soft and will result in a compôte texture being produced where the fruit structure breaks down. The fruit is soaked in a hot sugar solution, which rises slightly in density over time, to reach the centre of the fruit and so preserve it.

■ *Sugar-coated fruit* (*fruits déguisés*) – Fresh, dried or candied fruits or fruits shaped out of marzipan are covered in a protective shell of either crystallised sugar or cooked (coloured and flavoured) sugar.

■ *Fudge* – this is a soft caramelised sugar confection with added cream. It is usually cut into squares and served in many different flavour combinations, such as vanilla, chocolate, coffee or rum and raisin.

Fudge

MARZIPAN

Marzipan has been used for centuries by pastry chefs all over the world. It is a favoured delicacy in many European countries and can be used in baking, confectionery, biscuits, breads, gâteaux, torten and cakes. Marzipan is a sweet, pliable mixture of almonds and sugar. It is sometimes tinted with food colouring and modelled into a variety of decorative shapes.

Recent studies into the history of marzipan have shown that *marci panis* has had a long and complex journey. During the thirteenth century in such places as Venice, Naples, Sicily and Provence various spices and sweets were presented in thin wooden boxes. These boxes were called *mazaban* and eventually this word must have extended its meaning to cover its contents. In other languages this became *marzipan* (German), *marchpane* (English), *marzapane* (Italian) or *massepain* (French).

Marzipan is now known to have originated in Asia, where the delicate almond/sugar mixture was served at the sultan's table as the crowning of a meal. Through Arabian rule, marzipan reached Spain and Portugal, and during the crusades it spread through the rest of Europe via the largest trading port of the area, Venice.

Once in Europe, marzipan was produced in the early days by the apothecaries; it was well known as a remedy into the eighteenth century. In the fourteenth century, marzipan was used for artistic creations and figurines modelled by hand. Lübecker marzipan was first mentioned in the city's guild rolls in 1530. Lübeck's reputation as the City of Marzipan and its dominance in the production of marzipan was established after 1800. Much of this dominance was due to new production technology being introduced and the marzipan houses of the area being able to source the highest quality ingredients from around the world while still keeping to traditional recipes.

> **VIDEO CLIP**
> Moulding a marzipan rose

Lübecker marzipan

Lübecker marzipan has a great tradition and is world-renowned. Among the many companies that have set the standards for this type of marzipan, two stand out: Carstens and Niederegger. But what distinguishes Lübecker marzipan from other products?

The basic elements of marzipan are a marzipan paste and sugar. Marzipan paste is generally 75 per cent almonds and 25 per cent sugar, the almonds being roasted and blended together with the sugar. It is the relative proportions of marzipan paste and sugar that helps to determine the flavour and quality of Lübecker marzipan. A Lübeck Fine Marzipan contains up to 90 parts marzipan paste to 10 parts sugar.

Marzipan legislation

For a paste to be classified as a marzipan or almond paste it must not have less than 23.5 per cent dry almond content and not less than 75 per cent of the remaining content should be sugar. This standard does not, however, apply to items such as cake decorative figures and **petit fours**. With the high cost of almonds, other cake covering pastes are beginning to be used in place of traditional marzipan in some areas of confectionery. These have an almond content of less than 23.5 per cent and so cannot be called marzipan.

MARZIPAN RECIPES

Boiled marzipan

INGREDIENTS	900G MARZIPAN	2KG MARZIPAN
Caster sugar	400g	1kg
Water	240ml	600ml
Ground almonds	300g	750g
Egg white (lightly beaten)	1 egg	2½ eggs
Almond flavour (optional)	To taste	To taste
Icing sugar	100g (approximately)	225g (approximately)

Method of work

1 Place the sugar into a clean pan with the water and cook to 118°C (soft ball stage) and observe all the sugar boiling rules (see page 462).

2 Remove the pan from the heat and carefully add the almonds and flavour if required.

3 Add the lightly beaten egg white then return to the heat to cook for a further 2 minutes, stirring constantly.

4 Place the paste into an electric mixing machine with a paddle attachment and slowly beat, adding a little icing sugar, to create a smooth consistency to the paste.

5 Turn the paste out onto a marble work surface and knead until smooth and cool. Wrap the marzipan well in plastic film and store in a dry, cool area.

Raw marzipan *Pâte d'amande cru*

INGREDIENTS	700G MARZIPAN	1.6KG MARZIPAN
Icing sugar	450g	1kg
Ground almonds	250g	600g
Egg white (lightly beaten)	2 eggs	5 eggs
Additional icing sugar	50g (approximately)	100g (approximately)

Method of work

1 Sift the icing sugar and ground almonds together twice and place into a clean stainless steel bowl.

2 Make a well in the centre and add the lightly beaten egg white. Stir together to form a smooth paste.

3 Turn out onto a clean work surface and knead until smooth. Add the additional icing sugar if the paste is initially too wet. Wrap the marzipan well in plastic film and store in a cool area, such as a refrigerator.

Marzipan déguisés

INGREDIENTS	10 DEGUISES	20 DEGUISES
Cooked marzipan	50g	100g
Dried dates	10	20
Cointreau or kirsch (to flavour the marzipan)	To taste	To taste
Colour	As required	As required
Granulated sugar	250g	500g
Liquid glucose	30g	60g
Water	50g	100g

Method of work

1 Flavour and colour the marzipan as required.

2 Cut an incision lengthways into the date and remove the stone if still inside. Stuff the dates with small pieces of the marzipan and remould to their original shape. Leave to dry out for at least one hour.

3 Boil the sugar and water together, adding the glucose at 104°C. Cook the sugar solution further to 156°C and then immediately arrest the cooking by plunging the pan into a bowl of cold water for 10 seconds.

4 Carefully dip the dates into the hot sugar and leave to set on a lightly oiled marble worktop or a silicone baking mat.

5 Keep in a dry, airtight container until required.

Stuffing the dates with small pieces of marzipan

Plunging the pan into a bowl of cold water

Carefully dipping the dates into the hot sugar

Lemon and almond marzipan bonbons

INGREDIENTS	35 BONBONS	70 BONBONS
Granulated sugar	350g	700g
Liquid glucose	40g	80g
Water	100g	200g
Skinned whole almonds	350g	700g
Cooked marzipan	175g	325g
Sugar syrup (at 30B°)	100g	200g
Trimolene	30g	60g
Blanched lemon zest	1 lemon	2 lemons
Unsalted dry butter	60g	120g
Crystallisation syrup (saturated sugar solution)		
Granulated sugar	1375g	2725g
Water	500g	1000g

CHEF'S TIP

Cover the candissoire with a paper that will absorb the humidity (not silicone paper), if you notice a delay in the crystallization process. The size of the crystals on the paper will be the size they are on the candies.

Method of work

1 Boil the sugar and the water, adding the liquid glucose at 104°C. Continue boiling until 119°C has been reached.

2 Grind the almonds to a powder using a food blender, then slowly pour in the hot sugar solution and blend for 30 seconds.

3 Add the marzipan, trimolene and the syrup at 30B° and continue mixing for another 5 minutes using an electric mixing machine with the paddle attachment.

4 Add the blanched lemon zest, and when the mixture is cold add the unsalted **dry butter**. Roll into small, evenly sized bonbons.

Method of finishing

Very clean equipment and utensils are needed for this task.

1 Place the sugar and the water into a clean saucepan and slowly bring to the boil, stirring to dissolve the sugar solids.

2 Skim the sugar syrup just before it comes to the boil to remove any impurities. When the sugar boils, clean the sides of the saucepan with a clean brush and clean water. Skim off any impurities as it boils.

3 Boil the syrup for 1 minute, then cover with plastic film and allow to cool down without stirring, to prevent any premature crystallisation.

4 Place the bonbons to be candied on a wire rack that fits in a shallow tray (candissoire). Ensure the bonbons do not touch each other so that they can be evenly coated. Pour the sugar syrup over the bonbons very slowly (to help obtain small crystals) until the syrup reaches the top of the bonbons.

5 Invert a rack over the bonbons if needed to keep them in place and leave them in the candissoire at room temperature until the syrup has cooled to about 40°C.

6 Cover the candissoire with baking parchment. Do not move the container in which the bonbons are crystallising otherwise the crystals will shift and start growing on other parts, rather than on the actual bonbons.

7 Let the bonbons crystallise for 17–20 hours, or more, depending on how dry the surrounding environment is. When the crystals reach the desired size, drain the bonbons on the bottom of the rack for 1 hour and remove them to a clean rack to dry until they are not sticky (this can take up to 6 hours). Keep the bonbons in an airtight container in the refrigerator at 5°C until required.

Bonbons to be candied placed on a wire rack that fits a shallow tray

Pouring the sugar syrup over the bonbons very slowly

Draining the bonbons on the bottom of the rack

SUGAR CONFECTIONERY

Sucrose, the main constituent of cane and beet sugar, is one of a number of natural sweeteners used in the professional kitchen. These sweeteners form part of a larger group of commodities known as carbohydrates. Carbohydrate molecules are made up from atoms of carbon, hydrogen and oxygen and are arranged as chains of simple sugars:

■ *Monosaccharides* – a single sugar unit, such as glucose or fructose
■ *Disaccharides* – are made up of two joined monosaccharides, for example sucrose, lactose or maltose
■ *Polysaccharides* – these are long chains of monosaccharides and form starches

Sucrose is the most common sugar in our diet and consists of one molecule of glucose and one of fructose.

Glucose syrups are created by breaking down starch molecules found in wheat, maize and potatoes. The polysaccharides are broken down by heating the starch with an acid. When sugar (sucrose) is heated with an acid present (such as cream of tartar or lemon juice) a process called 'inversion' takes place. The sucrose is split evenly into fructose and glucose, which is termed 'invert sugar'. An invert sugar is sweeter than a sugar solution and will have a similarly small crystal size. Invert sugar inhibits crystal formation.

Cooking sugar

VIDEO CLIP
Boiling sugar for catering

When boiling sugar it is important to observe the correct procedures and rules to prevent the sugar re-crystallising:

1 Ensure cleanliness of the equipment and the ingredients at all stages of the boiling process. A copper pan should be cleaned with an acid (lemon juice) and scouring material (salt) and rinsed under cold water to ensure absolute cleanliness. All other equipment should be scrupulously cleaned. The sugar thermometer should be placed into cold water and brought to the boil on a stove.

2 Dissolve the sugar in the water completely over a low heat before boiling.

3 If scum forms on top of the sugar solution during boiling, remove it using a spoon or strainer (this could be the impurities from the actual sugar). Repeat until no more scum forms.

4 When the sugar solution begins to boil, brush the insides of the hot pan with a brush and clean cold water.

5 Add the glucose or invert sugar at 104°C.

6 Boil the sugar rapidly and continuously measure the temperature using a sugar thermometer.

7 Arrest the cooking once the desired temperature is obtained by dipping the base of the saucepan into some iced water for 8–10 seconds. Wipe the base of the saucepan dry.

Measuring the density of sugar solutions

Many different types of pâtisserie, dessert and confectionery goods require the use of a sugar solution, such as sorbets, ice creams and preserved fruits. The density of a sugar solution is measured using a saccharometer, and the units of measurement used are either degrees Baumé or degrees Brix.

Always ensure that the temperature of the sugar solution to be tested is 20°C. This is because the density changes with temperature. Put the sugar solution into a suitable container, a 500ml measuring jug is ideal, and place the saccharometer into the solution. Take the reading where the scale on the side of the saccharometer meets the surface of the solution. The density of the sugar solution can be adjusted as required: add a thicker syrup at the same temperature to increase the density or add water to decrease the density.

The following chart is designed to give the chef a working reference of the sugar to water ratios required to produce certain degrees of density. Although this book concentrates on degrees Baumé, the Brix measurements are also included:

WEIGHT OF SUGAR TO BE ADDED TO 450ML WATER	DENSITY REQUIRED	DENSITY REQUIRED
GRAMS	BAUMÉ: B°	BRIX: °Bx
51	5.6	10
74	7.8	14
100	10.0	18
144	13.3	24
204	17.0	31
255	20.0	36
317	22.5	41
480	28.0	51
742	33.5	62
1010	37.1	69
1083	40.0	75

During the sugar boiling process the water evaporates and so the solution becomes denser, which will result in the solution setting firm when cold. The thicker the sugar solution, the more the temperature increases, and it is by reading the changes in temperature that we can determine the physical change in the sugar solution. The chart below shows the changes that occur at different temperatures and the use of the sugar solution at each stage. The solution can be tested by dropping a small amount from a clean spoon into a bowl of very cold water and then quickly examining it or picking it up with the fingers to check the setting consistency.

TEMPERATURE: °C	NAME OF DEGREE	HOW TO TEST	USES
104	Boiling	Look for agitation of liquid surface	
107	Thread	At this relatively low temperature there is still a lot of water left in the syrup. Take a little of the solution between the thumb and finger and separate them to form an elastic thread of sugar	Stock syrup and some icings
110	Pearl	The thread formed by pulling the sugar solution may be stretched. When a spoon is dipped into the syrup and then raised, the syrup runs off in drops	Jelly, candies and some icings
113	Soufflé	The syrup spins a 5cm thread when dropped from a spoon	Delicate sugar candy and syrup
115	Feather	The film of sugar can be blown into feather-like pieces	Jams and confiture
118	Soft ball	A small amount of syrup dropped into chilled water forms a soft, flexible ball, but flattens after a few moments in the fingers	Fudge, fondant, pâte à bombe, Italian meringue and classic butter creams
121	Hard ball	The sugar concentration is much higher, which means less moisture in the sugar solution. Syrup dropped into chilled water may form into a ball that holds its shape on removal. The ball will be firm, but its shape can still be changed by squashing it.	Nougat, marshmallows
132–138	Soft crack	At this stage, the moisture content is low. Syrup dropped into chilled water separates into hard but pliable threads. They will bend slightly before breaking	Rock sugar
138–155	Hard crack	At these temperatures, there is almost no water left in the sugar solution. Syrup dropped into chilled water separates into hard, brittle threads that break when bent	Can be poured and pulled to make presentation displays
170	Light caramel	The sugar solution turns amber due to caramelisation. The sugar is beginning to break down and form many complex compounds that contribute to a rich flavour	Sauces and glazes
178–180	Dark caramel	A darker caramelisation has now occurred	Dessert decorations

SUGAR CONFECTIONERY RECIPES
Vanilla fudge

CHEF'S TIP

Derivatives of this recipe include:
Coffee – add diluted instant coffee to taste
Chocolate – add dark couverture (minimum 68 per cent cocoa solids) at the mixing stage. Do not add the chocolate earlier or it may burn.

INGREDIENTS	30–40 PIECES	80–100 PIECES
Granulated sugar	225g	450g
Soft brown sugar	225g	450g
Liquid glucose	110g	225g
Unsalted butter	110g	225g
Double cream	140ml	280ml
Vanilla extract	To taste	To taste

Method of work

1 Place all the ingredients into a large, clean saucepan and place on a medium heat. Boil steadily to 118°C. Remove from the heat.
2 Using a clean wooden spoon, stir constantly until the boiled mixture begins to grain.
3 Pour into a shallow tray that is lightly oiled (or lined with silicone paper) and allow to cool and set completely.
4 When set, cut into squares.

Pâte des fruits

INGREDIENTS	1 SMALL SLAB (18 × 18CM)	1 LARGE SLAB (36 × 36CM)
Raspberry purée	425g	850g
Apricot purée	250g	500g
Powdered pectin	20g	40g
Caster sugar	75g	150g
Granulated sugar	750g	1.5kg
Liquid glucose	175g	350g
Tartaric acid	5g	10g
Water	3g	5g

Method of work

1 Place the purées together in a clean heavy-based saucepan. Mix the powdered pectin with the caster sugar and whisk into the fruit purées. Bring to the boil.
2 Add the granulated sugar and the glucose. Stirring constantly, bring the temperature of the boiling mixture to 107°C.
3 Dissolve the tartaric acid in the water and add to the cooked fruit paste.
4 Line the bottom of a frame with silicone paper and pour the fruit paste into the frame. Leave to cool.
5 Remove from the frame, peel off the silicone paper carefully then cut the set fruit into 2.5cm squares and roll in granulated sugar.

Sugar candy lollipops

INGREDIENTS	10 LOLLIPOPS	20 LOLLIPOPS
Isomalt	100g	200g
Granulated sugar	350g	700g
Liquid glucose	150g	300g
Water	160g	340g
Yellow colour	As required	As required
Lemon flavouring	As required	As required

Method of work

1 Place the isomalt, granulated sugar, glucose and water in a heavy-based saucepan and boil to 140°C.

2 Add the colour and flavouring and continue boiling until 155°C has been reached. Arrest the cooking by plunging the base of the saucepan into cold water for a few seconds.

3 Pour the candy solution into lightly oiled individual stainless steel rings on a silicone baking mat and leave to cool slightly. Remove the rings and push lollipop sticks into each candy as required.

4 Leave to fully set and cool down. Remove from the silicone mat and store in an airtight container.

Mint chocolate caramels

INGREDIENTS	45 CARAMELS	90 CARAMELS
Double cream	350g	700g
Cubed sugar	200g	400g
Liquid glucose	200g	400g
Trimolene	50g	100g
Red colour	As required	As required
Dark couverture (minimum 64% cocoa solids)	120g	240g
Cocoa paste (100% cocoa solids)	60g	120g
Mint flavouring	To taste	To taste
Unsalted butter	40g	80g

Method of work

1 Boil together the cream, sugar, liquid glucose and trimolene in a heavy-based saucepan to 118°C.

2 Add the cocoa paste, couverture, colour, mint flavour and butter and stir in well off the heat.

3 Pour the mixture into a lightly oiled shallow stainless steel tray and leave to cool and set.

4 When it is cool enough, remove carefully from the tray and cut into 2.5cm slabs. Store in an airtight container prior to use.

Nougat Montélimar

INGREDIENTS	30 PIECES	60 PIECES
Granulated sugar	210g	420g
Clear honey	60g	120g
Water	50g	100g
Liquid glucose	60g	120g
Egg whites	25g	50g
Glacé cherries	30g	60g
Blanched pistachio nuts	30g	60g
Flaked almonds	20g	30g
Chopped hazelnuts	20g	30g

Method of work

1 Bring the sugar and water to the boil in a heavy-based saucepan. Add the honey and the liquid glucose at 107°C. Skim off any impurities that reach the surface of the boiling sugar solution.

2 Boil to 137°C. Meanwhile, aerate the egg whites to soft peaks and slowly pour in the hot syrup while still beating. Continue beating until the mixture becomes firm.

3 Warm the cherries and nuts in an oven for a few minutes and carefully combine into the cooked meringue mixture.

4 Pour the mixture into a shallow tray lined with rice paper. Place a further sheet of rice paper on the top of the nougat and weigh down with a flat board. Leave to set for 24 hours before turning out and cutting into small pieces.

5 Store in an airtight container if not required immediately.

Sugar-dipped fruit *Fruits glacés*

INGREDIENTS	20 DIPPED FRUITS	40 DIPPED FRUITS
Cube sugar	240g	480g
Liquid glucose	20g	40g
Water	70g	140g
Fruits to be dipped		
Grapes	As required	As required
Cherries	As required	As required
Mandarin orange	As required	As required
Strawberries	As required	As required

CHEF'S TIP

It is important to store these dipped fruits in a dry, airtight container. Sugar is hygroscopic and so will attract moisture in damp or cold environments. Dipped fruits are usually made at the last moment before being served.

Method of work

1 Prepare the fruit carefully, taking care not to bruise or cut the skins or membranes. Any leakage of liquid from the fruit will immediate begin to break down the sugar once the fruit has been dipped and will result in re-crystallisation. Cherries and grapes should be cut into pairs and kept on the stalk.

2 Place the fruit onto a wire rack and place on top of an oven or a warm place to dry their surfaces.

3 Bring the sugar and water to the boil in a heavy-based saucepan. At 104°C, add the liquid glucose. Continue boiling to 155°C (hard crack stage). Remove from the heat and arrest the cooking.

4 Dip the fruit into the sugar. Use a small set of tweezers to avoid burning the fingers. Ensure each fruit is fully dipped and that no part of the fruit is left without a covering of sugar.

5 Quickly transfer the dipped fruits onto a lightly oiled, clean marble slab or a silicone baking mat to set.

Vanilla macaroons

INGREDIENTS	40 MACAROONS	80 MACAROONS
Icing sugar	300g	600g
Ground almonds	75g	150g
Egg whites	90g	185g
Granulated sugar	85g	180g
Liquid glucose	45g	90g
Water	35g	70g
Egg whites	85g	180g
Vanilla	To taste	To taste

Method of work

1 Preheat an oven to 210°C.

2 Mix together the icing sugar, ground almonds and the larger quantity of egg whites to a paste.

3 Meanwhile, bring the sugar and the water to the boil in a heavy-based saucepan. Add the glucose at 104°C and continue boiling until 118°C has been reached.

4 Whisk the smaller quantity of egg whites to a soft peak. Slowly pour the boiled sugar syrup into the whisked egg white. Continue whisking until cold to create an Italian meringue.

5 Carefully fold in the meringue into the ground almond mixture. Add the vanilla at this stage. Place the mixture into a piping bag with a plain tube.

6 Pipe the macaroons onto a silicone baking mat and let them dry for 30 minutes at room temperature.

7 Place the macaroons into the oven. After 3 minutes reduce the heat to 170°C and bake for a further 6 minutes.

8 Remove the macaroons from the oven and place onto a wire rack to cool. Carefully remove the macaroons when they are cool. Pipe a little butter cream, ganache or apricot jam onto the underside of a macaroon and then stick two macaroons together.

CHEF'S TIP

It is simple to create different flavours to this recipe:
Lemon – add the finely grated zest of lemon
Orange – add the finely grated zest of orange
Pistachio – add some pistachio paste to taste
Raspberry – add raspberry flavour and colour

Florentines

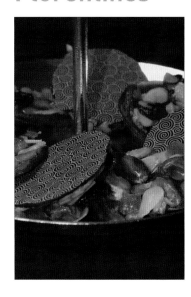

INGREDIENTS	70 FLORENTINES	150 FLORENTINES
Unsalted butter	150g	300g
Caster sugar	200g	400g
Clear honey	50g	100g
Double cream	100g	200g
Mixed peel	100g	200g
Chopped walnuts	100g	200g
Flaked almonds	200g	400g
Pistachio nuts	100g	200g
Raisins	50g	100g
Tempered dark couverture	500g	1000g

Method of work

1 Preheat an oven to 200°C.

2 Place the butter, sugar and cream into a heavy-based saucepan and bring to the boil. Add the clear honey at 104°C and continue boiling to 115°C.

3 Remove from the heat and add all the nuts and fruit. Stir in well and pour the mixture onto a silicone baking mat. Place another mat on top and spread the mixture evenly between the two mats. Place in a freezer.

4 When the mixture has just frozen, cut out 2.5cm discs and place onto a baking tray lined with a silicone baking mat.

5 Place into the oven and bake for 12 minutes.

6 When the Florentines are baked they may spread a little. Let them cool before cutting them back to the required shape using a plain cutter.

7 Dip the base of each Florentine into the melted chocolate and set on an embossed plastic chocolate mat until the chocolate has set.

8 Reserve in an airtight container until service.

ADDITIVES USED IN SUGAR WORK AND CONFECTIONERY

- *Ascorbic acid* – Ascorbic acid (vitamin C) is an **antioxidant** and is used to conserve the colour of a product (for example, poached fruits).

- *Tartaric acid* – This acid is found in many types of fruit, but it is always extracted industrially from grapes. The crystals are large and clear. One part of boiling water dissolves two parts of tartaric acid. Tartaric acid enhances flavours and brings tartness. It is also an antioxidant, so it improves colours and aromas. This is added to sugar to help prevent the sugar from crystallising.

- *Citric acid* – Usually extracted from lemons, citric acid is used with cream of tartar in fondants or cooked sugar to make them softer and more pliable. It is also used to stabilise the albumin in whipped egg whites.

- *Agar-agar* – Also called Japanese isinglass, agar-agar is derived from seaweeds found in the Pacific and Indian oceans. It expands in cold water but does not dissolve. It only dissolves in boiling water after a certain amount of cooking. Agar-agar is used in bonbons, jellies and even jams. The powdered form is the easiest to use.

- *Pectins* – Pectin is a gelling agent found in fruits. It is usually extracted from crushed apples but is also derived from citric fruit rinds. Pectin is used in powder form in gums, fruit jellies and jams. It maintains the moisture in gum candies and fruit jellies. Adding an acid such as citric, lactic or tartaric to a recipe using pectin causes the pectin to set:

  - *Pectin NH* is used in fruit glazes and fruit fillings; its gelling effect is reversible by heating and it holds well on fruit

  - *Pectin (medium rapid set)* is especially well-suited for making fruit preserves and jellies; setting does not occur too rapidly, thereby increasing the time a product can be worked, for example casting fruit jellies in individual starch or Flexipan moulds

  - *Yellow pectin* is used in fruit jellies; its gelling effect is not reversible by heating. When using this pectin, it should be 1–2 per cent of the overall weight of the mix

- *Gums* – These are neutral substances derived from trees. There are several varieties of gum of which three are used in sugar confections:

  - Gum Arabic
  - Gum tragacanth
  - Fruit-tree gum

  Dissolved gums provide an elastic consistency. Gums dissolve slowly in cold water but quickly in boiling water. The alcohol contained in gums is forced to evaporate, making the product thicker and gummier, until it finally solidifies into a transparent mass that shows no traces of crystallisation.

 CHEF'S TIP

Sweetening power is a measure of how much (in percentage) a substance will increase the sweetness of the product that it is being added to.

- *Gelatine* – Colourless when pure, gelatine is extracted from the bones and cartilage of animals. It is used in sugar confections to set whipped pastes and jelly candies. Bringing gelatine to the boil will not destroy its gelling property, but boiling the gelatine for an extended amount of time will reduce it gelling power. Gelatine is bloomed (softened) in cold water and will absorb from five to ten times its weight in water.

- *Sorbitol* – This is used to stabilise moisture and prevent mould and bacterial growth and as a sweetener in low-sugar or sugarless desserts. Sorbitol prevents the drying of cakes, macaroons and sponges. It also helps to preserve freshness and flexibility in almond paste, ganache, praline paste and fruit jellies. Sorbitol has a solid content of 95 per cent and a sweetening power of 55 per cent.

- *Dextrose* – A form of pure glucose (99.5 per cent), supplied as a fine white powder. Dextrose is used as a stabiliser and as an anti-crystallising agent in ice cream and sorbets, and it has many uses in baking. It has a solid content of 95 per cent and its sweetening power is 70 per cent.

- *Glucose* – A monosaccharide sugar produced by the breaking down of starch found in potato, wheat or maize. It is used as an anti-crystallisation agent in the cooking of sugar.

- *Sodium bicarbonate* – Also known as baking soda, sodium bicarbonate is a salt that acts as a leavening agent and conserving agent. It is used to raise the boiling point of a liquid, and therefore speed up the boiling process.

SUGAR RECIPES

Fondant

CHEF'S TIP

Convenience fondant is often used in the pastry kitchen because it is reliable, consistent and saves time. Fondant can be used for cooking in place of sugar – it has the advantage of already having undergone a degree of inversion.

INGREDIENTS	500G OF FONDANT	1KG OF FONDANT
Granulated sugar	480g	960g
Water	125ml	250ml
Cream of tartar	1tsp	2tsp

Method of work

1 Bring the sugar and water to the boil in a heavy-based saucepan. Add the cream of tartar at 104°C.

2 Continue boiling until 115°C has been obtained.

3 Pour the sugar solution on a very lightly oiled marble slab.

4 Splash the surface of the sugar with a little cold water and let the temperature drop to 100°C. Agitate the sugar with a clean spatula. The mass will become thicker as it cools and as the agitation continues.

5 When the sugar solution has become stiff and hard to work, knead by hand into a smooth, plastic paste.

6 Cover with plastic film or polythene to prevent skinning and use as required.

Assessment of knowledge and understanding

You have now learned about the use of the different types of complex hot, cold and frozen desserts and how to produce some garnishes and sauces utilising an array of commodities and techniques.

To test your level of knowledge and understanding, answer the following short questions. These will help to prepare you for your summative (final) assessment.

Quality identifications

1 Explain the importance of selecting the correct type, quality and quantity of ingredients when producing an ice cream.

2 State the quality points to look for when producing a crepe soufflé.

3 Explain why we need to pre-crystallise couverture.

Equipment and materials

1 State two advantages of using an electric mixer for producing a pâte à bombe.
   i) _____ ii) _____

2 Identify the difference between a Swiss and an Italian meringue.

3 State the ideal refrigeration temperature for setting chocolate.

4 Explain the importance of using a sugar thermometer.

Preparation methods

1 Briefly describe how to produce a vanilla ice cream.

2 Explain how pasteurisation plays an important part in ice cream making.

3 Explain the correct procedure for melting chocolate.

4 State the procedure for preparing sugar for boiling.

Cooking methods

1 State how a crème brûlée is tested in order to see if it is correctly cooked.

2 State the temperature for baking the following:
   (a) Chocolate fondant _____ (b) Vanilla soufflé _____

3 Identify the critical quality points for the following products:
   (a) Chocolate sorbet

   (b) Iced parfait of strawberries

   (c) Crème mousseline

CHEF'S PROFILE

Name: TONY HOYLE

Position: Head Pastry Chef

Current job role and main responsibilities: Managing the pastry kitchen of a 230-room five-star hotel, with three restaurants and large conference and banqueting facilities. We have 13 chefs in the pastry kitchen and 90 chefs in all in the kitchens. We produce all the food in house, from our vienoisserie, chocolates, ice creams, breads, petits fours, plated desserts and buffet desserts to our artistic chocolate and sugar showpieces.

When did you realise that you wanted to pursue a career in the catering and hospitality industry?

I enjoyed cooking from an early age. My father was a chef. He prompted me to work with him for a while when I left school and it took off from there. I started my career in the hot kitchen but I was soon captivated by the creativity and artistry of the pastry kitchen. It was in large hotel kitchens and Michelin-starred restaurants that I did most of my training and discovered the world of French pâtisserie. So the next step was to work in France, which totally opened my eyes to how wide and diverse the field of pastry work is. I then spent the next few years learning all I could about all aspects of my profession. I have since been fortunate to be Pastry Chef in some of the most renowned hotels in London.

What do you find rewarding about your job?

My greatest pleasure in the kitchen has to be chocolate work. I am a bit of an obsessive about chocolate, unfortunately it is little understood as an ingredient and is not the single-flavour commodity that most people perceive it to be. At The Grove we use a number of different chocolates blended from some of the finest cocoa in the world.

What do you find the most challenging about the job?

For me the most interesting field of pastry work is running a large five-star hotel pastry kitchen. There is always so much going on; every day is different and brings new challenges. You get to work with people of the same mentality, who strive to produce the best they can for our guests and to make The Grove a special place to visit.

Who is your mentor or main inspiration?

I draw my inspiration from many different sources: books, travelling, looking at what our competitors are doing by eating out, trade magazines and sometimes by just taking ingredients and playing around with flavour and texture combinations. Most importantly, I talk to the members of my team for their ideas and menu suggestions.

What traits do you consider essential for anyone entering a career as a chef?

Be obsessive about food, work in the best establishments you can and listen to your chef. Watch how they work. Try and have an idea of where you want to be and set yourself goals. Too many people enter this profession as a last resort and have no idea what they want to do with their careers. Learn by your mistakes and don't take criticism personally. Get used to working when most people are out enjoying themselves.

Can you give one essential kitchen tip or technique that you use as a chef?

Always treat people with respect and as you would like to be treated yourself.

Whipped milk chocolate ganache, spice cake, vanilla jelly and honeycomb ice cream

INGREDIENTS

Milk chocolate ganache

Whipping cream	225g
Milk chocolate (40% pistoles)	350g
Invert sugar	50g
Whipping cream	500ml

Tuile mix

Flour	100g
Butter	100g
Sugar	100g
Egg white	100g

Spice cake

Water	450ml
Sugar	200g
Honey	450g
Strong flour	450g
Baking powder	2g
Ground mixed spice	5g
Bicarbonate of soda	25g
Grated lemon zest	1 lemon
Grated orange zest	1 orange
Clarified butter	280g

Vanilla jelly

Bottled still water	600ml
Agar-agar	5g
Sugar	30g
Leaf gelatine	1 leaf
Tahitian vanilla pods	2
Orange blossom honey	100g

Honeycomb

Sugar	200g
Golden syrup	75g
Glucose syrup	225g
Bicarbonate of soda	30g

INGREDIENTS

Honeycomb ice cream

Milk	500ml
Whipping cream	250ml
Egg yolk	120g
Sugar	70g
Invert sugar	25g
Malt extract	35g
Horlicks	100g
Glucose powder	25g
Milk powder	25g
Stabiliser	3g
Chopped honeycomb	40g

Method of Work

1 To make the ganache, boil the 225g of cream and the invert sugar.

2 Pour the hot liquid onto the chocolate pistoles.

3 Using a handheld blender, mix together to form a smooth emulsion.

4 Cool to 40°C and blend in the other amount of cream. Refrigerate overnight.

5 Whip on the KitchenAid mixer to the consistency of soft whipped cream.

6 To make the tuile, mix the dry ingredients together.

7 Whisk in the egg white then the melted butter, then rest in the fridge for 1 hour.

8 Take a little of the mixture and colour red with powder colour.

9 Cut a 10cm plastic tuile stencil.

10 Place the stencil on a silpat and spread the red mix inside the stencil.

11 On top of this, spread the plain mix so the two mixes have a marbled effect.

12 Bake in a deck oven at 160°C for approximately 10 minutes .

13 When baked, take off the mat and wrap round a 25mm tube until set.

14 Pipe the whipped ganache to fill the tube then dip each end in chopped peanut brittle. This must be done at the last minute to avoid the tuile going soft.

15 To make the spice cake, boil together the honey, water, zests, sugar and spice.

16 Mix together the dry ingredients, then pour on the liquid and whisk together.

17 Add the butter and rest in the refrigerator overnight.

18 Spread in a biscuit frame 5mm thick.

19 Bake at 180°C for approximately 20 minutes.

20 When cool, cut into rectangles 30mm x 105mm.

21 To make the jelly, split the vanilla pods and scrape out the seeds.

22 Boil the water, vanilla and honey and leave to infuse for 1 hour.

23 Mix the sugar and the agar-agar. Whisk into the liquid and bring back to the boil.

24 Pass through a fine sieve.

25 Spread 3mm thick onto a tray lined with acetate.

26 When set, cut into rectangles 105mm x 35mm.

27 To make the honeycomb, boil together the sugar, glucose and golden syrup to 145°C.

28 Sieve the bicarbonate of soda into the hot liquid.

29 Mix well then pour onto a tray lined with silicone paper to cool.

30 When cold, chop up into 3mm pieces.

31 To make the ice cream, mix the dry powders with the sugar.

32 Whisk the milk into the powders.

33 Add the cream, malt and invert sugar and bring to the boil.

34 Whisk some of the liquid onto the yolks.

35 Whisk this into the rest of the liquid and cook gently to 82°C to pasteurise the mixture.

36 Pass through a fine sieve and leave to cool in the refrigerator overnight.

37 Freeze in the ice cream machine then mix in the honeycomb pieces.

38 To assemble, place the vanilla jelly on the plate.

39 Onto this put the spice cake rectangle.

40 Onto this put the ganache-filled tube.

41 You can decorate this with a chocolate curl garnish and gold leaf.

42 Serve with a fresh raspberry sauce.

43 Scoop the ice cream and sit on almond streusel pieces.

CHEF'S PROFILE

Name: BEVERLEY DUNKLEY

Position: Head of UK Academy

Establishment: Barry Callebaut UK Ltd

Current job role and main responsibilities: To plan and organise all activity which takes place in the Barry Callebaut UK training Academy. This activity includes a variety of courses for chocolatiers, bakers, pâtissiers and pastry chefs plus bespoke customer training days.

When did you realise that you wanted to pursue a career in the catering and hospitality industry? From a very early age – I told my parents when I was 8 years old that I wanted to be a cook. At that age I was making cakes, and by the age of 11 I was cooking the family Sunday roast!

Training:

1   Peterborough Technical College: City and Guilds 706/1 and 2 Food Preparation and Cookery
2   Birmingham College of Food, Tourism and Creative Studies: City and Guilds 706/3, Parts 1 and 2 Advanced Pastry
3   Grantham College of Further Education: City and Guilds 730/7 Teacher's Certificate
4   University of Central Lancaster: City and Guilds Certificate of Education
5   Lancaster and Morecambe College: TDLB Training Assessor Awards D32/D33/D34/D36

Experience:

1   Barry Callebaut (UK) Ltd, Global Chocolate Manufacturer: Account Manager/Head of UK Academy
2   Lancaster and Morecambe College of Further Education: Lecturer of NVQ Patisserie levels 1, 2 and 3
3   Cooper Group, Bakery Supply of Ingredients and Equipment: Sales and Demonstrator
4   Oberweis, Relais Dessert in Luxembourg: Pastry chef for petits gâteaux
5   Edward Notters Sugar School, Zurich: School technician
6   Hambleton Hall, Relais Chateaux Hotel in Rutland: Head Pastry Chef

What do you find rewarding about your job?

Meeting new people. Watching people learn new skills and develop their careers and businesses. The commercial side of the business is also engaging; controlling the planning and budgeting of the Academy courses as well as actually promoting the desire to work with chocolate.

What do you find the most challenging about the job?

Making sure a specific course meets the expectations and needs of all attendees. After two successful years the challenge is to continually raise the standards and variety of the courses we run, and to increase the chocolate skills of chocolatiers, pastry chefs and bakers.

What advice would you give to students just beginning their career?

Just enjoy – absorb as much knowledge as you can from all sources, be that from lecturers, work colleagues, websites, books and exhibitions. This information is invaluable. Catering is a fantastic career that can diversify into so many other areas of industry. It is also a wonderful opportunity to travel and work all over the world.

Who is your mentor or main inspiration?

In the early years it would have been the Roux brothers, but with each stage of my career development I have been lucky enough to have a mentor figure to learn from and who has given me inspiration.

What traits do you consider essential for anyone entering a career as a chef?

Catering is all about passion. People work well beyond their paid hours to gain satisfaction from their work and are not driven by a nine-to-five job.

- Have the motivation to be a team player, work well under pressure and like challenges.
- Be respectful to others and learn from their experience and knowledge.
- Be prepared to relocate and relish the opportunity to travel in order to gain experience, whether in England or abroad.
- Have high values and do your best everyday.
- Be flexible and accept change within your job role. Never accept complacency and embellish the latest trends in the marketplace with new ingredients and techniques.

Can you give one essential kitchen tip or technique that you use as a chef?

Preparation is the key to success.

Raspberry and Saffron Ganache

INGREDIENTS

Whipping cream	100g
Raspberry coulis	100g
Saffron fibres	0.5g
Callebaut 823 chocolate	600g
Freeze dried raspberry pieces to decorate	

Method of work

1 Bring the cream, raspberry and saffron fibres to the boil.

2 Sieve onto the melted chocolate.

3 Blend together to make an emulsion.

4 Pour into a frame (1cm in thickness) and allow to crystalise over night.

5 Spread a thin layer of pre crystalised chocolate on one side of the Ganache.

6 Cut into desired shape.

7 Cut 2cm squares of clear stiff clear transfer sheet.

8 Dip the individual chocolates into pre crystalised Callebaut 823 Chocolate.

9 Whilst the chocolate is still wet sprinkle with a few pieces of freeze dried raspberry and then place a clear transfer sheet square directly on top of the dipped chocolate.

10 Allow to cool at least twenty minutes before the clear plastic is removed.

CHEF'S PROFILE

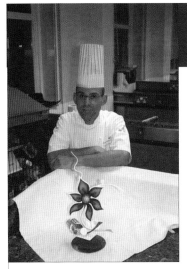

Name: JAVIER MERCADO

Position: Pastry Chef Lecturer

Establishment: Westminster Kingsway College

Current job role and main responsibilities: I am a tutor for a group of 16-year-old first year professional chefs (Diploma/NVQ). I also teach the pastry side of the foundation chef's degree course.

When did you realise that you wanted to pursue a career in the catering and hospitality industry? At the age of 19.

Training: Johnson E Wales University, Providence, Rhode Island, USA: AAS IBPI Applied Science Degree.

Experience:

1 R.D. Corporate Assistant Pastry Chef for Aibert Uster imports, Maryland, USA
2 Pastry Chef for the RitzCarlton Group, Virginia, USA
3 Pastry Chef for the Westin Hotel Group, St. Croix, US Virgin Islands

What do you find rewarding about your job?

The ability to create artistic impressions using my imagination and other inspirations.

What do you find the most challenging about the job?

The heat/rain, which acts as a reminder of what mediums I utilise to achieve a final end product.

What advice would you give to students just beginning their career?

Stay focused. Respect the instructors' advice, and if you work hard, always believe in yourself.

Who is your mentor or main inspiration?

Ewald Notter and Stephan Klein – I look up to them and they have given me the drive to push my skill level. Their works are simply awesome.

What traits do you consider essential for anyone entering a career as a chef?

The ability to remain practical and to never lose sight of their goals. If you are motivated, success will follow.

A personal profile:

My interests include airbrushing, sugar artistry and chocolate work.

- Best Taste Award, World Chocolate Masters 2006
- Most Creative Award, World Chocolate Masters 2004
- Best in Class, Sugar Category, Hotelympia 2006
- Best in Class, Sugar Category, Hotelympia 2004
- Gold Award, Chocolate Category, Hotelympia 2004

Can you give one essential kitchen tip that you use as a chef?

Place a sheet of silicone paper on top of an induction hob, underneath the saucepan. If a product (liquid) spills, carefully remove the sheet and dispose. This leaves the hob always looking clean.

CHEF'S RECIPE

Yellow submarine: banana and cinnamon ganache

INGREDIENTS	YIELD
For the filling	
Whipping cream	180g
Ground cinnamon	2tsp
Cocoa Barry Blanc Satin couverture coins	684g
Liquid glucose	10g
Fresh banana, very ripe, chopped	135g
Salt	Pinch
For the coating	
Cocoa Barry Excellence 55% couverture coins	100g
Cocoa Barry Blanc Satin couverture coins	800g
Yellow cocoa butter	30g

Method of work

1 To make filling, bring whipping cream and cinnamon to boil. Add white chocolate and glucose and stir until melted. Add banana and salt. Puree mixture and cool to room temperature.

2 Wearing disposable gloves, rub a little tempered dark chocolate for coating, into the moulds in a swirl and leave it to set slightly then rub the yellow cocoa butter evenly over the entire surface of mould. Leave to set fully.

3 To coat the moulds, fill with white tempered chocolate. Scrape top level. Tap moulds to release any air bubbles. Drain out excess chocolate. Scrape the top again and then place mould – still inverted – onto a sheet of baking parchment and leave for a few minutes.

4 Lift moulds off baking parchment and scrape off excess chocolate. Chill them until set. Remove from fridge and leave for about 5 minutes before filling.

5 Warm ganache slightly until runny and fill squeezy bottle or piping bag. Pipe into cavities. Return moulds to fridge until ganache skins over.

6 Remove chocolates from fridge for at least 10 minutes to allow plastic moulds to warm slightly. Pour a thin layer of tempered white chocolate over tops and quickly scrape smooth. Return moulds to fridge until chocolates have set. Then remove from fridge and un-mould.

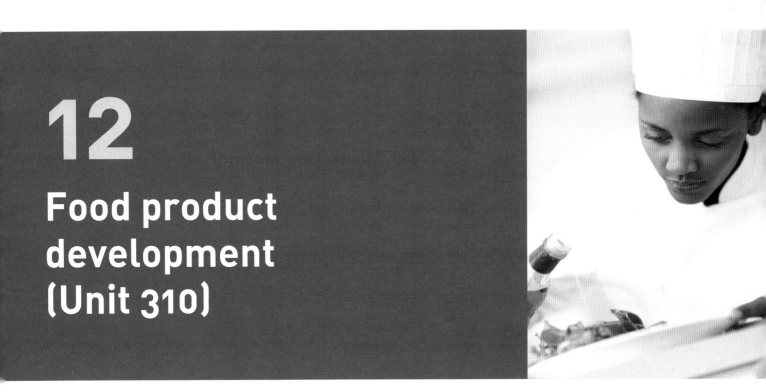

12

Food product development (Unit 310)

LEARNING OUTCOMES

The aim of this chapter is to help the candidate develop the necessary knowledge and understanding of how to research, design, develop and evaluate new food based products to meet current market requirements.

There is **one** principal outcome in this chapter. At the end of this chapter the candidate will be able to:

■ Research, design, develop and produce food products

INTRODUCTION

Developing new food products for commercial or restaurant high-street markets is a time consuming and complex process. Even after the successful introduction of a new product, recipe or dish, the quality must still be frequently improved to ensure continued success in an extremely competitive marketplace.

Innovation is a hot topic in the food industry. There are many different approaches to creating new innovative concepts, recipes and products, so what makes your approach unique in the commercial world of food development? Do you emphasise the commercial value of ideas? Do you create ideas that address the needs of consumers? Do you understand the business-related implications of those ideas, whether they be product development, scale-up, or production concerns? The figure below shows in schematic form the continual process of development and how the concept of development is cyclical and does not stop.

Diagram of the development cycle

The first area that needs to be explored is the concept of research and idea generation.

RESEARCH AND IDEA GENERATION

Brainstorming, or idea generation, is a critical process in new product development that needs to be planned and creatively managed. Idea generation can often be a neglected component of new product development efforts. Large companies invest heavily in research and development yet the emphasis always seems to be on pure research rather than the creative process of generating ideas. Successful idea generation is part of the pursuit for an undiscovered idea or a new dish to enhance your menu.

The first stage is to determine where you want your product to fit. You could be designing a product for any one of the following areas:

1 To enter a professional cookery competition.

2 To balance or enhance a new restaurant menu.

3 To create a new convenience product.

4 For a new airline, ferry or train menu.

Creative techniques that help to realise new opportunities can be: personal interviews, group reviews, brainstorming, written exercises or content analysis. The key to the idea generation approach is to:

▓ Capture a vision of your specific market from different angles (e.g. that of your customer).

▓ Create a positive environment to collaborate, create ideas and problem solve directly with customers and potential customers.

▓ See the problem from many different perspectives . . . of the customers, the production team (chefs), the food and beverage service workers and the complainers.

▓ Think big . . . without any constraints.

▓ Use data from as many sources as possible.

▓ Work in teams to successfully brainstorm.

Many creative-thinking sessions suffer through people trying to force ideas. It is best, therefore, if people work in groups to create a creative environment. Research on idea generation suggests that participants often have their best ideas after the session, not during it. It is important to be mindful about valuing the sessions for their contribution to the process, without pushing too hard for instant results.

Consumer insight

One of the most important factors in making innovative concepts successful in the marketplace is to understand consumer reactions to the concepts early in the development process. You should choose a relevant consumer service that will help you obtain insights on your concept. Questionnaires need to be designed not only so as to provide a strong quantitative analytical basis, but also to include qualitative research that helps you look beyond the data.

Various types of research activities can help obtain both research and data by establishing an extensive customer database to answer your questions and give opinions. From this, you can begin to gauge how well your concept will be received.

Sensory analysis (or **sensory evaluation**) is a scientific discipline that applies the principles of experimental design and statistical analysis to the five human senses (sight, smell, taste, touch and hearing) for the purposes of evaluating consumer products. The discipline requires panels of assessors, on whom the products are tested and the responses recorded. By applying statistical techniques to the results, it is possible to draw conclusions about the tested concept or product. Most large consumer goods companies have departments dedicated to sensory analysis.

 CHEF'S TIP

A **quantitative analyst** is a person who works using numerical data to give information based on questionnaires (e.g. how many people questioned liked vanilla).

Qualitative research is a method of investigation, traditionally found in market research. Qualitative researchers aim understand human behaviour in depth and the reasons that govern such behaviour (i.e. why a customer might like a certain flavour).

Market Trends

The food product and restaurant market is affected by changing social and economic patterns. Many people have a greater income today, for example, as compared with 20 years ago. People lead busier lives now, meaning they might do more shopping in supermarkets rather than in traditional shops and buy more ready-made meals or eat out instead of cooking for themselves.

In order to take account of these lifestyle changes food developers and chefs need to constantly rethink the type of foods and dishes required for supermarkets and restaurant menus. Customers expect to find a wide range of foods which includes overseas dishes and food ingredients. There are several reasons for this:

- We travel abroad more frequently and so are exposed to many new types of food.
- We live in a multicultural community made up of a number of different races and religions – many with their own traditional cuisines.
- There are numerous cookery programmes on television that encourage people to try new food ideas.

Many factors affect what people choose to eat. These include age, habits and the presentation of food. Consumers are becoming more concerned about what they eat.

This might be because they have special dietary requirements, which mean they cannot eat certain products for religious or political reasons, or because certain foods make them feel unwell. Some consumers are demanding healthier foods. Healthier diets have less fat, sugar, salt and more fibre. People who are concerned about health, diet and the environment look for products that are healthier and use specific ingredients such as organic and Fair Trade.

THE DEVELOPMENT STAGE

Actually producing the concept is the next stage in food product development. All data and analysis that has been collected should now be used to develop the dish or the concept. It is here that you will prepare, cook and present your product.

In order to achieve this stage you will need to provide accurate food orders containing the types of ingredient that you will be using. You will need to continually adjust and adapt the concept until you feel that it is ready to be presented for consumers to evaluate, using the development cycle described earlier in this chapter.

The following form can be used to help record and evaluate your dish or concept:

	Dish/Concept 1	Dish/Concept 2	Dish/Concept 3
Name of the product			
Presentation			
Flavour			
Texture			
Aroma			
Ease of service			
Additional comments			

Quality assurance and implementing your concept

Quality assurance is a promise from the manufacturer to the customer that their food meets a clear, consistent set of standards. There should be quality control checks at all key stages in the production of your concept and the results of the checks written down. This is called a quality assurance system.

Quality control (QC) checks will normally include the following:

- Weight checks to make sure the product is the prescribed weight.
- Visual checks to make sure that presentation is accurate.
- Temperature checks to make sure the product is being kept at an appropriate temperature.

- pH checks to make sure the food has the correct acidity/alkalinity. (This is used especially for products such as chocolates which may have a long shelf life.)
- Microbiological checks to make sure bacteria are not at harmful levels.
- Chemical checks to guard against chemical contamination.
- Ingredient checks to ensure the provenance of all ingredients.
- Final check the sampling of the final product to check its flavour, texture and aroma. This is sometimes undertaken during a kitchen service (in a restaurant environment).

Some of these QC checks are to do with food safety. Food manufacturers use a system called Hazard Analysis Critical Control Points (HACCPs) to help identify what could go wrong in the production process, and to establish checks that will prevent or reduce the risk of biological, physical or chemical hazards. Checks take place at three separate stages:

1 The design stage.
2 The manufacturing stage (including Hazard Analysis Critical Control Points [HACCP]).
3 The end of the manufacture process: checking consistency of shape, size, appearance, taste and textures of manufactured foods.

A quality management system (QMS) is a specialised way of documenting a quality assurance (QA) system to make sure it has been implemented properly. Companies that use a QMS to maintain high QA standards receive a certificate that is recognised within the industry, called ISO 9000. The QMS covers:

- The quality of raw materials used
- The details of the recipe used to make the product
- The processes and techniques used to make the product
- How the raw materials are stored
- How the finished product is stored
- Details of the procedures for risk assessment.

Glossary of terms

00 flour Speciality flour used in pasta making as it has a high gluten content

à la (French) 'In the style of', such as: à la Française (the style of the French)

à la bourgeoisie (French) The style of the family (family style)

à la broche (French) Cooked on a skewer

à la carte (French) Items on the menu that are priced individually and cooked to order

à la Florentine (French) 'In the style of Florence'. Generally refers to dishes served on a bed of spinach and gratinated with sauce Mornay

à la Française In a French style

à la minute (French) Cook food at the last minute

à la Provençal (French) Dishes prepared with garlic and olive oil

à la Russe (French) In the Russian style

à point (French) Food cooked just to the perfect point of doneness: when cooking beef steaks, 'à point' means that a steak is cooked medium

abats (French) Offal

acetic acid A natural organic acid present in vinegar and citrus juices

acidulate To give a dish or liquid a slightly acidic, tart or piquant taste by adding some lemon juice, vinegar, fruit juice. Also, one can acidulate fresh cream by adding lemon juice to get sour cream.

acidulated water Water to which a mild acid, usually lemon juice or vinegar, has been added to prevent sliced fruits (especially apples and pears) and peeled or cut up vegetables (such as artichokes and salsify) from turning dark during preparation

additives, food Substances added to food to maintain or improve nutritional quality, food quality and freshness. Additives are strictly regulated. Manufacturers must prove the additives they add to food are safe

agar-agar An extract of seaweed from the Indian and Pacific Oceans. When dissolved in water, it will set into a jelly on cooling. Often used as a vegetarian substitute for gelatine

ageing A term used to describe the holding of meats at a temperature of 1–4°C for a period of time to break down the tough connective tissues through the action of enzymes, thus increasing the tenderness

agneau (French) Lamb

al dente Italian for 'to the tooth': refers to the firm but tender consistency of a perfectly cooked piece of pasta

albumen The protein portion of the egg white, comprising about 70 per cent of the egg. Albumen is also found in animal blood, milk, plants and seeds

almond paste A confectionery preparation consisting of ground almonds mixed with a sugar solution to form a paste. Sometimes referred to as marzipan it can be a raw paste or a cooked paste

aloyau de boeuf Sirloin of beef

amandine (French) Prepared with or garnished with almonds

ambient temperature Room temperature

amuse bouche This is a pre-starter or mouth pleaser given as an opening for the coming menu

Anglaise (French) English style

antioxidants Substances that inhibit the oxidation of meat, vegetables and fruit. They help prevent food from becoming rancid or discoloured

Apicius Marcus Gavius Apicius, born around 25 AD, is credited with writing cookery books and devising recipes. His book *Cuisine in Ten Books* was used as a reference work for several centuries

appareil A mixture of different ingredients to be used in a recipe

aromates A mixture of herbs and spices used to increase or bring out flavours in a dish

arrowroot The starch extracted from the stems of certain tropical plants. A fine, white powder, it is used to thicken sauces and soups and certain desserts

ascorbic acid Vitamin C

aspic Clear savoury jelly

au blanc (French) Meaning 'in white'. Foods, usually meats, that are not coloured during cooking

au bleu 1. A term for the cooking method for trout: 'Truite au bleu'. The fish is taken from a fish tank, killed, gutted, trussed and slid into boiling court bouillon. The fish skin is not washed. This gives a characteristic silver blue finish to the finished dish.
2. A steak cooked very rare

au four Baked in the oven

au gratin (French) Food topped with a sauce and cheese or breadcrumbs, then baked or glazed under a salamander

au jus (French) Served with natural juices

au lait (French) With milk

au naturel (French) Food that is cooked simply, with little or no interference in its natural appearance or flavour

au vin blanc (French) Cooked with white wine

bacteria Micro-organisms that can cause food poisoning

baguette A French bread that is formed into a long, narrow cylindrical loaf. It usually has a crisp brown crust and light, chewy interior

bain marie (French) Water bath used to cook or store food

bake To cook in an enclosed oven

baking powder A raising agent consisting of bicarbonate of soda and cream of tartar. It is commonly used in the baking of cakes

ballotine A prepared meat, poultry, game or fish dish where the flesh is boned out, rolled and tied before cooking whole; sometimes stuffed with a farce or mousseline

bard To wrap meat, poultry or game with bacon or pork fat. The bard will render during cooking and impart succulence and flavour

barquette Boat-shaped pastry case or mould

baste To pour drippings, fat, or stock over food while cooking

Baumé The Baumé scale is a hydrometer scale developed by French pharmacist Antoine Baumé in 1768 to measure density of various liquids. Notated variously as degrees Baumé, B°, Be°, Bé°, Baumé

bavarois A cold dessert made from a cooked egg custard set with gelatine and lightened with whipped cream

beard The common name for the hair-like filaments that shellfish such as oysters and mussels use to attach themselves to rocks. They must be trimmed before the shellfish are prepared

beat To introduce air into a mixture using a utensil such as a wooden spoon, fork or whisk, in order to achieve a lighter texture beurre blanc A sauce made with reduced alcohol or vinegar and shallots into which butter is whisked

beurre fondue Melted butter

beurre manié A raw mixture of flour and butter in equal quantities used as a thickening agent

beurre noir Black butter; can be served with skate wings and brains

beurre noisette Nut-brown butter served with fish meunière

bicarbonate of soda An alkaline powder: used to soften water for cooking vegetables and is one of the main ingredients of baking powder

blanch To place foods in boiling water or oil briefly, either to partially cook them or to aid in the removal of the skin (e.g. nuts, tomatoes). Blanching also removes the bitterness from citrus zests

blend To mix together ingredients, usually of different consistencies, to a smooth and even texture, utilising a utensil such as a wooden spoon or blender

blind bake To bake pastry without a filling. Metal weights or dried beans are usually used to keep the pastry from rising

blinis Pancakes made from buckwheat flour and yeast

boil To bring a liquid to boiling temperature and to maintain it throughout the cooking time

boil rapidly Food is submerged into boiling liquid over a high heat and the bubbling state is maintained throughout the required cooking period. This method is also used to reduce sauces by boiling off the liquid and reducing it to a concentrated state

bouchee A small puff pastry case with high sides and a hollow middle

bouillon 1. Any broth made by cooking vegetables, poultry, meat or fish in water. The strained liquid is the bouillon, which can form the base for soups and sauces. 2. A salt paste used as a stock

bouquet garni A faggot of herbs and aromatic vegetables, usually parsley, thyme, bay leaf, carrot, leek and celery, tied together and usually dangled into a stockpot on a string. These herb bundles give the stew, soup or stock an aromatic seasoning. The bouquet garni is removed before serving

Braise A cooking method where food (usually meat) is first browned in oil and then cooked slowly in a liquid (wine, stock or water)

bresoala Beef cured in a wine-rich brine. It is then air dried and sliced very thinly for service

Brillat-Savarin Jean-Anthelme (1755–1826): French gastronome and author of the famous book *Physiologie du Goût*

brine A strong solution of water and salt used for pickling or preserving foods

Brix The Brix scale was originally developed by Adolph Brix. Degrees Brix (symbol °Bx) is a measurement of the mass ratio of dissolved sugar to water in a liquid. It is measured with a saccharometer, which shows the density of a liquid. It largely replaced the Baumé scale in the early 1960s

broil The American term for browning under the grill

brunoise 1 mm dice

buffet A buffet is a meal where guests serve themselves from a variety of dishes set out on a table or sideboard

butterfly To cut food (usually meat or seafood) leaving one edge joined and then open it out like the wings of a butterfly

buttermilk Milk product that is left after the fat is removed from milk to make butter

calorie Unit of energy; 1 calorie = 3.968 btu = 4.1868 joules. The heat required to raise the temperature of 1g of water by 1°C

canapé A base of bread, pastry or porcelain onto which savoury food is placed as a pre-dinner snack or as a course at the end of a meal prior to dessert

caper The flower bud of a shrub that is native to eastern Asia and is widespread in hot regions of the world. Capers are pickled in vinegar or preserved in brine

caramelise To allow the surface sugars of food to caramelise, giving a characteristic colour and aroma

carbohydrate There are three major groups of carbohydrates which are found in fresh fruits, vegetables and cereals: sugars (e.g. sucrose, fructose, glucose), starches and cellulose

Carême Marie-Antoine (1784–1833): 'The king of chefs and chef of kings.' Commenced his career as a pastry chef and was a personal chef to Tallyrand, the future King George IV and Tsar Alexander I. Responsible for many ground-breaking changes in the preparation and presentation of food and classical cuisine. Author of many books, including *L'Art de la Cuisine*

Caroline A savoury mini éclair that can be served hot or cold with a filling on buffets

carpaccio Originally, paper thin slices of raw beef with a creamy sauce, invented at Harry's Bar in Venice.
In recent years, the term has come to describe very thinly sliced vegetables, raw or smoked meats and fish

carte du jour Menu of the day

carving Slicing or cutting items, usually for customers or in front of customers

casserole To cook in a covered dish in the oven in liquid such as stock or wine

cassoulet A classic French dish from the Languedoc region consisting of white beans and various meats (such as sausages, pork and preserved duck or goose)

caul Also known as crepinette (lamb) or crepin (pork), it is a thin, fatty membrane that lines the stomach cavity of pigs or sheep. It resembles a lacy net and is used to wrap and protect foods such as pâtés, ballotines etc. The fatty membrane melts during cooking. It should be soaked in slightly salted water before use

chapelure Dried fresh breadcrumbs

charcuterie (French) cured or smoked meat items

chaud (French) Hot

chef (French) A culinary expert. The chief of the kitchen

chef de garde manger (French) The person in charge of the cold meat department

chef de partie (French) 'Chief of the section', a chef who leads a team of assistants in a section

chemiser To line or coat a mould with a substance (either sweet or savoury)

chiffonade (French) 'Made from rags'. A small chopped pile of thin strips of an ingredient, usually raw but sometimes sautéed

chine Removal of the backbone on a cut of meat such as a rack of pork

chinois A metal conical strainer used for straining

clamart Any dish that contains peas or pea purée

clarified butter Clarified by bringing to the boil until it foams and then skimming the solids from the top or straining through muslin before use

clarify To clear a cloudy liquid by removing the sediment

clouté An onion studded with cloves and bay leaf

coagulate To solidify protein with heat

coat To cover with a thin film of liquid, usually a sauce

coat the spoon When a substance is rendered thin/thick enough so that when a wooden or metal spoon is inserted into it and taken out, the substance leaves a thin film 'coating the spoon'

cocotte A fireproof dish usually made from porcelain

coddling Cooking just below the boiling point, for example coddled eggs

collagen White connective tissue that gelatinises with long slow cookery

collop Small thin slices of meat, poultry or fish, but mainly refers to slices across the tail of lobster

commis chef de partie (French) A qualified chef who is an assistant to a chef de partie

compôte Stewed fruit

compound salad A salad with more than one main ingredient

concassé Coarsely chopped, e.g. tomato concassé

concassé a cuit A cooked small dice of peeled tomatoes

confit A method of preserving meat (usually goose, duck or pork) whereby it is lightly cured and slowly cooked in its own fat. The cooked meat is then packed into a crockpot and covered with its cooking fat, which acts as a seal and preservative. Confit can be stored in a refrigerator for up to 6 months.

consommé Clear soup

coquille (French) Shell

cordon A dish that is surrounded by a thin line of sauce

Cordon Bleu (French) 'Blue ribbon'. A term used to describe high quality household cookery

correct To adjust the seasoning and consistency of a soup or sauce

coulis Fine purée of fruit

coupe A rounded dish of varying size. Often used classically for presenting an ice cream based dessert with accompaniments such as fruit, salads and biscuits

court bouillon A cooking liquor made by cooking mirepoix in water for about 30 minutes then adding wine, lemon juice or vinegar. The broth is allowed to cool before the vegetables are removed

couverture A type of chocolate used for the preparation of cakes, confectionery and a variety of desserts; containing at least 35 per cent cocoa butter and a maximum of 50 per cent sugar

cream The process where sugar and softened butter are beaten together with a wooden spoon until the mixture is light, pale and well blended. This process may also be carried out with a hand-held mixer or in a food processor

Crecy Any dish that contains carrots

crêpe (French) Pancake

crimp To seal the edges or two layers of dough using the fingertips or a fork

croquembouche A decorative cone-shaped presentation of choux buns glazed with caramel, usually placed on a base of nougatine and decorated with pulled sugar ribbons and flowers

cross-contamination The transfer of pathogens from contaminated food to uncontaminated food

croute A bread or pastry base that is used to hold sweet or savoury items

croûtons Shaped bread that is fried or toasted to accompany soups, entrées or as a base for canapés

crudites Raw vegetables, served with a dip

curdle When a liquid or food, such as eggs, divides into liquid and solids, usually due to the application of excess heat or the addition of an acid such as lemon juice

curing The preservation of food items, using acidic liquids, salt or marinating

cut in To incorporate fat into a dry ingredient, such as flour, by using a knife and making cutting movements in order to break the fat down

cutlet A cut of lamb or veal from the loin with the rib bone attached

dariole small mould used to cook individual portions of food, e.g. summer pudding

darne A cut of round fish on the bone

daube A slow-cooked stew, usually of beef in stock with vegetables and herbs. Traditionally cooked in a sealed daubiere

debone To remove bones from meat, fish or poultry

deep fry The process of cooking food by immersion in hot fat or oil in a deep pan or electric fryer to give a crisp, golden coating

deglaze To add liquid such as wine, stock, or water to the bottom of a pan to dissolve the caramelised drippings so that they may be added to a sauce, for added flavour

degrease Skim the fat from food, e.g. stock

demi glace A thick, intensely flavoured, glossy brown sauce that is served with meat

desalting The removal of salt from foods. Food is soaked in cold water or washed under running water to dissolve the salt. Some foods such as salt cod require long, overnight soaking

détrempe A mixture of flour and water for making a dough or a puff paste

diced Cut into cubes

disgorge To soak meat, poultry, game, offal in cold water to remove impurities

dock To prick or spike a raw pastry base using a metal pastry tool such as a fork or a specialised pastry docker

doria Food cooked with or garnished with cucumbers

dorure Glazing with an egg mixture on raw pastries and dough before baking to produce an attractive coloured finish

dredging To coat with dry ingredients, such as flour or breadcrumbs

drizzle To drip a liquid substance, such as a sauce or dressing, over food

dry butter European-style butter, with a fat content of 82 per cent or above, available in specialty pastry shops. It is used widely in the production of puff pastry and confectionery because it has reduced moisture content

drying off The removal of excess moisture from foods during cooking. Not to be confused with drying or reducing. An example of drying off is when potatoes are placed over a low heat after having been drained in order to dry them off before mashing

durian an oval fruit weighing up to 5kg. The flesh is cream coloured and textured and has a distinctive putrefying odour. It is found in Southeast Asia

dusting To sprinkle with sugar or flour.

duxelle Minced mushrooms and shallots cooked until dry

Ecossaise (French) Scottish

eggwash Beaten egg used to coat food as a glaze or as a binding agent

elastin Yellow connective tissue that does not break down during cooking

emincé (French) Cut fine, or sliced thinly

emulsify The blending of two liquids that would not naturally combine into each other without agitation. The classic examples are oil and water, French dressing and mayonnaise

en croute Cooked in pastry, e.g. beef Wellington

en papillote (French) Cooked in a folded greaseproof bag

enrober To completely cover a food item with a liquid

entrecôte A steak cut from the boned sirloin

entrée (French) A main course of meat or poultry that is not baked or roasted

entremet The sweet course. An entremet is usually a dessert of some distinction and can be presented with a showpiece (usually made from sugar or chocolate). Can be hot but are usually cold or iced and in the form of a layered gateau which is glazed to conceal its contents

escalope (French) A thinly sliced, boneless, round cut of meat that is batted until very thin

espagnole Basic brown sauce

étuvée French term to describe the slow stewing of a main ingredient (usually vegetable based)

farce (French) Forcemeat or stuffing

farci Stuffed

feuilletage Puff pastry

flake To separate segments naturally, e.g. cooked fish into slivers

flambé Ignite alcohol on a dish, e.g. crêpe Suzette or Christmas pudding

fleurons Crescent-shaped puff pastry used to garnish fish dishes

flute/fluting Used in pastry or biscuit making as a decoration. Pies and tarts are fluted around the edge by pinching the pastry between the forefinger and thumb to create v-shaped grooves

fold in To gently combine lighter mixtures with heavier ones usually using a metal spoon or spatula in a cutting or slicing 'J' movement whilst slightly lifting the utensil

forcemeat Ground meat or meats mixed with seasonings, used for stuffing

frangipane A pastry cream used in the preparation of various desserts, cakes and sweets. It is an almond based cream that was derived from the Italian Marquis Muzio Frangipani, who invented a perfume for scenting gloves based on bitter almonds. This inspired pastry chefs of the time to make an almond-flavoured cream, which was named 'frangipane'

freezer burn Food that is left uncovered in the freezer desiccates and becomes unusable

friand A small puff pastry case filled with sausage meat, minced meat, ham or cheese, baked in the oven and served as an hors d'oeuvre

friandise (French) A small delicacy, e.g. petit fours or small sweets

fricassée A white stew where the meat or poultry is cooked in the sauce

fritture Deep fat fryer

froid (French) Cold

fromage (French) Cheese

fume (French) Smoked

fumet A liquid obtained by reducing a stock or cooking liquid that can be added to a sauce to enhance the flavour

galantine A dish made from poultry, game, pork, veal or rabbit usually incorporating stuffings. The flesh is boned out and the whole meat (with the skin intact) is rolled and pressed into a symmetrical or sometimes a cylindrical shape. Galantines can also be made using fish

galette A flat round cake of variable size, can be sweet or savoury based

game Name given to wild feathered and furred animals hunted in certain seasons

ganache A flavoured chocolate-based cream used to decorate desserts, fill cakes and make petit fours

garnish To decorate. Also refers to food used as decoration

gastrique A reduced mixture of vinegar and sugar used in the preparation of sauces and dishes with a high degree of acidity. For example, tomato sauce

gastronomy The art of good eating and appreciation of fine food and drink

gelatine A colourless substance extracted from the bones and cartilage of animals. Supplied in powder or leaf form, it will dissolve into warm liquids and set the liquid when cooled. Widely used for making desserts

gingerbread A type of cake. British gingerbread is made using ginger and treacle and the French version, pain d'épiceuses, contains honey and a variety of spices

glacé Crystallised fruits in a syrup or liqueur

glaze To give a food a shiny appearance by coating it with a sauce or similar substance, such as aspic, sweet glazes or boiled apricot jam

glucose A clear simple sugar made by heating starch with an acid. Used in the production of jam and syrups, and also extensively used by the pastry chef in sugar work

goujons Small strips cut from a fillet of flat fish, often panéd or dipped in batter and then deep fried

gourmet (French) Food connoisseur

grate To reduce a food to very small particles by rubbing it against a sharp, rough surface, usually a grater or zester

grease To cover the inside surface of a dish or pan with a layer of fat, such as butter, margarine or oil, using a brush or kitchen paper

grill 1. To cook foods with radiated heat. 2. Cooking equipment that radiates heat from below, e.g. barbecue

hacher To cut very finely (often with a mincing machine).

hanging Hanging meat from a hook at a controlled temperature to facilitate ageing (see *ageing*)

hors d'oeuvres Small dishes served as the first course of the meal

hummus A Greek dish made from cooked chickpeas crushed with sesame oil; usually accompanies hors d'oeuvres

husk The tough outer casing of wheat, barley and rye. The French expression of *farine de gru* is used for wholemeal flour

icing A preparation of icing sugar used to coat cakes and confectionery

infusion The process of steeping an aromatic substance in a cool or warm liquid until the liquid has absorbed the flavour

iron An essential mineral that is found in food sources such as liver, red meat, spinach and egg yolks

jardiniere Batons of vegetables

jelly A cold dessert made of fruit juice, wine or liqueur to which sugar and gelatine have been added

julienne (French) A cut of meat, poultry or vegetables, which has the same dimensions as a match

jus (French) 'Juice', usually refers to the natural juice from meat

jus lie (French) Thickened gravy

knead A process where dough is made smoother, softer and more elastic by applying gentle pressing and stretching actions to it. One end of the dough is secured by the heel of one hand and stretched away then pulled back over the top. In bread making, two hands are used

knocking back To release pockets of gas in fermented dough before shaping and proving

lait (French) Milk

larding Larding is fat cut into strips and inserted into meat using a special needle. Used to add moisture to meat

lardons Bacon that is cut into small batons

levain (French) A dough that is used to make bread rise

legumes (French) Dried beans, peas, lentils etc.

liaison A binding agent made up of egg yolks and cream, used for enriching soups and sauces

Lyonnaise Refers to dishes accompanied by sautéed onions

macédoine A neat dice of mainly vegetables which measure 1/2cm square

macerate To soak a fruit in a liqueur or wine. This softens the fruit while releasing its juices and the fruit absorbs the macerating liquid's flavours

madeleine A small cake shaped like a rounded shell

marinade A mixture of wet and/or dry ingredients used to flavour or tenderise food prior to cooking

marinate To let food stand in a marinade (such as a liquid, dry cure or paste) before cooking. Some marinades add flavour, while those that contain acids or enzymes help to tenderise, e.g. made with fruits such as lemon, mangos papaya or kiwi fruits, or with wine, vinegar or yoghurt

marquise A chocolate dessert, a type of rich mousse that can be served chilled or iced

Melba toast Thin triangular pieces of crisp toast, classically served with pâté

menthe (French) Mint

minced Ground or chopped, usually refers to meat, fish or poultry

mirepoix A mixture of diced aromatic vegetables, e.g. carrots, onions, celery and leek

mise en place Basic preparation prior to cooking

miso A Japanese condiment of fermented soya

monosodium glutamate A type of salt used as a flavour enhancer

monte au beurre Addition of butter to create an emulsion of cooking liquor and butter

mousse A sweet or savoury preparation that has a very light consistency

nage An aromatic court bouillon in which shellfish are cooked. Dishes prepared in this way are often called 'à la nage'

nape To cover an item with either a hot or cold sauce

navarin A brown stew of mutton or lamb

noir (French) Black

noisette A cut from a boned loin of lamb

nori An edible scented seaweed used in Japanese cookery. Used as a powder, or pressed and dried for wrapping around sushi

nouilles (French) Noodles

nutrients The essential parts of food that are vital to health

oenology The study of wines

oeuf (French) Egg

offal The edible internal organs of an animal

open sandwich A sandwich that has a base only

organic farming A farming method which aims to maintain natural farming methods of growing crops or maintaining livestock without the use of chemicals

palatable Pleasant to the taste and edible

panache A selection of vegetables

panada A paste of various bases, either bread, flour or potato, used to thicken or bind products

pané à la Francaise Passed through seasoned milk and seasoned flour. Used as a coating for fried foods

pané à la Alglaise A coating of flour, eggwash and breadcrumbs

papillote (French) Cooked in foil or parchment paper to seal in flavour, then served and cut open at the table

parboil To cook partially by boiling for a short period of time

parfait (French) 'Perfect', a smooth pâté or iced dessert which can be sliced leaving an even and consistent appearance

pass Push liquids or solids through a sieve

pate (French) 'Paste'. 1. Pâté is either a smooth or coarse product made from meat, poultry, fish, vegetable, offal or game that has been blended and cooked with cream, butter and eggs. 2. Pate is different base pastry products: sweet, short, lining, puff, choux

pathogen Micro-organism that can cause food poisoning

pâtisserie Sweet or savoury pastries and cakes, generally baked in the oven

paupiette Rolled and/or stuffed fillet of flat fish

pavé A square or diamond-shaped piece of meat, poultry or fish, but can also be referred to pastry or cakes

paysanne Vegetables cut into thin slices

pectin A natural gelling agent found in plants and is abundant in certain fruits, such as apples, quinces, redcurrants and lemons. Pectin is an important ingredient when making jams and jellies

pesto Rustic Italian dressing made with basil, garlic, olive oil and pine nuts

petit (French) Small.

petit four A small biscuit, cake or item of confectionery, usually served after dinner with the coffee

petit pois (French) Small peas

pipe To shape or decorate food using a forcing bag or utensil fitted with a plain or decorated nozzle

piquante A dish or sauce that is sharp to the taste

pluche Small tips of salad leaves or herbs used as a garnish

poach To cook food in hot liquid over a gentle heat with the liquid slightly below boiling point

pressing To apply pressure to items to help shape or remove excess moisture, e.g. terrines to help them keep an even layering or sweatbreads to remove excess liquid

prove To allow yeast dough to rise

purée A smooth paste of a particular ingredient or a soup that is passed through a sieve

quenelle A poached dumpling, mousseline or cream presented in an oval shape. Classically made of veal or chicken

ragout A stew of meat or vegetables

ramekin Individual or small ceramic round baking dish.

rasher Thin slice of bacon

rechauffer Reheat food for service

reduce To concentrate the flavour of a liquid by boiling away the water content

refresh To plunge food into, or run under, cold or iced water after blanching to prevent further cooking.

roast To cook food in an oven or on a spit over a fire with the aid of fat

roux Fat and flour mixture used to thicken sauces and soups; can be cooked to white, blond and brown colours

rubbing in The incorporation of fat into flour. Butter is softened and cubed then gently rubbed into the flour between the thumb and forefinger, lifting the mixing at the same time. When the fat is fully incorporated the mixture resembles fine breadcrumbs

salad tiède A salad with the addition of warm or hot ingredients

salamander A small contact grill and poker used to brown or gratin foods, or a term to describe an overhead grill

salami An Italian charcuterie product made of ground pork or beef

sauté Cook quickly in shallow fat

savouries A small after-meal dish or item as an alternative to a dessert or cheese

savoury sorbet A flavoured water ice using savoury ingredients such as tomatoes

scald To heat a liquid, usually milk, until it is almost boiling, at which point very small bubbles begin to form around the edge of the pan

score To make shallow incisions with a small knife

seal To caramelise the outer surface of meat

sear To brown the surface of food in fat over a high heat before finishing cooking by another method, in order to add flavour

season to taste Usually refers to adding extra salt and pepper

sec (French) Dry

shallow fry To cook in oil or fat that covers the base of a shallow pan

shred To tear or cut food into thin strips

sift To pass a dry ingredient, such as flour, through a sieve to ensure it is lump free

simmer To maintain the temperature of a liquid at just below boiling

simple salad A salad with only one main ingredient, e.g. tomato salad

skim To remove impurities from the surface of a liquid, such as stock, during or after cooking

skin To remove the skin from meat, fish, poultry, fruit, nuts and vegetables

slice To cut food, such as bread, meat, fish or vegetables, into flat pieces of varying thickness

smoking Hot or cold method of curing and flavouring food using wood, herbs or spices

soak To immerse in a liquid to rehydrate or moisten a product

sorbet A smooth frozen ice made with flavoured liquid-based ingredients, such as fruit juices

sous chef (French) 'Under chief', second to the head chef

steam To cook food in steam, over rapidly boiling water or other liquid. The food is usually suspended above such liquid by means of a trivet or steaming basket, although in the case of puddings the basin actually sits in water

steep To soak food in a liquid such as alcohol or syrup until saturated.

stir fry To fry small pieces of food quickly in a large frying pan or wok, over a high heat, using very little fat and constantly moving the food around the pan throughout cooking, keeping it in contact with the hot wok

stock A cooked, flavoured liquid that is used as a cooking liquor or base for a sauce

sweat To cook gently in a little fat without colour

table d'hôte A set menu at a set price

terrine A dish used to cook and present pâté

thumbing up Producing an edge all the way around the top of a flan by pinching in with the thumb and forefinger

timbale A small high-sided mould

tronçon A cut of flat fish on the bone

truss To tie up meat or poultry with string before cooking

vegan Someone who will not eat any animal product

vegetarian Someone who will not eat meat or fish but will eat animal products such as milk, eggs and cheese

velouté (French) A sauce made with stock and a blond roux, finished with a liaison of cream and yolks

viande (French) Meat

whip To beat an item, such as cream or egg whites, to incorporate air

whisk To beat air into a mixture until soft and aerated

zester A hand-held tool with small, sharp-edged holes at the end of it, which cuts orange, lemon or grapefruit peel into fine shreds

Recipe Index

General Index